Islam and Good Governance

"In this insightful, passionate book, Muqtedar Khan focuses on the importance of the Islamic principle of *Ihsan* in revitalizing Muslim life and thought globally in the contemporary world. He observes—correctly—that although this concept has traditionally animated Islamic ethics and mysticism, it has rarely been deployed in the political sphere. Khan goes on to make a compelling case for addressing this deficiency and to demonstrate how striving for beauty and excellence—as implied by the term *Ihsan*—will allow Muslims to govern themselves effectively in accordance with the highest ideals of their tradition. In an age marked by shallow religio-nationalist identities and the cheap instrumentalization of religion, Khan offers a way out of this morass by going back to foundational Islamic values, primarily *Ihsan* and foregrounding it for application in today's polarized and amoral world. This is a book that deserves to be read widely by both Muslim and non-Muslim readers who share an equal concern for the attrition of moral and ethical values today, particularly in the public sphere, and can be read with profit even in the hard-nosed worlds of academia and policymaking."
—Asma Afsaruddin, *Professor of Near Eastern Languages & Cultures, Hamilton Lugar School of Global and International Studies, Indiana University, Bloomington, USA*

"Muqtedar Khan's *Islam and Good Governance* offers a political philosophy that is both refreshing and timely. In this era of fixation on identity politics, Khan rejects the standard choice between religious and secular identities as superficial. He focuses instead on process—the necessary means for achieving good governance, and finds it in cultivation of core Islamic values of love and mercy."
—Tamara Sonn, *Hamad Bin Khalifa Al-Thani Professor in the History of Islam at the Edmund A. Walsh School of Foreign Service in Georgetown University, USA*

"Muqtedar Khan's *Islam and Good Governance* is a noteworthy contribution to the literature on Islamic political thought. By mending the concept of *Ihsan*, doing beautiful deeds, to political practice, he champions a praxis in the public sphere that is more virtuous and pensive. The reader comes away with a better appreciation of the shortcomings of identity politics, and the astuteness of mystical readings of Islam. *Islam and Good Governance* advances the view that politics must bend the knee to morality."
—Mehrzad Boroujerdi, *Professor of Political Science at Syracuse University, USA*

"Muqtedar Khan's new work bridges the worlds of Islamic spirituality and politics. A great deal of research on Sufism has gone towards helping us locate Sufis as full social beings, politically active and engaged in their societies. This has helped us move beyond the older and inaccurate association of Sufis as being 'apolitical' or 'otherworldly,' characterizations which were often rooted in Protestant caricatures. Much less frequently have we seen political scientists, and politically science trained scholars take seriously the role of Sufism in today's world. Muqtedar Khan goes to the heart of the matter by focusing our attention on *Ihsan*, that spiritual paradigm of making goodness and beauty real encapsulated in the Prophetic tradition 'to worship God as we see Him, and if not, to remember that God sees us.' Khan's work is recommended for both scholars of Sufism and political science. May it find a wide audience among scholars and policy makers."
—Omid Safi, *Director, Duke Islamic Studies Center, Duke University, USA*

"In this audacious, provocative, and deeply hopeful book, Muqtedar Khan tries nothing less than to reconceptualize Muslim politics. He is following in the footsteps of Muhammad Abduh, Muhammad Iqbal, and Fazlur Rahman in challenging Muslims to understand their faith as an ethical, not legal system. If they do this, they will put *Ihsan*—the search for beauty and moral perfection—where it belongs, at the heart of both Islamic piety and politics."
—Sohail Hashmi, *Professor, Mount Holyoke College, USA*

"The violence and cruelty of radical groups like the Islamic State and Al-Qaeda have in recent years led many international observers to conclude that Muslim politics is inherently incompatible with democracy and modernity. In this wide ranging and profound book, Muqtedar Khan reminds us of an entirely different vision and practice of Islam in politics, one premised on the concept of *Ihsan*—the Quranic injunction to carry out beautiful, compassionate, and ethical deeds. Delving deep into the depths of the Qur'an, the traditions of the Prophet, and Islamic mysticism, the author presents a rich and compelling alternative to the failed vision of the proponents of so-called 'Islamic states.' The result is a book that is at once timely, urgently important, and, over its entire course, ethically moving."
—Robert Hefner, *Professor, Pardee School of Global Affairs, Boston University, USA*

"Muqtedar Khan's *Islam and Good Governance* is an original, thoughtful, and fresh approach in political philosophy that will intrigue as well as challenge many Muslim and non-Muslim scholars presuppositions and models for development."
—John L. Esposito, *Professor, Georgetown University, USA*

M. A. Muqtedar Khan

Islam and Good Governance

A Political Philosophy of Ihsan

M. A. Muqtedar Khan
University of Delaware
Newark, DE, USA

ISBN 978-1-137-55718-6   ISBN 978-1-137-54832-0   (eBook)
https://doi.org/10.1057/978-1-137-54832-0

Library of Congress Control Number: 2018968489

Cover image © The Protected Art Archive / Alamy Stock Photo
Cover design: Fatima Jamadar

This Palgrave Macmillan imprint is published by the registered company Springer Nature America, Inc.
The registered company address is: 1 New York Plaza, New York, NY 10004, U.S.A.

For Reshma, the love of my life.

FOREWORD

The symbols and benchmarks of modernizing societies in the mid-twentieth century were Western in origin. Modernization and development theory presumed that the path to modernity and development required the Westernization and secularization of society. The choice faced by developing countries like those in the Muslim world seemed to be between the polar dichotomies of tradition and modernity, or as a prominent social scientist put it "a choice between Mecca and mechanization."

To be modern meant to adopt Western and secular ideas, languages, institutions and values. Individuals were judged modern, as distinguished from "traditional," if they wore modern (Western) suits, dresses and jeans and spoke a modern (Western) language.

Two interrelated issues, national identity (nationalism) and independence, dominated the period between World War I and World War II. Both secular and Islamic reformers/Islamic modernists saw the West as both a positive and a negative force and influence. On the one hand, nationalism was a reaction against Western imperialism, European colonial rule. On the other hand, many who led nationalist and independence movements owed their education and training to the West and were influenced by liberal nationalist beliefs and ideals and modern Western political values and institutions such as nationalism, constitutional government, parliamentary rule and individual rights.

Islam played an important role in the development of anti-colonial movements and modern nationalism in diverse countries and to varying degrees from North Africa and Southeast Asia, taking different configurations depending on local and regional contexts. Ironically in the postcolonial period, while countries achieved independence, West-inspired colonial institutions, values, political ties and languages remained strong. Habib Bourguiba, "the Great Combatant" of Tunisia's nationalist struggle, aligned Tunisia with France and French culture. French not Arabic was the language of education and culture. Pakistan remained a member of the British Commonwealth and English served as the language of government and higher education. However, in the 1960s, the widespread dissatisfaction with monarchs and other authoritarian leaders and governments threatened as well as toppled some governments.

By the 1970s, Islamic movements, mainstream and extremist, emerged as an alternative to the dismal failures of secular nationalism, capitalism and socialism. The Muslim Brotherhood and Jamaat-e-Islami and Ayatollah Khomeini and Iran's Islamic opposition and other movements across much of the Muslim world from Egypt, Sudan and Libya to Iran, Kuwait, Turkey, Pakistan, Malaysia and Indonesia appealed to Islam to legitimate and to mobilize popular support in somewhat spectacular ways. Diverse Islamic ideologies inspired and legitimated the mujahideen victory in driving the Soviet Union out of Afghanistan, and the Iranian revolution and fall of the Shah. Islamically oriented candidates and parties participate in elections and are serving in government at local, provincial and national levels and serving in parliaments, cabinets and as prime ministers. However, the dark side, religious extremism and militant terrorist movements, national and global, epitomized by Al-Qaeda and ISIS or Daesh, have threatened the safety and security of Muslim and Western countries.

At the same time, major polling by organizations like the Gallup World Polls and Pew reported that large numbers of Muslims throughout the world are unhappy with the status quo and clearly want broader democratization. When asked what they admired most about the West, among the top responses of the mainstream majority were the West's rule of law, fair political systems, democracy, respect for human rights, freedom of speech and gender equality. Majorities of Muslims said that if drafting a constitution for a new country, they would include "free speech," freedom of assembly and religion as a fundamental guarantee.

Admiration for Western democratic values did not, however, translate into support for a Western secular model of government. Most Muslims also believe their own religion and values are essential to their progress. Thus, while some dismiss the relationship of religion to the state, arguing for a secular state, majorities expressed a desire for *Shariah*, the basis for religious values, as "a" source of law. Although perceptions of what the *Shariah* represents and the degree to which it is possible to implement its rulings in society vary enormously, most want democratic and religious principles and values to coexist in their government and thus see a role for religious principles in the formulation of state legislation.

The Arab Uprisings or Arab Spring 2010–2012 stunned governments in Muslim countries and the West as a totally unexpected series of pro-democracy uprisings in Tunisia, Egypt, Libya, Syria and Bahrain. One of its major results was regime changes that saw Islamic parties, the Muslim Brotherhood in Egypt and Ennahda in Tunisia come to power. Despite the fact that a broad base of groups and activists led the revolts in Tunisia and Egypt, at election time the Muslim Brotherhood and Ennahda prevailed. The Arab Spring turned into an Arab Winter with the chaos and violence in Libya and Syria, the overthrow of President Mohamed Morsi, the first democratically elected president of Egypt in a military coup led by General Abdel Fatah El Sisi and the subsequent restoration of authoritarian rule. The El Sisi government moved swiftly and violently in their attempt to thoroughly destroy the Muslim Brotherhood and any critics or opposition, implementing a massive violation of human rights. After the Arab Spring, many have questioned not only the future of democracy in the Middle East but also the role of Islam and Islamic movements in state and society.

M. A. Muqtedar Khan, a prolific scholar and expert, has boldly critiqued the recent past and proposed a state that is not based on a secular or Islamic model but rather on *Ihsan*. He argues that justice must be rescued from the limiting influence of law and it should be the Quranic conception of justice that defines both state and state laws rather than law defining the state and the concept of justice.

In the Quranic verse 13:11, structural change is tied to change in agency. The existing condition of a society will not change until there is a change within the citizens themselves. Khan explains this change in agency by identifying five principles that characterize a society of *Muhsins*; (1) citizenship as witnessing the divine, (2) citizens as character builders, (3) citizens as lawmakers, (4) citizenship as self-regulation and (5) citizens as rulers.

Khan, a Muslim social scientist and Islamic scholar, not only draws on but also critiques past experiences and experiments of traditional Islam and its emphasis on Islamic law and that of political Islam. The model of secular versus Islamic or Muslim state and the role of *Shariah*/Islamic law that was developed and appropriated in early Islamic centuries are critiqued as inappropriate. In its place, Khan advocates and presents a paradigm based on *Ihsan* and its application for a postcolonial relationship of Islam and politics.

Islam and Good Governance seeks to develop a political philosophy based on *Ihsan* that emphasizes love over law, process (Islamic governance) over structure (Islamic state) and self-annihilation (*Fanaa*) over identity or self-assertion. Recognizing that many Muslims are determined that Islam should play a role in the public sphere, Khan advances a vision of Islam that emphasizes virtue over identity, ethics over politics and makes Islam a force for the good in the global society. The book employs two methodological tracks: (1) deconstructing existing orthodoxy and (2) replacing it with a new and more mystical and compassionate narrative of Islamic principles and values. Khan offers an alternative way of thinking about Islam's role in politics that is especially distinct from that of Islamists and Jihadists. This book critiques the traditional focus of Islamic political thought on structure and law and instead argues that perhaps a focus on process will yield more benefits for society.

Khan's approach is based on a critical distinction and difference between *Shariah* and Islamic law; the two are related but should not be conflated or equated. *Shariah* is divine principles and values in light of which Islamic jurisprudence based on human interpretations developed the corpus of laws in specific political, social, economic and cultural contexts. Thus, the process of Islamization will vary in different political and social contexts.

Khan's *Islam and Good Governance* is an original, thoughtful and fresh approach in political philosophy that will intrigue as well as challenge many Muslim and non-Muslim scholars' presuppositions and models for development.

Georgetown University   John L. Esposito
Washington, DC

ACKNOWLEDGMENTS

Whoever does not thank people, has not thanked Allah.
—Prophet Muhammad (peace be upon him—pbuh)

In the name of God, most benevolent and most merciful. Everything that exists will perish, except His beauty, His love, His mercy and His majesty. As one who has received innumerable favors from Him, the Almighty, the Real, the Everlasting, I remain in a state of perpetual gratitude toward Him. It is no doubt in my heart that writing this book has been one of the greatest mercies that Allah has bestowed on me. It has allowed me to understand Him and his creation much better. I express my thanks first and foremost to the Lord of all the Worlds.

It has taken several years of research and retooling to write *Islam and Good Governance*. I am grateful to the opportunity the writing of this book has given me to not only understand the most beautiful elements of Islam but also to visit some of the spiritually uplifting places, people and books in the Islamic civilization. Whether this book will have any impact remains to be seen. But I bear witness that it has already changed me and my life. I now live a spiritually more enriching and rewarding life as I try to inculcate and practice what I have learned while writing this book. It has also informed how I engage with people. It has not only impacted my spiritual life but also my professional life as I have tried to refocus on researching and teaching that which I think will improve the conditions we live in, through good governance and away from identity politics and global conflicts.

The book has taken five years to write and I have benefitted from research support by several institutions and many individuals across the world who have reeducated me about Islamic mysticism, *Tasawwuf*, the Quran and *Ihsan*. I have been introduced to both practices and some secrets of mystical life and for this I am deeply grateful to the Sufi masters and scholars in the United States, Morocco, Egypt and Turkey. Along the way, many individuals also demonstrated to me what is the meaning of *Ihsan* through their generosity, kindness and unsolicited support. I wish to thank them all.

I am grateful to the International Institute of Islamic Thought for their generous grant that enabled me to take the full year of sabbatical in 2011–2012. I also wish to thank them for the several seminars and symposiums they hosted that allowed me to share my preliminary ideas and research and help fine tune my arguments. I am indebted to the Department of Political Science at my home institution, the University of Delaware, and its area studies research grant that sponsored trips to Morocco, Tunisia, Turkey and Egypt. I owe the Institute for Global Studies for a fellowship that helped me study classical Arabic for three years. I am also grateful to the University of Delaware for small grants that have helped me travel to share my work in progress at various academic conferences. And finally, I am also thankful to Creative Learning for funding support for the Muslim world conferences that I helped organize which allowed me to travel to East Asia, Philippines, Indonesia and Malaysia, to share and develop the ideas that are in this book.

I have benefitted from the wisdom and knowledge of several scholars who patiently worked around my ignorance and arrogance to make me understand Islamic sacred texts and the tradition better. In the United States, the late Dr. Jamal Barzinji was a big supporter of the project as well as a provider of thoughtful critique. His support was critical in the early days of this project. I owe thanks to Imam Mohamed Magid and Dr. William Chittick, who helped me understand the significance of the idea of *Ihsan* in Islam. I owe special thanks to Dr. Chittick's scholarship on *Ihsan* and Sufism without which I would have struggled much more than I did. I am grateful for Dr. John Esposito's mentoring, encouragement and guidance. For more than two decades, he has been a friend and I am also especially grateful to him for writing a foreword to this book. The friendship and guidance of Dr. Asma Afsaruddin and the feedback and input from Dr. Hisham al-Talib, Dr. Abubaker Shingetti, Maulana Abulfatah Syed Nusrat, Mufti Nawal-ur-Rahman, Imam Faisal Raouf and the late Dr. Irfan Khan were essential to the project in its early days as I searched for direction.

I owe a debt to the scholars and Sufis of Morocco who both taught and enriched me. Much thanks to the late Dr. Fatima Mernissi who not only helped me find rare Arabic books on *Ihsan* but also introduced me to many other scholars. Thanks are due to Dr. Ahmad Abbadi, Dr. Khalid Saqi, Dr. Mohammed Amine Smaili and Cherif Sidi Ibrahim Tidjani. I am also grateful to the Islamic Studies Department at Mohammed V University whose faculty and students heard my preliminary ideas on the subject and provided interesting and critical feedback.

Over the years, I have enjoyed a lot of support from friends and colleagues while writing this book. Special thanks are due to Dr. Ali Raza Mir, Javad Khan, Dr. Tahir Shad, Dr. Ali Hussain Mir, Dr. Kamran Bokhari, Dr. Bill Kruvant, Charito Kruvant, Dr. Stuart Kaufman, Dr. Robert Denemark, Dr. Alan Fox, Dr. James Magee, Dr. Wasif Qureshi, Dr. Omar al-Talib, Reverend Greg Jones, Dr. Dan Green, Dr. David Redlawsk, Dr. Gretchen Bauer, Mohammed Shakir, Khalid Ibrahim, Mustafa Tuncer, Mukaram Syed, Dr. Hummayun Ismail, Rabbi Michael Beals, Rabbi Douglas Krantz, Dr. Saleem Khan, Dr. Naveed Baqir, Shahid Bajwa, Reverend Jay Hutchinson, the late Tosun Bayrak, Dr. Sabri Ciftci and Senator Christopher Coons. I am indebted to the faith communities at Masjid Isa Ibn Maryam in Delaware, Islamic Community Center in Lancaster, PA, and the West Presbyterian Church in Wilmington for listening to me earnestly as I explored many of the themes in this book in sermons and lectures. I am grateful to Palgrave Macmillan's editorial staff, especially Alina Yurova and Mary Fata. I owe thanks to my graduate students who have help me grow intellectually as they take on increasingly more challenging research projects and to the staff who keep the wheels running smoothly, especially Barbara Ford. I owe special thanks to my Turkish students who travel miles, by train and bus, to meet me and take me to spiritually enriching places and Sufi lodges when I am in Turkey.

My visit to Jordan was critical in understanding the role of both democracy and Islam in politics. I am grateful to Dr. Fathi Malkawi who made it all happen. Thanks also to Majed Fawzi, Dr. Rohile Gharaibeh, Ms. Banan Malkawi and Dr. Ishaq Farhan and all those who attended my seminar on *Ihsan* and good governance in Amman and provided useful suggestions and critique. In Cairo, Sheikh Ahmed El-Hafez Al Tijany, Dr. Said Sadek, Dr. Sahibe Nade, Sheikh Ahmed Tayyeb, Dr. Ibrahim Negm and Abou Ela Madi were very helpful.

I made more than a dozen visits to Turkey while writing *Islam and Good Governance*. I am grateful to that country that has preserved the culture of *Tasawwuf* and *Ihsan* to some extent, unlike many other Muslim nations who have lost the beauty of tradition in their failed attempts to modernize. I owe special thanks to *Tekke* (Sufi center) of the Jerrahi order in Karagumruk Istanbul. The *Zikr* gathering in the *Zawiya* there on Thursday nights truly gave me a taste of the spiritual experience that did more to change my soul than all the books I read.

I owe a lot of debt to many scholars in Turkey who literally schooled me in the science of *Tasawwuf*. I want to particularly recognize Dr. Nuri Tinaz, Dr. Ibrahim Kalin, Dr. Mustafa Sinanoglu, Dr. Hikmet Yaman, Dr. Süleyman Derin, Dr. Ismail Kara, Dr. Lutfi Sunar, Dr. Halil Ibrahim Yenugen, Dr. Recep Senturk, Dr. Bilal Kuspinar, Dr. Kasim Kopuz, Dr. Ali Kose, Dr. Musa Tasdalen, Dr. Selime Leyla Gurkan, Dr. Serhat Ulagali, Dr. Ali Murat Yel, Dr. Ekrem Demirli, Dr. Erdem Ozluk and Dr. Duygu Ozluk. I am also grateful to University of Marmara's Department of Ilahiyat, Department of Sociology and International Studies and its Center for Middle Eastern Studies along with the Department of Ilahiyat at University of Ankara, Istanbul Sehir University and Necmettin Erbakan University for hosting my seminars on *Ihsan* and governance. Thanks also to the Department of International Relations at Seljuk University for hosting a lecture by me. I have benefited from the feedback given by the faculty and students of these universities.

Two people need particular mention: Sheikh Haitham Hamdan who spent five hours a week for nearly three years teaching me classical Arabic and Dr. Ikram Masmoudi who continued where he left off. This book is about *Ihsan*—understood as doing selfless, good and beautiful things. None has demonstrated it more dramatically in my life than Jane W. Goldblum. Not only is she the best at what she does—which is in itself a form of *Ihsan*—she also showed amazing character in what she did for me. Thank you, Jane.

I am fortunate to have a wonderful and supportive family. They not only demonstrate excellence in their worldly endeavors but also have a healthy desire for spiritual growth. I am especially grateful to have in my life my mother and spiritual friend, Afzalunnisa Begum, and Reshma's loving and supportive mother, Mohana. My thanks for their love and support to Rumi, Ruhi, Iqtedar, Arshia, Imtiaz, Sadia, Danish, Rana, Nabiha, Omar, Adnan, Nitin, Rachna, Anisha, Neal, Shailey, Ashwin, Rohit, Mohanica, Roshan, Akshay, Dogma, Kismet and Billo. I am sure my dad,

Abdul Hafeez Khan, and Reshma's dad, Shashi Kumar Mohile, would be proud of this book if they had lived to see it. This book is dedicated to my wife Reshma, who has been an unwavering friend and supporter and a great partner. The sacrifices she has made to make our lives a success here have taught me that *Ihsan* for some people is a way of life. She brings love, beauty and happiness—*Ihsan*—to our lives.

Praise for the Author

"Khan believes his more liberal voice highlights a historical tension between traditionalist Islamic theologians, who tend to furnish more conservative fatwas, and Islamic philosophers, who go for the more flexible rulings."

—*The Washington Post*

"UD professor Muqtedar Khan has been called the moderate voice of Islam. Thanks in no small part to his prolific writing, that voice is heard around the world."

—*Delaware Today*

"Muqtedar Khan is one of the rising stars among Muslim intellectuals in the West."

—*The Daily Star*

"Academic and fiery public intellectual, Muqtedar Khan believes that Muslims in America are ideally situated to not only spread Islamic values in the West, but also reshape the destiny of traditional Muslim societies."

—*ABC Australian Broadcasting Corporation*

"Muqtedar Khan is the Voice of Moderate Islam."

—*Los Angeles Times and the Boston Globe*

"Muqtedar Khan is a rare moderate voice."

—*The Daily Times*

Contents

About the Author

M. A. Muqtedar Khan is a professor in the Department of Political Science and International Relations at the University of Delaware. He is the Academic Director of the State Department's National Security Institute (2016–2019) at the Institute for Global Studies at the University of Delaware. He was a senior non-resident fellow of the Brookings Institution (2003–2008), a fellow of the Alwaleed Center at Georgetown University (2006–2007) and a fellow of the Institute for Social Policy and Understanding (2001–2016). He founded the Islamic Studies Program at the University of Delaware and was its first director from 2007 to 2010. He holds a PhD in international relations, political philosophy and Islamic political thought from Georgetown University. He is the author of several books: *American Muslims: Bridging Faith and Freedom* (2002), *Jihad for Jerusalem: Identity and Strategy in International Relations* (2004), *Islamic Democratic Discourse* (2006), *Debating Moderate Islam: The Geopolitics of Islam and the West* (2007) and *Islam and Good Governance: A Political Philosophy of Ihsan* (Palgrave, 2019). Khan is a frequent commentator in the international media. His articles and commentaries can be found at www.ijtihad.org. His research can be found at https://udel.academia.edu/MuqtedarKhan.

CHAPTER 1

Introduction: The Quest for a Political Philosophy of *Ihsan*

God is with those who do beautiful deeds. (Quran 29:69)

The Quran promises that God is with those who do beautiful things. Keeping in my mind this promise, this book is an attempt to bring *Ihsan*— doing beautiful deeds—into politics. In an age when the role of Islam in politics is maligned by the egregiously violent and cruel actions of terrorist groups like *Daesh* (the Islamic State) and Al-Qaeda and the authoritarianism of many so-called Islamic states that seek to legitimize their politics by claiming that they are driven by Islamic *Shariah* (divine laws), a book that seeks to reclaim the beautiful in Islamic teachings and Islamic governance is absolutely necessary. While I cannot predict if this book will have any impact on politics in the Muslim world and the political ideologies of Islamic groups, I am confident that it will at least articulate an alternate vision and understanding of the role of Islam in politics that can be inspirational, enlightening and even desirable.

This book deconstructs centuries of Islamic political-philosophical narrative that has eventually led to the idea of the modern Islamic state or Islamic Caliphate as the only legitimate form of Islamic governance. It also challenges the predominantly Islamist notion that the implementation of *Shariah*—Islamic law—is both the source of legitimacy and the purpose of an Islamic state. This book shows that there are diverse approaches to not only Islamic politics, such as realism, legalism and mysticism, but also those that include the highest form of idealism as understood in the cosmology

© The Author(s) 2019
M. A. M. Khan, *Islam and Good Governance*,
https://doi.org/10.1057/978-1-137-54832-0_1

of *Ihsan* and the worldview of *Al-Tasawwuf*, the science of Islamic mysticism. In doing so, this book seeks to channel and guide the fervor for Islam and Islam-based politics that is so prevalent in Muslim societies today onto the high road for a politics of aesthetics that will nurture compassion, mercy and love in societies rather than those that seek to forcibly implement divine laws in pursuit of divine justice which often devolve into harshness, intolerance, compulsion and violence.

This book deconstructs both the moderate discourse of political Islam and the radical discourse of Jihadism by delving into the depths of Islamic mystical thought, the Quran and hadith traditions and even the works of mystics like Sheikh Saa'di. By articulating a vision of a beautiful (*love*-based society) and a state of *Ihsan*, this book seeks to move away from the now failed vision of Islamic states without demanding radical secularization at the structural level or abandonment of faith at the level of agency. No single book of human authorship can be a blueprint for any state or a society. What a book can aspire to do is to invite, instigate and perhaps even inspire a conversation on a new way of thinking and doing politics. In that spirit and recognizing the limits of any discursive enterprise, this book encourages Muslims to engage in a conversation about thinking, realizing and working toward an *Ihsan* (beauty and goodness) based politics.

THE PHILOSOPHICAL AND THEOLOGICAL FOUNDATION

Prophet Muhammad (pbuh) teaches Muslims in a seminal tradition, that *God has ordained* Ihsan *(doing beautiful deeds) in all spheres of life* and so this book asks why not in politics? How would divinely inspired beautiful politics look? This book seeks to answer that question. This book dares to envision a politics based on a concern for the interests of others rather than just self-interest. For over 1400 hundreds since the beginning of Islam, Muslim scholars have written extensively about concepts of Islam including *Ihsan* but not much about the role of *Ihsan* in politics or in governance. Some scholars in recent years have thought of Sufi approaches to politics as an antidote to radicalism but not about *Ihsan* as a foundation for this philosophical and ethical departure.[1] There are a few pamphlets published by some contemporary traditional scholars who merely rehash what has already been written about *Ihsan* by prominent scholars like

---

[1] Muhammad Amir Rana, "Counter-ideology: Unanswered questions and the case of Pakistan," *Perspectives on Terrorism* 2.3 (2008): 3–5.

Al-Ghazali, Ibn Taymiyyah and Ibn Arabi, but their scope and intent are very limited. A lot of ink has been spent on understanding *Ihsan* but only in the context of personal manners and interpersonal relations or with regard to dedication in ritual prayers and in mystical practices. None of the books about *Ihsan* have ventured into politics. This will be a first and hopefully a major contribution to Islamic thought and political philosophy based on *Ihsan*.

According to a famous tradition, when Angel Gabriel asked Prophet Muhammad (pbuh), "What is *Ihsan*?," the Prophet responded, "To Worship Allah as if you see him, if you can't see Him, Surely He sees you." The concept of *Ihsan* though defined so simplistically is loaded with theological and mystical implications. It means perfection, goodness, to better, to do beautiful things and to do righteous deeds. Prophet Muhammad's (pbuh) answer seems simple, but it has had a profound impact on how Islam as a civilization has evolved over time and how Muslims have understood the divine purpose of creation. Those who pursued *Ihsan* as seeking to see God, they over time developed the Islamic mystical tradition of Sufism. *Tasawwuf* as it is understood in Islamic theology means literally to purify or perfect. It is essentially the science of Islamic mysticism and this beautiful tradition unfolded literally as an exegesis of the above tradition understood in the light of Prophet Muhammad's (pbuh) night journey to heaven (the *Meraj*), when according to Sufi beliefs Prophet Muhammad (pbuh) saw God, and Prophet Moses' beautiful prayer in the desert, "Oh my Lord, show thyself, so that I may gaze upon you" (Quran 7:143). This desire to see God has put *Muhabba* or love of God as the central concept of Sufi Islam.

On the other hand, Islamic orthodoxy developed by placing emphasis on the second part of the answer, "Surely He sees you" and rather than love, *Taqwa* or fear of a watching, judging God became the central focus of Muslim understanding of God and their faith. Since God is watching us, we must live up to his expectations and his expectations are articulated in the *Shariah* and therefore law rather than love became the purpose of life and society. The most conservative version of this approach to Islam is the contemporary *Salafi* understanding, characterized more by harshness unlike the Sufi movements, which seek to emphasize kindness.

This book, *Islam and Good Governance*, seeks to develop a political philosophy based on *Ihsan* that emphasizes love over law, process (Islamic governance) over structure (Islamic state) and self-annihilation (*Fanaa*) over identity or self-assertion. Many Muslims nearly everywhere are determined that Islam should play a role in the public sphere. I hope to advance a vision of Islam that will emphasize virtue over identity and ethics over politics and make Islam a force for the good in the global society.

The demand for Islamization is persistent and global. It definitely varies in intensity and nature in its manifestations, but it is safe to acknowledge that in every place where Muslims constitute a reasonably sized community, a section of the said community seeks a more prominent role for Islam. Some demand the incorporation of Islam in the sociopolitical structures of their societies, while others may desire Islam to play the role of a collective identity.[2] Moreover Islam, as understood and articulated by contemporary orthodoxies, may be incompatible with some of the key ingredients of the contemporary global order, values and institutions— secularism, the nation-state system, legal equality across religious communities, gender equality, to name a few. Islam's role in the global society will remain contentious and unsettled until either the global society becomes subservient to Islam as desired by some radical Muslim groups or the vision of Islam advanced by Muslims is so transformative that it renders Islam both compatible with the irreversible realities of history and becomes one of the many ethical traditions in the multi-paradigmatic ethos of global values.[3]

In *Islam and Good Governance*, I propose to revisit Islam's most fundamental sources and scriptures to rearticulate a vision of Islam that is at once authentic and transformative. I hope to articulate an understanding of Islam which is based on the Quran and the hadith tradition that will emphasize Islamic idealism and privilege it over Muslim realism. In my research, I have discovered that Muslims by pressing Islam in the service of politics and the state have allowed realist precepts (considerations of power) to systematically subvert the highest ethical, normative and compassionate aspirations of Islamic scripture. This was done by privileging sources and/or interpretations that lend themselves to *realpolitik* and by marginalizing ethical principles that encourage other-regarding behavior over self-regarding politics.[4] I hope to reverse this by making the concept of *Ihsan* constitutive of Islamic ethos, and privileging the highest and the most beautiful understanding of Islam.

---

[2] Ibrahim M. Abu-Rabi', *Intellectual origins of Islamic resurgence in the modern Arab world* (SUNY Press, 1996). John L. Esposito, ed., *Voices of resurgent Islam* (Oxford University Press, 1983). Olivier Roy, *Globalized Islam: The search for a new ummah* (Columbia University Press, 2006).

[3] Mohammed A. Muqtedar Khan, "Islam as an ethical tradition of international relations," *Islam and Christian-Muslim Relations* 8.2 (1997): 177–192.

[4] Bassam Tibi, "The politicization of Islam into Islamism in the context of global religious fundamentalism," *Journal of the Middle East and Africa* 1.2 (2010): 153–170.

For me, *Ihsan* is the antithesis of identity. Identity deals with external manifestations, with recognizable markers, but *Ihsan* is about interior excellence; it is about anonymous beauty. It is action, it is thought and it is a state of being where both beauty and excellence merge, where self-regarding behavior recedes to usher in other-regarding conduct. *Ihsan* is a state of enlightenment that is not only limited to the refinement of the mind, but it also includes the refinement of the heart. Can we make public policy based on finer emotions of compassion, forgiveness and sacrifice? Perhaps not always, but can we do it often enough to transform the public arena from a battleground of power players to realm of conscience where the impulse for the good frequently trumps the instinct for power. By deconstructing political Islamist ideology, I aspire to revitalize enlightened Islam, which was always there hidden in clear view in Quranic verses, in prophetic traditions and occasional Islamic moments such as the golden age of Islamic pluralism in Andalusia, under some of the Mughals emperors of India, especially during the rule of Emperor Akbar.[5]

The project is highly interdisciplinary in nature. It cuts across social sciences, humanities and theology. This book essentially employs two methodological gambits—(1) deconstructing existing orthodoxy and (2) reconstituting a new and more mystical and compassionate narrative of Islamic principles and values. From an epistemological standpoint, it is a normative theory project, but unlike most theoretical and philosophical reflections, *Islam and Good Governance* seeks to engage with policy in the areas of international security, conflict resolution, foreign policy, interfaith relations and social reform and development and most importantly for nation building in the post-Arab Spring era. I started working on this book in 2011. I spend nearly two years working on improving my classical Arabic and I spent a summer in Morocco refreshing my grasp of classical grammar. I also have traveled, thrice to Morocco, twice to Egypt, to Jordan, United Kingdom, Tunisia and France, and over a dozen times to Turkey, to study and interview teachers, activists, politicians and mystical teachers to learn from them about *Ihsan* and the challenges to good governance in the Muslim world. My book distills the learnings from my travels as well as includes extensive literature reviews and seeks to find a meeting point where mysticism, theology and political theory can be engaged.

---

[5] S. Frederick Starr, *Lost enlightenment: Central Asia's golden age from the Arab conquest to Tamerlane* (Princeton University Press, 2013) Christopher De Bellaigue, *The Islamic Enlightenment: The Struggle Between Faith and Reason, 1798 to Modern Times* (Liveright Publishing, 2017).

This book is unique because it develops a political philosophy based on mystical and spiritual values. It seeks to combine Sufism with political theory and this has never been done before in a systematic way. In this age, when the world is suffering from Salafi and Salafi Jihadi ideologies, a revival of the profoundest dimensions of Sufism can rescue both Islam and the world from Salafi anger, hate and intolerance. Contemporary scholar William Chittick has written several books, which explore the meaning of *Ihsan* in Islamic mystical poetry, and how Rumi and Ibn Arabi have developed the idea, but his work does not contribute to political theory or public policy. In the post-Arab Spring era as Muslims struggle to understand how to accommodate both, the instinct for democracy and the clamor for Islam, this book should come as a guide to the perplexed.

THE STRUCTURE AND CONTENTS OF THE BOOK

This book has six chapters besides the introduction and concluding thoughts. Chapter 2 makes the case that Islamic legal corpus has developed in such a way that it eschews *Ihsan* and compassionate interpretations of divine texts and sources. This chapter employs two case studies to make the point. One case study is about a contentious and highly politicized issue of punishment for blasphemy in Pakistan, and the other a routine simple issue of how to make up for breaking a Ramadan fast. In both cases, it is apparent that the most obvious understanding of sources is also the most compassionate one and yet scholars and jurists have canonized the harshest of possible interpretations. *The goal of this chapter is to show the absence of* Ihsan *in applied Islam.* This chapter examines the politics and the historical narratives that systematically exclude perspectives based on *Ihsan* in the understanding of divine sources and their legal interpretations.

Chapter 3 examines the challenge modernity presented to Muslims and identifies four Muslim responses—traditionalists, modernist, Islamist and secular. It critically examines these responses focusing on their understanding of modernity and their interpretation of Islam. These perspectives are examined in the light of the Islamic revival that has been taking place in many parts of the Muslim World. In this chapter, I demonstrate how this global Islamic revivalism has reduced Islam to an identity. Islam is used not as a source of normative values but as an instrument of political mobilization. The goal of this chapter is to show how contemporary Muslim politics, even in the name of Islam, has deviated from its normative purpose. Over a century of Islamic revivalism and the emergence of political Islam has reduced Islam from being a fount of civilization, ethics, values, norms, cultures and politics to essentially a political identity.

In Chap. 4, I explore how the Islamic tradition has understood *Ihsan* in the past and in the recent past. I examine how *Ihsan* has been understood and explained by grand Sheikhs like Ibn Arabi, Al-Ghazali and Ibn Taymiyyah and many more classical philosophers, theologians and mystics. I also review the only two substantial books (both in Arabic language) on *Ihsan* published in the past 25 years, one by a Salafi leaning scholar from Egypt and another one by a Sufi leader from Morocco. This chapter also examines in depth how the Quran and the hadith literature present *Ihsan*. The goal is to show the depth and complexity of the concept of *Ihsan* in Islamic thought and sources.

In Chap. 5, I introduce my understanding of *Ihsan*. I revisit the sacred sources of *Ihsan*, unpack them and define *Ihsan* beyond the classical understanding as a spiritual state. I envision *Ihsan* as a complex philosophy that includes an epistemology, the spiritual act of witnessing God, as political forgiveness, as anti-identity politics (*Fanaa*), as pursuit of excellence, as self-criticism and as steadfastness. *Ihsan* is presented as a process of perfection and as mystical composure in times of adversity. My rendition of *Ihsan* in this chapter allows me to reassemble the unpacked components as a political philosophy of good governance. Every aspect of *Ihsan* unveiled is based on Quran and tradition. I am not a member of any Sufi order nor have I pledged any allegiance to any Sufi saint or scholar, and so I am under no obligation to restrain my critical and rational faculties and I am not beholden to anyone else's vision. There are no unsubstantiated claims to knowledge, or gnosis in this book. Even when I write about mystical knowledge, I remain within the realm of reason and do not claim to advance any insight that is beyond the scope of rational arguments or empirical, historical or discursive analysis.

The next two chapters are on political philosophy. In Chap. 6, I offer a critical genealogy of Islamic political philosophy and the development of Islamic political thought from the age of the rightly guided Caliphs to the contemporary Arab Spring. I look at key classical thinkers like Al-Mawardi, Al-Farabi, Ibn Taymiyyah and Ibn Khaldun and key contemporary thinkers such as Syed Qutb, Maududi, Khomeini and Al-Nabbhani. This chapter concludes with a critique of Islamic political thought for privileging identity and power, structure and law and ignoring process and the mystical dimensions of Islam. In this chapter, I also explore the Islamic conception of democracy as advanced by several contemporary theorists. This chapter includes a review of Sufi understanding of politics and argues that the preliminary ideas advanced by Sufi thinkers like Saa'di indicate the potential to develop a political philosophy based on the concept *Ihsan*, specially the mystical understanding of *Ihsan*. This chapter exposes the diversity of approaches to Islamic political thought in order to emphasize that the *Shariah*-based approach to politics is only one Islamic way of thinking about politics.

Chapter 7 is the key chapter of this book. In this chapter, I try to outline a vision of transition from politics as we know to a politics of *Ihsan*. In this chapter, I offer an alternate way of thinking about Islam's role in politics, especially distinct from that of Islamists and Jihadis. This book critiques the focus of Islamic political thought on structure and law and instead argues that perhaps a focus on process will yield more benefits for society. Advocates of Islam are seeking power to "implement *Shariah*" and in the process are either leaning toward autocracy or making ethical compromises to accommodate democracy. In either case, the cause of the normative principles is lost. This chapter argues that rather than seeking power, advocates of Islam should seek to bring *Ihsan* into society. It submits that Muslims should focus on process, make it inclusionary and one that privileges the various dimensions of Islam and through criticism and activism keeps the social conscience alive. This chapter will lay out the Islamic principles that encourage good governance, and *politics in pursuit of goodness*. It imagines a state of *Ihsan* and a society of *Muhsins* (those who practice *Ihsan*).

CHAPTER 2

The Loss of *Ihsan*

قُلْ يَا عِبَادِيَ الَّذِينَ أَسْرَفُوا عَلَىٰ أَنْفُسِهِمْ لَا تَقْنَطُوا مِنْ رَحْمَةِ اللَّهِ
إِنَّ اللَّهَ يَغْفِرُ الذُّنُوبَ جَمِيعًا إِنَّهُ هُوَ الْغَفُورُ الرَّحِيمُ

Say: O my Servants who have transgressed against their souls! Despair not of the Mercy of Allah: for Allah forgives all sins: for He is Oft-Forgiving, Most Merciful. (Quran 39:53)

When I read Islamic sources, especially the Holy Quran and traditions of the Prophet Muhammad (pbuh), I am overwhelmed by the profound compassion they teach, the humility they demand and the existential comfort that they provide. Consider this verse from the Quran, *and my mercy embraces all things* وَرَحْمَتِي وَسِعَتْ كُلَّ شَيْءٍ (7:156), or the verse that describes both the message and the messenger of Islam in one spectacular statement as nothing but mercy—*We have not sent you (O Muhammad) except as mercy to all the worlds* (21:107) وَمَا أَرْسَلْنَاكَ إِلَّا رَحْمَةً لِّلْعَالَمِينَ.[1] Consider this authentic tradition from the most authentic collection *Sahih Bukhari* (93:473), "Allah will not be merciful to those who are not merciful to others." To me this is the essence of the teachings of Islam. I see the same message everywhere in the scripture. Here is another Quranic example:

---

[1] This verse for me describes both the message of Islam and the Messenger of Islam (pbuh) as nothing except mercy to all the worlds. For those who take the literalist approach insist that this verse only describes the Prophet as mercy, I refer them to the verse 16:64, which describes the Quran as nothing except guidance and mercy.

© The Author(s) 2019
M. A. M. Khan, *Islam and Good Governance*,
https://doi.org/10.1057/978-1-137-54832-0_2

Those who patiently persevere, seeking the countenance (the Face) of their Lord; Establish regular prayers; spend, out of (the gifts) We have bestowed for their sustenance, secretly and openly; and repel Evil with good: for such there is the final attainment of the (eternal) home. (Al-Quran 13:22)

وَٱلَّذِينَ صَبَرُواْ ٱبْتِغَاءَ وَجْهِ رَبِّهِمْ وَأَقَامُواْ ٱلصَّلَوٰةَ
وَأَنفَقُواْ مِمَّا رَزَقْنَـٰهُمْ سِرًّا وَعَلَانِيَةً وَيَدْرَءُونَ بِٱلْحَسَنَةِ
ٱلسَّيِّئَةَ أُوْلَـٰئِكَ لَهُمْ عُقْبَى ٱلدَّارِ

In my opinion this verse alone is sufficient to define a good life on Earth—one that is virtuous, rewarding and that which does no harm to anyone. Scriptures such as these, which invite us to ennoble ourselves through deeds that are compassionate and to respond to evil with goodness, are abundant.

Even popular Muslim folklore is infused with the ideas of compassion, mercy and tolerance. When I was a young man working in the Indian corporate sector in Bombay (the city since then has changed its identity and is now known as Mumbai), a co-traveler on the commuter train told me a very interesting Sufi tale. A Sufi mystic was once deep in meditation when he heard a voice say to him, "Shall I tell the people what I know about you? They will stone you to death?" Apparently, it was the voice of God telling the Sufi that God knew his past and his deepest of thoughts. The Sufi responded, "Shall I tell the people what I know about you? None will then ever pray, or fast or perform a good deed!" There are many subtexts to this story that critical analysts will surely discover, such as the suggestion that Sufis communicate directly with God. But the main point of the story is that if people discovered how forgiving, compassionate and merciful God really was, they would never ever fear hellfire and will live an unrestrained life fully assured that in the end all their transgressions will be forgiven. I remember this story very well. I have told it to many people and have heard it many times since then. The last time I heard it was most recently from a barber in Morocco. He told me this story to console me when I remarked in jest that perhaps my receding hairline was God's punishment for bad thoughts. The fact that mercy and compassion are the most definitive of God's defining attributes is a widely held belief among Muslims. Moreover, this is not exactly a secret. It is stated clearly in the Quran, in the form of a promise, and what can be more guaranteed than the promise of God himself.

قُلْ يَا عِبَادِيَ الَّذِينَ أَسْرَفُوا عَلَى أَنفُسِهِمْ لاَ تَقْنَطُوا مِن رَّحْمَةِ اللَّهِ إِنَّ اللَّهَ يَغْفِرُ الذُّنُوبَ جَمِيعًا إِنَّهُ هُوَ الْغَفُورُ الرَّحِيمُ

Say: O my Servants who have transgressed against their souls! Despair not of the Mercy of Allah: for Allah forgives all sins: for He is Oft-Forgiving, Most Merciful. (Quran 39:53)

But then when I look at the reality of the Muslim world, at Muslim politics and the actions and pronouncements of Muslim voices that purport to speak on behalf of Islam and God, I find a striking absence of this essence of Islam that I find so prolific in the text. The point that I am trying to make is not that Muslim behavior has departed from Islamic principles, but rather that the articulation of Islamic principles themselves, in contemporary Muslim discourses, have departed from the ethos of compassion and mercy so beautifully articulated in the Quran's disclosure of God's divine purpose in revealing Islam and sending Prophet Muhammad (pbuh) as his messenger. When I was conducting research for this chapter, the media was reporting that a woman, Amina Naser, was beheaded in Saudi Arabia for committing sorcery. In 2011, this was a second individual to be beheaded in Saudi Arabia for sorcery. The Ulema of Saudi Arabia deem it "a threat to Islam."[2] People are regularly accused of blasphemy against Islam in Pakistan, where the punishment for blasphemy is death, even when one repents.[3] As I browse the news from the Muslim world, examples of people being sentenced to death in the name of Islamic law on a regular basis are too numerous to cite. But then when we engage in debates with Islamophobes in the West who accuse Islam of intolerance or even inciting violence, we are quick to cite the Quran (5:32):

مَنْ قَتَلَ نَفْسًا بِغَيْرِ نَفْسٍ أَوْ فَسَادٍ فِي الأَرْضِ فَكَأَنَّمَا قَتَلَ النَّاسَ جَمِيعًا

Whoever kills an innocent soul, it is as though he has killed all of humanity.

[2] See BBC report, "Saudi Woman Beheaded for Witchcraft," Dec 12, 2011. Viewed on the World Wide Web on Dec 15, 2011 at http://www.bbc.co.uk/news/world-middle-east-16150381.

[3] Here is the most recent example that I found. There have been two accusations this week. http://tribune.com.pk/story/303165/mob-forces-police-to-book-christian-man-for-burning-pages-of-holy-quran/.

This verse is used to make the case as to how Islam does not condone violence or terrorism and highlights how abhorrent it is to kill innocent people no matter what the cause. The verse is indeed powerful; it asserts that killing for any other reason except two—as punishment for murder and for creating chaos, or terrorism on earth—is worse than genocide! But it is ironic that if this is indeed the case and we were to take the legal meanings of the verse seriously then one cannot pronounce death penalty for adultery, fornication, sorcery, apostasy or even blasphemy. But at this time in history, the distance between the beautiful aspects of Islamic religious texts and the reality of Islamic legal interpretations and Muslim societies is vast and ever increasing. I shall seek to demonstrate this by first exploring how a big segment of the Muslim community has become *Shariah* centered and then employ two cases to highlight the distance between divine values and their earthly realization.

The Development of *Shariah*

Since the rise of contemporary Islamic political movements, *Shariah* has become the most important Islamic concept. The implementation or absence of *Shariah* as a governing principle has become a litmus test for determining the Islamicness of Muslim institutions. Today many Muslims judge polity, economy and financial transactions for its religious identity and the so-called implementation of *Shariah* determines the religious identity of social things. An economy is Islamic if it forbids interest-based banking and transactions. A state is Islamic if it applies the *Shariah*, often reduced to the application of *hudud* laws, as in the case of Pakistan during General Zia-ul-Haq's Islamization campaign, or Iran after the Islamic revolution and Afghanistan under the Taliban. A woman is Islamic if she wears a Hijab, a school is Islamic if it too implements a handful of identity markers, such as include Quranic instruction as part of the curriculum. *Shariah* today has been reduced to a handful of identity markers that act as litmus tests about the religious identity of social things whose legitimacy comes from their perceived *Shariah* compliance (manifestation of relevant identity markers).

In this age of globalization, as Muslim societies in the traditional hinterland and diasporas are swamped by foreign cultures, fashions and trends, visible identity markers have become a way to conserve and sustain religious beliefs. Religiosity and identity have become synonymous. I explore how Islam has been reduced to an identity in the next chapter;

here however I wish to emphasize how *Shariah* has become the face of Islam. The concept of *Shariah* has become so ubiquitous that in the minds of Muslims and non-Muslims alike, being Muslim is all about implementing *Shariah*. In the West today, combating the application of *Shariah* has become a popular way to express dislike and animosity for Islam and Muslims. In a curious way the concept has been reified to such an extent that now Muslim scholars and individuals alike talk about what Islam says about various things. For example, Muslim scholars will routinely say, Islam says that such and such is forbidden, or Islam's position on terrorism, on women, on abortion is as follows. Muslims seeking legal Islamic rulings, or *fatwa*, often frame their questions in this fashion, for example, "What does Islam say about prayer during travel?"[4]

There are two things happening here—one, Islam and *Shariah* are treated as one and the same thing, and two, both *Shariah* and Islam are reified (made concrete) to such an extent that they are treated as a singular authoritative voice. In numerous interviews and conversations about Islamic *Shariah* in Turkey, the United States, Egypt and Morocco, I often caught prominent Muslim intellectuals and scholars reifying *Shariah*-Islam during and after a conversation in which we explored the diversity and even the sociopolitical construction of the concept of *Shariah*. How Muslims, especially authoritative Muslims, talk about Islam in the public sphere not only reveals how they think about it but also shapes how common Muslims will think about Islam going forward.[5]

Reification of *Shariah* and equating of Islam and *Shariah* has a rather emaciating effect on Islam. Islam is a *din*, and its scope is much wider than *Shariah*, which is generally understood as Islamic law. Islamic law explores the boundaries of Islam and tries to articulate what is permissible and what is not permissible. The law concerns itself with and often stipulates the minimal and necessary requirements of faith; it does not explore the depth and heights of Islamic faith, mysticism, philosophy or even emotions such as divine love (*Muhabba*). There is more to Islam than *Shariah*. Islam has answers to existential questions, to cosmic mysteries, to divine yearnings, and all of these elements are outside the purview of law. Law is important, but it is not everything. Law is a social necessity whereas faith is an existential

---

[4] Robert W. Hefner, ed., *Shari'a Politics: Islamic Law and Society in the Modern World* (Indiana University Press, 2011).

[5] Khaled Abou El Fadl, *Speaking in God's name: Islamic law, authority and women* (London: Oneworld Publications, 2014).

necessity. The Quran does not say that God sent Prophet Muhammad (pbuh) as conveyer of divine law; on the contrary Prophet Muhammad (pbuh) was sent as nothing but mercy to humanity. It is not accidental that the word *din* is used frequently in the Quran and the word *Shariah* only twice (Quran 45:18, 5:48). Indeed, a vast majority of legal scholars of the Quran agree that only 5% of the Quran or about 350 or more verses of the 6400 that are in the Quran are of legal nature (*Ayah Al-Ahkam*).[6]

Moreover, when we say Islam says this about any specific issue, we are missing two important characteristics of Islamic law—its diversity and its contingent nature. Islamic rulings are contingent upon many things, including culture (*'urf*), time and space. Understanding of Islamic law can vary from place to place and from time to time. Culture and local customs often have an important bearing on Islamic law. The manner in which Prophet Muhammad (pbuh) interpreted Islamic law is clearly indicative of his sensitivity to local customs. There are today extant many legal schools. The office of the Grand Mufti of Egypt has actually documented nearly 80 different legal schools of thought that shape how Muslims understand Islam in Cairo today. The Sunni branch of Islam recognizes four prominent and completely distinct schools of Islamic legal traditions, which vary not just in the interpretation of law but also vary in philosophy of law and jurisprudence. Diversity of understanding is an important and enduring characteristic of Islamic legal tradition and it is the first casualty of a discourse that asks and answers questions using the modality—what does Islam say about such and such and Islam says this about the same.

The popular usage of the term *Shariah* is often misleading. It is used to indicate a clear, unified, uncontested, monolithic and divinely ordained set of rules and regulations about life. It is also used to indicate the body of law itself. This is far from the truth. *Shariah* is a complex concept that includes three different things: (1) sources of Islamic law, (2) Islamic jurisprudence and (3) the rules and regulations that have been derived using the first two elements. Muslim scholars differ in their understanding of what constitutes each of those three elements. While nearly all Muslims and scholars believe that the Quran and the Sunnah of Prophet Muhammad (pbuh) are the primary sources of the *Shariah*, there is no consensus as to which verses of the Quran are legal verses and which traditions from the vast collection of *ahadith* (prophetic traditions, plural of hadith) are sources

---

[6] Mohammad Hashim Kamali, *Shari'ah law: an introduction* (London: Oneworld Publications, 2008).

of *Shariah*. Different legal schools add to the sources of the *Shariah*. Some believe that the consensus of the companions of the Prophet and their followers is also a source of the *Shariah* while other scholars disagree.[7]

When it comes to jurisprudence (*Usul al-Fiqh*), the philosophy and epistemology of *Shariah*, the differences among Muslim scholars are well known and the existence of different schools of law, such as the Hanafi, the Shafii, the Maliki and the Hanbali for Sunni Muslims, can be attributed primarily to the different philosophies of law that these schools expound. The philosophical differences between these legal schools are at times very profound, especially in their methodologies of interpreting the sources of *Shariah* and their theories about the balance between reason and revelation while articulating the rules of *Shariah*. These schools as they exist today have evolved over centuries and even their philosophies of law show a great degree of variety within the schools' paradigmatic umbrellas and across the various legal traditions.

Finally, the product of the Islamic legal schools, what they call as their understanding of the *Shariah*, or the derivative rules that they articulate from what they consider as sources of the *Shariah*, is the body of rules and laws that is known as *al-fiqh*. Modernist Islamic thinkers have emphasized the difference between *Shariah* and *fiqh* to drive home the point that while *Shariah* is divine, immutable and infallible, *fiqh* is essentially human and fallible and subject to reform and revision. What Muslims generally talk about when they say Islam says this about a particular issue, they are either referring to a source (a verse from the Quran or a prophetic tradition) of Islamic law, or a ruling from one of the many compendiums of Islamic *fiqh* in the heritage.

In this chapter, I seek to demonstrate how over the centuries, Islamic *fiqh* has evolved in such a way as to slowly but systematically exclude *Ihsan* (compassion, mercy, beauty) from Islamic rulings. Today if we survey Muslim voices in the media, we find ourselves confronted with two discourses of Islam, one where people are talking about the compassion and tolerance of Islam while others are interpreting their faith in extremely intolerant and sometimes even brutal fashion. A close scrutiny will reveal that those who emphasize the compassion and mercy of Islam are often speaking from original sources, namely the Quran and the Sunnah, whereas those who are advancing harsh and even intolerant interpretations

---

[7] Majid Khadduri and Herbert J. Liebesny, eds., *Origin and development of Islamic law* (New York: The Lawbook Exchange, Ltd., 1955). Also see Kamali, *Shari'ah Law*.

of Islam are often quoting specific scholars, Islamic legal rulings from various legal traditions, or countries, and or/using historical episodes as substitutes for law. The key takeaway is that those who are using the primary sources of the *Shariah* are also accessing the *Ihsan* that is deeply embedded in the Quran and the Sunnah of the Prophet Muhammad (pbuh), and those who are using *fiqh* and the historically evolved legal rulings are often accessing a reading of the *Shariah* divested of *Ihsan*.

Muslims have been articulating understandings of the *Shariah* for nearly 14 centuries. There have been many efforts to reform Islamic thought and legal approaches as there have been efforts to revive Islamic sciences. Every effort at revival and reform has acknowledged the corruption of Islamic values as a result of either political intervention or cultural developments and every call to revive is a testimony of the decline. Thus, it is safe to say that the manner in which Muslims understand and interpret Islamic sources has suffered several episodes of decline and corruption over the centuries and therefore my claim that the current understanding of Islamic *Shariah* too has been corrupted by politics and various cultural trends is neither unprecedented nor unusual. The numerous calls for reform and revival made by many prominent Muslim voices from many Muslim countries and communities in the past two centuries further underscore the extent of decline.[8] While many of these reformists' and revivalists' voices have sought comprehensive change, my concern is at once very simple yet very profound; I am lamenting the loss of *Ihsan* from the way we think and live Islam. My call to revive *Ihsan* while on the face of it is simple; it will, I am confident, have a transformative impact on how Islam is understood and will fundamentally change Muslim societies if *Ihsan* becomes a global aspiration of Muslims.

In the rest of this chapter, I examine two cases of how Islamic sources are used to articulate Islamic rulings. The first case is basically a discussion of how a completely non-political and non-contentious issue has led to an understanding of Islamic sources without the compassion inherent in the Prophet's practice (*Sunnah*), and the second case deals with issues that are highly political and in an environment that is pregnant with religious, cultural and geopolitical conflict. The first case is from the classical *fiqh*

---

[8] See Fazlur Rahman, *Revival and reform in Islam* (London: Oneworld Publications, 1999). Also see John L. Esposito, ed., *Voices of resurgent Islam* (London: Oxford University Press, USA, 1983). Ali Rahnema, ed., *Pioneers of Islamic revival* (New York: Palgrave Macmillan, 1994).

(rules) of fasting, the second the contemporary *fiqh of sabb al-rasool* or the vilification of the Prophet. The first case looks at the understanding of law that is nearly universal among Sunnis in the Muslim world and the other case looks at the specific application of *Shariah* in a Muslim country. Unfortunately, in each case, we find that the *Shariah* sources are very benign but the *fiqh* is very harsh.

Case Study I: The Recompense for Breaking Fast

The first case is about the consequence or penalty for breaking a fast in the month of Ramadan through sexual intercourse with one's spouse. If one breaks one's fast in the month of Ramadan by having sexual intercourse with one's wife, what does one do to make up this fast which is now void? All answers to this question on the Internet and several books of *Fiqh*[9] of fasting that I consulted have the same answer with minor variations. I looked at answers provided by the prestigious and influential Al-Azhar University,[10] prominent Pakistan scholar Taqi Usmani[11] and many other books of Islamic jurisprudence.[12] The answer was the same. In order to make up for the fast broken through sex with one's spouse, the culprit must manumit a slave. If one cannot free a slave, then one must fast for two months consecutively to make up for this fast. If one cannot do that, then one must feed 60 poor people. The remarkable consensus around this ruling across various Islamic legal schools suggests that the divine sources of this law must be crystal clear. Let us examine what the sources for this widely agreed upon *Shariah* ruling really are.

According to all Sunni Islamic schools of jurisprudence, the main *Usul al-Fiqh*, or sources of Islamic law are four: the Holy Quran, the *Sunnah* of

[9] The literal meaning of the Arabic term *Fiqh* is understanding. But it is widely used in Islamic law to indicate a particular understanding of the Islamic law or *Shariah*. The Islamic *Shariah* is a collection of sources and *Fiqh* is a body of rules and regulations extracted from these sources. Often Muslims equate the two in practice, but it is important to maintain the distinction since *Shariah* is divine and *Fiqh* is the human understanding of the divine law. See Fazlur Rahman, *Islam* (Chicago: University of Chicago Press, 1979), pp. 100–104.

[10] You can read the position of Al-Azhar's scholars and their justification on the World Wide Web at: http://www.alazhr.com/islamicpillars/Chapter4-4.htm.

[11] See the same position advanced by Taqi Usmani, a prominent Islamic scholar from Pakistan: http://www.alazhr.com/islamicpillars/Chapter4-4.htm.

[12] For example, see Laleh Bakhtiar, *Encyclopedia of Islamic Law: A Compendium of the Major Schools* (Chicago: Kazi Publications, 1996), pp. 138–139. Also see Muhammad Yusuf Islahi, *Everyday Fiqh*, Vol. II (Lahore: Islamic Publications, 1991), p. 98.

Prophet Muhammed (prophetic precedence), the *Ijma* (consensus) among Muslims and *Ijtihad/Qiyas* (independent or analogical reasoning).[13] Jurists are reluctant to use the third and the fourth source of Islamic law, since they believe it will open the door for human error. They are most comfortable primarily when relying on textual sources, the Quran and the corpus of hadith literature, which is operationalization of the concept of *Sunnah*. Besides, there is no consensus about *Ijma* itself. For some, for example Hanafi jurists, it is the consensus of the companions of the Prophet alone, for others it is the consensus of the first three generations of Muslims and then others consider it as the consensus of the entire Muslim *Ummah*.[14] On the issue that we are examining all jurists rely on textual sources alone. The Quran does not address the subject directly, but the prophetic traditions do and therefore they are the controlling authority on the juridical position on *Kaffarah* (compensation) for breaking of fast through legal sexual intercourse.

The Quran essentially lays out the *Shariah* of fasting in the verses 2:183–2:187. It forbids intercourse during fasts and allows those who are travelers or sick to miss fasts. The compensation for missing fasts for those who can fast is to make up the missed fasts with equal number of fasts, and for those who are unable to fast is to feed poor people (2:184). The Quran does not explicitly discuss the consequence of breaking fast through intercourse and hence we need to look at the next source of Islamic law, the prophetic traditions. But one can argue that the spirit of the law in the verse 2:184:

> So whoever among you is ill or on a journey [during them]—then an equal number of days [are to be made up]. And upon those who are able [to fast, but with hardship]—a ransom [as substitute] of feeding a poor person [each day].

suggests that when one misses a fast for whatever reason one should make up the fast if one is able or feed a poor person instead. Clearly the grace and blessings that one may earn through proper fasting may not be earned

---

[13] See Wael B. Hallaq, *A History of Islamic Legal Theory: An Introduction to Sunni Usul Al-Fiqh* (London: Cambridge University Press, 1997), pp. 36–81. Also see Mohammad Hashim Kamali, *Principles of Islamic Jurisprudence* (Cambridge: Islamic Texts Society, 1991). See Mohammad Hashim Kamali, *Shariah Law: An Introduction* (Oxford: Oneworld Publications, 2008). See Imran Ahsan Khan Nyazee, *Islamic Jurisprudence* (Islamabad: International Institute of Islamic Thought, 2000).

[14] See Wael Hallaq, *A History of Islamic Legal Theories*, pp. 75–81. Also see Imran Ahsan Khan Nyazee, *Islamic Jurisprudence*, pp. 182–194.

through the compensatory fasting, but nevertheless the obligation would be fulfilled. But the fact that there was a more specific case during the Prophet's time and it was recorded in the tradition has reduced the legal scope of the verse 2:184 to sickness and travel alone.

A search of the prophetic traditions reveals a particular instance when a man came and confessed to the Prophet that he had broken his fast by having intercourse with his wife, and all the scholars and schools of law that have advanced a compensatory ruling on this issue have relied on this particular source to base their judgments. I found this particular tradition repeated nine times in *Sahih Bukhari*,[15] three times in *Sahih Muslim*[16] and once in Imam Malik's *Muwatta*.[17] There is a similar hadith reported by *Sunan Abu Dawud*,[18] which has a slight variation but the substantive content of the tradition is the same as those reported by the others. Here is the tradition:

> Narrated Abu Huraira: A man came to the Prophet and said, "I am ruined!" The Prophet said, "Why?" He said, "I had sexual intercourse with my wife while fasting (in the month of Ramadan)." The Prophet said to him, "Manumit a slave." He replied, "I cannot afford that." The Prophet said, "Then fast for two successive months." He said, "I cannot." The Prophet said, "Then feed sixty poor persons." He said, "I have nothing to do that." In the meantime a basket full of dates was brought to the Prophet. He said, "Where is the questioner." The man said, "I am here." The Prophet said (to him), "Give this (basket of dates) in charity (as expiation)." He said, "O Allah's Apostle! Shall I give it to poorer people than us? By Him Who sent you with the Truth, there is no family between Medina's two mountains poorer than us." The Prophet smiled till his pre-molar teeth became visible. He then said, "Then take it."[19]

Muslim jurists have over the centuries written extensively in defense of the prophetic precedence, The *Sunnah*, as to how it was essential for

[15] See Book 31 #158, Book 47 #772, Book 64 #281, Book 73 #110, Book 79 #700, are some of those references from *Sahih Bukhari*.

[16] See Book 006, Hadith 2457, 2459 and 2461 in *Sahih Muslim*.

[17] See in Imam Malik's *Muwatta*, in book 018, Hadith #18.9.28.

[18] See Hadith #2207 in Ahmad Hasan (Trans.), *Sunan Abu Dawud*, Vol. II (New Delhi: Kitab Bhavan, 2005), p. 597.

[19] See Hadith #281, Book 64, Vol. VII in Muhammed Muhsin Khan (Trans.), *The Translation of the Meanings of Sahih Al-Bukhari*, Vol. VII (New Delhi: Kitab Bhavan, 1987), pp. 214–215.

understanding the practice of Islam correctly and not following the prophetic tradition was disobedience of not just the Prophet himself but also
of God. Even when the Quran is clear, the manner in which the Prophet
interpreted the Quranic text became the law since Islam's sources are
both, God's commandments as articulated in the Holy Quran and in the
prophetic understanding and explanation of the same as understood from
his *Sunnah*. The prominent Muslim jurists, Sheikh Yusuf Qaradawi very
eloquently captures the orthodox Islamic position on the Sunnah:

> The Sunnah of the Prophet comes as a source following along with the
> Quran and making it clear, as God said, addressing his messenger: 'We have
> sent down to you the Remembrance so that you make clear to humankind
> what has been sent down for them' (Al-Nahl, 16:44). Through the Prophet's
> sayings, his actions and his acceptance (*taqrir*), the Sunnah functions as the
> practical exegesis of the Quran, the application in reality, as well as the ideal,
> of Islam. In sum, the Sunnah is the Quran interpreted and Islam embodied.[20]

But in this case, it appears that the judgment advanced by the jurists
explicitly excludes the prophetic practice and selects only that part of the
tradition, which they assume is the law. Every jurist claims that the
Kaffarah for breaking the fast through intercourse with one's spouse is
the freeing of a slave, or fasting for 60 days (there is variance here, some
insist it must be continuous, while others allow discontinuity on grounds
of disability) or feeding 60 poor people. But the rest of the tradition, especially the part where the Prophet smiles at the man who claims that he can
neither free a slave nor fast for 60 days or feed poor people, and instead
gives him a basket of dates to go home and share with his own family, is
ignored. The man was unwilling to pay the compensation even from
received charity! Yet the Prophet neither got angry with him nor spoke
harshly with him. The net result of his going and confessing to the Prophet
was that he came home richer, with a basket of dates. If this man today
went to any Muslim jurist searching for expiation from his error, his experience will be vastly different from the Sunnah.

---

[20] See Yusuf Al-Qaradawi, *Approaching the Sunnah: Comprehension and Controversy*
(Herndon, VA: International Institute of Islamic Thought, 2006), p. 1. See also Mohammad
Hashim Kamali, *A Textbook of Hadith Studies: Authenticity, Compilation, Classification and
Criticism of Hadith* (Leicestershire: The Islamic Foundation, 2005). Israr Ahmad Khan,
Authentication of Hadith: Redefining the Criteria (Herndon, VA: International Institute of
Islamic Thought, 2010), p. xiii.

The difference between the Islamic law as applied by the Prophet and as understood by all jurists is stark. The prophetic precedent is full of compassion, understanding, tolerance, mercy and forgiveness. The juristic understanding of the same is devoid of all the beauty and compassion inherent in the *Sunnah*. The jurists read the tradition and without any explanation stripped it of its tenderness and gentleness and expressed it in its harshest form. Some schools of thought actually insist that if you miss the 60th fast after fasting for 59 continuous days, for whatever reason, one has to begin the sequence again![21] When I read this tradition, I see in it what is promised in the Quran—that the Prophet was sent as nothing but mercy to humanity. But when I read the law, articulated by Muslim jurists I find the same mercy systematically left out. The webpage of Al-Azhar University cites the above quoted entire hadith as the basis of their ruling but confine their ruling on the compensation to the three-tiered option discussed before and ignores the manner in which the Prophet himself dealt with the issue. It seems that jurists have become blind to the compassion inherent and apparent in the *Shariah*. Not only do they ignore the compassion in the prophetic tradition but also in the Quran itself: *So whoever sights [the new moon of] the month, let him fast it; and whoever is ill or on a journey—then an equal number of other days. Allah intends for you ease and does not intend for you hardship* (2:185). The Quran states that Allah does not intend hardship, but you would not get that message from the way the Islamic *Shariah* is articulated by jurists. Many jurists will respond to my critique by arguing that the divine law is the conditions for expiation that is in the tradition discussed, but the *Shariah* is a composite that includes the prophetic *Sunnah*, how the Prophet applied it. And if we are going to ignore the *Sunnah* then we need a very good explanation as to why—other than "we wanted the harshest punishment."

I find the manner in which the Prophet dealt with the situation very beautiful moving and inspirational. When the man states that he cannot fast for 60 days continuously, he does not explain why since he is healthy enough to fast in Ramadan, the Prophet does not subject him to any interrogation. And when he says that he cannot feed 60 people, the Prophet offers him the dates to feed 60 people. In a way the Prophet was paying the compensation for the man's misdeed. And when the man says his family is the poorest, the Prophet is neither irritated nor angry with him, but rather amused with him and tells him with a smile to keep it all for himself and his family! The entire interaction reveals the Prophet's profound understand-

---

[21] See Islahi, *Everyday Fiqh*, Vol. II, p. 98.

ing and accommodation of human frailty. Human nature (*fitrah*)[22] is a very important concept in Islamic discourses. Prophet Muhammad (pbuh) displays a great deal of understanding of human nature, unfortunately those who articulate Islamic law show neither an affinity to compassion nor any grasp of human nature. Now if the Islamic law was what the jurists say it is then the Prophet has violated the law in his adjudication of the case in the very instance, which is the principle basis for the law they stipulate.

The case also raises troubling questions about how Muslim scholars conclude what is divine injunction. What if the man was able to free a slave and answered yes, when the Prophet asked him if he could free a slave. The Prophet would have asked him to then go and free a slave and that would be the end of their interaction and Islamic law of expiation would be to manumit a slave. It is not difficult to imagine what its relevance would be for our age. What if the man could have fasted for 60 days, then the option to feed 60 poor people would not have been available to us. Jurists would probably respond that my counterfactual argument in this instance is really too hypothetical to deserve a serious answer. But then some would also argue that the entire episode is a form of revelation divinely orchestrated to enable the Prophet to teach us the law of expiation for deliberately breaking fast in Ramadan. Indeed, if the entire episode was divinely orchestrated then the compassion with which the Prophet dealt with the man is also a divine injunction to execute the law with mercy and understanding. Then the extant articulation of the ruling and its exclusion of the prophetic compassion would constitute selective application of law, and selective rejection of revelation.

There is a command in the Quran (39:18),[23] which explicitly invites us to follow the best interpretation of the text. We are told that those who derive the most beautiful meaning (*ahsanahu*) from the text are the ones whom Allah has guided and they are people of understanding.

الَّذِينَ يَسْتَمِعُونَ الْقَوْلَ فَيَتَّبِعُونَ أَحْسَنَهُ ۚ أُوْلَئِكَ الَّذِينَ هَدَاهُمُ اللَّهُ ۖ وَأُوْلَئِكَ هُمْ أُوْلُوا الأَلْبَبِ

---

[22] See Yasein Mohamed, *Fitrah: Islamic Concept of Human Nature* (London: Ta-Ha Publishers, 1996). Islam is sometimes described as *Din al-Fitrah*, Natural Religion.

[23] An exegetical discussion of this verse can be found at http://www.islamfortoday.com/khan10.htm.

In the case above, I have shown that rather than extracting the most beautiful meaning from the source text, scholars have in actuality extracted the harshest possible interpretation and over the centuries employed the concept of *Ijma* to make this *juristic preference*, divine law. Islamic laws by and large have been shaped by the corpus of hadith traditions more so than the Quran itself.[24] There are authentic traditions of the Prophet that can and should be used as epistemological basis for how jurists think about crime and punishment. They cannot and should not pronounce Islamic edicts as if God is a very harsh taskmaster on the contrary recognize that he is the Most Merciful and the Most Benevolent God.[25] The very sources they rely on to articulate these laws scream at them that Allah's mercy is boundless. I want to conclude this case study by citing a tradition that jurists must not ignore.

> Allah the Almighty has said: "O son of Adam, so long as you call upon Me and ask of Me, I shall forgive you for what you have done, and I shall not mind. O son of Adam, were your sins to reach the clouds of the sky and were you then to ask forgiveness of Me, I would forgive you. O son of Adam, were you to come to Me with sins nearly as great as the earth and were you then to face Me, ascribing no partner to Me, I would bring you forgiveness nearly as great as it."[26]

When one moves from textuality to legality, it is as if one is moving from light to darkness, from enlightenment to *jahiliyyah* (ignorance). I understand that one case study will not suffice to make the point that Islamic laws are often articulated in a way that excludes the mercy of God. Nevertheless, any cursory examination of how laws against blasphemy, on adultery and apostasy are legislated and executed by Muslim countries that call themselves Islamic, like Saudi Arabia, Iran, Pakistan and Afghanistan, will make it clear why so many contemporary Muslim scholars are calling for reform of not just the corpus of Islamic law (*Fiqh*) but the very

---

[24] Jonathan Brown argues that while the Quran is revered more than *ahadith*, it is the prophetic tradition which has a greater impact on making of Islamic law. See Jonathan Brown, *Hadith: Muhammad's Legacy in the Medieval and Modern World* (Oxford: Oneworld Publications, 2009), p. 3.

[25] All but one of the Quran's 114 chapters begin by invoking God—بِسْمِ اللّٰهِ الرَّحْمٰنِ الرَّحِيمِ. In the name of Allah the Most Merciful, and the Most Benevolent. These are the most dominant of God's many names and attributes.

[26] This is the 42nd hadith cited in Imam Al-Nawawi's famous collection of prophetic traditions. See Sheikh M. An-Nawawi, *Al-Arbaeen Al-Nawawi* (Chicago: Kazi Publications, 1982).

philosophy of *Usul al-Fiqh* (Islamic jurisprudence). The most prominent contemporary example of this call for reconstituting Muslim approach to Islamic law is the *Maqasid al-Shariah* movement that seeks to both revive the vitality of Islamic legal thinking but also correct some of the perceived deficiency in the extant corpus.[27]

Mohammad Hashim Kamali, one of the most prominent contemporary scholars of Islamic legal tradition, summarizes this aptly[28]:

> To say that alienation of Islamic values from law and governance has been a source of widespread dissatisfaction is to state the obvious. ... This tendency in Islamic juristic thought, and how it has been manifested in the practice of law and governance, namely to target externality at the expense of meaning and substance is due for a corrective.

The Muslim world in my estimate is suffering from a double deficit. There is a deficit in the realization of the highest divine principles that teach compassion, tolerance, charity and humility. And then there is also the deficit in the acceptance and internalization of evolving humane principles of democracy, freedom and human rights. We are neither invoking the depths of understanding and compassion proliferating in our sources, nor are we fully committed to embrace when similar humane principles and values are legislated and instituted by the global society. There is, I concede readily, nothing original or new about this claim. Muslim intellectuals, philosophers and commentators have been lamenting the absence of Islamic values in Muslim societies and along with secular commentators and students of the Muslim world, many Muslim scholars too have written on the human rights deficit in the Muslim world.[29]

---

[27] See, for example, Jasser Auda, *Maqasid al-Shariah as Philosophy of Islamic Law: A Systems Approach* (Herndon, VA: International Institute of Islamic Thought, 2008). Gamal Eldin Attia, *Towards Realization of the Higher Intents of Islamic Law; Maqasid al-Shariah: A Functional Approach* (Herndon, VA: International Institute of Islamic Thought, 2007). Ibn Ashur, *Treatise on Maqasid al-Shariah*, Trans. Mohammad al-Tahir El-Mesawi (Herndon, VA: International Institute of Islamic Thought, 2006).

[28] See Mohammad Hashim Kamali, *Shari'ah Law: An Introduction* (Oxford: Oneworld, 2011), pp. 6–7.

[29] See Saad Eddin Ibrahim, "The causes of Muslim countries' poor record of human rights," in Shireen Hunter, ed., *Islam and Human Rights: Advancing a US-Muslim Dialogue* (Washington, DC: CSIS, 2005), pp. 100–109. Abdullahi A. An-Na'im, *Toward an Islamic Reformation: Civil Liberties, Human Rights and International Law* (Syracuse, NY: Syracuse University Press, 1990).

In discussing this singular case, I am merely systematizing the impetus for this book, which is to point out the ever-enlarging chasm between the prolific presence of the most beautiful of values in Islamic texts and their profound absence from Muslim reality. I take comfort in the fact that I am not the only thinker concerned with this loss of beauty. Khaled Abou El Fadl, a prominent jurist also wrote a book a few years ago lamenting the loss of beauty in Muslim practice of Islam.[30] In this book, I shall explore, what went wrong? Where is the enlightenment that Islam brought to eliminate the *jahiliyyah* from this world? Where is the compassion that embraces all things? Where is the justice that reminds us of the one God who is both merciful and just? Why haven't Muslims succeeded in institutionalizing these values of Islam, which fall under the rubric of the Islamic concept of *Ihsan*? The concept of *Ihsan* will be discussed in great detail in this book, but it is sufficient to understand here that it means, excellent and the "good" as understood in political and normative philosophy. I understand *Ihsan* to be a composite of the values of beauty, excellence, compassion, charity, forgiveness and devotion.

There has come to you from Allah a light and a clear Book. By which Allah guides those who pursue His pleasure to the ways of peace and brings them out from darknesses into the light, by His permission, and guides them to a straight path. (Quran 5:15–16)

Case Study II: Blasphemy Against Prophet Muhammad (PBUH)

لَا تَقْنَطُوا مِن رَّحْمَةِ اللَّهِ إِنَّ اللَّهَ يَغْفِرُ الذُّنُوبَ جَمِيعًا إِنَّهُ هُوَ الْغَفُورُ الرَّحِيمُ

Do not despair of Allah's mercy, He forgives all sins. Indeed He is Most Forgiving and Most Merciful. (Quran 39:53)

In the first case study, I showed how perfectly well-meaning jurists of Islam essentially did away with the *Ihsan* that underpins the *Sunnah* of the Prophet while articulating Islamic laws based on the very same *Sunnah*. The exclusion of prophetic compassion, mercy and understanding of human nature from the law has widespread concurrence. In the second case study I want to show how the same exclusion takes place not just in

---

[30] See Khaled Abou El Fadl, *The Search for Beauty in Islam: A Conference of the Books* (Lanham, MD: Rowman and Littlefield, 2005).

the philosophical thinking of jurists but in the broad culture and how people from a wide array of social segments participate in it. The second case study is about how Muslims are responding to real or perceived insults to the Prophet of Islam. At the beginning I must confess that I am not approaching this subject from a detached and "objective" standpoint. I am an observant Muslim and I too am deeply offended and hurt by deliberate insults to the Prophet and the Quran. I have written several Op-Ed articles condemning such actions as unbecoming, offensive, malicious and hurtful.[31] But I am also appalled at the completely un-Islamic, undignified and violent responses of many of my coreligionists to episodes of insults to the sacred symbols of Islam.[32]

Professor Shemeem Abbas, herself a victim of false persecution under the blasphemy law of Pakistan, has published a book which tries to argue that the culture of intolerance and persecution of alleged blasphemers is a historical consequence of Muslim empires using religion to discredit and delegitimize dissent. She claims that criminalization of blasphemy cannot be supported from the Quran and is essentially an un-Islamic law exploited as Islamic by the continuing collusion of state and the clerical establishment, which started during the Ummayad and Abbasid empires and found a second wind in Pakistan under President Zia-ul-Haq. I am sympathetic to her claims and also applaud her personal courage in dealing with the horrors of persecution. I also support her call for more intellectual freedom, religious tolerance and gender equality in Pakistan.[33]

The basic purpose of her book is to show how the mixing of religion and politics has engendered a culture of intolerance that often backfires and rather than fostering homogeneity and solidarity leads to fragmentation and oppression. The book provides useful historical details

---

[31] See Muqtedar Khan, "The Verbal Assault on Islam," *Washington Post's On Faith Blog*, May 4, 2010. On the World Wide Web at: http://newsweek.washingtonpost.com/onfaith/panelists/muqtedar_khan/2010/05/freedom_of_expression_burqa_muhammed_and_cartoons.html. Also see Muqtedar Khan, "The Quran Burning: Sign of Things to Come," *Washington Post's On Faith Blog*, September 6, 2010. On the World Wide Web at: http://newsweek.washingtonpost.com/onfaith/panelists/muqtedar_khan/2010/09/the_quran_burning_sign_of_things_to_come.html.

[32] See Amélie Blom, "The 2006 Anti-'Danish Cartoons' Riot in Lahore: Outrage and the Emotional Landscape of Pakistani Politics," *South Asia Multidisciplinary Academic Journal* 2 (Summer 2008). See Hesham A. Hassaballa, "Why We Muslims are Angry," *Beliefnet*, February 2006. On the World Wide Web at: http://www.beliefnet.com/Faiths/Islam/2006/02/Why-We-Muslims-Are-Angry.aspx.

[33] Shemeem Burney Abbas, *Pakistan's Blasphemy Laws from Islamic Empires to the Taliban* (Austin, TX: University of Texas Press, 2013).

about blasphemy laws in the subcontinent and provides a context to understanding current challenges. The best chapter of the book is chapter five that deals with the case of the Sufi Al-Hallaj who was executed in a brutal fashion for blasphemy. In that chapter, which is both rich in historical detail and discussion of the various elements of the Al-Hallaj episode, Abbas successfully shows how politics has abused Islamic law and especially how blasphemy laws are used as the stick of the orthodoxy in collusion with state apparatus to punish the dissenting or subaltern voice which may speak up for justice.[34]

Blasphemy against the Prophet of Islam has become a global challenge. Two elements continue to agitate the crisis around this issue. One is the continuing provocation from Western Islamophobes who insult the Prophet of Islam to push an anti-Muslim political and immigration agenda in Western countries with Muslim minorities.[35] Some Muslims respond to the provocation with violence and provide the media images that are helpful to project Islam as an intolerant religion and Muslims as extremists and terrorists. The second element is the presence of blasphemy laws in some Muslim countries that are abused with regular frequency to harass both Muslims and non-Muslims. While only five Muslim countries have tough blasphemy laws, they provide enough examples on regular basis to generate global concern.[36] There have been several cases, which have garnered global attention. A young Christian girl in Pakistan was accused of blasphemy against the Prophet of Islam, when she made a spelling mistake in an exam on a question about the Prophet.[37] A wealthy Christian man in Egypt was prosecuted for tweeting a joke on his Twitter account about the Prophet, even

---

[34] See Abbas, *Pakistan's Blasphemy Laws*, pp. 87–108.

[35] See Anders Linde-Laursen, "Is something rotten in the state of Denmark? The Muhammad cartoons and Danish political culture," *Contemporary Islam* 1.3 (Fall 2007): 265–274. See also Peter Gottschalk and Gabriel Greenberg, "From Muhammad to Obama: Caricatures, Cartoons and Stereotypes of Muslims," in John L. Esposito and Ibrahim Kalin, eds., *Islamophobia: The Challenge of Pluralism in the 21st Century* (New York: Oxford University Press, 2010), pp. 191–210.

[36] See Asma T. Uddin, "Blasphemy Laws in Muslim-Majority Countries," *Review of Faith and International Affairs* 9.2 (2011): 43–47. See Umar Cheema, "Only Five out of Fifty Four Muslim States have Tough Blasphemy Laws," *The News*. See on the World Wide Web at: http://www.thenews.com.pk/NewsDetail.aspx?ID=9222.

[37] See Muhammad Sadaqat, "Girl Accused of Blasphemy for a Spelling Error," *The Express Tribune*, September 25, 2011. See on the World Wide Web at: http://tribune.com.pk/story/259907/girl-accused-of-blasphemy-for-a-spelling-error/.

after he apologized profusely for the error.[38] In Saudi Arabia a Muslim man was sentenced to lashes for allegedly insulting the companions of the Prophet of Islam.[39]

But the most egregious of recent affairs is the case of Asia Bibi in Pakistan that unleashed a sequence of terrible events that included the assassination of two prominent national leaders and led to much social unrest and political turmoil.[40] I researched the debates and the rhetoric in the Pakistani public sphere on the subject of blasphemy against the Prophet in the wake of this case.[41] I was profoundly horrified by the vehemence, the violence, the anger and the hatred with which Muslim scholars and intellectuals were approaching the issue. The intensity of intolerance for each other was astonishing. Prominent scholars instead of informing, enlightening and calming angry and confused masses were inciting people to violence and calling for the death of national leaders. In discussing the religiopolitical scenarios in Pakistan, I have divided all the players into four groups: secular nationalists, Islamic modernists, Islamists and traditionalists. I discuss the theological and political positions of these groups in much detail in the chapter "Islam as Identity."

The first thing I noticed was that this was not about religion at all; it was all politics. The traditionalists and the Islamists were on the same page on this issue. They were demanding that Asia Bibi, a Christian laborer accused of insulting the Prophet (*Sabb al-Rasul*), must be prosecuted and executed if found guilty. Their political position was vehement and uncompromising. It was clear that they were using the issue to achieve several political goals. Chief among them were (1) maximize their own individual political exposure and gain more followers, (2) expose the liberals and the secularists as anti-Islam, (3) prevent the steady secularization of Pakistani laws and polity, (4) project the ruling elite as the tools of Western culture and imperialism and highlight their "liberal and secular extremism,"

---

[38] See BBC news report, "Egypt Businessman Naguib Sawiris faces Blasphemy Trial," http://www.bbc.co.uk/news/world-africa-16473759.

[39] See BBC news report, "Australian Man faces lashes for blasphemy in Saudi Arabia," http://www.bbc.co.uk/news/world-asia-16064123.

[40] See Huma Imtiaz, "Aasia Bibi and the Blasphemy Law," a report posted by the Jinnah Institute based in Karachi and Islamabad; http://www.jinnah-institute.org/issues/secular-space/184-aasia-bibi-and-the-blasphemy-law.

[41] See M. A. Muqtedar Khan, "Islam and the Political Theology of Blasphemy," paper presented on August 12, at the Summer Scholars Institute at IIIT, Herndon, Virginia. A report on the presentation can be viewed at: http://blog.minaret.org/?p=5119.

(5) keep the issue of Islam in the front and center of national politics, (6) discredit the Islamic moderates as partners with the secularists and (7) send a message to the West that insults to Islam will not be tolerated. The internal competition for political mileage between Islamic groups further aggravated the situation and made the debates and protests more intense.[42]

The nationalists and the secularists were using the issue to highlight the threat of religious extremism and were hoping that they could garner enough domestic and international support to (1) change or abolish the blasphemy law in its current form, (2) expose the religious establishment as intolerant, extreme, against human rights and a threat to civil society and specially to religious minorities and (3) consolidate their political position by appearing to stand firm in the face of extremism.[43] The Islamic modernists[44] engaged the Islamist and traditionalist coalition and made a strong argument that a closer look at Islamic sources will reveal that Islamic sources do not demand punishment for blasphemy, at least not capital punishment. Their arguments and their critique while being very cogent did not change the opinion of the supporters of Islamists and traditionalists.

The controversy over Asia Bibi continued for several months and two episodes marked the nadir of this crisis. The first was the assassination of the Governor of Punjab Salman Taseer on January 4, 2011, a strong supporter of Asia Bibi and the leading critic of the blasphemy law. He wanted it repealed. Taseer was demonized by the religious establishment as a blasphemer because he opposed the law, and many members of the Ulema actually designated him as *Wajib Al-Qatl* (deserving of being killed). Mumtaz

---

[42] One of the most prominent traditionalist voices on this issue was the Barelvi Mufti Hanif Qureshi. Here is his sermon which inspired the assassin of Salman Taseer: http://www.youtube.com/watch?v=qxEouO7FjfM. Another prominent traditionalist voice was the Grand Mufti Ashraf Ul-Qadri. Here is one of his many public statements on blasphemy: http://www.youtube.com/watch?v=FJD8wVlSdU8. On behalf of the Islamists, the leader of Jamaat-e-Islami, Amir Syed Munawar Hassan, played the role of the point-man on organizing and coordinating the religious establishment's position on the blasphemy issue. See, for example, this news report "Blasphemy Law: JI Seeks Assurance from PM," *Dawn*, Dec 31, 2010: http://www.dawn.com/2011/01/01/blasphemy-law-ji-seeks-assurance-from-pm.html. See also the report, "The right comes together," *Dawn*, December 19, 2010. http://www.dawn.com/2010/12/19/the-right-comes-together.html.

[43] The prominent secular voices were those of legislator Sherry Rahman, Governor Salman Taseer and Minister Shahzad Bhatti. Think tanks like the Jinnah Institute too played an important role. See "Sherry Rahman: Blasphemy Law Needs Rectification," http://jinnah-institute.org/issues/210-sherry-rehman-blasphemy-law-needs-rectification.

[44] The most important Islamic modernist voice in Pakistan is clearly that of the Al-Mawrid Institute and its intrepid panel of scholars. See "Punishment for Blasphemy against the Prophet (sws)," http://www.al-mawrid.org/pages/articles_english_detail.php?rid=1157&cid=304.

Qadri, the police officer who was assigned to Governor Taseer's security detail, murdered him after he was convinced by a sermon from a rather bombastic traditional Muslim scholar Hanif Qureshi. The video of the sermon is still available on YouTube proudly announcing its achievement as the main inciter of the assassination.[45] The second episode was the assassination, on March 2, 2011, of the Federal Minister for Minority Affairs Shahzad Bhatti, a Christian who was a vocal critic of the blasphemy law because of its pernicious use against Pakistani Christians like Asia Bibi. These two assassinations underscored the gravity of the crisis, the extent to which it could undermine national security, and dismantle civil society. The two assassinations added fuel to an already raging fire.

A few weeks prior to this book going to press, the Supreme Court of Pakistan decided Asia Bibi's case in her favor. The three-judge bench determined that there was insufficient evidence to establish that she had indeed committed blasphemy. In its decision the court stipulated that there were several inconsistencies in the case presented by the prosecutors and in the accounts provided by the witnesses. While some segments of the society interpreted the decision as a sign of progress, the question remains, what if she indeed had said something insulting and then how would the court rule?[46] The decision was followed by days of protests and violence by religious groups. Prominent religious scholars called for the army to rebel against their commanders, people to rebel against the government and called for the assassination of the Supreme Court justices deeming them all *Wajib Al-Qatl*, deserving of death. Pakistani society is clearly polarized on this issue and the prospects for a fruitful national dialogue on the subject are remote. The chances of a dialogue in the diaspora communities also seem to be unlikely because a segment of the diaspora is on board with the religious groups while another is more interested in trying to preserve Pakistan's image rather than deal with the issue critically.

There were two debates about the blasphemy issue in Pakistan. One was theological, about the law itself wherein the issue at stake is does Islamic law prescribe the death penalty for blasphemy against the Prophet. The second debate was political. The law became the venue for a debate about the kind of state Pakistanis want, a liberal democratic one that

---

[45] The Hanif Qureshi sermon justify the killing of Salam Taseer can be seen here: http://www.wichaar.com/videos/hanif-qureshis-sermon-which-made-mumtaz-qadri-to-kill-salman-taseer-gustakh-e-rasool/hanif-qureshis-sermon-which-made-mumtaz-qadri-to-kill-salman-taseer-gustakh-e-rasool-video_c0c6e14bd.html.

[46] See report in Dawn.com at https://www.dawn.com/news/1442634.

respects fundamental human rights like freedom of speech and religion and one that treats both Muslims and non-Muslims as equal citizens; or a theological state where human rights will be curbed in the interest of religious ideology and where non-Muslims will be relegated to a second-class status.[47] The political philosopher in me finds the second debate very inviting but the theologian in my prevails in this instance. Therefore I shall confine my discussions to the first debate which demonstrates how for political purposes the prophetic attribute of *Ihsan* was excluded from the understanding of blasphemy that a vast majority of religious scholars in Pakistan were advancing.

There were four main groups engaged in the debate. The secular nationalists like the former Pakistan Peoples Party legislator and an Ambassador to the United States Sherry Rahman, and organizations like the Jinnah Institute wanted the law to be repealed or changed. The Islamic modernists like Allama Javed Ghamidi and Dr. Khaled Zaheer of the Al-Mawrid Institute argued that there was no capital punishment in Islam for insulting the Prophet and they provided a systematic counterargument to the religious establishment.[48] The traditionalists and the Islamists demanded death for those who are accused of insulting the Prophet and those who want the law changed or repealed. From within the religious establishment there were rare voices of sanity, like Dr. Tahir ul-Qadri who condemned the misuse of the blasphemy law and Maulana Fazlur Rahman a prominent voice among the Islamists who eventually conceded that the application of the law may be revisited. After reading dozens of newspaper articles, watching umpteen televised debates on Pakistani talk shows, listening literally to scores of YouTube videos of the prominent Islamic scholars from the Deobandi tradition, the Barelvi tradition and the Jamaat-e-Islami, I have managed to construct the main argument that the traditional and Islamist coalition advanced justifying capital punishment for insulting the Prophet of Islam.

The argument for death penalty for blasphemy made by the religious establishment in Pakistan is a bit dodgy. They usually start by simply asserting that there is a consensus among all scholars that one who insults the Prophet must be killed. The fact that the concept of *Ijma* is invoked right way telegraphs the confession that there is no direct Quranic or hadith text

[47] See Rasul Baksh Rais, "What Kind of Pakistan Do We Want?" *The Express Tribune*, May 31, 2011: http://tribune.com.pk/story/178863/what-kind-of-pakistan-do-we-want/.

[48] See for example Khalid Zaheer, "The Real Blasphemers," *The Express Tribune*, Jan 02, 2011: http://tribune.com.pk/story/06867/the-real-blasphemers/. See also Javed Ahmed Ghamidi, "The Punishment for Blasphemy Against the Prophet (sws)": http://www.ghamidi.net/article/Punishment%20for%20Blasphemy.pdf.

available to vindicate the said judgment. As I have pointed out while discussing Case Study I, the generally agreed upon juristic methodology is to first look for the answer in the Quran, and if the Quran is silent then the Sunnah and if the hadith traditions are silent then look for agreement among scholars. The fact that the scholars are going straight away to consensus of scholars is a clear sign that even they know that the sacred texts do not prescribe the death penalty for blasphemy. Second, they are wrong when they claim there is consensus on the issue.[49] First of all many contemporary scholars disagree, so there is no contemporary consensus on the issue. If they are claiming that there is a consensus among the classical scholars, then again they are wrong, because Imam Abu Haneefah (699–767 CE), the founder of the biggest and the oldest Islamic school of jurisprudence that bears his name, disagreed. He claimed that Islamic law does not prescribe the death penalty for non-Muslims who insult the Prophet of Islam. Most of the scholars who claim that there is a consensus on the matter invoke the two famous books that discuss the subject written by Ibn Taymiyyah, *Al-Sarim Al-Maslool ala Shatim Al-Rasool* (Drawn Sword Against the Insulter of the Prophet), and Qadi Iyad Ibn Musa al-Yahsubi, *Kitab Ash-shifa bi Ta'rif Huquq al-Mustafa*.[50] But both the books actually record the dissent of Imam Abu Haneefah. The fact of the matter is that the biggest Islamic legal School does not maintain that the non-Muslim blasphemer should be killed. Any scholar who claims that there is a consensus on the matter is most definitely equivocating.

The advocates of death penalty do try to buttress their claims by invoking verses 63–66 from the ninth chapter (*al-Tawbah*, (Repentance) in the Quran. The verses merely promise that those who oppose Allah and His Messenger will be disgraced and sentenced to hell forever. Ironically the verse (63) rather than prescribing death penalty on earth promises retribution in the hereafter; effectively taking the matter out of the hands of Muslims and kicking the can forward into the hereafter. Allah the almighty repeats the message for those who in their zeal to kill overlook the first message in 33:57. Both verses are clear. God is

---

[49] The religious establishment in Pakistan was helped by scholars from Saudi Arabia who wrote helpful *Fatwas* for them and also provided English and Urdu translations. See *Fatwa* of Sheikh Al-Munajjid: http://islamqa.info/en/ref/22809.

[50] See the relevant English translation from Qadi Iyad's Al-shifa on the World Wide Web, by a very reliable and able translator *Al-shifah* A Bewley: http://www.masud.co.uk/ISLAM/misc/alshifa/pt4ch1sec1.htm. See also the Urdu translation of Imam Ibn Taymiyyah, *Al-Sarim Al-Maslool ala Shatim al-Rasool*: http://www.scribd.com/doc/46845739/Al-Sarim-Ul-Maslool-Ala-Shatim-Ur-Rasool-by-Imam-Ibn-Tayyimia-URDU-Translation.

telling us that He will take care of the matter. But these days many of the scholars do not allow the Quran to get between them and "their *Shariah*."

$$\text{أَلَمْ يَعْلَمُوٓاْ أَنَّهُۥ مَن يُحَادِدِ ٱللَّهَ وَرَسُولَهُۥ فَأَنَّ لَهُۥ نَارَ جَهَنَّمَ خَٰلِدًا فِيهَا ۚ ذَٰلِكَ ٱلْخِزْىُ ٱلْعَظِيمُ}$$

Know they not that whoever opposes and shows hostility to Allah and His Messenger (SAW), certainly for him will be the Fire of Hell to abide therein. That is extreme disgrace. (Quran 9:63)

$$\text{إِنَّ ٱلَّذِينَ يُؤْذُونَ ٱللَّهَ وَرَسُولَهُۥ لَعَنَهُمُ ٱللَّهُ فِى ٱلدُّنْيَا وَٱلْءَاخِرَةِ وَأَعَدَّ لَهُمْ عَذَابًا مُّهِينًا}$$

Indeed, those who abuse Allah and His Messenger—Allah has cursed them in this world and the Hereafter and prepared for them a humiliating punishment. (Quran 33:57)

There are several other verses in the Quran that record how some people insulted the Prophet of Islam—see, for example, 2:104, 4:46—and then there are others that talk about hypocrites who mocked the beliefs of Islam. But nowhere, absolutely nowhere does the Quran prescribe the death penalty for someone who has blasphemed or insulted the Prophet.

The traditions of the Prophet (*Sunnah*) and his biographies (*Seerah*) record innumerable episodes in his life, in which he was insulted, harassed, vilified, beaten and even attacked with stones by those who refused to accept his message. But in all these cases he did not respond to them with violence, he did not curse them and he did not order those who vilified him to be killed. In fact, the Prophet is on record for commanding Muslims to not respond to harm with harm. The famous collection of 40 traditions by Imam Nawawi records this tradition[51]:

$$\text{لا ضرر و لا ضرار}$$

Do no harm; Do not reciprocate harm.

---

[51] See Ezzedine Ibrahim and Denys Johnson-Davies (Tr.), *An-Nawawi's Forty Hadith* (Riyadh, KSA: International Publishers House, 1992), pp. 106–107.

In addition to the above command, the Quran itself explicitly orders both
the Prophet (pbuh) and Muslims to respond to verbal provocations and
excesses in a better fashion. Consider the verse 23:96:

$$ ٱدۡفَعۡ بِٱلَّتِی هِیَ أَحۡسَنُ ٱلسَّیِّئَةَ نَحۡنُ أَعۡلَمُ بِمَا یَصِفُونَ $$

Repel evil with that which is best: We are well acquainted with the things they say.

For a true believer, this verse should suffice as God's command not to
respond to blasphemous statements with violence or even with verbal
responses of the same degree of offensiveness. Muslims are always expected
to occupy the moral high ground; after all they are servants of the Most
Merciful and the Most Benevolent God. But overlooking the overwhelming
example of forgiveness, set over and over again in his 23 years as Prophet,
the advocates of death penalty mined his life looking for episodes that they
could use to argue their case. They found a few episodes including two similar episodes in which a man kills a woman for repeatedly cursing and abusing
the Prophet.[52] Apparently when they reported this to the Prophet, he
announced that they were exempt from paying blood money in those cases.
This exemption from blood money is taken to mean that God has made
killing those who abuse the Prophet a divine rule. I find these traditions to
be problematic, even though scholars, namely Ibn Taymiyyah and
Muhammad al-Albani declared them as authentic. These men made their
confessions in public. They both claimed that the women they had killed
habitually cursed the Prophet. I wonder why no one asked them, why they
did not kill these women, when they cursed the Prophet the first time or the
second time and why did they wait and counsel these women to change
their habit. I also wonder why no one asked as to why one of them continued to have relationships with a woman who cursed the Prophet of Islam
repeatedly. And finally neither of the tradition reports that the Prophet ever
ordered them to be killed. Nor are there any traditions, which report that
the Prophet had announced the law that one who insults him must be
killed. So, these men, when they finally got tired of listening to the Prophet
being cursed, killed another human being *without actually knowing that it
was divinely permitted*, since we are deducing it was legal because the
Prophet waived the blood money after the fact. These two instances cannot

---

[52] These reports are in *Sunan Abu Dawud*, #4361 and #4362.

be a robust basis for deducing a law wherein death penalty is mandatory. Even if they are, it is perplexing as to how they are applicable in the case of Asia Bibi, who allegedly insulted the Prophet only once. Why does she not get the same benefit of being warned several times as did the two women in Medina? The reason is simple—those who use these traditions to deduce death penalty for blasphemy are only looking for plausible justification for their decision to kill anyone who in their view insults the Prophet.

The story of the covert operation to assassinate Ka'b Ibn Ashraf, a leader of the Jewish tribe Banu Al-Nadir, was also used by some of the preachers in Pakistan to justify the death penalty for blasphemy against Prophet Muhammad (pbuh). Ka'b Ibn Ashraf, a prominent leader of a Jewish tribe had a long list of offenses according to the authors of *Seerah* (Prophet Muhammad's (pbuh) biographies) and the *Al-Mufassiroon* (commentators of the Quran). He made a treaty with the Meccans to fight against the Prophet and the city state of Medina. He plotted to assassinate Prophet Muhammad (pbuh), and he slandered Prophet Muhammad (pbuh) and wrote pornographic poetry about Muslim women. According to historical accounts his assassination was necessary to restore the balance of power between the Muslim forces in Medina and the heavily fortified Jewish tribe of Al-Nadir. It also ended the military cooperation between Banu Al-Nadir and the Meccans after the death of the main link between the two.[53] In the traditions that are invoked the Prophet is quoted as saying "Who will rid me of K'ab Ibn Ashraf, who has harmed Allah and His messenger." The Arabic terms that are used for blasphemy, insult or cursed are "Sabb" or "Shatama" and the Prophet used neither of them in those traditions. He used the term "aza" which means harm, injury, trauma, violence, suffering and hardship, not blasphemy or cursed or even slandered.[54] The exact quote is "fainnahu aza Allaha wa rasoolihu." This again is a misappropriation of an episode that happened during a time of war and its inappropriate application to a lowly laborer from a minority community in a country with the world's fourth biggest army and eighth big-

---

[53] See A. Guillaume (Tr.), *The Life of Muhammad* (Karachi: Oxford University Press, 1967), pp. 264–369. Also see Ibn Kathir, Safiur-Rahman Mubarakpuri et al. (Trs.) *Tafsir Ibn Kathir* (Jeddah, KSA: Darussalam Publications, 2003), Vol. 9, pp. 542–550. For an interesting study of Ka'b Ibn Ashraf's assassination, see Uri Rubin, "The Assassination of Ka'b b. al-Ashraf," *Oriens* 32 (1990): 65–71. Norman Stiller, *Jews of Arab Lands: A History and Source Book* (The Jewish Publication Society, April 1, 1998), pp. 119–126.

[34] The traditions are reported in *Sahih Bukhari* and the references are Book 45 Hadith #687, Book 52 Hadith #270 and Book 59 Hadith #369.

gest nuclear arsenal—Pakistan. This is indicative of how Muslim scholars indulge in what can only be described as *jurisprudential malpractice.*

Now having found some textual basis for enforcing the death penalty, the advocates then move to ensure that there is no escaping the gallows through repentance. Unfortunately, they are unable to claim consensus on this issue. Only a minority of Muslim scholars, namely the founders of two of the smaller jurisprudential schools of Islam (in terms of followers), the Maliki school and the Hanbali school, argued that even if the accused were to repent and seek forgiveness, they must be killed. Their position is that it is possible that God may forgive them in the hereafter but in this world they must be executed. To justify this claim, the scholars refer to a prophetic tradition, from *Sunan Abu Dawud* (#2683). I am reproducing it here:

> *Narrated Sa'd:*
>
> On the day when Mecca was conquered, the Apostle of Allah (pbuh) gave protection to the People except four men and two women and he named them. Ibn AbuSarh was one of them. He then narrated the tradition. He said: Ibn AbuSarh hid himself with Uthman ibn Affan. When the Apostle of Allah (pbuh) called the people to take the oath of allegiance, he brought him and made him stand before the Apostle of Allah (pbuh). He said: Apostle of Allah, receive the oath of allegiance from him. He raised his head and looked at him thrice, denying him every time. After the third time he received his oath. He then turned to his Companions and said: Is not there any intelligent man among you who would stand to this (man) when he saw me desisting from receiving the oath of allegiance, and kill him? They replied: We do not know, Apostle of Allah, what lies in your heart; why did you not give us a hint with your eye? He said: It is not proper for a Prophet to have a treacherous eye.

This episode is read by the advocates of death penalty to establish that one who insults the Prophet must be killed, even if he or she repents for it. They draw this conclusion from the facts that Ibn AbuSarh came forward to pledge allegiance to the Prophet and still the Prophet hoped that someone had killed him. We must first realize that death penalty advocates are now suggesting the Allah's *Shariah* is derived through indirect hints! To take this episode and conclude that one who insults the Prophet cannot be forgiven in this world is blasphemous to the idea of the *Shariah* itself! The fact that the Prophet allowed AbuSarh to live and never ever actually ordered that he be killed, also negates the conclusion that death penalty advocates draw. If the contemporary Ulema are correct in their claims about what is *Shariah* then will this Ulema then also state that on this occasion *Shariah* was not upheld because this man was not killed. Just like in Case Study I, the law that the Ulema derive from the case was not upheld in the case itself. This tradition does not state that AbuSarh was a *Shatim al-Rasool* (Insulter of the Prophet) the advocates of death penalty assume that he was. According to another tradition in *Sunan Abu Dawud*, this man was an apostate, who used to be a Quran scribe for the Prophet and he subsequently left the fold of Islam. The hadith clearly states that the Prophet wanted him dead for apostasy, not blasphemy.

> *Narrated Abdullah ibn Abbas: Abdullah ibn AbuSarh used to write (the revelation) for the Apostle of Allah (pbuh). Satan made him slip, and he joined the infidels. The Apostle of Allah (pbuh) commanded to kill him on the day of Conquest (of Mecca). Uthman ibn Affan sought protection for him. The Apostle of Allah (pbuh) gave him protection. (#4345)*

But the second tradition was never involved in the debate, to the best of my knowledge, but #2683 was often repeated and with great eloquence and detail and literally "performed" for the masses by the Pakistani Ulema.

It is interesting that the role of Uthman Ibn Affan, a close confidant of the Prophet, he married two of the Prophet's daughters and eventually became the third rightly guided Caliph, is not examined critically or otherwise at all. He not only allowed Ibn AbuSarh, who was a foster brother and allegedly a blasphemer of the Prophet, to use his home to elude capture, but also brought him to the Prophet and advocated for clemency on his behalf. If the *Shariah* law was that one who blasphemes the Prophet must be killed and there should be no forgiveness for him, then would Uthman Ibn Affan plead against God's law? Would the Prophet allow an outcome that contradicts divine law? Salman Taseer the late Governor of Punjab too advocated for clemency on behalf of Asia Bibi and recognizing the unintended consequences of the law advocated for its change or repeal. He too was labeled as a blasphemer and declared *Wajib Al-Qatl* (deserving of being killed) and his assassin was declared as a hero of Islam and upholder of divine law. None stopped to think even for a moment that perhaps he was playing, in his own way, a role similar to what Uthman Ibn Affan played in the case of Ibn AbuSarh. Analogical thinking is a preferred method of *Ijtihad* (independent reasoning) for most Ulema; this was an opportunity to exercise that process.

The religious establishment of Pakistan composed of Muftis and Grand Muftis does not reflect on these issues at all. They do not look at the evidence closely. They are merely interested in using Islam for providing a semblance of support for their ideological and political claims. The countervailing evidence is overwhelming, but they completely ignore it. When the Prophet visited the city of Taif to invite its citizens to Islam, he was insulted, mobbed, attacked and even stoned by the city's population. He neither cursed them nor ever ordered anyone to be killed for what they did to him. For 13 years, the citizens of Mecca abused him, quarantined him, insulted him, mocked him, slandered him, waged several wars against him, attacked his immediate family and killed his relatives, but when he conquered Mecca, he forgave them all, including Abu Sufyan who for more than a decade demonized Prophet Muhammad (pbuh) raised armies and waged two wars against him.[55]

Hind Bint 'Utbah, the wife of Abu Sufyan, cursed the Prophet and when his dear uncle, Hamza Ibn Abu Mutallib, was killed by her slave in battle, she cut his liver and heart and ate it; she was so filled with animus toward Prophet Muhammad (pbuh) and his message. But after the surrender of Mecca he forgave her too. She was so overwhelmed by his gesture that she reportedly said: "O Messenger of God, no tent was more deserted in my eyes than yours; but today no tent is more lovely in my eyes than yours."

The *Seerah* of the Noble Prophet is full of such accounts of forgiveness to enemies who cursed him, harmed him and waged wars against him. But the advocates of death penalty for blasphemy in Pakistan claim that there can be no forgiveness for insulting the Prophet. They claim that since all those offenses were made against the person of the Prophet he chose to forgive them, but after his death no Muslim can forgive insults against the Prophet. But the *Sunnah* of the Prophet on how to deal with the insult against the Prophet is overwhelmingly to forgive. The learned Ulema choose to ignore the prophetic precedent to advance an Islamic legislation without compassion, without forgiveness and very simply without *Ihsan*. Forgiveness as an

---

[55] For accounts of Prophet Muhammad's examples of forgiveness see some of these biographies. Tariq Ramadan, *In the Footsteps of the Prophet: Lessons from the Life of Muhammad* (London: Oxford University Press, 2007), pp. 193–195. Muhammad Husayn Haykal, Ismail Ragi al-Faruqi (Tr.), *The Life of Muhammad* (New Delhi: Crescent Publishing Co, 1976). Martin Lings, *Muhammad: His life based on the Earliest Sources* (Rochester, Vermont: Inner Traditions International, Ltd., 1983). See also Ibn Ishaq, A. Guillaume (Tr.), *The Life of Muhammad* (Karachi: Oxford University Press, 1967).

Islamic virtue did not die with the Prophet; it lives on as his *Sunnah*, as a source of divine law and in the Quran as God's direct injunctions.

$$\text{خُذِ ٱلْعَفْوَ وَأْمُرْ بِٱلْعُرْفِ وَأَعْرِضْ عَنِ ٱلْجَٰهِلِينَ}$$

Show forgiveness; enjoin what is good, and turn away from the foolish. (7:199)

I do not want to conclude this section without sharing something positive. While there are many who demonize Prophet Muhammad (pbuh), there are also many non-Muslims who have honored him. Maharaja Kishen Prasad, the Prime Minister of Hyderabad from 1900 to 1912, wrote this beautiful couplet in Urdu about Prophet Muhammad (pbuh).[56]

$$\text{کافر ہوں کی مومن ہوں خدا جانے می کیا ہوں}$$

$$\text{می بندا ہوں انکا جو ہے سلطان مدینہ}$$

I may be an infidel, I Maybe a believer, I know not who I am; I am the servant of the one, who is the sovereign of Medina.

CONCLUSIONS FROM THE TWO CASE STUDIES

Both the cases, one about a simple non-controversial and basically a ritual issue and the other about a highly emotional, controversial and politicized issue, demonstrate one thing quite clearly—for some inexplicable reason Islamic scholars deduce legal rules which they then traffic as divine law by excluding the *Ihsan* that we find permeating the *Sunnah* of Prophet Muhammad (pbuh). While this may not be the case in every issue, but I found too many examples for comfort while selecting these two cases. While the first case shows how under normal circumstances the scholars have excluded the compassion inherent in the precedent of the Prophet, the second case shows how a politically charged atmosphere brings out the worst from the jurists who instead of moderating political passions with religious ethics, actually distort the spirit and the letter of the law and use law to incite extremism in politics.

There are many external factors that are clearly influencing how Muslim scholars are thinking about Islamic issues and impacting how they interpret Islam. The Asia Bibi controversy took place at a time when the United

---

[56] Quoted in Annemarie Schimmel, *And Muhammad is His Messenger: The Veneration of the Prophet in Islamic Piety* (Chapel Hill, NC: University of North Carolina Press, 1985), p. v.

States had been conducting many aerial attacks on Pakistani soil and in the process killing a large number of innocent civilians along with many extremists. There is a profound sense of insecurity in Pakistan. Many in Pakistan feel that Pakistan and Islam are under attack. There have been several attacks in the West on Islam's sacred symbols. The Danish cartoons about Prophet Muhammad (pbuh), the film *Fitna* which misrepresents and slanders Islam, the use of Quran abuse as a means to torture Muslims in Guantanamo and the Quran burning episode in Florida are some of the most prominent instances. Moreover, for many years now conservative Muslims have felt that the West, Muslim liberals and secularists have been conspiring to change Islam. They feel that if they did not stand up for traditional understanding of Islam from Western and modern assaults, Islam, religion and awareness of God will disappear from the Earth. This fear prevents them from accommodating compassion, tolerance and forgiveness. This is how Muslim scholars have allowed *Ihsan* to be forgotten.

The most cited book on blasphemy against the Prophet, *The Drawn Sword against those who insult the Prophet*, was written by Ibn Taymiyyah (1263–1328 CE) under similar circumstances. He lived in the age when the Islamic world was being invaded by the Crusaders from the West and the Mongols from the East, and Christians were slandering the Prophet of Islam. His book was an angry response to the religiopolitical environment of his time, and once again, nearly 800 years later it is in vogue because for many Muslims the time they live in is similar to the time Ibn Taymiyyah lived in. But the coalition of traditionalist and Islamist scholars in Pakistan by advancing an extremely intolerant interpretation of Islamic law has created a storm of controversy over a small argument between a few laborers (Asia Bibi and her Muslim colleagues). If they stopped to reflect on their conduct, they will realize that they have not only abused Islamic sources but spread *fasad* (mischief) in the land.

In the two cases that I explored I tried to show that given the Islamic sources, the Quran and hadith, Muslim scholars and jurist consults can articulate an alternate corpus of legal interpretations that are significantly more compassionate, tolerant and cognizant of human frailties. Using harsher interpretations of legal principles may appeal to those who think that these harsh penalties and punishments may act as deterrent. But unfortunately harsh interpretations merely end up making Islamic law look cruel and also make it more difficult to practice in real life. An interesting example of how interpreters err on the side of harshness can be seen in the commentary of the verse 7:45 that speaks of the Ten Commandments revealed to Moses.

وَكَتَبْنَا لَهُ فِى ٱلْأَلْوَاحِ مِن كُلِّ شَىْءٍ مَّوْعِظَةً وَتَفْصِيلًا
لِّكُلِّ شَىْءٍ فَخُذْهَا بِقُوَّةٍ وَأْمُرْ قَوْمَكَ يَأْخُذُوا۟ بِأَحْسَنِهَا سَأُو۟رِيكُمْ دَارَ
ٱلْفَٰسِقِينَ ﴿١٤٥﴾

And We wrote for him on the tablets [something] of all things—instruction and explanation for all things, [saying], "Take them with determination and order your people to take the best of it. I will show you the home of the defiantly disobedient."

I looked at the commentary of this verse by Ibn Kathir and Fakruddin Al-Razi, both prominent classical commentators and Maulana Maududi a popular contemporary interpreter who made a profound impact on how Islamic law is understood in Pakistan. The key element of this verse is that it commands Moses to advise his followers to "take the best" (*ya'khuzu biahsanuha*) of what was revealed to him. Ibn Kathir cites a tradition to interpret the same phrase to say "Musa peace be upon him was commanded to adhere to the toughest of what was ordained to his people." He interprets best to mean toughest.[57] Similarly Maududi, who translates it accurately as "best sense,"[58] however in his commentary on it explains that it means in such a way that an individual with average intelligence can grasp its meaning.[59] The Quranic verse as I read it clearly invites the followers of Moses to take the best interpretation of what was revealed to them—it is an invitation to show *Ihsan*. But the two commentators I discussed reduce this invitation to something beautiful to something harsh and average. I was however delighted to note that Al-Razi however interpreted the verse precisely as I am advocating and to my delight actually uses the verse, *Who listen to speech and follow the best of it* (39:18), to explain the meaning of to take the best of it.[60] I have discussed this verse in my discussion of the first case in this chapter but I shall revisit these verses and discuss them in further detail in the section

---

[57] See Ibn Kathir, *Tafsir Ibn Kathir*, Vol. 4, Trans. Sheikh S. Al-Mubarakpuri (Jeddah, KSA: Darussalam Books, 2003), p. 160.

[58] See Syed Abul A'la Maududi, *Meaning of the Quran*, Vol. IV–VI, Trans. Ch. Muhammad Akbar (Lahore, Pakistan: Islamic Publications, 1993), p. 69.

[59] See Syed Abul A'la Maududi, *Meaning of the Quran*, Vol. IV–VI, p. 71.

[60] See Fakhruddin Al-Razi, *Tafsir Al-Fakr Al-Razi*, Vol. 5 (Beirut, Lebanon: Dar Al-Fikr, 2003), p. 3055.

"*Ihsan* as Epistemology" when I unpack the concept of *Ihsan*. Unfortunately, Al-Razi has not had the same impact on Islamic thought as Ibn Kathir or even Maududi. The task of articulating laws is a serious responsibility; I hope Muslim scholars will always keep in mind this very thoughtful summary of Islamic faith and its relation to life advanced by Prophet Muhammad (pbuh).

خير دينكم أيسره

The best of religion is that which brings ease to the people.[61]

---

[61] See Mohammad Hashim Kamali, *Principles of Islamic Jurisprudence* (Cambridge: Islamic Texts Society, 1991), p. 247.

CHAPTER 3

Islam as Identity: After a Century of Islamic Revivalism

إن الله يبعث لهذه الأمة على رأس كل مائة سنة من يجدد لها دينها

The Messenger of Allah said: "Indeed, Allah will send at the beginning of every century, to this community, one who will revive their religion for them."[1]

Inspired by the above prophetic tradition, or as vindication of its veracity, Muslim revivalists have frequently sought to revive Islam and reform Muslim society, producing a continuous tradition of revival and reform. The tradition has not always been transformative, but it certainly has existed. It is difficult to identify which individual was the *Mujaddid*— one who revives—in any given century. There is no agreed upon list. Islam in its current form has been extant for over 14 centuries, but there are certainly over 14 claimants to the title of *The Mujaddid*. Claims about the status of any individual as reviver is often a disputed and contentious affair, but there are some who are widely considered and accepted as indeed true revivers of the faith of Islam. Imam Abu Hamid Al-Ghazali (1056–1111 AD) is an excellent example of a reviver of Islam. His *magnum opus, The Revival of Religious Sciences (Ihya Uloom Al-Deen)*, is considered as one of the greatest books in Islamic heritage.

---

[1] See the first hadith in "The Book of Great Battles" in the collection *Sunan Abu Dawud*. I found that different collections number them differently. Some number it as #4291 and others as #4278. This is the reference to the edition I used. Muhammed Mahdi Al-Shariaf (Tr.), *Sunan Abu Dawud: English-Arabic Text*, Vol. V (Beirut, Lebanon: Dar Al-Kotob Al-Ilmiyyah, 2008), p. 34.

© The Author(s) 2019
M. A. M. Khan, *Islam and Good Governance*,
https://doi.org/10.1057/978-1-137-54832-0_3

He played a pivotal role in reconciling contentious debates between rationalists and traditionalists, between the orthodox and the Sufis and between the orthodox and the philosophers. Similarly, there have been many great scholars who have been declared as *Mujaddids* by their followers and have been accepted as such by many for several centuries. Some famous examples include Sheikh Muhammed Ibn Arabi (1165–1240 AD), Sheikh Ibn Taymiyyah (1263–1328 AD), Sheikh Ahmad al-Sirhindi (1564–1624) and Shah Waliullah Dehelvi (1703–1762 AD). In recent times, there are rumors that one of the founding fathers of Islamism, Maulana Maududi of Pakistan, thought of himself as the *Mujaddid* of the last century. He did not explicitly make that claim, but his understanding of the role of the *Mujaddid* does appear to be autobiographical. His followers have certainly thought of him so and have not shied away from making those claims.[2] Maududi, in the modern era, was the principle reviver of the idea of "the reviver" and in the process made the entire tradition of revival and reform (*Tajdid wa Islah*) in Islam, the Islamic justification for contemporary revivalist movements which needed Islamic justification for their break from traditional Islam without inviting the often fatal accusation of innovation (*bid'a*). Even though modern revivalist movements were proliferating across the Muslim world for nearly 100 years, the theory of revivalism was revived primarily through the narratives of Maududi and his followers and was then picked up by other movements.[3] The most recent attempt at advancing another new reformist paradigm by Tariq Ramadan too grounds the legitimacy of his enterprise in this tradition.[4]

[2] See Syed Abul A'la Maududi, *A Short History of The Revivalist Movement in Islam* (Kuala Lumpur: The Other Press, 2002). This is a translation of Maududi's Urdu work on the subject titled *Tajdid Wa Ihya Al-Deen*. Seyyed Vali Reza Nasr, *The Vanguard of the Islamic Revolution: The Jamaat-I Islami of Pakistan* (Berkeley, CA: University of California Press, 1994), p. 136.

[3] The concept of the *Mujaddid* has special resonance to Islam in Pakistan because of the controversy about the Ahmediyyah movement. The Ahmediyyah movement was declared as heretical by the government of Pakistan after concerted agitation by tradition Islamists and Maududi and his followers. The founder of the Ahmediyyah movement, Ahmed Qadiani (1835–1908), had claimed that he was the *Mujaddid* of the thirteenth century of Islam. His ideas which were seen as heretical by the orthodoxy attracted special attention to the concept of revivalism, since it was Qadiyani's principle instrument for leveraging his ideas as legitimate. See Syed Abul A'la Maududi, *The Finality of Prophethood*. The pamphlet is available on the World Wide Web at: http://alhafeez.org/rashid/finalprophet.htm.

[4] Tariq Ramadan, *Radical Reform: Islamic Ethics and Liberation* (London: Oxford University Press, 2009), pp. 12–14.

In this chapter, I explore the modern manifestation of the Islamic tradition of revival and reform as a response to the challenge of modernity, to the decline of Muslim societies and their relative powerlessness vis-à-vis the West. It is my contention that Muslims have responded to these challenges in multiple ways and over time crystallized four contemporary Muslim traditions—Islamists, traditionalists, modernists and secularists. While these traditions are easily observable in Sunni Islam, they can be found among Shia Muslims, too. Nearly 100 years of Muslim revivalism has provided partial success to all traditions, none enjoying hegemonic domination on Muslim culture and society, even though traditionalists have the numbers and Islamists are currently ascendant. All traditions have enjoyed some success, some traditions more so than others, but together they all have succeeded in generating a global environment of acute Islamic consciousness and awareness and made "Islamic Identity" a global issue which is contested vigorously among Muslims and between Muslims and non-Muslims, in domestic and global politics.

THE SEARCH FOR THE ROSETTA STONE
FOR CIVILIZATIONAL REVIVAL

For nearly two centuries, Muslims worldwide have been searching for the *Rosetta Stone* that will give them the clue to understanding why the great Islamic civilization and its attendant Islamic empires declined. The loss of power, global leadership and the decline of spiritual, intellectual and cultural vitality that was the hallmark of the Islamic past, continues to rankle with Islamic scholars, intellectuals and poets. The relative underdevelopment of the Muslim world in terms of science and technology, the political instability, the absence of freedom and dignity and the overall security situation, in vast swaths of the Islamic world is a profound source of spiritual and philosophical discontentment among Muslims everywhere.[5] After all God had promised Muslims sovereignty over the Earth (Quran 24:55), if they believed in him and did good deeds. But the reality is far from that promise. Muslims seem to have loss divine favor and many are concerned with how to regain that lost favor.

---

[5] The publications of Arab Human Development Reports on an annual basis now provide a glimpse into the state of development in the Arab world. See http://www.arab-hdr.org/. See also Ali A. Allawi, *The Crisis of Islamic Civilization* (New Haven: Yale University Press, 2009). Also see specially the work of Chapra who is one of the most prominent of Muslim economists, M. Umer Chapra, *Muslim Civilization: Causes of Decline and the Need for Reform* (Leicester, UK: Islamic Foundation, 2010).

وَعَدَ ٱللَّهُ ٱلَّذِينَ ءَامَنُواْ مِنكُمْ وَعَمِلُواْ ٱلصَّلِحَتِ
لَيَسْتَخْلِفَنَّهُمْ فِى ٱلْأَرْضِ كَمَا ٱسْتَخْلَفَ ٱلَّذِينَ مِن قَبْلِهِمْ
وَلَيُمَكِّنَنَّ لَهُمْ دِينَهُمُ ٱلَّذِى ٱرْتَضَىٰ لَهُمْ وَلَيُبَدِّلَنَّهُم مِّنۢ بَعْدِ
خَوْفِهِمْ أَمْنًا يَعْبُدُونَنِى لاَ يُشْرِكُونَ بِى شَيْئًا وَمَن كَفَرَ
بَعْدَ ذَٰلِكَ فَأُوْلَٰئِكَ هُمُ ٱلْفَٰسِقُونَ

Allah has promised to those of you who believe and do good that He will most certainly make them rulers in the earth as He made rulers those before them, and that He will most certainly establish for them their religion which He has chosen for them, and that He will most certainly, after their fear, give them security in exchange; they shall serve Me, not associating aught with Me; and whoever is ungrateful after this, these it is who are the transgressors.

Globalization, which has also brought Muslims closer to each other, further contributes to this shared consciousness of civilizational discontent. This collective angst can be captured in a simple question—*We have God's Truth on our side, so why is political, moral and temporal leadership in the hands of those who are not Muslims?* At another level this same feeling is articulated in terms of Muslim suffering at the hands of the West, which first colonized it and then continues to dominate it.[6] Civilizational anxieties are not limited to the Muslim psyche alone. In the past few years we have witnessed the emergence of a genre of scholarship that either laments are prognosticates the imminent collapse and ongoing decline of the Western civilization. This is a condition separate from the Christian longing and prognostications of the end of creation itself.[7]

Muslim thinkers have advanced several theories seeking to explain the decline of the Islamic civilization. Many Islamic movements have emerged with the explicit goal to revive the Muslim *Ummah*, reform Muslim societies

---

[6] See Khalid Bin Sayeed, *Western Dominance and Political Islam: Challenge and Response* (Albany, NY: SUNY Press, 2009).

[7] See, for example, Patrick J. Buchanan, *The Death of the West: How Dying Populations and Immigrant Invasions Imperil Our Country and Civilization* (Boulder, CO: St. Martin's Griffin, 2002). As for the discourse on the end of creation itself, see an excellent analysis by Frederic J. Baumgartne, *Longing for the End: A History of Millennialism in Western Civilization* (Boulder, CO: St. Martin's Press, 1999).

and restore them.[8] There is no consensus about what was the primary reason for the decline, but remarkably there is a near global consensus that the Islamic world has been in decline for centuries. Some intellectuals have argued that the reason why Muslims have lost their *mojo* is because they have abandoned the path of the *Shariah*. They hypothesize that if Muslims implemented the true *Shariah*, they would once again be glorious like their Muslim predecessors. They believe that the best way to order society is according to the divine *Shariah* and because Muslims have departed from this divinely ordained path to success, they declined. This is the basic premise behind movements that are broadly defined under the rubric of political Islam,[9] such as *Jamaat-e-Islami* in South Asia and the Muslim Brotherhood (*Al-Ikhwaan al-Muslimeen*) in the Arab world.[10] They believe that a systematic implementation of the *Shariah* will once again restore global leadership and moral sovereignty to Muslims. They envisage an Islamic state as the vehicle that will re-implement *Shariah* in the lives of Muslims and bring them back their lost glory.[11]

The traditional Ulema too share the perception that Muslims are in decline and have been so for a while. They too insist that the cause for Muslim decline is a wholesale abandonment of Islamic way of life, particularly of Islamic rituals. The emergence in India of the *Tablighi Jamaat*, a spiritual revivalist movement which has remained steadfastly devoted to the ritual aspects of Islam, and its subsequent globalization is one of the most promi-

---

[8] For a comprehensive bibliography on the subject, see Yvonne Y. Haddad, John O. Voll, and John L. Esposito, *The Contemporary Islamic Revival: A Critical Survey and Bibliography* (Westport, CT: Greenwood Press, 1991). For theory and history, see Fazlur Rahman, *Revival and Reform in Islam: A Study of Islamic Fundamentalism* (Oxford: Oneworld, 2000).

[9] I have lately started to prefer the term Islamists to political Islam. Rather than describing or identifying the characteristics of a specific group, the term political Islam essentially qualifies Islam itself.

[10] For an excellent summary and analysis of the ideas of Islamists, see Nazih Ayubi, *Political Islam: Religion and Politics in the Arab World* (London: Taylor & Francis, 2004). For a summary of the ideas of the key thinkers of political Islam such as Maulana Maududi, Syed Qutb, Ayatollah Khomeini, including the views of Khurshid Ahmed and Hassan Turabi, see John L. Esposito, ed., *Voices of Resurgent Islam* (New York: Oxford University Press, 1983). For a systematic review of political Islam in Pakistan, see Seyyed Vali Reza Nasr, *The Vanguard of the Islamic Revolution: The Jamaat-I Islami of Pakistan* (Berkeley, CA: University of California Press, 1994). See also Shahram Akbarzadeh, ed., *Routledge Handbook of Political Islam* (London: Taylor & Francis, 2012). Also see M. A. Muqtedar Khan, "The Political Philosophy of Islamic Resurgence," *Cultural Dynamics* 13.2 (Summer 2001): 213–231.

[11] See M. A. Muqtedar Khan "The Islamic States," in M. Hawkesworth and M. Kogan, eds., *Routledge Encyclopedia of Government and Politics* (New York: Routledge, 2004), pp. 265–278. Also see Noah Feldman, *The Fall and Rise of the Islamic State* (Princeton, NJ: Princeton University Press, 2009).

nent responses to Islamic decline by traditional Islam. Unlike the political Islamists who lament the departure from the Islamic way in the arena of *muamalat* (mundane and worldly affairs), the traditional scholars bemoan the lack of adherence to the Islamic way in the area of *Ibadaat* (rituals and relations with the divine). The philosophical wisdom behind this theory is not based on any systematic empirical analysis of history or social decline but a simple belief that God favors those who follow the straight path and since Muslims have abandoned it, they have lost the *Nusrah of Allah*—divine favor and grace—and hence they are condemned to worldly indignities which include domination by non-Muslims in the here and now and ultimately more punishment in the hereafter. This view is also supported by Muslim struggle to understanding why the promised sovereignty once granted was taken away by God (see the Quranic verse cited earlier 24:55). The Islamists are worried about the loss of the *Duniya* (world), while the traditional Ulema fear that Muslims have lost both the *Duniya* and the *Aakhira* (the hereafter).[12]

Unlike the Islamists and traditionalists, the modernist Muslims neither lament the loss of power nor piety. They worry over the disappearance of key principles and processes from Muslim society. Modernist Muslim intellectuals primarily focus on the intellectual decline of the Muslim society, which to them is both the cause of its overall decline and also the reason why Muslims have failed to fully adjust to the new challenges presented by the emerging conditions of modernity and postmodernity.[13] Unlike the Islamists who have rejected modernity as a Western artifact and the materialization of an inherently un-Islamic ideology, and the traditionalists who see modernity as merely a decline of spirituality, modernists understand it as a historical trend that is more or less inevitable and therefore deserves a

---

[12] For examples of traditional Islamic responses to modernity, see Seyyed Hossein Nasr, *The Need for a Sacred Science* (Albany, NY: SUNY Press, 1993). See Jan Ali, "Islamic Revivalism: The Case of Tablighi Jamaat," *Journal of Muslim Minority Affairs* 23.1 (Spring 2003): 173–181. Also see essays included in Joseph E. B. Lumbard, ed., *Islam, Fundamentalism, and the Betrayal of Tradition* (Bloomington, IN: World Wisdom Press, 2004). For a sense of Sufi revival in modern times, see Martin Van Bruinessen and Julia Day Howell, *Sufism and the 'Modern' in Islam* (New York: I. B. Tauris, 2007). See in particular chapter five from Seyyed Hossein Nasr, *Traditional Islam in the Modern World* (London: KPI Publications, 1987).

[13] See Fazlur Rahman, *Islam and Modernity: Transformation of an Intellectual Tradition* (Chicago: Chicago University Press, 1982). See John Cooper, Ronald Nettler and Mohamed Mahmoud, eds., *Islam and Modernity: Muslim Intellectuals Respond* (London: I. B. Tauris, 1998). See Tariq Ramadan, *Islam, the West and the Challenge of Modernity* (Leicester: Islamic Foundation, 2001). Also see Tariq Ramadan, *Radical Reform: Islamic Ethics and Liberation* (London: Oxford University Press, 2009).

comprehensive response and not a self-defeating rejection. The modernists who have since Sir Syed Ahmed Khan sought to demonstrate that Islam is not incompatible with science, modernity, democracy and human rights are primarily concerned with the loss of the principle belief that Islam is a progressive religion. They also are deeply concerned with the decline of *Ijtihad*, understood broadly as a process of reinterpretation of Islamic sources in the light of new existential conditions.[14]

While traditional scholars have always been there, the Islamists and the modernists are new types of thinkers who emerged as vanguards of Islamic response to modernity. They are both relatively new to the terrain of Islamic thought. They have clocked less than 200 years in history, yet they have transformed the way most Muslims think and speak about Islam. While they have diametrically opposite views about modernity, the Islamists reject it and the modernists seek accommodation with it. They have both provided comprehensive analysis of modernity and its impact on the Muslim world and culture. They have also sought to advance new interpretations of Islam and maintained that Islam is relevant to our time and can be practiced in spite of the structural changes that have come with modernity. This re-interpretive element in their narratives has prompted many analysts to label them collectively as reformist movements and tendencies. They are also united in their view of the traditional Ulema; they are both very critical of the traditional Ulema and see them as part of the problem. They both believe that the traditional Ulema's narrow vision of Islam, often reduced to a relentless focus on rituals alone, has emaciated Islam and divested it of its intellectual power and the Muslim society from its creative and productive potential. The traditionalists on the other hand are both dismissive and suspicious of the Islamists and the modernists. Dr. Seyyed Hossein Nasr once remarked that the so-called reformers of Islam were in actuality *deformers* of Islam.[15] He was critical of the accommodation of modernity he saw in the ideas of Islamists who embraced the idea of the state and the modernists who he saw as those who

---

[14] To get a sense of Islamic modernist thought, see the two anthologies by C. Kurzman— Charles Kurzman, ed., *Liberal Islam: A Source Book* (London: Oxford University Press, 1998) and Charles Kurzman, ed., *Modernist Islam: A Source Book* (London: Oxford University Press, 2002). See also Sheila McDonough, *Muslim Ethics and Modernity: a comparative study of the ethical thought of Sayyid Ahmad Khan and Mawlana Mawdudi* (Waterloo, Canada: Wilfrid Laurier University Press, 1984). For a summary of Arab modernist thought, see Albert Hourani, *Arabic thought in the Liberal Age 1798–1939* (New York: Cambridge University Press, 1984).

[15] These observations were made by Dr. Seyyed Hossein Nasr at a conference I had organized in 1998 at Georgetown University on Contemporary Islamic Philosophy. Dr. Nasr had delivered the keynote address at this conference.

surrendered to the epistemology of modernity. In his view traditional Islam rejected modernity in preference for an alternate, theocentric worldview, which transcended the materialist and temporal obsessions of modernity.[16]

The three groups of thinkers discussed here, who also represent the three dominant worldviews that shape current Islamic thought, constitute in themselves very complex discourses and there are many diverse trends within each of these groups.[17] This complexity and diversity within each of these trends underscores the extent and depth of Islamic intellectual tradition and also points to the tremendous intellectual effort that Muslims have applied in their endeavor to come to terms with structural transformations, shifts in balance of power and with theories of knowledge that modernity brought with it. For example, within the Islamists we find groups that advocate change peacefully through education and persuasion—*Dawa* (invitation and peaceful activism), such as the *Jamaat-e-Islami* in South Asia and *Al-Nahda* party in Tunisia. But there are also political Islamists who advocate the use of force such as *Al-Qaeda*. Political Islamists also vary according to their goals. While some like the Muslim Brotherhood in Egypt seek to establish an Islamic state in Egypt, others like the *Hizb ut-Tahrir* seek to re-establish a global Islamic Caliphate.[18]

Unlike the Islamists who started political movements and parties, modernists at best either reformed university curricula or established universities. The variance within modernist activism is limited. Modernist thinkers are either traditionally trained scholars with a progressive outlook or often academics in either Western or modern Muslim Universities. While they bring a plethora of new methods and ideas to Islamic thought, their impact remains limited. Because their language and their methods are often far from what Muslims traditionally considered as Islamic tropes and epistemologies, they have more impact on Western scholarship about Islam than Muslim practice of their faith. The modernist Islamic genre however does

---

[16] Seyyed Hossein Nasr, *Traditional Islam in the Modern World*, pp. 75–118.

[17] For a rather interesting and illuminating discussion of how all the three traditions interact and negotiate the meaning of Islam in Muslim society, see Muhammad Qasim Zaman, "Pakistan: Shariah and the State," in Robert W. Hefner, ed., *Shari'a Politics: Islamic Law and Society in the Modern World* (Bloomington, IN: Indiana University Press, 2011), pp. 207–243.

[18] To assess the nature of diversity within Islamist movements, see Francois Burgat, *Face to Face with Political Islam* (London: I. B. Tauris, 2003). See also Mohammed Ayoob, *The Many Faces of Political Islam: Religion and Politics in the Muslim World* (Ann Arbor: University of Michigan Press, 2007). See John L. Esposito, ed., *Political Islam: Revolution, Radicalism or Reform?* (Boulder, CO: Lynne Rienner Publications, 1997).

have a unique feature that is not so readily apparent in the other discourses—the healthy and vigorous engagement of Islamic sources by women.[19] In the past few decades, the modernist genre has also become more complex and has developed different streams within itself. For example, now one finds that there are both liberal and progressive tendencies within the modernist genre and the range of their methods varies from the use of postmodern epistemologies to reconstruct new narratives of Islam to traditional modernist approaches that privileged reason as a means to understood Islam.[20] Intellectually, the broad modernist tradition from Syed Ahmed Khan to Fazlur Rahma remains the most vibrant, but on the ground the Islamists and the traditionalists continue to garner more support and enjoy vast and wide following. But in the aftermath of the Arab Spring, as Islamists won elections in the post-authoritarian Middle East,[21] the ideas advanced by Islamic modernists about Islam and democracy, Islam and human rights, on pluralism and gender equality are gaining ground specially as Islamists seek legitimacy in the eyes of the international community and also seek to allay fears among fellow citizens at home.[22] The best example of the shift from Islamism to modernism can be seen in the politics of Al-Nahda in Tunisia as it struggles to survive and remain relevant in Tunisian politics.

The traditionalist camp has more or less remained true to its traditional roots and rituals. Their thinkers and scholars have failed to provide a comprehensive analysis of the plight of the Muslim *Ummah* except to assert that the problems of the community stem from its loss of divine grace because of its departure from strict adherence to rituals and the embrace of many modern and un-Islamic perspectives. Traditional Muslims constitute

[19] See, for example, Fatima Mernissi, *Beyond the Veil: Male-Female Dynamics in Modern Muslim Society* (Bloomington, IN: Indiana University Press, 1987). Also see Asma Barlas, *Believing Women in Islam: Unreading Patriarchal Interpretations of the Qur'an* (Austin, TX: University Texas Press, 2002). See Amina Wadud, *Qur'an and Woman: Rereading the Sacred Text from a Woman's Perspective* (New York: Oxford University Press, 1999). And also see Leila Ahmed, *Women and Gender in Islam: Historical Roots of a Modern Debate* (New Haven, CT: Yale University Press, 1992).

[20] See Omid Safi, ed., *Progressive Muslims on Justice, Gender and Pluralism* (Oxford: Oneworld Publications, 2003). M. A. Muqtedar Khan, ed., *Debating Moderate Islam: The Geopolitics of Islam and the West* (Salt Lake, Utah: Utah University Press, 2007). See also Chales Kurzman, *Liberal Islam; A Source Book.*

[21] See "Political Islam: Everywhere on the Rise," *The Economist*, Dec 12, 2011.

[22] See Marc Lynch, "The Big Think Behind the Arab Spring: Do the Middle East's Revolutions Have a Unifying Ideology?" *ForeignPolicy.com* (December 2011). On the World Wide Web at: http://www.foreignpolicy.com/articles/2011/11/28/the_big_think?page=full.

the biggest segment of the global Muslim community, with the modernist the smallest. If voting patterns in Muslim countries can be used as an indicator, then we can surmise that 30–40% of the community directly or indirectly supports the Islamists while the rest includes the modernists, the secularists and the traditionalists. The traditionalists are the most diffused and somewhat amorphous group in spite of their size and the fact that the biggest and oldest religious institutions everywhere belong to them. The traditionalist Muslims are also the most diverse of the three groups identified here. They include within their ambit great diversity in the interpretation of Islamic laws and also vary in institutionalized practices to the extent that there are many adversarial pairs like the Deobandis and Barelvis who despise each other even though in the bigger scheme of things they are both part of the traditional Islam. The only major modern response to modernity and its ravaging of spirituality that has come from the traditionalists has been the group widely known as the *Tablighi Jamaat*. True to its premodern pedigree, the *Tablighi Jamaat*, despite its modern birth and global reach, shows none of the characteristics that Max Weber associated with modernization, such as institutionalization, rationalization and specialization. It is a movement without institutions, without any formal organizational structure or coordination. Yet thanks to the long shadow of traditional Islam, the *Tablighi Jamaat* has found it relatively easy to sprout roots in the West, in Africa and in the Arab world. The movement is primarily focused on bringing Muslims back to the mosque to offer prayers five times a day. They believe that if Muslims performed the obligatory rituals with dedication, all will be well in the world and in the hereafter.[23]

In spite of the many differences in their methods and in their conclusions, all these movements belong in the big umbrella of Islamic responses to modernity and they are united in their belief that Islam and its teachings are central to Muslim individual and social existence and must remain so in the present and in the future. Besides the three trends identified above, which I see as those that can be classified as Islamic responses to modernity, there is also a significant secular response from Muslims to the challenges of modernity and beyond. Both periods of decolonization and

[23] See Muhammed Tahir, *The History of Jamaate Tabligh* (Karachi: Printing Press Karachi, 1987). Mufti A. Haq, *The Tablighi Jamaat Movement* (Lahore, Pakistan: Aziz Printing House, 1987). Mumtaz Ahmed, "Islamic Fundamentalism in South Asia: The Jamaat-i-Islami and the Tablighi Jamaat," in Martin Marty and Scott R. Appleby, eds., *Fundamentalisms Observed* (Chicago: Chicago University Press, 1991).

post-decolonization in the Middle East have been dominated by Arab nationalist socialism exemplified by the transnational Baath party and by popular leaders who gradually became self-serving dictators like Jamaal Abd Al-Nasser in Egypt, Habib Bourguiba in Tunisia, Saddam Hussain in Iraq, Muammar Gaddafi in Libya and Hafez Al-Assad in Syria.[24] For nearly half a century secular authoritarianism has dominated the Muslim world with occasional moments of democratization[25] (Pakistan, Turkey, Malaysia and Indonesia) and Islamization (Iran, Sudan, Saudi Arabia and Afghanistan). The most spectacular Muslim experiment with secular ideas was in Turkey with the rise of Attaturk and secular nationalism that has lasted for nearly 100 years.[26] But with the rise of the AK Party (Justice and Development Party) to power there was hope that a moderate and modernist form of Islamism, described by some as post-Islamism, will politically democratize, economically liberalize and culturally Islamize Turkey. But unfortunately, the coup in 2016 and its aftermath has pushed Turkey more into the category of authoritarian and increasingly there is fear that democracy in Turkey may not survive. The close association between secularism and authoritarianism in most of the Muslim world except Pakistan—where secularism is associated with democracy thanks primarily to the Pakistan Peoples Party—has more or less discredited secularism.[27] But one still finds that secular ideas particularly those that emphasize equality between people of different religions, human rights, women's rights and democratic civil governance still enjoy popular

[24] For a historical analysis about the dynamics between secular nationalism and Islamism, see Michaelle Browers, *Political Ideology in the Arab World: Accommodation and Transformation* (Cambridge, UK: Cambridge University Press, 2009). See Nazik Saba Yared, *Secularism and the Arab World: 1850–1939* (London: Saqi, 2002). See P. Salem, "The Rise and Fall of Secularism in the Arab World," *Middle East Policy* 4 (Fall 1996): 147–160. See specially Ira Lapidus, *A History of Islamic Societies* (Cambridge, UK: Cambridge University Press, 1988).

[25] See Shiping Hua, *Islam and Democratization in Asia* (Amherst, MA: Cambria Press, 2009).

[26] Nur Yalman, "Some Observations on Secularism in Islam: The Cultural Revolution in Turkey," *Daedalus* 102.1 (Winter 1973): 139–168. See Andrew Davidson and Joel Weinsheimer, *Secularism and Revivalism in Turkey; A Hermeneutic Reconsideration* (New Haven, CT: Yale University Press, 1998). M. Hakan Yavuz, *Secularism and Muslim Democracy in Turkey* (Cambridge, UK: Cambridge University Press, 2009).

[27] See Benazir Bhutto, *Reconciliation: Islam, Democracy and the West* (New York: Harper, 2008). For the dynamics between secularism and Islamism in Pakistan and Malaysia, see Vali Reza Nasr, *Islamic Leviathan: Islam and the Making of State Power* (New York: Oxford University Press, 2001).

support. They may not be dominant but they certainly have a vibrant and significant constituency as is apparent from the events unfolding as a result of the Arab Spring of 2011. The public discussions about the nature of the future state in the Arab world have once again revived the debates between the concept of *Dawlah Madaniyyah* (civil state) and *Dawlah Islamiyyah* (Islamic state).[28] Islamic Democratic liberalism that is informed by Islamic values and envisions a public role for Islam, but unlike the authoritarian vision of Islamists, is the only alternative to Islamism. Only time will tell if they triumph or become a part of a historical synthesis in the future.[29]

Unlike all the Islamic approaches, which lament loss of past glory or piety because of Muslim departure from true Islam, the secularists have tended to blame religion for the continued development deficit and the absence of democracy and modernization in Muslim societies.[30] Secularists see traditional Islam as a barrier to modernization and Islamism as barrier to democracy and human rights for non-Muslim minorities, for women and for those Muslims who may want to practice an Islam different from the vision advanced by Islamists. The secular approaches have always had a problem with Islam in the public sphere. Even when they try to accommodate Islamic principles like in Pakistan, the worldview of the two approaches varies so much that it is difficult to imagine the two tendencies finding a way to work together. One sees Islam as the solution and the other sees it as part of the problem. Secular approaches do have diversity and have recognized material reasons for the backwardness and other problems in the Muslim world and have advanced materialist solutions. But, persistent bad governance, lack of

---

[28] See "؟ماذا تعني الدولة المدنية" "What do you Mean by Dawlah Madaniyyah?" by Ahmed Zayed published by http://www.dawlamadaneya.com. The entire website is dedicated to the advocacy of a civil state.

[29] Here are some examples of attempts at political theory to advance a vision of democracy with a significant role for Islam and Islamic values in both the architecture of the polity and in politics as well. See Joshua Cohen and Deborah Chasman, eds., *Islam and the Challenge of Democracy* (Princeton: Princeton University Press, 2004). M. A. Muqtedar Khan, ed., *Islamic Democratic Discourse: Theory, Debates and Philosophical Perspectives* (Lanham, MD: Lexington Book, 2006). Abdullahi A. An-Na'im, *Islam and the Secular State: Negotiating the Future of the Shari'a* (Cambridge: Harvard University Press, 2008). Nader Hashemi, Islam, *Secularism and Liberal Democracy: Towards a Democratic Theory for Muslim Societies* (New York: Oxford University Press, 2009).

[30] A recent book illustrates beautifully how secularists blame Islam for all ills in society. See Dan Diner and Steven Rendall (Tr.), *Lost in the Sacred: Why the Muslim World Stood Still* (Princeton: Princeton University Press, 2009).

freedoms, deeply embedded corruption, underperforming economies, poverty, widespread unemployment and security failures under the rule of secular regimes have discredited secular nationalism and made Islamism a popular ideology in the Muslim world.[31]

IMPACT OF MUSLIM REVIVALISM

All these historical responses have been partially successful. I define success not in any absolute, theological or metaphysical sense, but primarily in the sense that it is about achievement of stated and desired goals. I also see success as an enduring impact on Muslim society. The experiment with secularism in Turkey ultimately has led to a historical synthesis allowing the emergence of a pro-democracy Islamic political culture that allows Muslims to practice their faith, feel proud of their Muslim identity and culture and also give a positive face to Islamism at least to many Muslims suffering from authoritarianism. The rise of moderate Islamism in Turkey inspired and provided a role model for Islamists in the Arab world during and after the Arab Spring. But recent trends in Turkey have been troubling. It has witnessed a spike in authoritarian and populist politics and human rights and democratic ideals have suffered relegation. It is the fond hope of this author that this democratic decline is temporary, as consequence of a failed coup, and Turkey will continue its march toward more democratization. Secular ideals and political values, especially about democracy, human rights and gender equality, have deeply influenced Muslim intellectuals from every tradition. Everyone now talks at least about Islam's compatibility with democracy and human rights if not insisting outright that any genuine implementation of Islamic principles cannot be achieved without democracy and human rights. Even those traditionalists, especially from the Salafi-Wahhabi tradition,[32] who reject the conceptions of universal human rights and democracy, still argue that Islamic legal tradition does a better job of conceptualizing and safeguarding the rights of human beings.[33] They recognize the significance

[31] See John Esposito and Azzam Tamimi, eds., *Islam and Secularism in the Middle East* (London: Oxford University Press, 2000).

[32] See Natana J. Delong-Bas, *Wahhabi Islam: From Revival and Reform to Global Jihad* (London: I. B. Tauris, 2007). Also see Khaled Abou El Fadl, *The Great Theft: Wrestling Islam from The Extremists* (New York: Harper Collins, 2007).

[33] See, for example, this lecture by Dr. Muhammed Musa Al-Shareef entitled, "Islam and Human Rights" (*Islam wa Huquq Al Insaan*). It can be viewed on YouTube at http.//www.youtube.com/watch?v=XmECQ4QgeGg.

of the idea of human rights, they are merely disputing the sources of those rights. Secularists and their penchant for authoritarian dictatorship in the Arab world in particular have given secular ideals a really bad name in the Muslim world; nevertheless, they have succeeded in ushering a strong awareness for the necessity and importance of individual and collective rights. In the aftermath of the Arab Spring, secular liberals lost in a big way to Islamists in most of the elections held in 2011–2012, but their presence and international scrutiny compelled Islamists to show a concern for individual rights and freedom of religion in their campaign promises and when they govern they will have to ensure that their religious zeal does not trample on human rights. The citizens of the Muslim nations are struggling to restore their individual dignity; they have not struggled against secular tyranny only to see it replaced by religious authoritarianism.

IMPACT OF ISLAMISM ON MUSLIM SOCIETY

The Islamists clearly have had the most significant impact on the culture and political evolution of Muslim societies in the last 100 years. After the debacle in Egypt and the return of secular authoritarianism there, Islamists appeal has become weaker but they still remain influential. Islamist discourse has shaped the Muslim consciousness in many ways. It has provided new vocabulary to how Muslims think and converse about Islam, politics and the world itself. Terms like God's sovereignty are now routinely used by Muslims, even if they are not fully committed to or associated with the Islamist project of establishing Islamic states/Caliphate. Islamists have also redefined traditional Islamic terms, for example, *jahiliyyah*. Islamic sources defined the term as unawareness of the God, his unity, his message and his expectations of his creation. But now, many Muslims think of it as absence of *Shariah*-based governance.[34]

Islamists have succeeded in providing a rudimentary public philosophy around which Muslims can organize their resistance to foreign political and cultural domination and also combat internal inertia in pursuit of political and social change. Islamism without doubt has been the most vibrant social and political mass movement in the Muslim world. It has truly created a global Muslim consciousness, albeit around political issues such as Palestine, *Shariah* and Islamic state and not around faith issues. For example, we have

[34] See M. A. Muqtedar Khan, "Islam, democracy and Islamism after the counterrevolution in Egypt," *Middle East Policy* 21.1 (2014): 75–86.

global movements to fight demonization of Islamic symbols by Westerners, but no movement to combat lack of fidelity to one of the five pillars of Islam—*Zakat* (obligatory Islamic distributive justice).

The biggest impact of Islamism, in my analysis, has been the reduction of Islam to the status of ideology. Islam in the eyes of Islamists is an alternative to capitalism and communism. By the mere fact of positing Islam as an ideology, they have made politics central to religion. Mian Tufayl Muhammad, the former *Amir* of the *Jamaat-e-Islami* of Pakistan stated it very succinctly: "Our religion is our politics, our politics is our religion."[35] Ideologies are political worldviews. Even if the worldview is taken more broadly, in order to encompass ethos, culture and private morality, it is still about the world. Islam as a faith is both about this world and more importantly about the other world. Rendering it as an ideology makes it solely of this world.

Islamism has also had, in my view, another debilitating impact on the Muslim community. It has made those who are moved by its slogans, such as "Islam is the solution," profoundly conscious of their Muslim identity.[36] By making politics a part of the religion, political posturing, power and political considerations, political strategies and concerns have all become important and have equal significance to other values that the faith espouses such as charity, worship and purification of the soul. The global tendency to talk about Islam and the West—literally thousands of books and articles have been written on this theme in many languages (yours truly is also guilty of this[37])—has also made Islam a political identity.[38] "The West" is a political construct. It is the collective identity of a group of nations that share certain cultural values, perhaps history and have a common global political agenda. By positing Islam as a potential antagonist of the West, Islam is represented as a collective political identity. The discourse that emerged after Sam Huntington presented his much discussed and controversial thesis, "The Clash of Civilizations?," further

[35] Quoted by Vali Reza Nasr in his book, *The Vanguard of the Islamic Revolution*, p. vii.

[36] See M. A. Muqtedar Khan, "Constructing Identity in Global Politics," *American Journal of Islamic Social Sciences* 15.3 (Fall 1998): 81–106. Also see M. A. Muqtedar Khan, "Islamic Identity and the Two Faces of the West," *Washington Report on Middle East Affairs* 19.6 (August/September): 71.

[37] M. A. Muqtedar Khan, "Constructing the American Muslim Community," in Y. Haddad, J. Smith and J. Esposito, eds., *Religion and Immigration* (New York: Altamira Press, 2003), pp. 175–198.

[38] See Abul Hasan Ali Nadwi, *Islam and the West* (Lucknow: Pub: Academy of Islamic Research & Publications, 1991). Norman Daniel, *Islam and the West: The Making of an Image* (Oxford: Oneworld, 2009). Bernard Lewis, *Islam and the West* (London: Oxford University Press, 1994).

cemented Islam as a collective political identity in the minds of Muslims and non-Muslims alike.[39] The culture of "Us versus Them," Islam versus the West, Muslims versus non-Muslims and Islamists versus liberals or secularists has reduced Islamic politics to *identity politics*. Islamic politics instead of becoming political activism in pursuit of social justice and realization of Islamic virtues has become a politics that seeks to defend and advance the material interests of a collective identity. The use of violence, terrorism and assassinations as strategies and instruments of politics by Islamist groups uncovers the reality that Islamism is not about Islamic values or ethics or social justice but rather about power and domination. Islamism has become a counter-hegemonic movement. Islamists parties won elections in the countries that experienced dramatic regime changes and reforms in the aftermath of the Arab Spring of 2011. But their brief record of governance was less than exemplary. In the countries where so-called Islamic governance exists, like in Saudi Arabia, there is little civilizational revival emanating. The wealth generated from oil has hidden the potentially devastating consequences of bad governance and erroneous domestic and international policies in those nations.

Another major negative consequence of Islamism has been the engendering of extreme hostility to Islam and Islamism globally. Since the end of the cold war, partially because the West needed an enemy to sustain its own strategic coalition, a cultural "other" to sustain its own cultural cohesion and reproduce the so-called Western secular, developed, democratic modern identity, and partially because of the anti-West rhetoric coming from Islamists everywhere who blamed the West for nearly all Muslim problems, the West has started perceiving Islamism as an enemy of Western culture, values and civilization. Islamists have relished this perception, using it to bolster their own legitimacy and expand their influence. The consistent anti-Western rhetoric from Islamists has succeeded as a large segment of the Western population sees Islamism and Islamic resurgence as a threat to Western interests, their allies in the region and to global stability. Many Western academics and scholars have tried to debunk this notion that Islamism is essentially anti-Western, and many policymakers understand this, but nevertheless the numbers of those who fear Islamism is very high. In the process of building support for Islamic revivalism, Islamists have made enemies, which has made it in turn more difficult for them to achieve their goals of Islamic revival.

---

[39] See Samuel P. Huntington, "The Clash of Civilizations?" *Foreign Affairs* 72.3 (Summer 1993): 22–49.

The Impact of Islamic Modernism

I assess Islamic modernism as an underachieving tradition. It is the richest one when it comes to ideas generation and Islamic modernists, like Muhammad Abduh, Sir Syed Ahmad Khan, Muhammad Iqbal, Fazlur Rahman and Abdolkarim Soroush, to but name a few, who have provided more systematic and more nuanced understanding and analysis of the impact of colonization and modernity on the Muslim world. They all have prescribed excellent pathways out of the contemporary maladies that plague the Muslim world.[40] But their ideas have not had the same mass appeal or even popular impact as those of Maulana Maududi and Syed Qutb. I feel that there are four reasons why the modernists have failed to have the same impact and reach, as do the Islamists.

Most modernists do not come from within the traditional religious academies and therefore they are not perceived to have the same legitimacy as traditional scholars who sport the religious paraphernalia—turban, flowing robes and bushy beards—symbols that Muslims associate with sacred authority.[41] Often they are academicians and research scholars whose language, theories and methodologies are either foreign or too obtuse for popular consumption. They cannot reduce what Islamic modernism stands for in a simple bumper sticker that Islamism did with the slogan—الإسلام هو الحل Islam is the solution. Even though Sir Syed Ahmed Khan did come up with a pretty good slogan when he described how both the Quran and creation were of divine origins—one as *The Word of God* and the other as *The Work of God*. But his slogan did not have the same impact as that of the Islamists. It required the exertion of intellectual effort to connect science with creation and then the Quran.[42] Science and

---

[40] Fazlur Rahman, "Islamic Modernism: Its Scope, Methods and Alternatives," *International Journal of Middle East Studies* 1.4 (Winter 1970): 317–333. For samples of the writings of the modernists, see Charles Kurzman, *Liberal Islam: A Source Book.*

[41] On May 26, 2010, the Oxford Islamic Society hosted a conference titled "Rethinking Islamic Reform." The key speakers were Sheikh Hamza Yusuf, a very charismatic traditionalist, who true to traditional Islam is infused with Sufi tendencies, and Tariq Ramadan, the bearer of the torch of reform and shaper of contemporary Islamic modernism. The conference can be viewed on YouTube. Sheikh Hamza epitomizes traditional Islam resplendent with turban and robe and a well-manicured beard. Ramadan was wearing an expensive western suit and a barely visible beard. Their discourse exemplifies all the observations I made about the traditions they represent. To my delight, Ramadan actually quoted the hadith in his talk that I start this chapter with. See http://www.youtube.com/watch?v=qY17d47hY8M&feature=related.

[42] See Dietrich Reetz, "Enlightenment and Islam: Seyyid Ahmad Khan's Plea to Indian Muslims for Reason," *The Indian Historical Review* XIV.1–2: 206–218.

religion were compatible because one was the word and the other studied the work of the same creator. The erudition and complexity of modernist thought has of necessity limited their outreach to Muslims familiar with concepts from Western thought, Islamic history and the intricacies of Islamic theological, philosophical and jurisprudential traditions.

Islamic modernists also failed to create high-impact institutions and movements that could have a deep and wide influence among Muslim masses to bring about the change that they sought. Aligarh Muslim University is perhaps the only major example of a modernist institution, which unfortunately quickly lost its purpose and direction.[43] In contemporary period we can now identify many modernist-leaning think tanks and research institutions but none that has the reach and scope of Islamic movements. Modernism despite its intellectual strength failed to become a vibrant and cohesive movement. It is also possible that many of the individuals, who could potentially be part of a modernist Islamic movement, become either moderate Islamists or moderate secularists.

Perhaps the most important reason why Islamic modernism does not have the appeal that Islamism and even secular nationalism enjoy is their critique of the realities of the Muslim world and Islamic intellectual heritage. While Islamists are focused on revival that necessarily requires glorification of Islamic past and all things Islamic, secular nationalists too indulge in national self-glorification, but modernists critique not just the culture but also what has long been taken as sacred—Islamic laws, traditions and practices. Often modernist calls for reform are seen as a clarion call to "change Islam itself" and this is the single most important reason why Islamic modernism remains a limited and even elitist endeavor. Every modernist's rallying cry is *Ijtihad*,[44] and common Muslims have great difficulty in relating to this. Often they are ill-informed about their faith, but their fervor runs strong and deep. Their lack of deep knowledge of their own tradition makes them nervous when they find modernists critiquing traditions, methods and sources, which they thought were sacred. Modernists will continue to have a limited impact in the traditional Muslim world where literacy rates are lower, but in the West they may succeed in having a palpable impact as can

---

[43] S. K. Bhatnagar, *History of M. O. A., Aligarh* (Bombay: Asia Pub. House, 1969).

[44] Moment for self-disclosure; the address of the website that I maintain and which hosts many of my short articles is www.ijtihad.org.

be seen from the growing popularity of many reformers.[45] The success of many Western Muslim preachers and intellectuals and their growing impact in the Muslim world, such as Sheikh Hamza Yusuf from California, also suggests limited portability of modernist ideas.

Nevertheless, despite their lack of transformative impact on Muslim societies, Islamic modernism has had a huge impact on how contemporary Muslims think about key issues such as the continuing advance of Western culture into Muslims societies. Many Muslim communities are beginning to recognize the importance of both democratic governance and science. The growth of university systems and the teaching of Islam in university setting both in the West and in Muslim countries have allowed the writings of modernists to enter into Islamic curricula. While you may not find books by Fazlur Rahman in libraries at *Madrassahs* or in their curricula, you will find literally hundreds of dissertations by Muslim researches on his work across the Muslim world, especially in the more developed countries like Turkey, Pakistan and Malaysia.

THE CONTINUED SALIENCE OF TRADITIONAL ISLAM

The best way to think of traditional Islam is to imagine Muslim society unsullied by modernity. This is my understanding of how Seyyed Hossein Nasr, the most prominent and eloquent spokesperson of traditional Islam, thinks about it. The very idea of traditional Islam makes several binary assumptions; the most fundamental of which is that traditions, therefore traditional Islam, are good and modernity in as much as it opposes traditions is bad. Traditionalists, like Islamists, see modern priorities as an impediment to a religious life, and the modern culture as inimical to religious beliefs and values. Traditionalists, in my view, commit two fundamental oversights that undermine their case. One, they fail to see that rather than eviscerating religion, modernity has energized religion in America, Asia and Africa. Religious revivalism across the world, while often seen as a reaction

---

[45] I recall a very interesting conversation about this phenomenon with Dr. Sherman Jackson, a prominent Islamic scholar both in the academy and in the community. He agreed with my point of the problem of knowledge deficit in the community and claimed that, it was the prime motivation, to provide "religious literacy," behind an initiative that he was part of ALIM, American Learning Institute for Muslims. See https://www.alimprogram.org/. There are many such initiatives in the United States, Canada and the United Kingdom, which may be able to increase the religious literacy of the communities to levels necessary to make arguments for reform and from Islamic modernists potent.

to or backlash against modernity, is actually a modern phenomenon and is triggered, facilitated and nurtured by the new historical conditions brought about by modernity. Religious revivalism is not a rejection of modernity, but indeed a major (albeit contradictory) facet of modernity.

Two, the proponents of traditional Islam, Nasr included, fail to employ the rigorous critical aptitude they bring to bear on modernity, on traditional Islam and traditional Muslim societies. They see no decline in the vitality of traditional Muslim society and only see the departure from traditional culture and rituals under the impact of modernity. While Islamists, secularists and specially modernists pondered over what Muslim societies have done to themselves to become "colonizable,"[46] Nasr does not advance any coherent thesis on why the traditional Muslim world had become relatively weaker and then ultimately subjugated by the modern West. There is no recognition that premodern Muslim societies may have departed from true traditional values and existed in strange emaciated conditions neither true to tradition nor ready for reform and modernization.

Nasr glorifies traditional Islamic beliefs and criticizes modernity. But his accounts are ahistorical. He does not examine historical facts and therefore the traditional Islam that he presents is not what was practiced in the Muslim world before the advent of modernity, but really a selective reading of Islam's intellectual tradition. He begins a chapter on Sacred Science in his book *The Need for a Sacred Science*, with a prophetic prayer—"*O Lord, show us things as they really are.*" He then proceeds to provide a critique of modernity, by highlighting the negative consequences of modern science. But he and other traditionalists like Ashraf Ali Thanvi and Ali Mian Nadwi of India or Sheikh Muhammad Al-Buti of Syria do not really provide a systematic analysis of the state of the Muslim world before the advent of modernity. Was the reality of the Muslim world then consistent with the ideals, principles and beliefs of traditional Islam? Nasr actually wrote a book with the title *Ideals and Realities of Islam*,[47] but it too is without any empirical content. I understand that my critique is unfair, after all social sciences are a modern phenomenon. It is unfair to demand

[46] Malik Bennabi in the Arab world and Ali Hasan Nadwi in India tried to understand why the Muslim world became colonizable. Malik Bennabi, Abdul Wahid Lu'Lu'a (Tr,), *The Question of Culture* (Kuala Lumpur: Islamic Book Trust, 2003). See Abul Hasan Ali Nadwi, *Islam and the World: The Rise and Decline of Muslims and Its Effect on Mankind* (London: UK Islamic Academy, 2003).

[47] Seyyed Hossein Nasr, *Ideals and Realities of Islam* (London: George Allen and Unwin, 1966).

an empirical analysis from traditionalists who relied mostly on history, philosophy, law and religion, and the methods of writing history then were very rudimentary.

The lack of appreciation of empirical facts stands out in Nasr's analysis of the Muslim women who aspire for gender equality. Arguing that there are fundamental differences between the natures of men and women, comparing them is like comparing "rose to jasmine," he criticizes, nay chastises them vehemently for going against their sacred nature for aspiring to an equal status with men. If he had examined the reality of women in the Muslim world, the vast distance between their idealized status in Islamic law and their actual material conditions would have given him serious pause. Even if one had taken the ideals of traditional Islam without any criticism and compared them to the realities of Muslim women in traditional societies, one would have been appalled at the demeaning status of Muslim women. As early as 1899, an Egyptian Islamic modernist wrote a book, *Tahrir al-Mara'a, (The Liberation of Women)*, in which he contrasts the actual low status of Muslim women in Egypt to their idealized status in Islamic *Shariah*.[48] Many of the rights granted to women by the *Shariah* were not and are not available to women by and large in traditional Muslim societies. The rise of Islamic feminism is a belated recognition of this shameful reality.[49] Traditionalists in their critique of modernity are not defending any reality, but an imagined ideal, which certainly does not exist anywhere. The appeal and success of Islamism is a direct consequence of the traditionalists' unanchored romance with idealized traditions, and the modernists' complex theories that few can understand and appreciate and even fewer can act upon.

Traditional Islam has become the default status of Muslim societies. Take any community, subtract the secularists, the Islamists and the modernists and what will be left over is traditional Islam. It is composed of weak networks of Sufi traditions and vestigial orthodoxy. Some might dispute my categorization of the *Tablighi Jamaat* as a traditional Islamic movement, but given that it does not fit with the other three categories I have discussed and is opposed to all of them, I believe that it can be

[48] See an edited English translation; Qasim Amin, "The Liberation of Women," in Mansoor Moaddel and Kamran Talattof, eds., *Contemporary Debates in Islam: An Anthology of Fundamentalist Thought* (New York: St. Martin's Press, 2000), pp. 163–182.

[49] See Margot Badran, ed., *Feminism in Islam: Secular and Religious Convergences* (Oxford: Oneworld Publications, 2009). See also Saba Mahmood, *Politics of Piety: Islamic Revival and the Feminist Subject* (Princeton: Princeton University Press, 2005).

categorized as a traditional Islamic movement. Given that it is essentially a modern phenomenon it can be considered as a modern, not modernist, manifestation of traditional Islam. It is easily the biggest Islamic movement on the planet with huge following in the United Kingdom, South Asia, East Asia, North America and even in the Arab world. It adopts a minimalist approach to Islam, focusing only on basic rituals, and hence its impact is minimal. All it succeeds in achieving is delaying the advent of modernity and preserve traditional gender relations. It actively discourages Islamic literacy, political engagement and activism for social justice issues. It has succeeded in creating several vast swathes of traditional ghettoes in the world determined to delay modernization. They offer no social or political vision for this world. They encourage a superficial engagement both with the world and with the faith of Islam and promise salvation based on this minimalist engagement with the mundane and the sacred. But there are unintended consequences. The movement often drags individuals from their secular existence into the orbit of faith. The awakening of an Islamic consciousness through encounters with the *Jamaat* can often lead to other exciting Islamic pathways.

Tablighi Jamaat is in many ways a soft Sufi movement. Sufi movements (*Tareeqas*) along with traditional orthodoxy constitute the core of traditional Islam in most parts of the world. In vast regions of South and East Asia and Africa, traditional Islam is more or less Sufi Islam. Even though commentators in the West and some in the Muslim world argue that Islam spread by the sword,[50] Islam spread in most of Asia and Africa through the work of Sufi and mystical masters[51] and remains deeply influenced by mystical practices and attitudes. But over the centuries Sufi masters have become rare and in their place one finds charlatans profiting from the faith and ignorance of the poor masses in Asia and Africa who turn to them for guidance to connect to the heavenly world and for comfort in this world. In place of deeply mystical and devotional traditions we find that there are now vestigial traditions that celebrate ignorance and superstition rather than enlightenment and spirituality (*Al-Ruhaniyyah*). One of the primary reasons for the decline of the Muslim community worldwide has been the inability of traditional Islam to adapt to the challenges

---

[50] One of the best works on how Islam spread, not by sword but by missionary work by Muslims, is T. W. Arnold, *The Preaching of Islam* (Delhi: L. P. Publications, 1990).

[51] See John L. Esposito, *Islam the Straight Path* (New York: Oxford University Press, 1998).

of modernity and late modernity. Sufi Islam with its overt focus on the other world took the eye of the ball in this world. The strong aversion that both modernists and Islamists show toward Sufism is because they feel that Sufi values, especially the excessive belief on God's providence (*tawakkul Allah*), are one of the reasons behind the decline of Islamic civilization.[52] They also maintain that the Sufis, their incessant protests notwithstanding, have corrupted Islamic beliefs and also undermined the purity of Islamic beliefs and thought. Professor William Chittick who is easily one of the most important authorities on Sufism in Western academia makes an interesting observation, sympathetic to Sufism, while comparing the three Islamic traditions discussed here[53]:

> *Today grass-roots Islam is more likely to be inspired by Sufi teachers more than modernist intellectuals, who are cut off from the masses because of their western style academic training. However, the presence in most Islamic societies of demagogues who have no qualms about manipulating religious sentiment for political ends complicates the picture immensely.*

Nevertheless, despite their many weaknesses and limitations, the Islamic responses to modernity have succeeded in revitalizing the intellectual and political landscape in the Muslim world. Muslim intellectuals and masses, regardless of their orientation, are unwilling to remain passive passengers as history progresses. They are determined to grab the steering wheel and guide history in a direction that is consistent with whatever they think is Islamic. They will not be silent witnesses to their own time. They are determined to leave an Islamic imprint on history once again. Even though Muslim secularists have had an impact, they have shown that secularism, unlike in the liberal West, does not necessarily lead to democracy and freedom. It remains to be seen if Islamists can demonstrate that perhaps politics based on religion, especially Islam, is capable of succeeding where secularism failed.

---

[52] See Muhammad Abduh, Kamran Talattof (Tr.), "The Necessity of Reform," in Mansoor Moaddel and Kamran Talattof, eds., *Contemporary Debates in Islam: An Anthology of Fundamentalist Thought* (New York: St. Martin's Press, 2000), pp. 45–52.

[53] See William C. Chittick, *Sufism: A Beginner's Guide* (Oxford: Oneworld Publications, 2005), p. 37.

UNDERSTANDING THE PHENOMENON
AND CHALLENGE OF MODERNITY

Except for some modernists like Sir Syed Ahmad Khan, Muhammad Abduh and Fazlur Rahman, most of the Islamists and traditionalists have not conceptualized modernity in a way that would allow them to respond to it effectively. Other traditional societies in Japan and India have more or less taken a different attitude toward modernity than many Muslims.[54] They have modernized but without becoming culturally alienated or abandoning their faiths entirely. Most Muslim thinkers have either embraced modernity uncritically, like Mustapha Kamal Attaturk of Turkey,[55] or like Syed Qutb rejected it outright.[56] The reason why many Muslim thinkers rejected and opposed modernity was because they conceived of it as a product of Western culture and often did not distinguish between "the West" and modernity. Many elements of modernity came to the Muslim world through colonialism. The anger and resentment that Muslim thinkers felt toward the West that dominated and exploited their lands and the accompanying Western discourse that demeaned and demonized Muslim religion and values have primarily shaped how Muslims responded to modern ideas, institutions and its impact on social structures.

One witnesses the same phenomenon among Muslims who, like Abdullah Jan, reject democracy as both un-Islamic and anti-Islamic.[57] When one engages Muslims who oppose democracy, one quickly discovers that they are, more often than not, angry at Western foreign policy, not democracy as a governing process. They are responding in anger at what democracies did to them and not the concept of democracy itself. One encounters the same reaction when one advocates freedom of speech. Muslims angry at the publication of cartoons about Prophet Muhammad (pbuh) in Europe and the desecration and abuse of Islam's sacred symbols in the name of freedom of expression reject the idea of free speech.[58] They argue

---

[54] See Hiroichi Yamaguchi and Haruka Yanagisawa, eds., *Tradition and Modernity: India and Japan Towards the 21st Century* (New Delhi: Munshiram Manoharlal Publishers Pvt. Ltd., 1997).

[55] See Andrew Mango, *Ataturk* (London: John Murray, 1999).

[56] See Seyyid Quṭb, *Milestones* (Damascus, Syria: Dar Al-Ilm, 2000).

[57] See Abid Ullah Jan, *The End of Democracy* (Canada: Pragmatic Publishers and Distributors, 2003).

[58] See, for example, Enver Masud, Cartoons of Prophet Muhammad, Aljazeerah.Info on Feb 10, 2006. On the World Wide Web at: http://www.aljazeerah.info/Opinion%20editorials/2006%20Opinion%20Editorials/February/10%20o/The%20Cartoons%20of%20Prophet%20Muhammad%20By%20Enver%20Masud.htm.

if the denial of Holocaust and genocide of the Armenians by the Turks can be banned legally by Western countries then why not blasphemy against the Prophet of Islam? Freedom of speech, in the view of many Muslim critics of the West, means nothing more than license to abuse and demonize Islamic symbols.

If only Muslims can see these values independent of Western hypocrisies they will develop a better understanding and appreciation for modernity. How can one call for *Ijtihad* or *Tajdid* without freedom of speech? How can Muslims realize Islamic values in their own societies without freedom of religion or freedom of association? These are values essential for human social, spiritual and political well-being. The fact that Muslims did not pay as much attention to them in the past does not mean that they are not as essential for Muslims as for the rest. When Muslims divorce modernity from the forms it takes in Western culture and especially in Western policies toward the Muslim world, they will find in it much to admire and emulate. The West did not invent modernity nor does the West own modernity. Many of the ideas and values of modernity are aspirations, which have not been realized even in the West. Rather than seeing modernity as Western culture, Muslims must recognize it for what it is. *It is a historical condition.* While the historical elements that underpin modernity remain constant, it does manifest differently in different cultures. Modernity is a complex confederation of contemporary realities that together produce the global condition called modernity. The modern Western culture, politics and all its realities too are a response and consequence of modernity.[59]

The West is not driving or shaping modernity, on the contrary modernity is shaping the West and the rest. Rather than responding to modernity by rejecting the West, Muslims should respond to the challenge of history regardless of the West. Many Muslim thinkers claimed that they did separate modernity from Western culture, and while they accepted the former, they rejected the later. However, they reduced acceptable modernity to science and rejected everything else as "atheistic materialism" and Western culture.[60] I find it perplexing that these brilliant Muslims assumed that the

---

[59] See Stephen Toulmin, *Cosmopolis: The Hidden Agenda of Modernity* (Chicago: The University of Chicago Press, 1990). See Jurgen Habermas and Frederick G. Lawrence (Tr.), *The Philosophical Discourse of Modernity* (Boston: The MIT Press, 1990). See Anthony Giddens, *The Consequences of Modernity* (Stanford, CA: Stanford University Press, 1990). See also Anthony Giddens, *Modernity and Self-Identity: Self and Society in the Late Modern Age* (Stanford, CA: Stanford University Press, 1991).

[60] See Ibrahim M. Abu-Rabi, *Intellectual Origins of Islamic Resurgence in the Modern Arab World* (Albany: SUNY Press, 1996), pp. 18–23.

West is powerful enough to shape global history. It is genuinely befuddling to me as to why traditional Muslims, even deeply philosophical and theoretically complex Muslims, so vehemently reject everything modern as if modernity is a product of Satan's will. It is not Satan but Allah who determines history. I understand the ambiguity of Islamists on this issue, because the Islamists do not acknowledge it but they too are modern and modernized. Their vision of the Islamic state is a modern idea. They embraced modernity the day they started aspiring for an Islamic (modern) state. Islamists have gradually embraced most aspects of modernity and their main challenge remains lack of Muslim power, and the impact of Western political and cultural domination. But the traditionalists continue to reject all things modern. Why reject the progress of history? Isn't that a rejection of God's will? Why not conceive of modernity as a divine challenge?

It is important that Muslims realize that the core of modernity is a historical reality that is irreversible. We can move beyond modernity but many of the structural changes brought about by modernity are irreversible. We cannot willingly return to an era before computers, air travel, cars or even institutionalized government and corporations. Modernity is not a choice. Modernity is many things, especially when we examine modern cultures. The first thing about modern cultures and even modern politics is that it is neither unified nor monolithic. There are many modern cultures and many modern political ideologies. There is now even a modern Muslim culture and there are many modern Muslim ideologies, too. Both Islamists, who are often blind to their modernist genesis, and traditionalists treat modern cultures and ideologies as monolithic. This posture is un-reflexive and superficial. The lack of recognition of the diversity within modernity leads to a rather caricaturized understanding of modernity sans any nuance. The traditionalists' critique of modernity is identical to postmodern critique of modernity. Postmodernity is a product of modernity, not tradition. Modernity on the other hand is what emerged from tradition in dialectical opposition to it. Some see modernity as a rupture, a complete breakaway, from tradition but others acknowledged continuity. Anthony Giddens rather elegantly describes modernity as a "post-traditional order."[61] More importantly, the new self-conception and self-definition of tradition, particularly advanced by those who oppose or reject modernity, like Seyyed Hossein Nasr, for example, is ironically *modern traditionalism*—an ideological or ideational response to modernity that idealizes an imagined

---

[61] See Giddens, *Modernity and Self-Identity*, p. 20.

tradition and seeks to use the same binary reasoning as modernity to construct tradition in opposition to modernity.[62] Like postmodernism, contemporary notions of traditional Islam are the product of and response to modernist thinking. It stems from the embrace of the most fundamental of modernist characteristic—binary logic. Even though the term traditional in traditional Islam is a modern concept, it means not modern.

The core of modernity consists of the fundamental structural shifts that have taken place in many of the key elements of human life. In politics, it was the shift to territorial sovereignty after the Treaty of Westphalia that ultimately led to the creation of the modern nation state—tribes with defined territorial boundaries. The modern state remains a key constitutive element of modernity. The shift in the epistemological basis of society was from traditional religious sources to reason, empiricism and the development of modern science. The scientific outlook remains one of the driving forces behind the endurance of modern historical structures. The shift in culture was primarily driven by the rise of individualism. This cultural trend may have weakened the institution of family and kinship-based community, but it is also responsible ultimately for the development of liberalism as a political and cultural ideology and the emergence of modern normative traditions like democratic governance, religious tolerance, pluralism and human rights. The idea of personal and individual freedom is the most powerful element of modern cultures and it underpins much of modern politics, ethics and values. Finally, the explosion of technology and industrial and postindustrial capitalism literally powers the spread and durability of modernity. Globalization or high modernity is essentially modernity with a greater geographical reach and more political, economic and cultural intensity.

Together, these core elements of modernity constitute a complex reality. Modernity is not an ideology that can be countered with another ideology, as the Islamists seem to think. They have made Islam into a totalitarian ideology by often repeating this refrain: "Islam is not just a faith it is a comprehensive system that includes politics, economics, science etc...." This notion of Islam as a comprehensive system was advanced by Islamist ideologues, Maulana Maududi and Syed Qutb after the modern systems theory of social science became popular in the West. Modernity is not just an immoral and

---

[62] Nasr acknowledges that the very idea of tradition has been constructed as an antithesis to modernity in Seyyed Hossein Nasr, *Knowledge and the Sacred* (Albany: SUNY Press, 1989), pp. 65–67.

unethical departure from religious norms. Modernity is in its own right a bundle of normative traditions and like the Islamist's Islam totalitarian in nature. We have modern ethics about everything, from the rights of animals to the rights of the environment. In traditional era you could buy and sell human beings, today you could go to jail if you kicked a dog. Modernity is best understood as "an age," a historical structure—*a longue durée*—the kind envisioned by Fernand Braudel.[63] But while Braudel emphasized continuity, I see change as an integral part of the structure itself, thus to me modernity is a discernable structure of history which is distinct from the past but it is not static, change is a fundamental part of it. Modernity is a historical structure that emerged as a consequence of the coalescing over centuries of a set of conditions, norms and regimes the most prominent of which are the nation state, capitalism, science, democracy and individualism.

Most Muslim intellectuals and scholars from the Islamist and the traditional genre reacted negatively to modernity because they essentially saw it as an effect of the West. For the former the main issue was politics, they resent Western domination and the latter fear its cultural hegemony and the devastation it brought to traditional society. Colonialism and imperialism were clearly possible because of the material advantages that early modernity brought to European powers. Muslim failure to recognize that the golden age of the Islamic civilization in many ways was one of the antecedents of modernity is a grave tragedy.[64] Modernity did not emerge independent of Islamic input. The failures to separate what is Western culture and what is essential modernity; to recognize the profound compatibility, at the level of principles, between modernity and Islam; and to both quickly reform and adopt are the key reasons why Muslim societies continue to be the backbenchers as the caravan of history trudges along. The traditionalists hate the caravan, but they cannot get off it. The Islamists want to drive the caravan, but before that they want to paint it green with a crescent and star and call it the *Islamic Caravan*. Little do the Islamists realize that there is no one really driving history. Some modernists think they know how the caravan works and are confident that they can build another one for Muslims, more efficient and moral, than the current one; while others believe that with few changes Muslims can not only be comfortable on the caravan but would actually enjoy the ride.

---

[63] See Fernand Braudel, Sarah Matthews (Tr.), *On History* (Chicago: University of Chicago Press, 1982), pp. 25–55.

[64] See M. Basheer Ahmed, Syed A. Ahsani and Dilnawaz Siddiqui, *Muslim Contributions to World Civilization* (Herndon, VA: International Institute of Islamic Thought, 2005).

THE FAILURE TO THEORIZE HISTORY

Ultimately, it is the failure to develop a robust theory of history that has disabled Islamists and traditionalists from coming to terms with modernity. They rely on scriptural pronouncements of past events as substitutes for a systematic understanding of history. For example, consider Maududi's provocatively titled essay "The Self-Destructiveness of Western Civilization," in which he develops a cyclical theory of history—he essentially summarizes Quranic narratives like the fall of pharaoh—and predicts that if a world war was fought it would be the end of Western civilization. He wrote this in 1932 but did not revisit his position in 1945.[65] The fact that World War II did occur and did not lead to the end of the Western civilization did not compel Maududi to revisit his own predictions or his understanding of the Quran. Ibn Khaldun, the famous Muslim philosopher of history, did advance a theory of civilization.[66] It is not exactly comprehensive and will not suffice to explain the complexity of the postindustrial order in which technology and political institutions like the state too play the role of engines of change. Those Muslims who have tried to make sense of the present using Ibn Khaldun's theories are mostly critical modernists such as Mustapha Pasha.[67] Beyond Ibn Khaldun the traditionalists have produced many prominent historians but not theorists of history.

One of the most prominent revivalists of Islamic historiography was the most conservative of Islamic modernists from India: Shibley Noamani, the successor of Syed Ahmad Khan. But his approach to history was designed to reignite pride in Islamic past and Islamic identity, but it did not provide understanding of the contemporary historical condition. Yvonne Haddad provides an exceptionally good survey of contemporary Arab efforts at developing an "Islamic theory or approaches to history."[68] I concur with her conclusion that much of the works she surveys is apologetic and seeks to construct narratives of the past that serve the politics and support the ideological assumptions of Islamism. Even though they rely heavily on the Quran, they

---

[65] The essay has been translated and published in English; see Syed Abul A'la Maududi, "Self-Destructiveness of Western Civilization," in Moaddel and Talattof, eds., *Modernist and Fundamentalist Debates in Islam*, pp. 325–333.

[66] See Ibn Khaldun, N. J. Dawood, ed., and Franz Rosenthal (Tr.), *Muqaddimah: An Introduction to History* (Princeton, NJ: Princeton University Press, 1989).

[67] See Mustapha Pasha, "Ibn Khaldun and World Order," in Stephen Gill and James H. Mittelman, eds., *Innovation and Transformation in International Relations* (London: Cambridge University Press, 1997), pp. 56–74.

[68] See Yvonne Yazbeck Haddad, *Contemporary Islam and the Challenge of History* (Albany, NY: SUNY Press, 1982).

fail to advance a philosophy of history that will simultaneously explain the rise of the West and the decline of Muslims. Most of these historians while acknowledging the decline of the Muslim world also simultaneously construct doomsday scenarios about the future. They too have allowed an ideological goal, their intense commitment to prove Islam is right and the West is wrong, to subvert their efforts to theorize or understand history.

The first thing that Muslims need to understand about history is that there is only one history. There is no such thing as Islamic history or Western history. Islam and Muslims are part of the history of humanity.[69] What do exist are Muslim narratives and non-Muslim narratives of history that clearly serve the identity, cultural and political needs of the societies that these narratives are constructed for. But if histories are written merely to serve the purpose of constructing identity without much attention to observable realities, then it will only exacerbate the intellectual crises. A critical perspective is necessary to ensure that the study of history serves the minimal goal to help us develop some meaningful understanding of the past, and not construct our present alone.[70]

My goal here is not to advance a systematic theory of history, but only to underscore my point that modernity is a historical condition and we can comprehend its origins, its continuity and its transformation in a meaningful way only if we can conceptualize history beyond trends and events and as much as possible free from ideological subversions. I understand history as a continuously evolving order co-constituted by two key elements, the existing historical structure and its interaction with human agency. Human agents—individuals, groups, states and supra-state institutions—are both produced and shaped by history, but as they interact with historical structures—capitalism, democracy, nation state—science—new ideas, new technologies and new agencies, reshape those historical structures sometimes gradually and sometimes in dramatic ruptures. Today the modernity that we are experiencing is not the same modernity that Muslim intellectuals encountered more than 100 years ago. Modernity is not a static condition it is a continuously evolving, sometimes smoothly and sometimes contentiously. The so-called postmodern challenge to modernity is essentially a glimpse of the transformative changes taking place in the modern

---

[69] See Louay Safi, *Tensions and Transitions in the Muslim World* (Lanham, MD: University Press of America, 2003), p. 51. Safi shows that reformist thinkers do recognize that histories, in this case Muslim and Western are difficult to separate.

[70] Soguk makes a rather interesting observation that Muslims have yet to tell their story. They not only have failed to develop a theory of history but have also not done a good job of just telling the Muslim story. See Nevzat Soguk, *Globalization and Islamism: Beyond Fundamentalism* (New York: Rowman and Littlefield Publishers, 2011).

condition. Perhaps we already are living in a postmodern era. I believe we are now in an age so profoundly complex that it renders both space and time less meaningful. It has expanded to enable the coexistence of both past and future in the present and thus we see the present as a braid composed of tradition, modernity and postmodernity.

ISLAM AS IDENTITY

In my view, and several Muslim scholars of Islam and contemporary historians of Islam concur with me on this, the biggest impact of the Islamic revivalism is the reduction of Islam to an identity. For many Muslims of every persuasion, the revival of Islam essentially translated into the revival of Islamic identity. For the Islamists it is at a social structural level, for the modernists it is at an intellectual level and for the traditionalist it is at the spiritual level. All the traditions in seeking to revive Islam have employed the globalization of Islamic symbolism as a tool to spread their ideas, their politics and their visions. The black and white *Kaffiyah* (headdress) became a global symbol of political solidarity with the Palestinian cause. The red *Kaffiyah*, worn by Saudis as part of their national cultural costume, has spread in South Asia and parts of Africa indicating sympathy for Salafi/Wahhabi Islam. The *Hijab*, which in the early modern era was relegated to the rural areas of Arab society, has now gone global. It has become a symbol of Muslim resistance to Western culture and a flag bearer of Islamic resurgence. Now many Muslim women in nearly every part of the world wear it. It is an instant signifier of both religiosity and a public statement of cultural rebellion against modernity. One day you are wearing a shirt and jeans, you are a modern Western woman, the next day you don a *Hijab*, and *Alhamdulillah* (praise be to Allah), you are a spiritual, religious Muslim woman. There is nothing more effective than the phenomenon of the *Hijab* for illustrating how at some levels Islamic resurgence has become about identity projection (Islamic) and cultural rejection of modernity and the West even among modern Western Muslims.

Islam has become a powerful source of identity—whether it is in the form of an individual attribute like the *Hijab*, or a collective attribute deserving of a special kind of state, the Islamic state. Students of politics and sociology have belatedly realized the power of identity as a factor that shapes and determines outcomes in human affairs; but since the end of the cold war, and with the rise of Islamism globally, Islam has become the most powerful and most contentious source of individual and collective identity. Today Muslims everywhere are demanding things "Islamic." In the Muslim world they want Islamic states, Islamic economies, Islamic democracy and Islamic universities.

In the West they want Islamic schools, Islamic centers, Islamic societies and Islamic mortgages. Secularists alone do not seek to reconstruct or assert Islamic identity; their principal goal has been national identity. The only concession that the secularists have extended to any other identity other than national identity has been to a supranational identity, namely Pan-Arabism.

The demand for Islam as a prefix runs from the profound to the profoundly mundane. While there are some, like yours truly, who once sought to revive Islamic philosophy,[71] there are those who wish to establish Islamic tourism, and others who are launching Islamic games and even Islamic speed dating. "Islamic" has become the dominant trope in Muslim discourses and narratives. The amount of literature that is now produced on and around the theme of Islamic identity construction in traditional Muslim literature and Western academia is overwhelming. Muslim consciousness, it appears, is now consumed with constructing and defending the Islamic identity. Even as Islam becomes a global obsession and Muslim presence becomes global, thanks primarily to international migration, Muslims are acting as if there is some grave global existential threat to things Islamic in the present world. Even after 100 years of revivalism, Muslims are still defending their identity from the assault of modernity, the subversion of postmodernism, Western domination and Muslim deviation. The defense and the reproduction of Islamic identity have become a global Muslim priority so much so that being a Muslim today tantamount to constructing, defending and projecting Islamic identity. Islam has been reduced to "identity." I must at this stage confess that, until a few years ago, I too have been a very active protagonist of the Islamic identity and its various *avatars* such as American Muslim, Indian Muslim, rational Muslim and moderate Muslim.

Clearly, what constitutes "Islamic" is highly contested. No two things Islamic look alike. Iran, Saudi Arabia and Pakistan all claim to be Islamic Republics and yet there is a lot of diversity in their understanding of what that means. What is common is only the jingoistic proclamations and claims to identity markers such as *Shariah* as source of laws, cosmetic legislations on blasphemy and apostasy (they do have serious consequences for those on whom these laws are used for purposes of symbolic politics)

---

[71] See M. A. Muqtedar Khan, "The Need to Revive Islamic Philosophy," *Intellectual Discourse* 6.1 (Spring 1998). I also hosted two conferences, one in 1998 and the other in 1999, to review what I then called was a contemporary Islamic philosophy. See Ahmad Iftheqar Hussain, "First Contemporary Muslim Philosopher's Conference," *American Journal of Islamic Social Sciences* 15.3 (Fall 1998): 167–172.

and the mandatory restrictions on women. While Muslims in the past have always made the distinction between believers and non-believers, the manner in which Muslims now discourse about Islamic identity, even making its construction and preservation a primary goal in education (especially in the West), is modern. In fact, the common denominator to all Muslim responses to modernity and Western political and cultural domination has been to react defensively. Defending Islamic identity has become a slogan for defending a set of values, cultures and ethos, whose substance may be disputed but whose potential for extinction is agreed upon.

In this chapter, I explored Muslim responses to modernity and sketched out how Islamic responses disagree profoundly on diagnosis of the Muslim condition, and how to redress it, but ultimately, they all agree upon the need to assert the Islamic identity. There is nothing wrong or even especially unique about Muslims seeking to proliferate their cultural and religious symbols, all healthy and thriving cultures do that. But if Islamic revivalism is reduced to Islamic identity production, then all it will achieve is to create literally a bazaar for Islamic artifacts, including religious books and pilgrimages, but fail to precipitate the profound transformation at the social and individual level that reformers and revivalists are dreaming about. The Islamic revolution of Iran is now forty years old. Women wear chadors (still the state needs to enforce it) and the Mullahs control everything. To the question has Iran achieved success in proliferating Islamic symbols in Iran and promoting Islamic politics abroad? The answer is a resounding yes. But has Iran revived the Islamic civilization and spirituality it sought? The green revolution of 2009 and the ongoing struggle for freedom and liberalization in every sphere of domestic society suggest otherwise.[72] It is my contention that the disproportionate attention that Muslims pay to identity formation and symbolism detracts from a focus on substantive issues such as the revival of Islamic spirituality, Islamic ethics and values, and the goodness that Islamic sources teach. Identity is an external attribute and not necessarily a mirror of the internal self. It is ultimately a form of narcissism. Identity is often constructed in such a way as to project a political message. One way to think of identity is to think of it as a political view from the outside. This leads to *performativity*, where the projecting subject is performing for the benefit of an external observer.[73] What others think of the self becomes the

---

[72] See Hamid Dabashi, *The Green Movement in Iran* (New York: Transaction Publishers, 2011).

[73] See James Loxley, *Performativity* (New York: Routledge Publishers, 2006).

dominant criteria for determining political and cultural choices. I believe Identity politics gives tremendous power to the other over the self, since the self itself is constructed in opposition to and in competition with the other. If performativity inspires the self to explore the self, even through externalities, then it is beneficial and even transformative.[74] But if it is motivated by the desire to distinguish from the other then it is pernicious. The transcendent sources of Islamic self are set aside in order to accommodate political machinations. Islamic scriptures teach Muslims to worry about only what God thinks of them, and not what others think of them. Someone who is busy serving his or her lord with complete devotion, and focused on the purification and beatification of the self—on interior decoration—should not have too much time to devote to painting the façade.

Muslims specially should know better that external manifestations of religiosity and even sustained religious life can sometimes be both shallow and mendacious—a mere performance. The Quran speaks of the hypocrites—*Al-Munafiqeen*—who give witness of their belief, perform all rituals of Islam including the obligatory prayers, but their hearts are empty of belief. There is an entire chapter on the hypocrites in the Quran (Chap. 63), which tells us that they were so good at projecting their Islamic identity that even Prophet Muhammad (pbuh) did not know who they were. I am not suggesting that any or all Muslims who seek to construct their Islamic identity and project it are hypocrites. I am merely pointing out that external confirmation of faith is not what God is looking for; He looks at what is in their hearts. It is not identity that needs to be revived, but it is the self that needs to be purified. Performativity can be deceptive, even the Quran warns about it. It should therefore not be used as a barometer for measuring civilizational revival.

بِسْمِ ٱللَّهِ ٱلرَّحْمَٰنِ ٱلرَّحِيمِ إِذَا جَاءَكَ ٱلْمُنَٰفِقُونَ قَالُوا۟ نَشْهَدُ إِنَّكَ لَرَسُولُ ٱللَّهِ وَٱللَّهُ يَعْلَمُ إِنَّكَ لَرَسُولُهُۥ وَٱللَّهُ يَشْهَدُ إِنَّ ٱلْمُنَٰفِقِينَ لَكَٰذِبُونَ

When the hypocrites come to you (O Muhammad SAW), they say: "We bear witness that you are indeed the Messenger of Allah." Allah knows that you are indeed His Messenger and Allah bears witness that the hypocrites are liars indeed. (Quran 63:1)

[74] See, for example, Azam Torab, *Performing Islam: Gender and Ritual in Iran* (Amsterdam: Brill Publishers, 2006).

CHAPTER 4

Ihsan: Classical and Contemporary Understanding

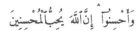

Perform beautiful deeds. Indeed Allah loves those who perform beautiful deeds.—Quran 2:195

Ihsan is the final destiny of the true believer. It is that state of human existence and experience where the here and the now begins to merge with the hereafter. It is sometimes that fleeting moment when time becomes still and the believer has this profound awareness that he is in the throes of a powerful experience that brings with it a sense of awe, amazement and fulfillment. Such moments are rare and only very few fortunate individuals experience it, and even fewer have been able to record and describe it for others. It is also a state of being when one is at peace with oneself and with the circumstances of one's existence. One is neither insecure about the future nor one grieves the past. Life itself becomes a reward, a beautiful fulfillment. This is *Ihsan*, the final destiny of the true believer, the more fortunate of them experience it here, and others will know it hereafter.

The idea that *Ihsan*—a state of divine beauty and a place of divine beauty—is the final destination of those who do good deeds is expressed very eloquently and frequently in the Quran. I shall discuss a few instances to underscore this idea. In Chapter 13 of the Quran, Surah Al-Ra'd (The Thunder), verse 18 reads as follows:

© The Author(s) 2019
M. A. M. Khan, *Islam and Good Governance*,
https://doi.org/10.1057/978-1-137-54832-0_4

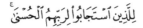

Those who answer the call of their Lord, for them (the destination is) *Al-Husna* (The beautiful, the good). Both *Ihsan* and *Husna* are conjugations of the same root h-s-n. The former literally means to make more beautiful, or better, while the latter literally means "the good." A review of the exegetical literature on this verse shows that nearly all classical commentators, including Al-Tabari, Ibn Kathir, Al-Razi and the two Jalals (Jalalain), understand and explain *Al-Husna* as the reward—paradise—that is promised to the true believers.[1] Only Al-Zamakshari and the contemporary Muhammad Asad, who follows Al-Zamakshari, disagree and suggest that *Al-Husna* here is an adjective that describes the quality of the believer's response to his Lord's call. But the text of the verse does not explicitly describe the reward as obtaining in the hereafter, even though the rest of the verse clearly states that those who do bad deeds will go to hell (*Jahannum*). Therefore, it is but logical that the classical commentators concluded that *Al-Husna* implies the opposite of hell, that is, heaven or paradise.

Interestingly other contemporary commentators like Syed Qutb, Maulana Maududi and Maulana Mufti Muhammad Shafi have all chosen to be vague and described the term as "good reward" without making the leap to paradise. Clearly some commentators are concluding that the destiny of those who believe (in Islam) and do good deeds is heaven, and their conclusion is also supported in many other verses in the Quran, for example, 11:23 and 29:58, while others have chosen to stay with the literal translation and conclude that the reward for faith and deeds is a good one. I generally agree with this understanding, except that along with Shabbir Ahmed Usmani, a prominent South Asian commentator and theologian, I interpret *Al-Husna* to mean a beautiful reward both in this world and in the next.

When one becomes fully conversant with my discussion of the concept of *Al-Ihsan*, the reader will realize that I think it is a temporal taste of divine perfection and beauty. It is a condition that will be permanent and in

---

[1] Their source is Prophet Muhammad's (pbuh) companion Ibn Abbas, who said that *Al-Husna* is *Al-Jannah*, the paradise. Since I will be using the same edition of each of the Quranic commentaries in their physical form that I am referencing, I will mention them only by the names of the authors, such as Al-Tabari or Al-Zamakshari. I have provided an index of all the Quranic commentaries used at the end of the book. Where necessary I shall however mention volume and page numbers, but for all Quranic references, the chapter and verse will be the main indicators.

abundance in the hereafter, but is a rare and more aspiration than reality in the here and the now. Additionally, the rewards for a life spent in pursuit of beautiful deeds are obtained both in the life and in the life after. Thus, based on the understanding *Al-Husna* as reward for faith and good action, both now and later, I submit that *Ihsan* is the final destiny of the true believer. This idea is repeated and cemented in 13:22 and 10:26 and in the following verse of the Quran:

ٱلَّذِينَ ءَامَنُواْ وَعَمِلُواْ ٱلصَّٰلِحَٰتِ طُوبَىٰ لَهُمْ وَحُسْنُ مَـَٔابٍ

Those who believe and do good deeds, for them there is a blessed and beautiful place. (13:29)

IHSAN: A SHORT REVIEW OF A LONG TRADITION

I spent nearly two years traveling across the Middle East, speaking to academics, scholars, intellectuals, traditional scholars (the Ulema) and practitioners of Islam and Islamic mysticism (Sufi masters and dervishes), seeking an understanding of the concept of *Ihsan*.[2] I was not interested in the superficial and academic answers that I received initially from them; I got as much from reading basic texts about Islam and *Tasawwuf* (the science of Islamic mysticism)—that *Ihsan* is the "highest form" of Islam or that it was a "dimension of Islam" that sought to highlight goodness, virtue and beauty in devotion. I was interested in grasping how Muslim understanding of *Ihsan* had over the centuries shaped Muslim understanding of Islam itself, how it had shaped their lives and how that manifested in the evolution of the Islamic civilization. My ultimate goal was to unveil the secrets of *Ihsan* to unravel its divine potential.

I found that the Muslim heritage had a bipolar approach to the concept of *Ihsan*. On one hand it was an unattainable ideal that was mentioned only in passing albeit with great reverence, while scholars focused on what they thought as the more important aspects of faith and creed of Islam or

---

[2] I did not conduct interviews as such; I listened and when possible I participated in practices. I also basically sat with these scholars, often for hours, and learned from them. Most of the experts that I engaged with, I consider them as my teachers, who taught me the traditional disciplines of Islam. Since I spent time with Western-style modern academics and traditionally trained scholars, my traveling personal University of Islam had a diverse and rich faculty and pedagogy.

on exploring the intricacies of divine law—the *Shariah* and its sciences.[3] Most of the scholars and practitioners I met and interviewed subscribed to one of two approaches—the religious and the spiritual. The ideals that the first approach to Islam pursued were *Taqwa*, understood as fear of God,[4] and *Adl* that is justice, and conversations with this group lead us either to discussing global politics and the suffering of the *Ummah* in a Western-dominated global order, or into the realms of the discourse on *Shariah* and the need to implement it. For those with the second approach on the other hand, *Ihsan* was everything, the alpha and the omega of Islam. Indeed *Ihsan*, for them, is the most comprehensive and only adequate understanding of the basic relationship between the human being and the Almighty God. Needless to say, the advocates of the latter position were essentially those who are associated with *Tasawwuf*—the science of Islamic mysticism, also known as *Sufis*. The proponents of the first approach were traditional and orthodox Muslims, devout, but not mystical, more concerned with obeying divine law than with seeking divine love. The former reduced *Ihsan* to deep devotion and dedication in prayers (*Khushu*) and excellence in manners and social interaction (*Akhlaq*). The latter developed it into a science of approaching God and a cosmology and an ontology of the Divine.

The textual history of *Ihsan* begins with the famous hadith of Gabriel, which is reported in the two most important canonical collections of Islam, *Sahih Bukhari* and *Sahih Muslim*, in which the Prophet Muhammad (pbuh) in response to a query from Angel Gabriel defines *Ihsan* as "To worship Allah as if you see him, for if you cannot see him, surely He sees You." This hadith is in the opinion of many Islamic scholars the most important hadith that encapsulates the meaning and purpose, the articles of faith, the beliefs and essential obligatory practices of

---

[3] Such as jurisprudence or *Usul al-Fiqh*, and *Kalam* or theological metaphysics.

[4] Increasingly in the West, English-speaking Muslims are translating *Taqwa* as God consciousness, but when I spoke with traditional Muslim scholars in Muslim countries like Morocco, Turkey and Egypt, they consistently explained *Taqwa* as *Khashiyah Allah*, or fear of Allah. Consider the exegetical discourse on the adjective *Al-Muttaqeen* in the Quran (2:2) most commentators explain it as God fearing. Ziauddin Sardar, a prominent British Muslim intellectual, defines *Taqwa* as God consciousness in his *Reading the Quran: Contemporary Relevance of Sacred Text* (New York: Oxford University Press, 2011), p. 72, but Abdulaziz Sachedina defines *Taqwa* as reverential fear of God; see his *Islam and the Challenge of Human Rights* (New York: Oxford University Press, 2009), p. 98. The idea of God consciousness, I believe, incorporates elements of *Ihsan* into an understanding of *Taqwa*.

the religion of Islam.[5] It is in this hadith that Prophet Muhammad (pbuh) explains the meaning of *Islam* (rituals), *Iman* (beliefs) and *Ihsan*. Nearly everyone who seeks to explain or understand *Ihsan* begins with this prophetic tradition and we too will examine it in detail in the next section of this chapter.

Classical Understanding of Ihsan

A review of classical literature revealed some interesting aspects of how *Ihsan* was treated by Muslim scholars. For example, when one looks at the work of the great jurist and founder of the oldest and biggest existing Islamic school of law Imam Abu Haneefah (699–767 AD), one is surprised at how he completely ignores the concept of *Ihsan*. In his book, *The Greater Knowledge* (*Al-Fiqh Al-Akbar*),[6] he discusses Islam and *Iman* and everything else that he thought were essentially elements of the religion of Islam, but skips the concept of *Ihsan*. Imam Abu Haneefah began his intellectual life as a *Mutakallimun*, a theologian engaged in debates between the rationalists (*Mu'tazila*) and the traditionalists, and then gravitated toward jurisprudence and law. Thus, he began his intellectual life in the domain of *Iman* and then moved toward the domain of Islam. So, he speaks of Islam and *Iman*, he skips *Ihsan* and talks about the *Shariah* and *Din*, which he defines as the sum of Islam, *Iman* and *Shariah*.[7]

والدين اسم واقع على الإيمان و الإسلام وال شرائع كلها

Sheikh Ibn Taymiyyah (1263–1328 AD), a prominent Hanbali jurist, who is in the present times very popular with the Islamic trend widely referred to as the *Salafi* movement essentially anchored his most distinctive and definitive work, *Kitab Al-Iman*, on the hadith of Gabriel. His goal in

---

[5] The significance of the hadith of Gabriel is evident from its selection in Imam Nawawi's *Forty Hadith* (*Al-Arbaeen Al-Nawawiyyah*), and the eminent scholar himself argues in his introduction that he included in his collection only the most important *ahadith* that pertain to Islam and can be considered to constitute half of the entire religion. See Ezzedine Ibrahim and Denys Johnson-Davies, *An-Nawawi's Forty Hadith* (Riyadh, KSA: International Islamic Publishing House, 1992), p. 22. Imam Al-Nawawi placed this hadith at number two.

[6] There are some Muslim and some orientalist scholars who contend that Imam Abu Haneefah may not be the author of *Al-Fiqh Al-Akbar*, but it is a minority view. See Abdur-Rahman Ibn Yusuf (Trans.), Imam Abu Haneefah, *Al-Fiqh Al-Akbar* (Santa Barbara: White Thread Press, 2007), p. 171.

[7] See Ibid., p. 171.

that book was to clarify the true meaning of the term *Iman*, differentiate it from the concept of Islam and enshrine the elements of faith and creed based solely on the Quran and Sunnah. It appears that Ibn Taymiyyah essentially sought to make the definitions of Islam and Iman provided in the hadith of Gabriel as orthodoxy. The book more or less makes the point that all Islamic concepts must derive from the Quran and Sunnah and nothing else, especially not from human reasoning. In principle I agree with his privileging of the hadith of Gabriel, and my own humble endeavor can be seen as an extension of Ibn Taymiyyah's *Kitab al-Iman*. He sought to elucidate on Islam and Iman from the said hadith and I am trying to unveil the multiple meanings of *Ihsan* and their relevance to the global public sphere from the same source.

Ibn Taymiyyah explains that the hadith of Gabriel identifies three ranks of the religion and he places *Ihsan* as the highest rank (*darajah*) followed by Iman and then Islam. This understanding of *Ihsan* as the highest rank or form of the religion of Islam is now the orthodox position and a systematic survey of contemporary sermons, lectures, short articles on the World Wide Web and answers by scholars to queries about the meaning of the word *Ihsan*, one finds that all non-Sufi sources follow the view of Ibn Taymiyyah. Interestingly, the great Sheikh himself makes contradictory statements. At one place he argues that Islam and *Iman* together constitute the entire religion (اعلم أن «الإيمان، والإسلام، يجتمع فيهما الدينُ كلّه،)[8] and at another place he argues that *Ihsan* is the highest level in religion.[9] It appears that his primary concern is Islam and *Iman* and for him they are more than sufficient. Similarly most orthodox scholars today are preoccupied with the practice of the religion (Islam) and the articles of faith (*Iman*) and the pursuit of perfection (*Ihsan*) is forgotten or mentioned only as an afterthought. Nevertheless, we are grateful to Sheikh Ibn Taymiyyah for so emphatically stating the significance of *Ihsan*, as the highest level of the religion of Islam, now even the most stringent critics of *Tasawwuf* cannot deny the profound importance of *Ihsan*.

While jurists either ignored or paid brief attention to *Ihsan*, the Sufi-leaning scholars truly immersed in it. For them it was all about *Ihsan* and indeed they viewed *Ihsan* as synonymous with *Tasawwuf* and Sufism. Frithjof Schuon (1907–1998), also known as Sheikh Isa Nuruddin, a prominent metaphysician and thinker of the school of perennial philosophy,

---

[8] See Ibn Taymiyyah, Naseer Al-Din Albani, ed., *Kitab Al-Iman* (Beirut: Al-Maktab Al-Islami, 1992), p. 7.

[9] See Ibid., p. 8.

writes that *"Ihsan* is synonymous with *Tasawwuf"*[10] and Sheikh Hisham Kabbani, a prominent Naqshbandi Sufi scholar, writes *"Ihsan* and the process that leads to it are known as *Tasawwuf."*[11] Both Schuon and Kabbani derive and develop their discussions on *Ihsan* and *Tasawwuf* from the hadith of Gabriel. Nearly all writings by Sufi scholars and poetry by Sufi practitioners are about how to reach the ultimate station of *Ihsan.* I found during my extended discussions with scholars and practitioners of *Tasawwuf* and through my numerous visits to various *Zawiyas* (circles of remembrance) and Sufi *Tekkes* (spiritual lodges), that there are three distinct ways in which they sought to reach the station (*maqaam*) of *Ihsan.*[12] Sufis seek *Ihsan* through (1) the pursuit of knowledge of God and his attributes (*Al-Maarifa*), (2) through the perfection of one's adherence to the *Shariah* through humility and dedication (*Khushu wa Khudu*) in performance of obligatory duties and (3) through indulgence in pursuit of practices that inspire, love and ecstasy often with the help of music, poetry and dance (*Sama*). I see the great mystical philosopher, Ibn Arabi (1165 to 1240 AD), as the exemplar of the first type of approach to *Tasawwuf,* philosophical mysticism. I see Abu Hamid Al-Ghazali (1058–1111 AD) as the most important proponent of the second type, the divine law-based mysticism, and Jalaluddin Rumi, the famous spiritual poet and mystic, as the epitome of the third approach to mysticism.[13]

Al-Ghazali (1058–1111 AD) had two academic careers separated by ten years of mystical pursuit. In the first he was a theologian and jurist who advanced the Ashari theology and challenged the impact of Aristotelian philosophy and Greek metaphysics on Islamic thought.[14] In his second

---

[10] Frithjof Schuon, *Understanding Islam* (Bloomington, IN: World Wisdom Books, 1994), p. 171, n. 67.

[11] See Sheikh Hisham Kabbani, *Self-Purification and the State of Excellence* (Mountain View, CA: As-Sunnah Foundation of America, 1998), p. 4.

[12] I have visited Sufi lodges in Egypt, Tunisia, Morocco, Turkey, Singapore and the United States. In my younger days I had visited many Sufi places in India, but then I was not a student of *Tasawwuf.*

[13] All the scholars mentioned here are giants of Islamic intellectual heritage, who are read and revered nearly a thousand years after the passed away. Ibn Taymiyyah is remembered as *Sheikh al-Islam* (The grand teacher of Islam), Ibn Arabia is revered by the people of *Tasawwuf* as *Sheikh al-Akbar* (The Greatest Teacher), Al-Ghazali who enjoys respect and popularity across many Islamic schools of thought is enshrined in the tradition as *Hujjat al-Islam* (Proof of Islam) and Rumi, he is simply *Mevlana*—"Our Master."

[14] For a brief introduction to Al-Ghazali's life and thought, see his intellectual autobiography, *Al-Munqidh min al-Dalal, Deliverance from Error.* See R. J. McCarthy (Trans.), *Al-Ghazali's Path to Sufism his Deliverance from Error* (Louisville, KY: Fons Vitae, 2000).

tenure as an academic and scholar, he taught and wrote primarily about a *Shariah*-based approach to realizing *Ihsan*. Al-Ghazali is the greatest synthesizer of knowledge in Islamic heritage and in his mystical thought too he sought to strike a balance between law and mysticism. His *Ihya Uloom al-Deen* (*The Revival of Religious Sciences*)[15] is a magisterial magnum opus that seeks to show how excellence, beauty and perfection (*Ihsan*) can be realized in nearly every aspect of life; in worship, in conduct of business, in marriage and interpersonal relations and finally in understanding law and the nature of the divine. Al-Ghazali too refers to the hadith of Gabriel, but does not rely on it as much as others in order to explain the essence and scope of *Ihsan*. Clearly, he was more interested in how *Ihsan* can be realized rather than what is *Ihsan*. In fact, when he does refer to the hadith, he does to do exactly what Ibn Taymiyyah uses it for 200 years later—to distinguish between Islam and *Iman*.

Al-Ghazali's contribution to Islam and the cause of *Ihsan* (*Tasawwuf*) is immeasurable. Sufis and Sufism have experienced two major moments of criticism in history. Once during the classical age when the orthodoxy deemed Sufi ideas, Sufi practices and prominent Sufis (like Mansur Al-Hallaj 858–922 AD) as heretics and in the modern era when modernists have viewed Sufis as the cause of the material decline and weakening of the power of the Islamic civilization.[16] Al-Ghazali's work, specially the *Ihya*, not only restores the theological legitimacy of spirituality and the inner and unseen dimensions of worship and faith,[17] but also articulates a moderate, law-based approach to *Ihsan*. Annemarie Schimmel, a very prominent voice on Islamic mysticism, writes, "This teaching—a marriage between mysticism and law—has made Al-Ghazali the most influential theologian of medieval Islam."[18] *Ihsan* in the Ghazalian framework is the station (*maqaam*) that one reaches only through meticulous attention to both, exoteric (*fiqh*) and esoteric (*Tasawwuf*) elements of worship.

---

[15] While reading the *Ihya*, I used a physical copy of the Urdu translation and the Arabic and English version published on the Al-Ghazali portal on World Wide Web at www.ghazali.org. For the translation in Urdu, see Abu Hamid Al-Ghazali, *Ihya Uloom al-Deen*, Allama Faiz Ahmed Owaisi (Trans.) (New Delhi: Maktabah Radhwiyyah, 1999).

[16] See the chapter on "Sufi Doctrine and Practice," in Fazlur Rahman, *Islam* (Chicago, IL: University of Chicago Press, 1979), pp. 128–149.

[17] See, for example, Abdul Hamid Al-Ghazali, *The Inner Dimensions of Islamic Prayer*, M. Holland (Trans.) (Leicester, UK: Islamic Foundation, 1983).

[18] See Annemarie Schimmel, *Mystical Dimensions of Islam* (Chapel Hill, NC: University of North Carolina, 1975), p. 95.

One cannot talk about Islamic mysticism or *Ihsan* without mentioning the enormously deep, extensive and profound works of Sheikh al-Akbar Ibn Arabi (1165–1240 AD). I do not feel fully qualified or competent to provide a concise and accurate understanding of Ibn Arabi's take on *Ihsan*. He is too difficult to easily summarize and very elusive. He has constructed an entire language of his own, with new concepts and metaphors, which he deploys often in poetic style and in very subtle ways. One has to first become a student of Ibn Arabi and understand him in order to be able to read him meaningfully. Traditional scholars dissuade individuals from reading Ibn Arabi's work without a teacher or a guide. A couple of Sufi masters who are students of Ibn Arabi looked at me in complete horror when I told them that I had been reading parts of both *Futuhat Al-Makkiyah* and *Fusus Al-Hikam*. I am not alone in this situation. Even more senior and accomplished scholars of Islamic mystical thought than me have expressed difficulties understanding Ibn Arabi.[19] One of the most prominent translators and commentators of Ibn Arabi, William Chittick himself acknowledges the challenges and difficulties in understanding Ibn Arabi.[20] A lot of what Ibn Arabi writes is based on the premise that his readers are also cotravelers on the spiritual journey and if you have not visited the spiritual stations that Ibn Arabi has, you will find it difficult to relate to the spiritual landscape he describes.

Nevertheless, there are many aspects of Ibn Arabi's work that both illuminate as well as embody the concept of *Ihsan*. The ones that appeal to me are those that are epistemological in their nature. He constructs an entire cosmology of *Ihsan*, a beautiful view of everything beautiful. His pursuits, in spite of his spiritual claims, are more philosophical than spiritual. He is seeking to understand and know the secrets of God, the purpose behind creation and the meaning of things as they are. He is remorseless in his quest and critical pursuit. When he discusses how God wills creation and explains the divine command of creation *Kun fa ya kun—Be and it exists*—Ibn Arabi suggests that things exist even before they exist, for they are able to listen to the divine command "be" and are able to obey and come into existence (Quran 36:82, 2:117).[21] As you read

[19] See, for example, John Renard, *Knowledge of God in Classical Sufism: Foundations of Islamic Mystical Theology* (Mahwah, NJ: Paulist Press, 2004), p. 56.

[20] For his observations on the difficulties in understanding Ibn Arabi, see William Chittick, *The Self-Disclosure of God: Principles of Ibn al-Arabi's Cosmology* (Albany: SUNY Press, 1998), pp. xi–xii.

[21] For example, verse 2:117, which says: "Originator of the heavens and the earth. When He decrees a matter, He only says to it, 'Be,' and it is."

his work, you find his ideas gripping you, shaking you and compelling you to reassess everything you think you know about God, about Islam and about the basic relationship between the Creator and his creation.

Ibn Arabi uses the idea of perfection, another meaning of the concept of *Ihsan*, in a way that is very compelling. He uses a *Hadith Qudsi* that is very popular with Sufis and rejected by the orthodoxy, in which God says, "I was a hidden treasure but I was not known, so I loved to be known; I created the creation and made myself known to them, So they came to know me."[22]

كنت كنزا مخفيا فأحببت أن أعرف فخلقت الخلق وتجليت عليهم فعرفوني

The entire story of life and creation is in essence the self-disclosure of God. God is the Ultimate Creator and the Ultimate Knower and the Ultimate Object of Knowledge, we are merely his slaves, who know him by his command, by his leave and as his slaves. We are the mirrors and he is the subject and the object of vision. In Ibn Arabi's words, "He is the viewer and we are His mirrors."[23] Our goal as seekers is to perfect our souls so that we can become perfect mirrors and that is the purpose of life, the meaning of *Ihsan*, becoming perfectly polished mirrors that reflect divine reality.[24] This idea as the human soul as a mirror that can reflect the divine light is not limited to Ibn Arabi, Sheikh Abd al-Qadir al-Jilani (1077–1166 AD), a very prominent Sufi master and founder of the Qadiri order, expressed similar views in his book *Sirr al-Asrar*, Secret of Secrets.[25] Jalaluddin Rumi wrote many poems with the soul as mirror metaphor, like this one[26]:

> *Love wants its tale revealed to everyone,*
> *But your heart's mirror won't reflect this sun,*
> *Don't you know why we can't perceive it here?*
> *Your mirror's face is rust—scrap it clear.*

---

[22] See William Chittick, *The Self-Disclosure of God: Principles of Ibn al-Arabi's Cosmology* (Albany: State University of New York Press, 1998), p. 21.

[23] Chittick, *The Self-Disclosure of God*, p. 82.

[24] This reading of Ibn Arabi's use of the metaphor of the mirror is based on the readings of Chittick, *The Self-Disclosure of God*, p. 82. Also see Ibn Al-Arabi, *The Bezels of Wisdom*, R. W. J. Austin (Trans.), (Mahwah, NJ: Paulist Press, 1980), p. 35.

[25] See Abd al-Qadir Al-Jilani, *The Secret of Secrets*, Tosun Bayrak al-Jerrahi al-Halveti (Trans.), (Cambridge: Islamic Texts Society, 1992), p. xlvii and p. 51.

[26] See Jawid Mojaddedi (Trans.), *Rumi: The Masnavi, Book One* (London: Oxford University Press, 2004), p. 6.

While Ibn Arabi epitomizes philosophical mysticism in Islam and Al-Ghazali defines a mystical path that follows that straight path of the *Shariah* in a rather exoteric fashion, Mevlana Jalaluddin Rumi (1207–1273 AD) is the jewel in the Sufi crown. While Ibn Arabi's thought, except when he is in his poetic mood, transforms the heart into a seeing and thinking organ of the mystic and Al-Ghazali endows this seeing and thinking heart with a visible fear and respect of the divine law that sometimes remains invisible to the perceptions of the literalists in the discourses of most Sufis, the Mevlana does not restrain his longing heart. It sprouts poetry, it sings and dances with abandon, creating perhaps the most sustained moment of ecstasy not only in Islamic history but in the entire love story of humanity with God.

Islamic mysticism is wedded to poetry. While poetry is not constitutive to mystical life, without it *mahabba*—divine love—one of the most important elements of the pursuit of *Ihsan* would not find expression. Poetry not only gives mysticism an attitude, but it also makes it accessible to all. While philosophical discourses may not be everyone's cup of tea, the power of *Sama*, mystical singing and remembrance of God in accompaniment of music, does melt the hearts of all dervishes and gives them a taste of divine union. In nearly every major Islamic language, Sufis have written poetry that brought the idea of *Ihsan* and the pursuit of *Ihsan* to the common man. Mansur Al-Hallaj (858–922 AD), Umar Ibn al-Farid (1181–1235 AD) and Ibn Arabi in Arabic, Farid Al-Attar (1145–1221 AD), Hafiz Al-Shirazi (1325–1390 AD) and Mevlana Rumi (1207–1273 AD) in Persian, Amir Khusroe (1253–1325 AD), Khawaja Mir Dard (1721–1785 AD), Mirza Ghalib (1797–1869) in Urdu all exemplified mystical thought. I contend here and will argue later that aesthetics is one dimension of *Ihsan* and one way in which it was pursued was through poetry.[27]

Rumi shared his view of *Ihsan* through discourses and through poetry. His poetry is considered of the highest quality in Persian, indeed his Masnavi is often referred to as the Quran in Persia. Rumi essentially expressed the key themes of *Tasawwuf* in his poetry, the sorrow on separation from the divine, the longing for union with the beloved and he also gave commentary on aspects of the Quran and told stories of the Prophets (Muhammad, Moses and Jesus were his favorite subjects, peace be upon them), and the companions of the Prophets. Some of the highlights of his poetry are

---

[27] A brief biography and translations of some of their poems of most of these poets can be found in Mahmood Jamal, *Islamic Mystical Poetry: Sufi Verse from the Early Mystics to Rumi* (London: Penguin Classics, 2009).

parables that advance the theme that the purpose of life is to connect with the divine. While Rumi did not advance a theory or a discourse on *Ihsan*, he showed through his poetry how *Ihsan* could be manifest in reality. I present here a very tiny selection of his poetry that speaks of *Ihsan*.

> *Whoever recognizes his own faults*
> *Towards perfection rapidly then vaults*
> *But if you think you are perfect as you are*
> *You won't reach God for you have strayed too far....*
> *Much blood will flow from your heart and eyes*
> *Before your self-conceit completely dies*

In this poem, Rumi is talking of the need for perfection of the self, a commentary on the verse that I began this chapter with "*Ahsinu—Inna Allah yuhibbu Al-Muhsineen*," it commends one to perfection, to do good deeds to become better, because God loves those who do beautiful things (Quran 2:195). Rumi talks about *Fanaa fi Allah* to perish in the love of God. The union between the slave and the Master cannot happen as long as the slave is plagued with conceit. It is only through self-annihilation that the slave becomes one with One. I conclude this section with a quatrain from Rumi that to my mind summarizes his conception of *Ihsan*.

> *On this path of love sublime,*
> *Anything else is idolatry,*
> *Anything else but light of union,*
> *On this path is unbelief.*[28]

Ihsan is the path of love toward the divine union; it is furthest from idolatry and unbelief. A key Sufi understanding of *Ihsan* involves the concept of *Fanaa*, self-annihilation, the effacement of the ego to such extent that one disappears and merges in God and then continues to subsist in this state of union with the divine (*Baqaa*). Mevlana Rumi wrote ecstatically and frequently about this state of being. Chittick translated and contextualized some of this poetry in his book *The Sufi Path of Love*[29]:

> *No one will find his way to the court of magnificence*
> *Until he is annihilated...*
> *He alone is perfect in attribute (achieved Ihsan*[30]*).*

[28] See Mahmood Jamal, ed., *Islamic Mystical Poetry*, p. 139.
[29] See Chittick, *The Sufi Path of Love*, p. 179.
[30] Observations in parenthesis are mine.

Who has become the prey of annihilation
A single hair will not find room
In the circle of Uniqueness

It is impossible to capture the essence of Rumi's thought and the beauty of his expression in a few pages. I can only hint at his sublime contribution to Muslim understanding of *Ihsan* and its various derivatives like beauty and love. One has to read him. Reading Rumi is a spiritual journey by itself.

Contemporary Understanding of Ihsan: Insights from the Muslim World

A lot has been written on *Ihsan* in the past few decades. The World Wide Web is brimful with short articles, lectures and sermons, on the meaning and significance of *Ihsan*. While there are abundant discourses, the poverty in the content is startling. Most discussions are limited to either the hadith of Gabriel or the notion that there are three levels of Islam and that *Ihsan* constitutes the highest form of Islam. *Ihsan* is a great virtue and Muslims must aspire for it. Some sources are more comprehensive than others; they site Quranic and hadith sources of *Ihsan*, in reality they are just commentaries discussing those verses and traditions in which the word *Ihsan* appears. These sources essentially underscore the rather narrow view that only those sources in which the word *Ihsan* is used, speak of *Ihsan*. I hope that through this discussion, I will be able to deepen how we think about *Ihsan*, its scope and how it is certainly the most beautiful element of all things—thoughts, emotions and actions.

I have chosen to review the works of a few contemporary scholars, from the East and the West, primarily because they are the ones who have written about *Ihsan* more extensively than others and they represent many different schools of thought. From the Muslim world I chose the work of Sheikh Muhammad bin Hassan and Sheikh Abdessalam Yassine on *Ihsan* and from the West, I chose the work of Sheikh Hisham Kabbani and Professor William Chittick. While traveling through Europe and the Middle East, I met and learned about *Ihsan* from many contemporary Muslim scholars and practitioners of *Tasawwuf*, they are too numerous to list them all here, but I have recognized many of them in the acknowledgment to this book. I examine here Sheikh Muhammad bin Hassan's recent book, *Al-Ihsan*,[31] and Sheikh

---

[31] See Sheikh Muhammad Bin Hassan, *Al-Ihsan: An Ta'budu Allaha Kannaka tarahu Fa In Lam Takun Tarahu Innahu Yaraka* (Mansoura, Egypt: Maktabah Fayad, 2010).

Abdessalam Yassine's book, also named *Al-Ihsan*.[32] The former is a prominent Scholar and preacher, associated with the orthodox Salafi approach to
Islam.[33] He was trained in Egypt and Saudi Arabia and is a prominent conservative voice in the Arab public sphere. The late Sheikh Yassine
(1928–2012 AD) was a prominent Sufi master who also founded the anti-
monarchy Islamic movement *Al-Adl wa Al-Ihsan* (Justice and Spirituality).
He was a Sufi with a political vision who strove to bring back justice, compassion and God consciousness into Moroccan political culture.[34] Like the
late Sheikh Yassine, Sheikh Hassan also does not shirk from entering the
political arena and in 2011 he became a spiritual mentor of the political
party Al-Nour in Egypt that had cornered 28% of the Egyptian electorate
and with the Muslim Brotherhood maintained for a while the Islamist hegemony in post-Arab Spring Egypt.[35] The late Sheikh Yassine and Sheikh
Hassan are polar opposites in their theological orientation, one was a Sufi
and the other is a Salafi; but they also have much in common: both wrote a
book on *Ihsan* and neither withdrew from the world; on the contrary, both
brought their religion into the political arena.

Sheikh Hassan's *Al-Ihsan* is a very interesting book. It is extraordinarily
meticulous in its documentation. In keeping with the Salafi methodology,
it relies primarily on the Holy Quran and the prophetic traditions. It occa-
sionally refers to commentaries, such as the *Fath al-Bari*, a highly respected
commentary by Al-Hajar Al-Asqalani on the *Sahih Bukhari* collection of
ahadith.[36] He also frequently refers to Ibn Al-Qayyim Al-Jawzi,[37] a prominent antecedent to the contemporary Salafis, who was known for his
severe criticism of Sufi practices but also recognized for his insights into
the science of *Al-Tasawwuf*. Hassan's book is long and systematic, but
unfortunately it disconnects knowledge from contemporary reality and he

---

[32] Sheikh Abdessalam Yassine, *Al-Ihsan* (Casablanca, Morocco: Matbooaat Al-Afaq, 1998).

[33] For a thorough, lucid and systematic discussion of what is the Salafi orthodoxy, how it
has emerged and evolved, see Khaled Abou El Fadl, *The Great Theft: Wrestling Islam from the
Extremists* (New York: HarperOne, 2007), pp. 45–112.

[34] His biography is available on the World Wide Net at http://yassine.net/en/docu-
ment/4729.shtml.

[35] See Farrag Ismail, "A Salafi Tremor in Egypt," *Al-Arabiya News*, June 02, 2011. On the
WorldWideWebitcanbefoundat:http://www.alarabiya.net/articles/2011/06/02/151576.
html.

[36] See p. 30 of Sheikh Hassan's *Al-Ihsan*.

[37] See, for example, Ibid., pp. 213, 419 and 451.

does not venture to explore how his understanding of *Ihsan* could impact Muslim realities or how it shapes his own forays into politics. I understand that the book was written and published before Egypt became free of the dictatorial regime of Hosni Mubarak and that there were possibly limits to how much Sheikh Hassan could have written about politics. But it does seem that he was determined to limit the discussion of *Ihsan* to the realm of worship. He could have talked of *Ihsan* in relation to issues of social justice, democratic reforms, political reforms and other human affairs (*muamalat*), but he chose to abstain.

He starts with the definition of *Ihsan* from the hadith of Gabriel, accepting the definition of *Ihsan* as "an ta'budu Allaha kannaka tarahu…" —*To worship Allah as if you see Him, and if you cannot see Him, He surely sees you.*[38] Indeed the famous hadith is the subtitle of his book. But unlike Sufis who focus on exploring what seeing Allah means, Hassan problema- tizes the concept of worship. He thinks that the thing to be explained in this tradition is *Ibadah* or worship and he proceeds for the next 600 and odd pages to discuss the exoteric nature of a dedicated and humble approach to worship.[39] He does flirt with mystical and spiritual themes, such as *Farar ila Allah* (Flee to Allah),[40] *Darajat Al-Tawakkul* (Levels of trust in God),[41] *Anwa' Al-Zikr* (Types of Remembrance of God),[42] but his approach remains clinical and does not provide one any spiritual reward. Reading the book is like visiting a very clean hospital that deals with only outpatients and physical injuries and certainly not like visiting a *Zawiya* or a garden that comforts the soul and heals the heart. The book is like a very thorough catalog of Islamic sources on *Ihsan* and concepts associated with rituals of worship. Perhaps given the apprehensions that Salafi scholars have about human reasoning, the book naturally lacks richness and depth in analysis and discussion of the listed sources. Indeed Sheikh Hassan's book on *Ihsan* demonstrates why one needs the science of *Tasawwuf* to flush out the profound depth of spiritual and cosmological meanings hid- den in the idea of *Ihsan*. No other Islamic science can do justice to it.

[38] Ibid., pp. 9–10.
[39] Ibid., p. 30.
[40] Ibid., pp. 330–342.
[41] Ibid., pp. 431–438.
[42] Ibid., pp. 657–658.

The late Sheikh Yassine's *Al-Ihsan* is a simple and interesting book that reads basically like a primer on *Tasawwuf* with occasional gems of genuinely original thought. The book has six sections which seek to introduce the reader to the science of *Tasawwuf* and to various concepts of Sufi beliefs and practices,[43] such as miracles of the friends of God, *Tafakkur*, to contemplate and reflect,[44] *Zikr*, remembrance of God[45] and so on and so forth. Clearly the book is a composition of discourses rather than a singular sustained argument. Nevertheless, his approach to the understanding of *Ihsan* itself is fascinating. Unlike the Salafis, he does not see it as a quality of ritual worship, and unlike most Sufis, even though Sheikh Yassine was a lifelong practitioner and a Sufi master, he does not see it as just a spiritual path.

Sheikh Yassine describes *Ihsan* as the cumulative conduct and dealings of a believer with his Lord, with people and with all other things.[46] Thus worship, politics, social activism and environmentalism would all fall under the rubric of *Ihsan*. He draws this understanding not from the hadith of Gabriel, which he addresses only in the fifth chapter of the second part of the book, but from a pair of traditions and a pair of Quranic verses. He discusses the traditions before he discusses the verses. Yassine's concept of *Ihsan* as the quality of human interactions with the Creator, the creation, the self and others, is shaped by these sources:

The first hadith is إن الله يحب إذا عمل أحدكم عملا أن يتقنه, which means *Surely Allah loves when any of you seeks perfection in whatever endeavor he takes up.* It is very interesting that Sheikh Yassine began his discussion with this tradition. I have had tutorial like discussions with literally scores of scholars of *Tasawwuf*, but this tradition, whose authenticity is questioned by the traditionalists, rarely came up as an important source for understanding *Ihsan*. I find its use compelling because it combines God's love and pursuit of perfection even in mundane matters.[47] While in most Sufi discourses, the love of God is the mover and God's love is the destiny, in this hadith, pursuit of perfection in action is the goal and God's love is the earned reward. For Sheikh Yassine, *Ihsan* is a station (*maqaam*) in life which enables the individual to live a life of heightened consciousness for spirituality as well as social justice. A believer in the state of *Ihsan* works toward

---

[43] See Sheikh Yassine, *Al-Ihsan*, p. 27.
[44] See Ibid., p. 304.
[45] See Ibid., p. 257.
[46] See Ibid., p. 17.
[47] See Ibid., pp. 17–21.

a better life here, for both the individual and the community and for a better life in the hereafter.[48]

The second hadith that he uses is better known and is often cited in any discussion of Ihsan—إن الله كتب الإحسان ألا كل شيء—Surely God has ordained Ihsan in all things. There is more to the hadith than just the command to excel in all things. The verses from the Quran that Sheikh Yassine employs (2;195, 3:134) are well-known proofs of the importance of Ihsan, both of which say that Allah loves those who are Muhsineen, (those who do Ihsan).[49] I shall discuss these sources a little later in this book. Sheikh Yassine discusses the hadith of Gabriel in the fourth chapter titled, Islam, Iman and Ihsan.[50] But here he merely reviews the early theological discussions on whether Islam and Iman are the same categories or are they different concepts. He agrees with Ibn Taymiyyah and concludes that Islam is a public manifestation of religion while Iman is located in the heart. He then proceeds to discuss the idea that first faith enters the heart of the believer and then the Quran follows suit and provides textual evidence to this claim. In essence he does not anchor his conception of Ihsan on the hadith of Gabriel, a very unusual thing for someone so deeply engaged in Tasawwuf and in the effort to realize Ihsan both at the individual and the communal level.

Contemporary Understanding of Ihsan Insights from the Western World

Western scholars of Islam and Sufism have indeed written quite extensively about Ihsan. For many reasons not germane to this discussion, Western academia has been fascinated with the people of Tasawwuf for a long time. Jalaluddin Rumi and his poetry, Ibn Arabi and his esoteric philosophy and Al-Ghazali and his theological synthesis have been dominant themes in the academic study of Islam. No doubt other themes, such as Islamic political movements and Islamic politics, do attract a lot of attention, but they are event-driven pursuits, whereas Sufism and Islamic philosophy are

[48] For a very useful summary of Sheikh Yassine views on Sufism and social activism, see Henri Lauzière, "Post-Islamism and the Religious Discourse of Abd-al-Salam Yassine," International Journal of Middle East Studies 37.2 (2005): 241–261.

[49] Sheikh Yassine refers to 2:195 and 3:134. The phrase Allah loves those who are Muhsineen—those who do Ihsan occurs in three more verses in the Holy Quran, 2:148, 5:13, 5:93.

[50] See Sheikh Yassine, Al-Ihsan, pp. 110–116.

perennial subjects. Many Western scholars have also done tremendous service to the understanding of Islamic mysticism by collecting, translating and making known the profound works of Islamic philosophers and mystics. Indeed, today many practicing Muslims and Muslim mystics are indebted to Western academy for helping them connect and remain engaged with their tradition.[51] I have looked at many scholars in the West who have written about *Tasawwuf* (the science of *Ihsan*) and *Ihsan* itself. The roster of prominent scholars of *Tasawwuf,* from whose work I benefitted considerably, includes the late Annemarie Schimmel,[52] Seyyed Hossein Nasr, Henry Corbin, Idris Shah, Frithjof Schuon,[53] Feisal Raouf and Sheikh Tosun Bayrak al-Jerrahi al-Halveti. I have chosen here to review Professor William Chittick and Sheikh Hisham Kabbani's discussions of *Ihsan*, because I found that they provide a very comprehensive and deep analysis of the meaning and sources of *Ihsan*.

Sheikh Kabbani is the leader of the Naqshbandi Sufi Order in the United States. He has published an entire volume on *Ihsan*, titled *Self-Purification and the State of Excellence* (*Tazkiyyah Al-Nafs, Tasawwuf, Ihsan*).[54] Sheikh Kabbani does not really make any distinction between purification of the soul and the state of *Ihsan*, he sees both of them as the goal of the science of *Tasawwuf* and following medieval greats like Al-Ghazali sees *Tasawwuf* as a religious obligation of Muslims.[55] I find this book useful because the Sheikh in it follows a very traditional methodology. He starts by explaining the linguistic, then the legal and then the esoteric meanings of the term *Ihsan*. He explores the various linguistic derivatives of *Ihsan*, such as *hasuna* (become beautiful and make excellent), *ihsanan* (to do excellently), *ahsana* (he did a great good), *Ihsan* (kindness), *husna* (reward), *hasan* (excellent and beautiful) and *hisanun* (beautiful ones). He then shows how the concept of *Ihsan* is firmly

---

[51] For example, see the extraordinary and voluminous translation in four volumes of Rumi's work, a landmark in Western studies of Islamic mysticism, Reynold A. Nicholson, *Mathnawi of Jalaluddin Rumi* (London: Gibb Memorial Trust, 1926). Another example is R. W. J. Austin's translation of Ibn Arabi's *Fusus Al-Hikam.* See R. W. J. Austin, *Bezels of Wisdom* (Mahwah, NJ: Paulist Press, 1980).

[52] See Annemarie Schimmel, *Mystical Dimensions of Islam* (Chapel Hill, NC: University of North Carolina, 1975), and also see Annemarie Schimmel, *And Muhammad is His Messenger* (Chapel Hill, NC: University of North Carolina, 1985).

[53] Frithjof Schuon, *Understanding Islam* (Bloomington, IN: World Wisdom Books, 1994).

[54] This is volume five of a seven-volume *Encyclopedia of Islamic Doctrine.* See Sheikh Muhammad Hisham Kabbani, *Self-Purification and the State of Excellence* (Mountain View, CA: As-Sunnah Foundation, 1998).

[55] See Ibid., p. 25.

grounded in both the primary sources of Islam, the Quran and the hadith, and concludes that *Ihsan* is indeed the highest state of Islam.

Kabbani also discusses the hadith of Gabriel, which he says is recognized by scholars of Islam as the mother of prophetic practice and the mother of prophetic traditions (*Umm Al-Sunna wa Umm Al-Hadith*). He relies primarily on the commentary on it by Imam Nawawi (1234–1278 AD). Imam Nawawi had described *Ihsan* as the station of witnessing the divine (*Maqaam Al-Mushahada*) and the station of truthful saints (*Maqaam Al-Siddiqin*) and Kabbani argues that this is vindication of the science of *Tasawwuf* since only it can lead to *Ihsan*.[56]

Sheikh Kabbani provides a very extensive survey of what prominent Islamic scholars have said about *Ihsan* and *Tasawwuf* in Islamic history. Even though the author does not construct a cohesive narrative one can treat his review as a decent genealogy of *Tasawwuf* and glean the contours of debate and contentions about the meanings and scope of *Ihsan* as it evolved over time in Islamic thought. He also connects the dots between the two concepts of *Ihsan* and the greater *Jihad* or *Jihad* against the ego (*Jihad-Al-Nafs*). According to a tradition, the Prophet (pbuh) on returning from a campaign remarked to his companions "You have come from the lesser Jihad to the greater Jihad." When his companion inquired, "What is the greater Jihad?" he replied, "The striving (*mujahadah*) of Allah's servants against their idle desires."[57]

Thus, Shakyh Kabbani concludes that *Ihsan* is the state one reaches after one wages *Jihad* against one's own self, in order to purify it. When one achieves the station of *Ihsan*, one manifests virtues, such as God-wariness (*Taqwa*), abstention (*zuhd*), reverence (*Khushu*), humility (*khudu*), patience (*sabr*), truthfulness (*sidq*), reliance (*tawakkul*), good character (*adab*), repentance (*tawba*), forbearance (*hilm*), modesty (*haya*) and courage (*shajaa*).[58] Finally, Sheikh Kabbani makes an excellent point for tying *Ihsan*, with Islam and *Iman*, he argues that *Ihsan* is that state of the heart that will determine if *Iman* and Islam will ultimately bear fruit or not[59]; it is *Ihsan*, in his view, that gives depth to Islam and *Iman*.

One of the most prominent scholars of Sufi Islam and of the concept and practice of *Ihsan* is Professor William Chittick. He has translated the works of some of the most prominent Sufi luminaries like Ibn Arabi and

[56] See Ibid., p. 35.
[57] See Ibid., p. 43.
[58] See Ibid., p. 31.
[59] See Ibid., p. 31.

Jalaluddin Rumi, and has written about both the philosophy and history of Islamic mystical thought. The Islamic tradition of naming scholars to emphasize their significance is not much in vogue in the West. If it were, William Chittick would surely be called *Sheikh Al-Ihsan*. Nobody has studied or written as much about *Ihsan* as he has. Two of his books, *Vision of Islam* coauthored with Sachiko Murata and *Faith and Practice of Islam*, use the hadith of Gabriel as a paradigm to organize their contents. It is rather fascinating to see how Professor Chittick divides Islamic values and practices around the three dimensions of *Din*—Islam, *Iman* and *Ihsan*.

William Chittick's most comprehensive discussion of *Ihsan* is in the *Vision of Islam*; it contains most of the ideas found in *Faith and Practice of Islam* and goes beyond them. Chittick and Murata make a compelling case that the best way to study Islam is to start with the hadith of Gabriel and use it as an organizational tool. I agree and this is vindicated by canonical Muslim scholars like Imam Muslim who starts his revered collection of hadith, *Sahih Muslim* with this hadith and Imam Nawawi who collected the 40 most critical traditions of the faith, placed it at number two. Chittick has consistently referred to Islam, *Iman* and *Ihsan* as three "dimensions" of *Din* and has, unlike many others in the tradition, resisted the temptation to place them in a hierarchy with *Ihsan* as the highest stage of Islam. Traditional Muslim scholars like Ibn Taymiyyah and Al-Ghazali see them as progressive levels and stages (*darajaat*). Chittick sees them as dimensions, Islam as works or deeds, Iman as faith or beliefs and *Ihsan* as perfection. By doing so he puts the three concepts at the same level but differentiating them metaphysically.

In *Vision of Islam*, he and his coauthor borrow from theoretical physics the idea that creation has four dimensions, three physical dimensions and time is the fourth dimension. As you will see in the next section, in the hadith of Gabriel, Angel Gabriel asks the Prophet Muhammad (pbuh) five questions, the last two were about "the hour," the time and signs of the Day of Judgment. Chittick and Murata argue that Islam, like the creation, has four dimensions, Islam, *Iman*, *Ihsan* and time. While I am not sure if this analogy adds to our understanding of the hadith or the creation, but it does add to the aesthetics of the explanation and that is a form of *Ihsan* in itself. Elsewhere Chittick notes that the words for both creation (*khalaq*) and ethics (*khuluq*) in Arabic are written in the same way and finds this linguistic equation of creation with ethics meaningful. Chittick and Murata proceed in their discussion of *Ihsan* in a very traditional fashion. They start with its linguistic meanings like most other scholars before them. They do make an interesting and important distinction between *Khayr* (goodness), often used as the antonym of *Sharr* (bad or evil) and *husn*. They argue convincingly that while *khayr* means goodness, *husn* also means goodness but necessarily with the additional implication of beauty. Chittick in all his discussions of *Ihsan* emphasizes the marriage of good and beauty in *Ihsan* and has often translated *Ihsan* as doing beautiful things. The authors discuss the Quranic sources of *Ihsan* and based on them conclude that *Ihsan* includes worship (*Ibadah*), seeing God, sincerity (*Ikhlas*), God-wariness (*Taqwa*), love (*hubb*) and wholesomeness (*Salih*).

The two authors bring an empirical element to the discussion of *Ihsan*. Unlike most scholars who are content to explore the theological, philosophical and mystical dimensions of *Ihsan*, its depth and its boundaries, Chittick and Murata also look at how *Ihsan* has manifest in history. They show how *Ihsan* has shaped Muslim supplications, practice of remembrance of God (*zikr*), in art and poetry and finally in practical Sufism. Unfortunately in their discussion of practical manifestations of *Ihsan*, they focus only on manners and ethics and their discussion of ethics is very limited and centered around interpersonal conduct more than anything else. But it was encouraging to me, who seeks to develop a political philosophy of *Ihsan* and good governance, to see that someone has recognized that the values associated with *Ihsan* can have implications beyond the sacred and onto the mundane dimensions of life.

Contemporary Attitudes and Insights on Ihsan

Four years ago, I decided to write a book called *Ihsan and Good Governance* with the intention of advancing the most beautiful, compassionate and thoughtful interpretation of Islamic sources that could help build an Islamic political philosophy based on an enlightened understanding of Islam. My goal is to offer an enlightened vision of Islam, distinct from that caricature advanced by groups like the Taliban and *Daesh*. I was quite moved by Immanuel Kant's definition of absence of enlightenment as voluntary refusal to reason and I understood the Muslim condition today as an age of *neo-jahiliyyah* (new ignorance) in which Muslims were suffering from a self-imposed *jahiliyyah*, and I conceived of *jahiliyyah* as not ignorance but as refusal to reason.[60] I decided to start from scratch and spent three years

---

[60] See Muqtedar Khan, "What is Enlightenment? An Islamic Perspective," *Journal of Religion and Society* 16 (2014).

working on my classical Arabic and reading the Quran and prophetic traditions as if for the first time. When I read the hadith of Gabriel again, even though I was quite familiar with it, I had an epiphany and I realized that the idea of *Ihsan* was the key to the enlightened understanding of Islam that I sought. The next moment I asked myself, but then why do we hear so little about *Ihsan* in Islamic discourses, which are all about *Shariah* and Islamic rulings. I had found my calling; it was to not only explore *Ihsan* but to articulate it in a way that it would profoundly inform the public and private life of Muslims. But first I had to understand *Ihsan*.

So I read up everything that I could on *Ihsan* and then traveled several times to Morocco, Jordan, Tunisia, Egypt and Turkey to study *Ihsan* and learn from traditional scholars, Islamic preachers, Muftis, public intellectuals and from practitioners of *Tasawwuf*. I had the opportunity to meet and learn from several Sufi masters and teachers. I also interviewed several Western academics and traditional Islamic scholars in the United States. I encountered some very interesting responses. Academics everywhere, especially in the United States and in Turkey, were fascinated by the idea of developing a political philosophy based on *Ihsan*. They wished me luck and answered all my questions as well as they could and I really enjoyed my conversations with them. They also gave me references and suggestions for further reading. Some Muslim academics specially found the idea unique and truly encouraged me to pursue this research agenda.

The responses from traditional scholars and practitioners and leaders of the faith were on the other hand much varied and often surprising. I cluster their responses into puzzlement, bewilderment, disdain and excitement. Salafi-leaning scholars were either genuinely puzzled or disdainful. Those who were puzzled argued that *Ihsan* was a limited idea that could only be applied in perfecting the ritual prayer with (*Khudu wa Khushu*) reverence and humility and in improvement of manners (*Aqlaq*). Others took me for a Sufi and often responded with disdain and condescension arguing that there was no such science as science of mysticism (*Ilm Al-Tasawwuf*) in Islam and Sufism was basically a deviance (*bid'ah*) and would merely guide Muslims away from *Shariah* and *Jihad*. I did prescreen the people I had conversations with and avoided people who would give me such responses. I did make presentations to scholars and intellectuals with some preliminary ideas about *Ihsan* and politics in Istanbul, Ankara, Amman, Rabat, Ifrane, Cairo, Washington, DC, and Providence and often ran into very conservative or Salafi-leaning scholars in the audience. Even though I expected it I was nevertheless surprised by how deeply anti-Sufi sentiments are embedded in some Muslim communities and scholars.

Even Ulema with reputation for being moderate and tolerant showed a surprising degree of intolerance for thinking of *Ihsan* as anything more than a quality of ritual prayer, lest it extends legitimacy to *Tasawwuf.*

The response from Sufi-leaning scholars and Sufi masters (*Shuyookh*) was either puzzlement or excitement. A prominent Sufi master in the United States looked at me bewildered and said, "*Ihsan* has no place in politics. Politics is corrupting and a Sufi, if he cares about his spiritual wellbeing would stay away from politics." When I persisted by suggesting that two of the four rightly guided Caliphs, the first, Abu Bakr, and the fourth, Ali Ibn Talib, who are both seen as Sufi masters by Sufi traditions did engage in politics and governed. He responded by suggesting that there was something fundamentally sick and corrupt about modern politics that is detrimental to spiritual life. Many Sufi masters tried to impress the point that Sufis must be detached from this world and political engagement is a sign of desire for this world. They also explained the lack of impact of the concept of *Ihsan* on Islamic political thought by arguing that the purpose of *Ihsan* in life is to detach oneself from the seductions of this world, power and wealth, and not to find fulfillment in them.

I would gently remind them that Prophet Muhammad (pbuh) reminded us that "Allah has ordained *Ihsan* in all things" (*kataba Allahu al-Ihsan ala kulli shai*). This often elicited irritation. Sufi Sheikhs are not used to being argued with. You ask a question, they answer, you obey. They would look at me, as if I was too dense, and say it does not mean in pursuit of the world. But unlike Sufi masters, Sufi-leaning scholars were immediately excited by the idea and would talk about the above tradition and agree that we must find a way to bring Islam's mystical values, its most beautiful manifestations into politics. These scholars, usually of Turkish or South Asian origins, would then talk about Muslim sultans and emperors who were guided by *Ihsan* and who were themselves poets and mystics. Turkish historians of the Ottoman Empire took special pride in informing me that a vast majority of Ottoman emperors were themselves Sufis and would have tried to bring some aspects of *Ihsan* into their governance. Clearly the passion for building beautiful mosques was one example of pursuit of *Ihsan* since *Ihsan* also meant beauty. The same was also true of the early Moghul emperors who were pluralistic in their approach, valued mystics and beautiful things, the peak of their contribution is the Taj Mahal considered by many as the most beautiful building ever built.

After understanding the profound linkage between *Tasawwuf* and *Ihsan* the goal of *Tasawwuf* is *Ihsan* or that *Tasawwuf* is the science of *Ihsan*—I spent a lot of time with Sufi masters and participated in *zikr* (remembrance) ceremonies in *Zawiyas* (Sufi lodges) in Fez (Morocco), Istanbul and Konya (Turkey) and in Cairo (Egypt). But I was very disappointed and puzzled by the lack of theoretical knowledge about *Tasawwuf* in general and *Ihsan* in particular among the rank and file dervishes. Many who claimed that they had been attending Sufi lodges for years regularly would look bewildered when I asked them about *Ihsan* and how it could influence mundane affairs (*muamalat*). Even Sufi masters were reluctant to discuss the nuances and subtleties of *Ihsan* that one found in discussions and in classical Sufi texts. The master would respond with great reverence when I asked them about Ibn Arabi or Al-Ghazali and their discussion of *Ihsan*. But while they insisted that *Ihsan* was the most important of not the only true goal of Islam and Sufism, they had little to offer in terms of theoretical understanding. A very prominent Sufi master of a major North African *Silsila* (school) told me bluntly that *Ihsan* was not about books or knowledge it was about experience and knowing about God, through remembrance and experience of God.

There is a new evolving tradition of "soft Sufism" in the West. We can see it in the rise in appeal of preachers and Imams like Sheikh Hamza Yusuf Hanson, Dr. Umar Farooq Abdullah, Sheikh Ninowy in the United States, Sheikh Abdul Hakeem Murad (Dr. Timothy Winter) in the United Kingdom and Sheikh Faraz Rabbani in Canada.[61] The faith leaders are reluctant to use the "S" word but if one were to read their writings and listen to their discourses on various websites that carry their videos, one will find that they are richer in their use and deployment of theoretical concepts from the science of *Ihsan*. Nearly every one of them has given more than one major discourse on *Ihsan* and with a great degree of sophistication and depth. A parallel development, which further enriches this emerging informal Sufi tradition, is the translation and publication of many Sufi classics by great Sufi masters. I also found that along with the emerging informal Sufism, traditional formal Sufi orders are also thriving and increasing in their influence on Muslims in the West.

Traditional scholars and Ulema, who constitute the vast majority of the Muslim world's middle ground between Salafis and Sufis, were the most bewildered by my questions about *Ihsan* and its potential role in the public sphere. These traditional religious leaders tended to be secular in the sense that they were apolitical in their orientation and religiosity was about

---

[61] Muqtedar Khan, "Future of Islam in America: A Uniquely American Sufism," *Ijtihad*, January 22, 2016.

rituals, prayer, fasting, reciting the Quran and going on pilgrimages. They were wary of the mystical excesses of Sufis and were reluctant to discuss *Ihsan* beyond the idea that it was about achieving a high quality of prayer. They also were reluctant to discuss the role of Islam in politics, much less, *Ihsan* beyond pointing to Islamophobia and lamenting the excesses of extremist groups like the Taliban. Interestingly, more than the Salafi or even the Sufi scholars, these middle of the road traditionalists, much to my delight, often recited the entire hadith of Gabriel in Arabic.

I had my most engaging and fascinating conversations about *Ihsan* and politics with the Islamists in Jordan. I found Islamists in Egypt, Tunisia and Morocco, all countries with strong Sufi traditions, surprisingly contemptuous of Sufis and of the discipline of *Tasawwuf* even though they often reminded me that Sheikh Hassan al-Banna was a Sufi who entered the political arena and in a way gave birth to *Ikhwan al-Muslimeen* (The Muslim Brotherhood), the most prominent modern political Islamic movement in the Arab world. The Islamists in Jordan were in the wake of the Arab Spring very excited about the prospects of Islamism and the coming role of Islam in politics. Because many of them had served in the government and held high-level positions, including cabinet-level positions, they had some experience with governance and understood the challenges of balancing ideals with political realities.

I engaged about five prominent Jordanian Islamists and all of them, while expressing reservations about Sufism, expressed great interest in exploring how Muslims could advance a morally and ethically guided paradigm of politics that would simultaneously safeguard Islamic identity and promote human rights. They alone, of all the Islamists I spoke with, did not contest or suggest that *Ihsan* could not possibly be realized in the public sphere. While they could not give concrete examples of how *Ihsan* can shape politics, some of them actually shared that they too strive to realize *Ihsan* in their public lives through charity and social service even if not through public policy. Needless to say my conversations with Jordanian Islamists was the most encouraging, even more than my many engagements with Sufi scholars who remain more skeptical about politics. Sufis in Cairo have been so disillusioned with the post-Arab Spring politics and the misuse of Islam for political purposes that many of them discouraged me from trying to even write this book.

From an academic perspective, I learned most from Turkish university professors. They know their stuff. Turkish academia is very different from those in the other parts of the Muslim world where the focus seems to be on the study of Islamic law and the Quran and hadith, and related disciplines. In Turkey, I found diversity of interest. There were those who studied the legal discipline and Islamic law, the Quran and hadith, but I also found Islamic philosophers, students of traditional theology (*Ilm Al-Kalam*) and historians of mysticism and related disciplines. In the same departments I ran into those who were studying Al-Farabi and Ibn Arabia, Mevlana Rumi and Ibn Taymiyyah. I did meet a few rare scholars of mysticism who were also members of mystical orders and travelers in the Sufi path. Conversations with them were the most fruitful, since they could speak from both theoretical and experiential perspectives.

But despite my extended engagement with scholars and experts of Islam, I found that the awareness of *Ihsan* and its place in Islamic value systems was minimal. Scholars, teachers and spiritual masters were all familiar with the hadith of Gabriel and they all, across the board, accepted in principle the assertion that *Ihsan* was the highest form of Islam, or that *Ihsan* was essentially the perfection of Islam and Iman. The Sufis argued that Sufism was all about *Ihsan* but beyond that nothing. Consider these two classic Sufi treatises, *Al-Risala al-Qushayriyya fi ilm al-Tasawwuf* (*Al-Qushayri's Epistle on Sufism*) and *Kitab al-Ta'arruf li-madhab ahl al-Tasawwuf* (*The Doctrine of the Sufis*), well known and highly regarded; both provide a good summary of a wide array of Sufi views and concepts but do not discuss *Ihsan* at all.[62] The purpose of an extended discussion of my conversations about *Ihsan* with scholars in the Muslim world is to emphasize how *Ihsan* has slowly disappeared from the Muslim collective memory. Yes, we know its basic definition but beyond that what shapes and agitates Muslim thinking about Islam is Islamic identity and Islamic law, the rest are all seen as good things to talk about but not to act upon. In the next chapter I will not only unpack the concept of *Ihsan* from the perspective of a Muslim political philosopher but also reflect on how *Ihsan* can become the basis for political ethics.

> *Have mercy Beloved,*
> *Though I am nothing but forgetfulness,*
> *You are the essence of forgiveness.*
> *Make me needless of all but You.*
> —Sheikh Abu Saeed Abil Kheir

[62] See Abu'l-Qasim al-Qushayri, *Al-Qushayri's Epistle on Sufism*, Trans. Alexander D. Knysh (Reading, UK: Garnet Publishing, 2007). *Abu Bakr al-Kalabadhi, The Doctrine of the Sufis*, Trans. A. J. Arberry (Lahore, Pakistan: Suhail Academy, 2011). Al-Qushayri does discuss quote the entire hadith of Gabriel in his discussion of *Muraqaba*, which is a dimension of *Ihsan*, on p. 202. Indeed, he writes about all elements of *Ihsan* without talking about *Ihsan*.

CHAPTER 5

Unveiling *Ihsan*: From Cosmic View to Worldview

To Worship Allah as if you see him, if you cannot see Him, surely He sees you.

THE HADITH OF GABRIEL

The spiritual relevance and significance of *Ihsan* was fully revealed in the hadith of Gabriel. In a very succinct and mystical fashion, Prophet Muhammad (pbuh) describes what *Ihsan* is. This well-known and oft-quoted hadith is the only source that defines the concept of *Ihsan* both comprehensively and concisely and within the context of the entire faith. Let us begin by examining this invaluable source of Islamic belief and the cornerstone of Islamic mysticism. There are many sources in the hadith literature and in the Quran, which are all windows and doorways to the world of spirituality. The hadith of Gabriel in itself constitutes a veritable highway to the spiritual world. It encompasses all that matters and leaves out nothing. From the necessary commitments (Islam), the essential beliefs (Iman), via the limits of human knowledge (knowledge of the hour) to the ultimate potentiality of spiritual reality (*Ihsan*), the hadith of Gabriel is a sufficient and complete discourse on how the relationship between the human self and the Divine Self can be perfected.

The hadith is so central to our argument that it is important to quote it fully in both Arabic and English translation.

© The Author(s) 2019
M. A. M. Khan, *Islam and Good Governance*,
https://doi.org/10.1057/978-1-137-54832-0_5

عَنْ عُمَرَ رَضِيَ اللهُ عَنْهُ أَيْضًا قَالَ : بَيْنَمَا نَحْنُ جُلُوسٌ عِنْدَ رَسُوْلِ اللهِ صَلَّى اللهُ عَلَيْهِ وَسَلَّمَ ذَاتَ يَوْمٍ إِذْ طَلَعَ عَلَيْنَا رَجُلٌ شَدِيْدُ بَيَاضِ الثِّيَابِ شَدِيْدُ سَوَادِ الشَّعَرِ لَا يُرَى عَلَيْهِ أَثَرُ السَّفَرِ وَلَا يَعْرِفُهُ مِنَّا أَحَدٌ حَتَّى جَلَسَ إِلَى النَّبِيَّ صَلَّى اللهُ عَلَيْهِ وَسَلَّمَ فَأَسْنَدَ رُكْبَتَيْهِ إِلَى رُكْبَتَيْهِ وَوَضَعَ كَفَّيْهِ عَلَى فَخِذَيْهِ وَقَالَ : يَامُحَمَّدُ أَخْبِرْنِيْ عَنِ الْإِسْلَامِ ، فَقَالَ رَسُوْلُ اللهِ صَلَّى اللهُ عَلَيْهِ وَسَلَّمَ : الْإِسْلَامُ أَنْ تَشْهَدَ أَنْ لَا إِلَهَ إِلَّا اللهُ وَأَنَّ مُحَمَّدًا رَسُوْلُ اللهِ ، وَتُقِيْمَ الصَّلَاةَ ، وَتُؤْتِيَ الزَّكَاةَ ، وَتَصُوْمَ رَمَضَانَ ، وَتَحُجَّ الْبَيْتَ إِنِ اسْتَطَعْتَ إِلَيْهِ سَبِيْلًا . قَالَ : صَدَقْتَ فَعَجِبْنَا لَهُ يَسْأَلُهُ وَيُصَدِّقُهُ . قَالَ : فَأَخْبِرْنِيْ عَنِ الْإِيْمَانِ ، قَالَ : أَنْ تُؤْمِنَ بِاللهِ وَمَلَائِكَتِهِ وَكُتُبِهِ وَرُسُلِهِ وَالْيَوْمِ الْآخِرِ وَتُؤْمِنَ بِالْقَدَرِ خَيْرِهِ وَشَرِّهِ . قَالَ : صَدَقْتَ قَالَ : فَأَخْبِرْنِيْ عَنِ الْإِحْسَانِ ، قَالَ : أَنْ تَعْبُدَ اللهَ كَأَنَّكَ تَرَاهُ فَإِنْ لَمْ تَكُنْ تَرَاهُ فَإِنَّهُ يَرَاكَ . قَالَ : فَأَخْبِرْنِيْ عَنِ السَّاعَةِ ، قَالَ : مَا الْمَسْؤُوْلُ عَنْهَا بِأَعْلَمَ مِنَ السَّائِلِ . قَالَ : فَأَخْبِرْنِيْ عَنْ أَمَارَاتِهَا ، قَالَ : أَنْ تَلِدَ الْأَمَةُ رَبَّتَهَا وَأَنْ تَرَى الْحُفَاةَ الْعُرَاةَ الْعَالَةَ رِعَاءَ الشَّاءِ يَتَطَاوَلُوْنَ فِي الْبُنْيَانِ ثُمَّ انْطَلَقَ فَلَبِثْتُ مَلِيًّا ثُمَّ قَالَ : يَاعُمَرُ أَتَدْرِيْ مَنِ السَّائِلُ؟ قُلْتُ : اللهُ وَرَسُوْلُهُ أَعْلَمُ . قَالَ : فَإِنَّهُ جِبْرِيْلُ أَتَاكُمْ يُعَلِّمُكُمْ دِيْنَكُمْ – رَوَاهُ مُسْلِمٌ .

Also on the authority of 'Umar, radiyallahu 'anhu, who said: "While we were one day sitting with the Messenger of Allah, sallallahu 'alayhi wasallam, there appeared before us a man dressed in extremely white clothes and with very black hair. No traces of journeying were visible on him, and none of us knew him. He sat down close by the Prophet, sallallahu 'alayhi wasallam, rested his knee against his thighs, and said, O Muhammad! Inform me about Islam." Said the Messenger of Allah, sallallahu 'alayhi wasallam, "Islam is that you should testify that there is no deity save Allah and that Muhammad is His Messenger, that you should perform salah (ritual prayer), pay the zakah, fast during Ramadan, and perform Hajj (pilgrimage) to the House (the Ka'bah at Makkah), if you can find a way to it (or find the means for making the journey to it)." Said he (the man), "You have spoken truly." We were astonished at his thus questioning him and telling him that he was right, but he went on to say, "Inform me about iman (faith)." He (the Messenger of Allah) answered, "It is that you believe in Allah and His angels and His Books and His Messengers and in the Last Day, and in fate (qadar), both in its good and in its evil aspects." He said, "You have spoken truly." Then he (the man) said, "Inform me about Ihsan." He (the Messenger of Allah) answered," It is that you should serve Allah as though you could see Him, for though you cannot see Him yet He sees you." He said, "Inform me about the Hour." He (the Messenger of Allah) said, "About that the one questioned knows no more than the questioner." So he said, "Well, inform me about the signs thereof (i.e. of its coming)." Said he, "They are that the slave-girl will give birth to her mistress, that you will see the barefooted ones, the naked, the destitute, the herdsmen of the sheep (competing with each other) in raising lofty buildings." Thereupon the man went off. I waited a while, and then he (the Messenger of Allah) said, "O 'Umar, do you know who that questioner was?" I replied, "Allah and His Messenger know better." He said, "That was Gabriel. He came to teach you your religion."[1]

This tradition is also referred to as *Umm al-Hadeeth*, the mother or the core of traditions. It is the first hadith reported in the *Sahih Muslim* collection and is also reported in the *Sahih Bukhari* collection, two of the most important canonical scriptural sources of Islam. The hadith also enjoys the second place in Imam Nawawi's collection of 42 traditions, which he thought were the key to understanding the true and complete essence of the Islamic faith. The tremendous popularity and widespread acceptance of Imam Nawawi's collection and use of his collection to teach Islam's fundamental principles to students and to inspire believers to understand their

---

[1] See Imam Muslim, *Sahih Muslim*, trans. Abdul Hamid Siddiqui, Vol. I (New Delhi, India: Idara Isha'at-e-Diniyat, 2007), pp. 7–9.

faith further contributes to the popularity and acceptance of this tradition. The authenticity of this hadith is beyond question and its significance to Islamic faith can hardly be overstated. Nearly every major scholar and commentator of Islam has reflected and written about this hadith.

The hadith is remarkable in its structure and in its various elements. First, let me speak to the critical elements in the tradition. It is narrated by perhaps one of the most important of all Muslims after Prophet Muhammad (pbuh), Umar bin Al-Khattab, the second righteous Caliph of Islam and one of the most important, revered and authoritative companions. According to a tradition, that truly elevates the status of Umar, reported by *Sunan Al-Tirmidhi* (#3686), the Prophet said that if there was to be a prophet sent after himself it would be Umar bin Al-Khattab.[2] The very fact that he is the first narrator in the chain gives the tradition a lot of gravitas. The episode described in the tradition happens in the mosque with many witnesses. There were so many witnesses that Abu Hurayra's recollection of the episode has one difference from Umar's; he misses the response of Angel Gabriel to Prophet Muhammad (pbuh),[3] when he says softly *saddaqta*—you answered truly,[4] to each of Prophet Muhammad's answers. The reason for the difference is the distance—Umar was sitting near Prophet Muhammad (pbuh) when Gabriel approached him and Abu Hurayra was sitting further away.

The tradition ends with Prophet Muhammad (pbuh) informing his companions that the mysterious man who had the audacity to question him and authenticate his answers, was indeed Gabriel, the leader of all angels, who had come to "teach them their *Deen*." There are symbolic dimensions to this event. This was in a way a public revelation. The angel came to the Prophet and summarized the essence of the divine message publicly and authenticated the veracity of the message—leaving no secrets, no room to accuse the Prophet of adding or withholding the fundamental elements of the faith. It is the most extraordinary example of transparency and inclusiveness possible in matters of religion. Some of the opponents of Prophet Muhammad (pbuh) would often ask him sarcastically to produce an angel to validate his claims of being a messenger.[5] I see this public appearance of Angel Gabriel in such remarkable circumstances as a symbolic answer to those criticisms.

---

[2] Al-Tirmidhi, Abu Isa Muhammad, *Jami' Al-Tirmidhi* (2007), #3686.

[3] Imam Muslim, *Sahih Muslim*, trans. Abdul Hamid Siddiqui, Vol. I, pp. 9–11.

[4] Imam Muslim, *Sahih Muslim*, trans. Abdul Hamid Siddiqui, Vol. I, pp. 7–8.

[5] These instances are referred to in the Quran (15:7–8). Clearly the critics were being sarcastic, but the hadith of Gabriel is so remarkable and so uncontested by Muslim sources that within the Muslim universe of belief it is truly miraculous.

Finally, an interesting element highlighted in this tradition is the relationship of Prophet Muhammad (pbuh) and Gabriel that is revealed by this encounter. The Prophet must have recognized Gabriel the instant he saw him. The sequence of questions would have given him away, even if he had appeared in a form that he had never assumed before. Two things struck me as outstanding—the absence of hierarchy in the dialogue and the obvious familiarity with each other's *maqaam* (spiritual status) so clearly manifest in their physical and intellectual proximity. Prophet Muhammad's (pbuh) answer to the final question that acknowledges the awareness of the extent of knowledge that each possesses and the shared awareness that there is more to existence than what they know are so reminiscent of meetings between great spiritual seers and saints who respect and love each other.

It is specially endearing if one contrasts it with the Quranic narration of the encounter between Prophet Moses (pbuh) and the teacher of teachers, Khidr.[6] Khidr is a knowledgeable servant of God, much revered by Muslim mystics, who taught Prophet Moses among other things that there is knowledge of the unseen that can inform how we live in the perceivable world. During the entire encounter, Moses remained bewildered and suspicious of the former, while Khidr was neither patient nor content with Moses. While the lesson in this encounter underscored the limits of knowledge possessed by Moses, and was designed to educate him primarily, the encounter between Prophet Muhammad (pbuh) and Gabriel was to authenticate and validate the knowledge of Prophet Muhammad (pbuh) and was designed to teach all of humanity in general. Khidr was in a way Moses' spiritual guide, helping him advance in his understanding of the miraculous ways of God, while Gabriel was to Prophet Muhammad (pbuh) more akin to a spiritual companion, a messenger of God to the Messenger of God. Together they were teaching the rest of humanity the essence of divine religion and divine realities.

The structure and the contents of the hadith are singularly critical to the understanding of Islam. The hadith collections as discussed in Chap. 2 supplement and complement the Quran. While all key elements of the Islamic faith are revealed in the Quran, which was revealed over an extended period of 23 years, they are not collated in the form of an easily absorbable summary. The hadith of Gabriel summarizes the *Deen* of Islam succinctly and clearly, and imparts on it a seal of finality and authenticity.

---

[6] In the Quran, the meeting between Khidr and Prophet Moses is revealed in chapter 18 from verses 65–82.

But most importantly, the hadith of Gabriel not only permanently identifies what the key elements of the *Deen* of Islam are but also identifies and
elevates *Ihsan* as the jewel in the crown.[7] If this hadith did not exist, I am
convinced that Islamic orthodoxy, which has given lip service to *Ihsan*,
barely acknowledging it in discourse and ignoring it in practice and in
legal thought, would have simply denied the concept even though its
essence permeates the Quran and the hadith literature. The Sufis would
have discovered *Ihsan*; they seem to be predisposed to its meaning, but
the tradition of *Tasawwuf itself* would have been blackballed more than it
is at the moment and with much more vehemence. The hadith of Gabriel
legitimizes the science and the practice of mysticism in Islam more than
anything else. Without it, the legitimacy of Islamic mysticism would be
further undermined. As it is, a broad section of the contemporary orthodoxy continues to denigrate mystical practices and denies mystical knowledge entirely.[8] It is only because of the hadith of Gabriel that the orthodoxy
reluctantly concedes that there is an inner spiritual world and the desire to
purify the self remains an important part of Islamic belief system.

The traditional understanding of the hadith of Gabriel, as manifest in the
discussions by a vast array of scholars on the World Wide Web and on
YouTube, is consistent with the way Ibn Taymiyyah understood it. There
are three levels of the religion of Islam, with Islam the basic and *Ihsan* the
highest of its stages. A more sophisticated understanding would be to see all
three dimensions as necessary elements of the *Deen*. *Deen* here implies religion and Islam is just one element of that. It is best to think of these three
dimensions as *co-constitutive* of each other, rather than dimensions that can
stand alone. This idea will become clearer if we think of Islam as constituting actions, testifying, and performing obligatory acts of devotions, prayer,
fasting, *Zakat* (distributive justice) and *Haj*. Iman as constituting thought or
belief; when one accepts and internalizes the truth of God, His Angels, His
Prophets, His Books, the inevitability of the Day of Judgment and the

---

[7] Even Imam Ibn Taymiyyah, who was very critical of Islamic mysticism, acknowledges that
Ihsan is the highest state of Islam. See Imam Ibn Taymiyyah, *Kitab al-Iman*, trans. Salman
Hassan Al-Ani, Shadia Ahmed Tel (Selangor, Malaysia: Islamic Book Trust, 1999),
pp. 18–23.

[8] I was often surprised at how often many traditional scholars, even those trained in places
with long history of mystical teachings like Al-Azhar, would simply tell me that there was no
such thing as *Ilm al-Tasawwuf*. Sometimes after discussing with me the meaning of *Ihsan*
and grudgingly conceding that *Ihsan* refers to the internal dimensions of belief and religion,
they would then proceed to deny the legitimacy of Islamic mysticism.

reality that all things good and bad are from God. We should think of *Ihsan* as a measure of the quality of the spiritual state. While Iman rests in the mind, *Ihsan* is in the spirit or the heart.

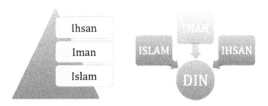

Without faith, there is no meaning in actions and without actions there is no way of knowing if there is belief indeed. Actions (Islam) vindicate belief (Iman), and belief authenticates action. Similarly without faith and without action, the state of the heart cannot be transformed. One cannot embark on a spiritual journey in search of salvation without a belief in the destination and without performing the necessary acts that move one along the path, past various stations (*maqamat*) toward that ultimate state of *Ihsan*, where neither time nor place, where neither being nor annihilation, neither stillness nor motion matters anymore as one becomes one with The One. It is in this state of union with the divine that one worships/serves God as if one sees Him.

The hadith of Gabriel is indeed the mother of Islamic sciences. Three of Islam's biggest disciplines have emerged to address each of *Deen*'s three dimensions.[9] Islamic legal tradition, *Shariah* sciences (*Fiqh* and *Usul al-Fiqh*) developed in order to explain the meaning, the critical importance of the five pillars of Islam. Islamic rational theology (*Ilm Al-Kalam*) on the other hand developed around several debates about the elements of Iman, such as the debates about the essence (*zaath*) and attributes (*sifa'ath*) of Allah, and free will and predestination. Islamic spiritual tradition (*Al-Tasawwuf*) evolved to understood and realize *Ihsan*. Thus, in a way the hadith of Gabriel is a fount of many Islamic disciplines.[10]

The term *Ihsan* has limited legal meaning (in the *Shariah* sense), but it is rich in its linguistic connotations and is like an ocean without a shore when it comes to the mystical truths. Tomes can be written and have been written

---

[9] Abdullah Saeed, *Islamic thought: An Introduction* (New York: Routledge, 2006).
[10] See M. A. Muqtedar Khan, "Islam as an Ethical Tradition of International Relations," *Islam and Christian-Muslim Relations* 8.2 (1997): 177–192.

about what all it encompasses and hints at. Linguistically it means several things including perfection, goodness, charity, good, better, develop, improve, beautify and beautiful. Its Arabic root is *h-s-n*, which means beautiful, and in the Quran this root occurs in several forms, the most common of which are *ahsanu*, *Muhsin*, *Muhsineen*, with occasional instances of *Al-Ihsan*. Translators usually translate the terms as 'do good' (*ahsanu*) and those who do good deeds (*Muhsin*, *Muhsineen* is one of its plural forms). William Chittick on the other hand has consistently translated *Ihsan* as 'to do beautiful deeds' and *Muhsin* as one who does beautiful things.[11]

Whether read in the original Arabic or in translation, the way the term *Ihsan* is understood has tremendous implications for understanding and interpreting the very message of the Quran. I have chosen to abstain from coloring what the text says via translation and have decided that from this chapter on, I will abstain from rendering the term in English and retain its Arabic form. After all, this entire book is an attempt to explain the term and in my humble view no single term in any language will suffice to communicate the meanings loaded in the cosmology called *Ihsan*. Thus, *ahsanu* will be translated as to do *Ihsan*, and *Muhsin* and *Muhsineen* as those who are in the state of *Ihsan*. *Ihsan* in its various forms occurs 191 times in 175 verses of the Quran and there are three important prophetic traditions in which it occurs. Interestingly, the spiritual definition of the term *Ihsan* can only be found in the famous hadith of Gabriel. Once one becomes familiar with the mystical secrets of *Ihsan*, the verses in the Quran that use the term open unbelievably transcendent vistas of mystical and cosmological truths.[12]

IHSAN: A NEW VISION?

أَنْ تَعْبُدَ اللهَ كَأَنَّكَ تَرَاهُ، فَإِنْ لَمْ تَكُنْ تَرَاهُ فَإِنَّهُ يَرَاكَ

To Worship Allah as if you see him, if you cannot see Him, surely He sees you.

---

[11] See William Chittick, *Sufism: A Beginner's Guide* (Oxford: Oneworld Publications, 2007), p. 4. Also see William C. Chittick, *The Self-Disclosure of God: Principles of Ibn Al-'Arabi's Cosmology* (Albany, NY: SUNY Press, 1997), pp. 122 and 309. Also see M. A. Muqtedar Khan, "Prophet Muhammad was the Best of *Muhsins*," *The Huffington Post*, Jan 1, 2013.

[12] See M. A. Muqtedar Khan, "Ihsan," in Richard Martin, ed., *Encyclopedia of Islam and the Muslim World* (New York: Cengage, 2016), pp. 497–498.

When Angel Gabriel asked Prophet Muhammad (pbuh) what is *Ihsan*, he replied, to worship Allah as if you see him, and if you cannot see him, know that he sees you. At face value, it appears to be such a simple answer. But its depth is unfathomable and for over 1400 years, Muslim mystics have been plumbing its depths with no end in sight. It's like swimming in an ocean with no shore in sight for as far as the eye can see, no matter how much distance you cover. In the previous chapter, I tried to summarize to the best of my understanding and ability how the Muslim tradition tried to understand *Ihsan*. I want to take another look at the sources to advance a fresh philosophy of *Ihsan*. What does it mean and how can we unpack it to make it more relevant to the life of ordinary Muslims today? Does it speak to humanity at large? Can it be understood in such a way that both our political and civil society institutions can enrich their quality and governance by adopting some of the elements of *Ihsan*? If *Ihsan* is pursuit of perfection, then can our institutions not become better by adopting some of the values that are associated with *Ihsan*? The new vision of *Ihsan* I am trying to advance is jointly influenced by my reading of the tradition and my experiences as a globetrotting mystic-curious.

To begin with, I strongly feel that when we translate the term *ta'budu* as worship, we invariably quarantine *Ihsan* to the realm of worship. The term with the root *a-b-d* has many meanings and the dominant one is that of servant-hood. Therefore, *ta'budu* can also be understood as to serve Allah or to be in the servant-hood of Allah as if you see him. Once we start thinking of *Ihsan* as servant-hood of God, then the relationship widens because service includes worship and more, and that additional element is service. In a widely known authentic hadith, God equates service to others with service to Himself, opening a completely new way of thinking about the relationship between the servant and his Lord through service to his other servants.

The Messenger of Allah said, "Truly, Allah, the Exalted, and Glorious will say on the Day of Resurrection: 'O son of Adam, I was ill but you did not visit Me.' He would say: 'O my Rubb (Lord), how could I visit you and You are the Rubb of the worlds?' Thereupon He would say: 'Did you not know that such and such a slave of mine was ill but you did not visit him? Did you not realize that if you had visited him (you would have known that I was aware of your visit to him, for which I would reward you) you would have found Me with him? O son of Adam, I asked food from you but you did not feed Me.' He would submit: 'My Rubb, how could I feed You and You are the Rubb of the worlds?' He would say.

'Did you not know that such and such a slave of Mine asked you for food but you did not feed him? Did you not realize that if you had fed him, you would cer- tainly have found (its reward) with Me? O son of Adam, I asked water from you but you did not give it to Me.' He would say: 'My Rubb, how could I give You (water) and You are the Rubb of the worlds?' Thereupon He would say: 'Such and such a slave of Mine asked you for water to drink but you did not give it to him. Did you not realize that if you had given him to drink you would have found (its reward) with Me?' [13]

The hadith establishes an interesting correspondence between visiting the sick with visiting God Himself. The example has special meaning in the light of the hadith of Gabriel, for what can be more like being with Allah than visiting with Him. The hadith of Gabriel literally says "as if" you see Him, not "see him." Those who are less mystical and more legal- istic in their approach to faith, should find an interesting analogy in this hadith which says to *serve his* servants is like, or *"as if"* one *has served God Himself.*

Two other prophetic traditions establish the principle of *Ihsan* as serv- ing Allah in the most beautiful and most perfect way possible. They are:

عَنْ أَبِي يَعْلَى شَدَّادِ بْنِ أَوْسٍ رَضِيَ اللهُ عَنْهُ عَنْ رَسُولِ اللهِ صلى الله عليه و سلم قَالَ: "إِنَّ اللَّهَ كَتَبَ الإِحْسَانَ عَلَى كُلِّ شَيْءٍ، فَإِذَا قَتَلْتُمْ فَأَحْسِنُوا القِتْلَةَ، وَإِذَا ذَبَحْتُمْ فَأَحْسِنُوا الذَّبْحَةَ، وَلْيُحِدَّ أَحَدُكُمْ شَفْرَتَهُ، وَلْيُرِحْ ذَبِيحَتَهُ".

Indeed Allah has prescribed Ihsan in all things. So if you kill then kill well; and if you slaughter, then slaughter well. Let each one of you sharpen his blade and let him spare suffering to the animal he slaughters.

God Almighty has commanded *Ihsan* in all things. He did this while speaking in the context of slaughtering animals for food, but the principle is universal. God has commanded *Ihsan* in all things, which would include worship and service, divine matters and mundane issues, sacred and secu- lar affairs. Traditional legal scholars, *fuqaha,* divide human affairs into *Ibadah* (worship) and *muamalat* (mundane affairs) and *Ihsan* is ordained

---

[13] See the hadith collection, Imam Al-Nawawi, *Riyadh –al-Saleheen,* trans. S. M. Madani Abbas (Riyadh, Saudi Arabia: International Islamic Publishing House, 2002), p. 466.

in both the realms. Most scholars and teachers of Islam are aware of this tradition, it is included in *Sahih Muslim,* one of the most canonical collections and two of the most read and valued subcollections by Imam Nawawi, *Riyadh-us-Saleheen* and *Arbaeen* (Forty traditions).[14]

Another hadith reported by Al-Tabarani is very fascinating, it says:

يحب الله العامل إذا عمل أن يحسن

Surely Allah loves a worker when the worker does his work beautifully.

The hadith is inviting workers to seek perfection in their work in reward for God's love.[15] The hadith is remarkable in that it does not distinguish between religious deeds and mundane actions; in fact it treats them both as worthy of utmost attention and perfection. The message is clear that God loves those who seek perfection and beauty (*Ihsan*) in every endeavor they launch and in conjunction with various verses in the Quran that send the message that God loves those who do *Ihsan* (2:195) or are in the state of *Ihsan,* we can conclude that *Ihsan* is the way to earn God's love. Who would want to seek God's love other than those who love Him? Thus, in a rather intriguing fashion, we can recognize that the love affair between the creator and his creation is manifest in the dedication with which the servant performs all her duties toward his Lord and toward the rest of the creation. We will explore these themes again when we discuss *Ihsan* as love, but for now the main takeaway is that *Ihsan* applies to all forms of actions, those that may count as *Ibadaat* (religious duties) and those that may count as part of *muamalat* (mundane affairs).

IHSAN IN THE QURAN

ٱلَّذِينَ ءَامَنُوا۟ وَعَمِلُوا۟ ٱلصَّٰلِحَٰتِ طُوبَىٰ لَهُمْ وَحُسْنُ مَـَٔابٍ

Those who believe and perform righteous deeds, Tuba is for them and a beautiful place of (final) return. (Quran 13:29)

---

[14] See Hadith #17 from the al-Nawawi collection on the World Wide Web at: http://abuaminaelias.com/forty-hadith-nawawi/.

[15] See Sheikh Abdessalam Yassine, *Al-Ihsan* (Casablanca, Morocco: Matbooaat Al-Afaq, 1998), pp. 17–21.

When discussing the concept of *Ihsan* in the Quran with various traditional scholars and Sufi practitioners, I frequently got two answers; either
that the concept of *Ihsan* in the Quran is different from that in the hadith
of Gabriel—the former is good deeds and the latter is humility and dedication in prayers—or that *Ihsan* is everywhere in the Quran and that the
Quran speaks to *Ihsan* in nearly everything that it says. Clearly while the
second answer was not very helpful to an academician who was seeking
specific renderings of *Ihsan* in the Quran, I find myself in disagreement
with the first answer. To think of *Ihsan* in the Quran as different from
Ihsan in hadith is a strange idea. We do not maintain the same assumption
about any other Islamic concept that it has different meanings in different
sources. Indeed, the principle that the Quran takes precedence and abro-
gates the Sunnah is based on the requirement that hadith reports be consistent with the text and meaning of the Quran. Additionally, we rely on
the hadith literature to explain and supplement the meanings of things in
the Quran; therefore, I believe that *Ihsan* is and must be the same in the
Quran and the hadith collections. Indeed, the only explicit definition of
Ihsan that is available to us is from the hadith of Gabriel and it gives profound depth and meaning to the use of the term *Ihsan* and its various
conjugations in the Quran and in other *ahadith*.[16]

There are over 190 mentions of the various conjugations of the Arabic
root *h-s-n* in the Quran and they occur as nouns, verbal nouns, verbs,
and in singular, plural, masculine and feminine forms. I have selected a
few verses to convey what I hope is a summary of how the Quran reveals
the idea of *Ihsan* around a few key themes. Based on these selections, we
can argue that according to the Quran, achieving the state of *Ihsan* is the
purpose for which we were created. Allah is close to those who seek to
better themselves in pursuit of *Ihsan*, and he loves them and is with
them. Without *Ihsan*, even justice is incomplete and *Ihsan* is not only the
goal but a forgotten condition of the human being, because God created
all his creation in the state of *Ihsan*—perfect, and it is only the human
beings who become heedless of this reality and must endeavor to return
to the state of *Ihsan*. Ultimately, *Ihsan* is a state in which the soul of the
believer finds contentment as if it is in a state of continuous remembrance of God.

---

[16] *Ahadith* is the plural of hadith.

Ihsan *as the Purpose of Creation*

In two verses, 67:2 and 11:7, the Quran says that God created the human subject to test if she would attain the state of *Ihsan* and do beautiful things.

الَّذِى خَلَقَ ٱلْمَوْتَ وَٱلْحَيَوٰةَ لِيَبْلُوَكُمْ أَيُّكُمْ أَحْسَنُ عَمَلًا

He is the One who created death and life so that he may test which of you has reached the state of Ihsan *(best) in your deeds.* (Quran 67:2)

وَ هُوَ ٱلَّذِى خَلَقَ ٱلسَّمَٰوَٰتِ وَٱلْأَرْضَ فِى سِتَّةِ أَيَّامٍ وَكَانَ عَرْشُهُ عَلَى ٱلْمَآءِ لِيَبْلُوَكُمْ أَيُّكُمْ أَحْسَنُ عَمَلًا

And He it is, Who has created the heavens and the earth in six Days and His Throne was on the water, that He might try you, which of you has reached the state of Ihsan *(the best) in deeds.* (Quran 11:7)

In 67:2, the concept of creation of death has intrigued classical commentators and much of the discussion around this verse is about creation, death and resurrection. Most commentators have interpreted *liyabluukum ayyukum ahsanu amlan* in both the verses as to test which of you is best in conduct or deeds and these deeds have been understood as those that have been performed sincerely, with good intentions and correctly, according to the law. But the Quran also refers to good deeds as *amila salehan* (e.g. in 2:62 and 16:97) and commentators also understand the meaning of the term without making any interpretive distinction between "righteous deeds" and "beautiful deeds."[17] There must be a reason why the Quran uses the words *ahsanu amlan* while talking about the purpose of creation and righteous deeds when talking about those who have Iman (faith) as in 2:62 and 16:97. I humbly submit that this difference is so because the intention is to suggest that the purpose of life is to attain the state of *Ihsan* when one does beautiful deeds (*ahsanu amlan*) and the proof of faith (Iman) is righteous deeds—*amila salehan*. *Righteous deeds* are proof of Iman and *beautiful deeds* are proof that the doer or *Muhsin* is in a state of *Ihsan*.

---

[17] I reviewed several commentaries including Ibn Kathir, *Tafsir Ibn Kathir*, Vol. 5, pp. 26–27, and Sahl al-Tustari, *Tafsir al-Tustari*, pp. 240–241.

Islam, Iman and Ihsan in the Quran

While many verses speak of each of the components of the *Deen* separately, the following two verses of the Quran are remarkable in that I see the summary of the hadith of Gabriel in both of them. One of them is 13:29 and the other one is 16:97.

الَّذِينَ ءَامَنُوا وَعَمِلُوا الصَّٰلِحَٰتِ طُوبَىٰ لَهُمْ وَحُسْنُ مَـَٔابٍ

Those who believe, and work righteousness, Tuba is for them and a beautiful place of (final) return. (Quran 13:29)

مَنْ عَمِلَ صَٰلِحًا مِّن ذَكَرٍ أَوْ أُنثَىٰ وَهُوَ مُؤْمِنٌ فَلَنُحْيِيَنَّهُ
حَيَوٰةً طَيِّبَةً وَلَنَجْزِيَنَّهُمْ أَجْرَهُم بِأَحْسَنِ مَا كَانُوا يَعْمَلُونَ

Whoever does righteousness, whether male or female, while he is a believer—We will surely cause him to live a good life, and We will surely give them their reward according to the best of what they used to do. (Quran 16:97)

The two verses do not talk about the end of time, but both refer to Islam, Iman and *Ihsan*. Verse 13:29 states that those who believe (have Iman) and do righteous deeds (submit to Islam) for them is *Tuba* and they are in the state of *Ihsan*. In 16:97, those who do righteous deeds are in a state of submission (Islam) and while they are believers (Iman), they will be rewarded according to the state of their *Ihsan* regardless of their gender. *Tuba* has been explained by some companions of Prophet Muhammad (pbuh) as perhaps a tree in paradise that will be a reward for the righteous. Ibn Kathir reports that according to one companion, Ibn Abbas, who has been hailed by the Islamic tradition as one of the scholar companions, *Tuba* means comfort and reward for the eyes.[18] I find this reference to comfort of the eyes as an echo of the extra reward promised to those who have achieved the state of *Ihsan* in 10:26—*For those who are in a state of* Ihsan *is the best (husna) reward and more.* In 10:26, it is *husna* and more and, in 13:29, it is *husna* and *Tuba.* As discussed earlier, this extra reward is indeed the ultimate comfort for the eyes—a vision of the divine. This reference to the ultimate reward as something that constitutes a possible divine vision helps establish the idea in the hadith of Gabriel that *Ihsan* is the highest state that can be achieved—it is also the highest reward and

[18] See Ibn Kathir, *Tafsir Ibn Kathir*, pp. 276–277.

that is as if one is seeing God. Discovering these verses of the Quran that more or less endorse the message of the hadith of Gabriel also confirms in my view the promise that the Quran has been sent as good news (46:12) and mercy (31:3) to those who are in a state of *Ihsan*.

Ihsan *Is a Spiritual State and Mystical Station*

God has special relationship with those who reach the state of *Ihsan*. There are many verses in the Quran that speak of God's love and nearness to those who have attained the state of *Ihsan*.

وَٱلَّذِينَ جَٰهَدُواْ فِينَا لَنَهْدِيَنَّهُمْ سُبُلَنَا وَإِنَّ ٱللَّهَ لَمَعَ ٱلْمُحْسِنِينَ

And those who strive for Us—We will surely guide them to Our ways.
And indeed, Allah is with them who are in the state of Ihsan. *(Quran 29:69)*

وَأَحْسِنُوٓاْ إِنَّ ٱللَّهَ يُحِبُّ ٱلْمُحْسِنِينَ

And do beautiful deeds (Ihsan) Allah loves those who do beautiful deeds (who
are in the state of Ihsan). *(Quran 2:195)*

وَهُوَ مَعَكُمْ أَيْنَ مَا كُنتُمْ وَٱللَّهُ بِمَا تَعْمَلُونَ بَصِيرٌ

And He is with you wherever you are and Allah sees everything you do. (57:4)

إِنَّ رَحْمَتَ ٱللَّهِ قَرِيبٌ مِّنَ ٱلْمُحْسِنِينَ

Indeed Allah's mercy is near those who are in the state of Ihsan. *(7:56)*

إِنَّ ٱللَّهَ مَعَ ٱلَّذِينَ ٱتَّقَواْ وَّٱلَّذِينَ هُم مُّحْسِنُونَ

Indeed Allah is with those who are conscious of him and those of them who are
in a state of Ihsan. *(16:128)*

The sample of verses provided above establishes a profound and deep relationship between one who is in the state of Ihsan and Allah. The one who is aspiring for the state of Ihsan is one who does beautiful things, who seeks to manifest beauty and perfection in everything that she does. He is always aware of his actions and his existence being in the glare of God's eyes. In 57:4, the Quran describes the closeness of God to his creation and emphasizes that God is seeing whatever one does, echoing what Prophet Muhammad (pbuh) says in his definition of Ihsan—*if you cannot see Him, surely he sees you.* In 16:128, the state of *Ihsan* is tied to the concept of *Taqwa*, which is understood by many as God-fearing and by others such as Muhammad Asad as God consciousness. Thus, God is with the one who is God conscious (aware that God is seeing him) and is in a state of *Ihsan* (acting as if He is seeing God or is being seen by God).[19]

From the prophetic traditions and the Quranic verses that we have reviewed, we can conclude that *Ihsan* is more of a state than an action. While the concept of Islam is clearly a collection of actions and Iman is clearly belief in the validity of certain truths, *Ihsan* is a state of being—a spiritual condition wherein one is part of a two-way relationship with the Truth and the Reality (*Al-Haq*) of the Divine. One believes with unshakeable certainty that God is and that one is with God. It is an uninterrupted awareness of God and recognition that he is also aware of us; indeed our very existence is for and because of this divine awareness of us (*Tawajju*). If God did not see us, was unaware of us, was not with us wherever we are, then neither would we exist in reality nor would we exist in the divine imagination. We exist first in God's imagination and then he creates us in reality and sustains us in reality through his benevolence, and when we become aware of this truth and look for him and connect with him and seek his love, his mercy and his vision then we are in the state of *Ihsan*. The desire for *Ihsan*, I understand, when pursued with sincerity and with deep longing, is rewarded with *Ihsan* in this world and in the next. For the novice, the state of *Ihsan* rewards with visions, the best of which are dreams about Prophet Muhammad (pbuh) and the ultimate is to see God in dreams or in a state of awakening. Mystics recount tales of mystical and spiritual encounters with Prophets and Angels and with Jinns and Khidr, the teacher of Prophets. These visions are preparatory and as the seekers move along in the journey toward the final destination of ultimate union with the divine, these visions are milestones of encouragement and assurances that one is on

---

[19] See Muhammad Asad, *The Message of the Quran* (Gibraltar: Dar al-Andalus, 1980).

the right path. The relationship between the One and his seeker is best summarized in a *Hadith Qudsi* collected by Ibn Arabi[20]:

> *God, ever Mighty and Majestic is He, says:*
> "*I am present in my servants thoughts of Me, and I am with him when he remembers Me. If he mentions me in his self, I mention him in My self, and if he mentions me in an assembly, I mention him in a better assembly than that. If he approaches me by a hand's breadth, I draw near to him by an arm's length; and if he draws to me by an arm's length, I draw to him by a fathom. If he comes to me walking, I come to him running.*"

VEILING *IHSAN*

I looked at various contemporary and classical commentaries of the Quran to examine how various commentators understand the term *wa hua Muhsin*—while he is a *Muhsin* or while he is in a state of *Ihsan*—using 2:112, 4:125 and 31:22 as case studies. I chose these three verses because they are important to my understanding and explanation of the concept of *Ihsan* in the Quran. I found these verses by a straightforward reading of the Quran.[21] I reviewed Al-Tabari, Ibn Kathir, Al-Zamakshari, Al-Razi, Al-Tustari and Ibn Arabi from among the classical commentators and from among contemporary commentators, I examined Syed Abul A'la Maududi, Syed Qutb, Muhammad Asad,[22] Muhammad Shafi, Maulana Daryabadi[23] and Al-Sadi.[24]

---

[20] A *Hadith Qudsi* is a special type of hadith in which God is reported as saying something unlike others in which Prophet Muhammad (pbuh) is reported as seeing, saying or doing something. This is the 27th hadith in Ibn Arabi, *Divine Sayings: The Mishkath al-Anwar of Ibn Arabi*, trans. Stephen Hirtenstein and Martin Notcutt (Oxford: Anqa Publishing, 2008), p. 28.

[21] I am especially grateful to my former student Onur Tanay, who worked with me in the summer of 2011 in mining the Quran for all verses that contained words such as good, beautiful, charity, better, all the possible meanings of the term *Ihsan* in many languages. This research was funded by a grant from the Department of Political Science and International Relations at the University of Delaware.

[22] See Muhammad Asad, *The Message of the Quran* (Gibraltar: Dar al-Andalus, 1980), pp. 23–24.

[23] Abdul Majid Daryabadi, *The Glorious Quran: Translation and Commentary* (Leicester, UK: Islamic Foundation, 2001), pp. 39, 191, 738.

[24] Sheikh Abd-Ar-Rahman b. Nasir As-Sadi, *Tafsir As-Sadi*, trans. S. Abd Al-Hamid (Floral Park, NY: Islamic Literary Foundation, 2012), p. 63.

بَلَىٰ مَنْ أَسْلَمَ وَجْهَهُۥ لِلَّهِ وَهُوَ مُحْسِنٌ فَلَهُۥٓ أَجْرُهُۥ عِندَ رَبِّهِۦ وَلَا خَوْفٌ عَلَيْهِمْ وَلَا هُمْ يَحْزَنُونَ

Yes [on the contrary], whoever submits his face in Islam to Allah while being a
Muhsin *will have his reward with his Lord. And no fear will there be concern-*
ing them, nor will they grieve. (Quran 2:112)

وَمَنْ أَحْسَنُ دِينًا مِّمَّنْ أَسْلَمَ وَجْهَهُۥ لِلَّهِ وَهُوَ مُحْسِنٌ

And who is better in religion than one who submits himself to Allah
while being a Muhsin. (4:125)

وَمَن يُسْلِمْ وَجْهَهُۥٓ إِلَى ٱللَّهِ وَهُوَ مُحْسِنٌ فَقَدِ ٱسْتَمْسَكَ بِٱلْعُرْوَةِ ٱلْوُثْقَىٰ

And whoever submits his face to Allah while he is a Muhsin—*then he has*
grasped the trust worthiest handhold. (31:22)

It is interesting to note that a vast majority of the commentators interpret
the word *Muhsin* as a doer of good or one who does good, without much
discussion of what good means. I think this discussion of *Muhsin* without
referencing *Ihsan* is like explaining the meaning of the term *Mujahid* as one
who strives hard or partakes in *Jihad*, without ever explaining what *Jihad*
means. Ibn Arabi and Ibn Kathir are outliers and polar opposites in their
understanding of these verses. Among the classical scholars, Al-Zamakshari,[25]
well respected for his linguistic expertise and also known for his Mu'tazila
leanings, connects the verses 2:112 and 31:22 without attaching any significance to the term *Muhsin*. Al-Tustari connects all three, to my initial delight,
but only because all these verses use the phrase "submits his face to Allah."
Clearly none, including the Sufi commentary by Al-Tustari, seeks to connect *Muhsin* and *Ihsan* in these verses.[26]

Ibn Arabi's commentaries are very brief but so very deep. In three sen-
tences he explains a *Muhsin* as one who is steadfast (*Mustaqeem*) in his
condition of *Baqa* after *Fanaa*. He adds that a *Muhsin* is one who witnesses his Lord in all his actions. Every action is witness to the Lord to
whom he has submitted his complete self. He links the action of witness-

[25] Mahmud bin Umar Al-Zamakshari, *Al-Kashaaf* (Beirut, Lebanon: Darul-Kitab, 2008),
pp. 136–137.
[26] Sahl B. Abd Allah al-Tustari, *Tafsir al-Tustari: Great Commentaries on the Holy Quran*,
trans. Annabel Keeler and Ali Keeler (Louisville, KY: Fons Vitae, 2011), p. 22.

ing the Lord, which Sufis have understood as *Mushahada*, to *Al-Ihsan*. He finally links the concept of being steadfast (*Al-Istiqamah*) as a station where one is sincere in worship and completely unaware of one's self.

مستقيم في أحواله بالبقاء بعد الفناء، مشاهد ربّه في أعماله، راجع من الشهود الذاتيّ إلى مقام الإحسان الصفاتيّ الذي هو المشاهدة بالوجود الحقانيّ لمكان الاستقامة والعبادة، لا بالوجود النفساني

In the short passage above,[27] Ibn Arabi develops a profound philosophy of *Ihsan* and to understand it, one needs to turn to *Al-Qushayri's Epistle on Sufism*, in which Al-Qushayri explains some of the ideas used by Ibn Arabi. The first thing one realizes is that while *Istiqamah* is a *Maqaam* (spiritual station), *Baqa* and *Fanaa* are *Ahwal* (spiritual states). Al-Qushayri describes uprightness as a station in which one perfects all affairs,[28] in a sense that one does not withdraw from the devotion one has achieved in their submission to their Lord. *Fanaa* is a state in which blameworthy traits in the person are eliminated (annihilated) and *Baqa* means that praiseworthy qualities are retained (subsist).[29] Thus, in a sentence, *Muhsin is one who is in a state of* Ihsan. The key difference between Ibn Arabi and nearly all other commentators is that Ibn Arabi here connects the Quranic understanding of *Ihsan* with the Hadith of Gabriel.[30] To me the remarkable thing is not that Ibn Arabi connects *Muhsin* with *Ihsan*, what is remarkable is that so many others don't.

Ibn Kathir on the other hand not only does not make this linkage between *Muhsin* and *Ihsan* but it does appear to me as if he is trying to preclude such a linkage. Ibn Kathir consistently interprets *Wa hua Muhsin*—while he is in a state of *Ihsan*, as if he is not aware of the hadith of Gabriel. In his commentary of 2:112, Ibn Kathir explains the meaning of the phrase as doing good deeds which are in conformity with the *Shariah* and only if these acts are done for Allah's sake alone.[31] In the dis-

---

[27] Muhyi-Al-Din Ibn Arabi, *Tafsir Ibn Arabi* (Beirut, Lebanon: Dar Sader Publishers, 2002), p. 42.

[28] Al-Qushayri, *Al-Qushayri's Epistle on Sufism*, p. 219.

[29] See Al-Qushayri, *Al-Qushayri's Epistle on Sufism*, p. 89.

[30] Ibn Arabi is consistent and his commentary on the term *Muhsin* is consistent, and in 4:125 too, he connects it with *Ihsan*.

[31] See Ibn Kathir, *Tafsir Al-Quran Al-Azeem* (Beirut, Lebanon: Dar Al-Kotob Al-Ilmiyah, 2006). Also see an abridged translation: Ibn Kathir, *Tafsir Ibn Kathir*, trans. Sheikh Safiur-Rahman Al-Mubarakputi et al. (Riyadh, Saudi Arabia: Maktabah Darussalam, 2003), pp. 338–339.

cussion, Ibn Kathir introduces a less known hadith from the collection of *Sahih Muslim*, the very collection whose first hadith explains *Ihsan*, to insist that good deeds must be done exactly the way prescribed by Prophet Muhammad (pbuh). It seems his main goal is to argue that even if Jews and Christians perform good deeds sincerely and for the sake of Allah, they are still not acceptable because they are not done according to the way of Prophet Muhammad (pbuh). He has sadly allowed his antipathy for the people of the book to completely miss the beauty and the depth of the verse. Lost in the particularities of the verses before and after it, he misses the transcendent message of verse 2:112. Ibn Kathir's commentary of the term *Muhsin* in 2:112, and 4:125 and 31:22 also supports the point that I make in the first chapter of this book, that Islamic legal thinking has a blind spot when it comes to *Ihsan*. In trying to bring *Shariah* into a conversation that is about *Ihsan*, Ibn Kathir forgets to talk about *Ihsan*. He is aware of the hadith of Gabriel and refers to it more than once in his vast commentary on the Quran (see 49:14) but not in a way that shows an appreciation for *Ihsan* described by his teacher Ibn Taymiyyah as the highest level of Islam.[32]

Among the contemporary commentators, the South Asian commentator Mufti Muhammad Shafi and the Saudi Arabian commentator As-Sadi follow Ibn Kathir and describe a *Muhsin* as one who follows the *Shariah*.[33] Maududi sometimes follows the lead of Ibn Kathir and at other times describes a *Muhsin* as a doer of good. The point here is not that a *Muhsin* is not a follower of the *Shariah*—one cannot be a *Muhsin* without also being a Muslim (one who adheres to the five pillars) and a *Mu'min* (one who has Iman), that is, one cannot reach the state of *Ihsan* without first submitting completely (Islam) and truly believing (Iman). But to describe a *Muhsin* as one who is *Shariah* compliant is like describing someone who has a Ph.D. as a high school graduate. There is a reason why Allah promises in the Quran to reward those who do *Ihsan* in a beautiful way *and more* (10:26) for they have exceeded well beyond the call of duty.

---

[32] For example, he refers to the hadith and the three terms Islam, Iman and *Ihsan* in his discussion of verse 49:14. This verse makes a distinction between a Muslim and a Mu'min, one who has submitted (state of Islam) and one who believes (has achieved Iman).

[33] See Maulana Mufti Muhammad Shafi, *Ma'riful Qur'an: A Comprehensive Commentary on the Holy Quran*, trans. Muhammad Hasan Askari and Muhammad Shameem (Karachi, Pakistan: Maktaba-e-Darul-uloom, 2005), pp. 290–291. Sheikh Abd-Ar-Rahman b. Nasir As-Sadi, *Tafsir As-Sadi*, trans. S. Abd Al-Hamid (Floral Park, NY: Islamic Literary Foundation, 2012), p. 63.

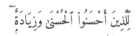

For those who have do Ihsan *is the best reward and even more.*

In the minds of Sufi scholars and philosophers, *Tasawwuf* and *Ihsan* are one and the same thing, and many practicing Sufi masters have told me as much. "*Sari Quran, Ihsan hai, sara tareeqah Ihsan hai*"—the entire Quran is *Ihsan*, the entire path is *Ihsan*—said one famous Sufi teacher from the subcontinent. In Cairo, a prominent Sufi master was puzzled that I was trying to isolate and contain the idea of *Ihsan*; "*Ilm al-taswwuf wa Ilm al-Ihsan nafs shai*," knowledge of mysticism and knowledge of *Ihsan* are the same thing, he said. Perhaps, the reason why there is so much written on *Tasawwuf* and so little on *Ihsan* is explicitly because the discourse on *Tasawwuf*, its various stations, methods, states, rituals, ceremonies, liturgies and *zikrs* (rememberance), is essentially an unpacking and explication of the meaning and condition of *Ihsan*. Perhaps it is a more recent development that Muslims are seeking to engage more with the concept of *Ihsan* itself without necessarily submerging in the ocean of Sufism entirely. Perhaps because *Ihsan* is an important dimension of Islam to even those who chose not to traverse the mystical trails.

If one browses *Al-Qushayri's Epistle on Sufism*, one will notice that he divides his work in three sections. The first section is a collection of biographies of early Sufis, the second explains a long list of key terms used by Sufis and the third is an even longer list of stations (*maqamat*) that a seeker may find on the path of *Tasawwuf*.[34] Neither the second nor the third list addresses *Ihsan*. I have argued that *Ihsan* is the final station, the ultimate goal of the seeker, but Al-Qushayri does not feel the need to discuss it. In contrast, when we look at Fethullah Gulen's book *The Key Concepts of the Practice of Sufism*, a book that may have been inspired by Al-Qushayri's *Epistle*, it does have a brief chapter on *Ihsan*.[35] Given the ambivalence of Gulen's status as a Sufi and the lack of clarity over whether his movement is a Sufi order or a civil society institution (the Turkish government now labels it a terrorist group), it might seem that only those who are not completely immersed in the mystical tradition or are not part of a Sufi order actually write about *Ihsan* as a separate concept. The best example is perhaps the book *Al-Ihsan* by Sheikh Muhammad

---

[34] See Al-Qushayri, *Al-Qushayri's Epistle on Sufism*, pp. v–ix.
[35] See M. Fethullah Gulen, *Key Concepts for the Practice of Sufism*, p. 133.

Hassan, which was discussed in the previous chapter. The few excep-
tions are Sheikh Kabbani, who wrote an excellent and comprehensive
section on *Ihsan*, and Sheikh Tahirul Qadri of Pakistan, who wrote a
short booklet on it.

Murata and Chittick are among the few who have sought to unpack the
concept of *Ihsan* while identifying different sources of *Ihsan* in the Quran.
They present *Ihsan* as a composite of worship, seeing God, sincerity, God-
wariness, love and wholesomeness.[36] They discuss these six dimensions of
Ihsan from predominantly a Quranic perspective, essentially because these
dimensions have been identified in their quest to demonstrate the Quranic
roots of *Ihsan*. Surprisingly much of the discussion of these concepts,
including *Ihsan* as seeing God, is very consistent with orthodox Islamic
understanding. Given their vast contributions to the study of Sufi thought
and specially Chittick's magnificent scholarship on Ibn Arabi and Jalaluddin
Rumi,[37] I expected a more mystical unpacking of *Ihsan*. Nevertheless, they
provide an excellent base to build on and my discussion and unveiling of
Ihsan owes much to their pioneering work. Some of Chittick's books in
themselves constitute a discourse on each of the above-identified dimensions of *Ihsan*, from which I shall borrow abundantly, such as his most
recent book on *Divine Love*, which is also an important dimension of *Ihsan*.[38]

Unpacking *Ihsan*: From Cosmology
to Sociopolitical Philosophy

In the previous chapter, I summarized how *Ihsan* has been understood in
the vast and diverse Islamic tradition and by contemporary academic
scholars and faith scholars. This chapter established that there was and is
deep and enduring interest in the concept of *Ihsan* and demonstrated its
profound impact on the evolution of Islamic thought and practice, particularly on the mystical interpretation of Islam and the development of
Sufi discourse and ways.[39] In this chapter, I have attempted to look at the
concept of *Ihsan* afresh, revisiting the key sources of Islam, the Quran and

[36] See Murata and Chittick, *The Vision of Islam*, pp. 265–295.

[37] See, for example, William C. Chittick, *The Self-Disclosure of God: Principles of Ibn al-
Arabi's Cosmology* (Albany, NY: SUNY Press, 1998). Also see William C. Chittick, *The Sufi
Path of Love: The Spiritual Teachings of Rumi* (Albany, NY: SUNY Press, 1984).

[38] See William C. Chittick, *Divine Love: Islamic Literature and the Path to God* (New
Haven: Yale University Press, 2013).

[39] See William C. Chittick, *Faith and Practice of Islam* (Albany, NY: SUNY Press, 1992).

Sunnah. It is up to the readers to judge if any new insight has been added or if more light has been shed on any hitherto understudied dimension. In the next section of this chapter, I will attempt to unpack the concept of *Ihsan* and try to *translate its depth into spread*. Clearly, *Ihsan* constitutes a cosmology, but by invoking the traditions that invite believers to do everything beautifully or while in a state of *Ihsan* and try to perfect and beautify their work no matter what they attempt, I hope to elucidate some of the dimensions of *Ihsan* as principles that can become the foundations of a worldview and the building blocks of a political philosophy of good governance.

After much reflection on everything that has been reviewed on *Ihsan* and discussions with many scholars and practitioners of *Tasawwuf*, I focus on the following eight aspects or elements of the state of *Ihsan*: (1) *Mushahada* (witnessing), (2) *Muraqaba* (vigilance) and *Muhasaba* (reflection), (3) *Muhabba* (love), (4) *Husn* (aesthetics), (5) mercy (including charity) and forgiveness (*Rehmah, Sadaqa*), (6) *Ma'rifah* (epistemology) and (7) *Fanaa* (self-annihilation). The task is daunting for each concept is worthy of a book; nevertheless, I shall try and both elucidate the cosmological aspects of the above mystical concepts, values and practices and then extract insights for worldly affairs from them.

The goal in this section of this chapter is not to secularize Islamic concepts by divesting them of their sacred and spiritual content. Political Islamists, by rejecting secular space and claiming that Islam has something to offer for both the worlds also desacralize the sacred by treating the secular and the sacred as similar if not the same sphere. Our endeavor here is to retain and *extend the sacred* into the public arena without depriving it of its sacred and mystical content. Spiritual values shall remain spiritual, thus in a way the goal is to *spiritualize politics* rather than *politicize spirituality*. Our endeavor here is the opposite of what Plato called soul-craft, using the state's educational policies and laws to produce better people, moral citizens and ethical societies. The idea here is to produce better— ethical, compassionate and beautiful—polity and politics as a result of bringing the mystical spirit into the political arena, in a way by bringing light to darkness.

MUSHAHADA|WITNESSING

When Prophet Muhammad (pbuh) described *Ihsan* as "to serve/worship Allah as if you see Him; if you cannot see him know that he sees you," he introduced the idea of vision of God as the highest state of *Deen*. Even though in the tradition Prophet Muhammad (pbuh) uses the term whose root is r-a-y رای which has the meanings of to see, to view, to consider, to discern, to conceive, to set eyes upon, much of the discussion of the idea expressed in this tradition employs the concept of *Mushahada* (witnessing) and the use of the root sh-h-d interestingly ties seeing to witnessing and to testifying. Therefore, the first part of the definition of *Ihsan* can now be read in the following ways: (1) *Ihsan* is to worship/serve Allah as if you see Him; (2) *Ihsan* is to worship/serve Allah as if you are witnessing Him and (3) *Ihsan* is to worship and serve Allah as if you are testifying (to Him and/or about Him).

When one looks at seeing as testifying, then it leads to a rather extraordinary linkage between Islam, Iman and *Ihsan*, making witnessing God the common or basic starting point of all the three dimensions of the *Deen*. William Chittick points out that *Mushahada* is similar to unveiling and that it involves "both sight and insight."[40] I agree with him because traditional debates about whether Prophet Muhammad (pbuh) actually saw God talk about seeing or witnessing God with the physical eyes and the eyes of the heart. The first type of *Mushahada* is promised to all *Muhsineen* after the Day of Judgment. Prophet Muhammad (pbuh) said that those who are in the state of *Ihsan* in that world will see God as if they are seeing the full moon on the horizon[41] and those who are in the state of *Ihsan* in this world may have divine visions in which they will see the mysteries of the unseen (*Al-Ghayab*) and the unveiled (*mukashafa*) with the eyes of their spirit either in dreams or in visions. When someone comes close to God through fulfilling the obligatory and the supererogatory prayers (*Nafl*), through extensive remembrance (*Zikr*), meditation and fasting, and above all by perfecting one's conduct, one is rewarded with mystical and spiritual experiences that unveil some of the mysteries of God and the unseen or the spiritual world.[42] It is this experience of *mukashafa* or unveiling that is a reward as well as a milestone in the journey toward the final destination, which is the complete unveiling of the "Face of Allah" the goal of every

---

[40] See William C. Chittick, *The Sufi Path of Knowledge* (Albany, NY: SUNY Press, 1989), pp. 225–228.

[41] See Hadith #529, in *Sahih Bukhari*, trans. Muhammad *Muhsin* Khan, Vol. 9 (New Delhi, India: Kitab Bhavan), p. 389.

[42] See Annemarie Schimmel's discussion of *Kashf-i-Ilahi*, God's unveiling, in *Mystical Dimensions of Islam*, pp. 192–193. See the chapters on *Mukashafa* and *Mushahada* in Fethullah Gulen, *Key Concepts in the Practice of Sufism*, pp. 107–113. See also Al-Qushayri's discussion of *Mukashafa* and *Mushahada* in *Al-Qushayri's Epistle on Sufism*, pp. 97–99.

Muhsin, to witness the ultimate Beauty, the only Reality, and the Absolute Truth that is *Al-Haqq*.[43] *Al-Haqq* is one of the 99 names of Allah and is preferred by Muslim mystics because it at once unites Truth and Reality in one concept.

The definition of *Ihsan* that suggests "as if you see him" is neither poetic nor metaphorical, rather it is a profound statement of the highest form of relationship between the Creator and the created. *Ihsan* is the state in which no matter what one does—worship, interact with other people, conduct business or engage in politics—one is doing so as if and only in order to perform *Mushahada*, that is, witness the reality of God. At a simple level, it is to see God and divine manifestations in everything that one sees and perceives. After all, this wonderful universe, this incredible thing that we call life, is a manifestation of divine mercy and miracles. Ibn Arabi sees the universe as essentially a continuous and miraculous self-disclosure of God—(*Tajalli*) and the human being as a knowing being takes cognizance of this self-disclosure and her existence becomes an existential witnessing—*Mushahada*.[44] Thus we can humbly submit that the creation, that is, as it exists is *Tajalli*, God's manifestation, and the human subject's sole purpose is to witness it, to give *Shahada*, to the infinite beauty, grace, creative power, compassion and love of Allah the One and Only God worthy of worship. Ibn Arabi writes in his *Futuhat Al-Makkiyah* that there is God's *Tajalli*, or manifestations, everywhere so that our *Mushahada* never ends, or we never take our vision (*nazar*) away from the divine.[45]

Even though it is an act of worship, *Mushahada* cannot be just an action or a series of actions. It is a complete immersion of the self, both external and internal, in witnessing the divine. The mystics described the state as a psycho-spiritual condition in which one is increasingly aware of the divine and unaware of the self. Thus, the process of knowing the divine, of recognition of divine manifestations, consumes so much attention of the *mushahid* (the witness) that there is no more awareness of the self—indeed,

---

[43] The Quran refers to those who seek his countenance—*Wajhahu Allah*, in several verses; for example, see 2:272, 13:22, 30:38–39, 76.9 and 92:20. The first number refers to the chapter and the second verse.

[44] See the chapter on *Tajalli*, in Fethullah Gulen, *Key Concepts in the Practice of Sufism*, p. 114.

[45] See the English translation of *Futuhat Al-Makkiyah*, Ibn Al-Arabi, *The Meccan Revelations*, Vol. I, Michael Chodkiewicz, ed., trans. William Chittick and James Morris (New York: Pir Press, 2005), pp. 182–183.

the self does not matter, the self is annihilated (*Fanaa*) and what remains (*Ba'qaa*) is the sole awareness of the divine reality. One is alive to the mystical, to the spiritual, to the internal and unseen world, while one is dead indeed to the external, material and mundane world.

There are several key Quranic themes that address the state of *Mushahada*.

1. God himself is witnessing his own reality and the reality of his creation. This witnessing the reality and oneness of Allah is a divine *Sunnah* (precedent).

شَهِـدَ ٱللَّهُ أَنَّهُۥ لَآ إِلَهَ إِلَّا هُوَ

Indeed Allah witnesses that there is no God but He. (Quran 3:18)

2. God has created Adam and his progeny to witness Him as their Lord and witness his essence and attributes, as they are unveiled in the unfolding of his Creation. In a very important verse in the Quran, God invites the entire progeny of Adam to witness him by asking them "Am I not your Lord" and the entire humanity responds, "Yes, Indeed we witness."

أَلَسْتُ بِرَبِّكُمْ قَالُوا بَلَى شَهِـدْنَآ

Am I not your Lord, they said Yes We Witness. (Quran 7:172)

In a cosmological sense, humanity has already testified to the reality and oneness of God and in this life they merely have to remember (*Tazakkur*) and thus witnessing can be understood as a state of continuous remembrance of the divine (*Zikr*).

3. Human beings have been created for the sole purpose of witnessing him, worshipping him and knowing Him. In the Quran God says he created Jinns and Humans only to worship him alone and classical commentators of this verse have understood worshipping God as knowing him and thus witnessing him.

وَمَا خَلَقْتُ ٱلْجِنَّ وَٱلْإِنسَ إِلَّا لِيَعْبُدُونِ

I did not create Jinns and Humans except to worship me. (Quran 51:56)

4. At least three Prophets (Peace and Blessing on all of them), Adam, Moses and Muhammad have had a spiritual vision of God that far transcends any mystical experience of any other human being. The narratives of these Prophets actually witnessing God in some form are chronicled in the Quran. Adam, according to the Quran, was created by God's own "two hands" and thus experienced the divine touch (Quran 38:75). God spoke to Moses and even let him have a glimpse of Himself in the form of a mountain-leveling flash (Quran 7:143) and in chapter 51, the first 18 verses describe what many Muslims consider the description of when Prophet Muhammad (pbuh) saw God (Quran 53:1–18). The Muslim community is divided over this issue. While all Muslims do believe that Prophet Muhammad (pbuh) had visions of God, they disagree on whether he saw God with his human eyes.[46]

Without getting into an extensive discussion, arguments and counter-arguments about whether Prophet Muhammad (pbuh) did have a vision of God, I want to state simply what I believe and how it shapes therefore my idea of *Mushahada* or witnessing. Along with Ibn Abbas, the companion of Prophet Muhammad (pbuh) whose account of the Prophet's spiritual and miraculous night journey to Jerusalem and then to heaven, I believe that Prophet Muhammad (pbuh) did have some kind of a vision of God.[47] I understand the following verses from the Quran as referring to that vision on the night of spiritual journey.

فَأَوْحَىٰ إِلَىٰ عَبْدِهِۦ مَآ أَوْحَىٰ

And he revealed to His Servant what he revealed. (53:10)

مَا كَذَبَ ٱلْفُؤَادُ مَا رَأَىٰ

The heart did not lie about what he saw. (53:11)

أَفَتُمَٰرُونَهُۥ عَلَىٰ مَا يَرَىٰ

Will you then dispute with him what he saw. (53:12)

---

[46] Frederick S. Colby, "The Subtleties of the Ascension: al-Sulamī on the Mi'rāj of the Prophet Muhammad," *Studia Islamica* (2002): 167–183.

[47] See Josef van Ess, "Vision and Ascension: Surat al-Najm and its Relationship with Muhammad's Mirj," *Journal of Qur'anic Studies* 1 (1999), pp. 47–62.

مَا زَا غَ ٱلْبَصَرُ وَمَا طَغَىٰ

The sight [of the Prophet] did not swerve, nor did it transgress [its limit]. (53:17)

لَقَدْ رَأَىٰ مِنْ ءَايَتِ رَبِّهِ ٱلْكُبْرَىٰ

Indeed he did see, one of the greatest signs of his Lord. (53:18)

While Ibn Abbas believed that Prophet Muhammad (pbuh) did have a vision of God, there are others who attach greater significance to traditions and the view of Ayesha, the Prophet's youngest wife, that no man in this life could see God. Over time many of those who follow the Sufi tradition have adopted the view of Ibn Abbas and those who are more orthodox have canonized the view of Ayesha, both of whom back their views with reports from the Prophet.[48]

My view is simple: if we can believe that the Prophet did travel from Mecca to Jerusalem on a winged beast, led all the Prophets in prayer, then traveled through various levels of heavens meeting many Prophets of God including Abraham, Moses, Jesus and Adam, and visited heaven and hell, and in his ascent going beyond the point which was the limit of Angel Gabriel's access to God, all in a blink of an eye, then why can't we believe the rest that indeed he had a vision of God? Those who do not believe that Prophet Muhammad (pbuh) saw Allah, they maintain that it was Gabriel he saw in his true form. I do not find this argument compelling for the following reasons.

By the time of the night journey, Prophet Muhammad (pbuh) had seen, met and interacted with Angel Gabriel for over ten years. Going all the way to heavens to see Gabriel in his true form is incredible for us but for the Messenger of God can this be the ultimate mystical experience? The Quran in 53:10 says, "And he revealed to his servant what he revealed." Prophet Muhammad (pbuh) was not the *abd* (slave, servant) of Gabriel, no one is. Prophet Muhammad (pbuh) and all of creation are the servants of God and God alone. In 53:18 the Quran states, "Indeed he did see, one of the greatest signs of his Lord." I find it difficult to accept that Gabriel is

---

[48] Frederick S. Colby, *Narrating Muhammad's Night Journey: Tracing the Development of the Ibn' Abbas Ascension Discourse* (Albany, NY: SUNY Press, 2008).

God's greatest sign. The human being is God's greatest creation and that is why everyone including Gabriel was ordered to bow before Adam (Quran 2:34, 17:61, 18:50). It makes sense then what the Prophet saw was certainly greater than Gabriel, and that can only be God or one of His manifestations. This is important because it was on this night that Prophet Muhammad (pbuh) returned with the five obligatory prayers for Muslims and since he did have a vision of God, he and he alone could pray as if he was seeing God everytime—*in a true state of Ihsan.*

5. Finally everything in this creation testifies and witnesses Him (Quran 17:44) and believers witness him in the form of a verbal testimony of faith—*The Shahada*—or through the ultimate pursuit of *Ihsan* and a vision of divine secrets and mysteries. The concept of witnessing is very complicated and one can get lost in its cosmological and philosophical explorations.[49] But in order to provide a limited grasp of it to enable actors to bring it into their lives, their politics and their actions, I recommend that we understand witnessing as a phenomenon that has two broad elements—one is witnessing the Creator and the other is witnessing the creation. The former is the highest state of *Ihsan* wherein one is indeed able to witness God and be in possession of what mystical philosophers call *Ayn Al-Yaqeen*, the first step toward the union with the divine which provides more comprehensive experience of God and leads to what mystical philosophers call as *Haqq Al-Yaqeen*—the true and absolutely certain knowledge of God, which can come only from sustained experience and union with Him.

Mushahada *as Service and Other-Regarding Politics*

And they who give preference to others over themselves.
They will be successful. (Quran 59:9)

---

[49] See Ibn Al-Arabi, *On the Mysteries of Bearing Witness to the Oneness of God and the Messengership of Muhammad*, trans. Aisha Bewley, from the *Futuhat Al-Makiyyah* (Chicago: Kazi Publications, 2010).

One can argue that the purpose of human life is to bear testimony to God and to witness him, his creation and his manifestations. Very few of us and that too on a few occasions can be in a mystical state witnessing the *Tajalli* of our Lord while in a state of complete oblivion of the self. Our existence is both corporeal and spiritual. The corporeal side needs to satisfy appetites that are neither spiritual nor mystical but are physical, psychological and intellectual. It is here that understanding worship as service and equating witnessing creation with witnessing the Lord gain profound meaning. It is Al-Qushayri who makes a direct connection between *Mushahada* and service. He makes a distinction between servant-hood (*ubudiyya*) and servitude (*ubuda*) and worship (*Ibadah*). While worship is worship, servant-hood he defines as a higher quality of worship but servitude he insists is witnessing (*Mushahada*). Al-Qushayri quotes a couplet from an unknown Sufi to embellish his argument[50]:

> If you ask me, I will say: I am his servant
> If you ask him, he will say: he is my slave

By serving the creation of Allah, visiting the sick and feeding the poor, nourishing the animal kingdom and conserving the environment, we serve God and if we are self-conscious about it, we do so as if we are witnessing our Lord. In politics and government, I understand witnessing the divine as advancing a moral-political vision that is designed to support a polity and politics that pursues the *good of others* as a divine mandate. By advocating the good of others rather than the good of the self or even on the basis of the common good that is derived from self-interest we bring *Ihsan* into politics. The alternative is other-regarding politics. It is in my mind a spiritual form of politics. When you struggle for others, you witness their pain, their marginalization and their needs, and when you act for them, you are acting as a deliverer of the divine grace. To serve others without an axe to grind is to worship God as if you see him.

Muraqaba and Muhasaba | *A Critical Society*

Muraqaba is the other side of *Mushahada*. While the latter is to witness, the former is to be witnessed. Literally the word Muraqaba means to be awake, to be aware, to be watchful, vigilant and alert. It is to be conscious

---

[50] See Al-Qushayri, *Al-Qushayri's Epistle on Sufism*, p. 213.

of being watched. To be aware constantly that one is the object of the divine gaze. Prophet Muhammad (pbuh) described *Ihsan* as to serve Allah as if you see him, and if you cannot see him, know that surely *He sees you.* This awareness that one is being watched or one is seen is *Muraqaba.* Thus, we can develop a simple understanding of "being seen" by the One who sees all and knows all, and some interpret this as becoming conscious of Islamic laws and being afraid to violate them. Here it would mean to develop *Taqwa* or fear of God that translates into obedience and adherence to law. This is how scholars such as Ibn Kathir have interpreted the concept of *Muhsin,* one who is in a state of *Ihsan.* But practitioners of Islamic mysticism have understood it as meditation.

The concept of *Muhasaba,* to take into account or exercise critical self-scrutiny, is a related practice that in my understanding is critical to *Muraqaba*—self-awareness or vigilance. To my mind, they are inseparable—a two-step process that makes one both aware of the self from a critical perspective and this criticality is defined by the awareness that the divine gaze is also examining us and holding us accountable for our actions, but above all is completely aware of us, our thoughts, our desires and our intentions. While many scholars, such as Fethullah Gulen, study these two processes separately, I feel that we must study them together.[51] What I am suggesting is not novel; even Imam Al-Ghazali in his *Alchemy of Happiness* combines both *Muhasaba* and *Muraqaba* in one section.[52] Both Al-Qushayri and Gulen also link *Muhasaba* with *Muraqaba,* indicating that *Muhasaba* is an important aspect of *Muraqaba.*[53]

The practice of *Muhasaba* and *Muraqaba* can have a profound effect on an individual.[54] They make the practitioner self-critical and focused on self-improvement. In addition, the practice of meditation or concentration on the reality of being watched perpetually by God is a state of focused vigilance that prevents the individual from doing something that may dis-

---

[51] See Gulen, *Key Concepts in the Practice of Sufism,* Vol. I, p. 6 for *Muhasaba* and p. 57 for *Muraqaba.*

[52] See Abu Hamid Muhammad Ghazali Tusi, *Alchemy of Happiness,* trans. Jay R. Crook (Chicago: Kazi Publications, 2008), p. 825.

[53] Al-Qushayri, *Al-Qushayri's Epistle on Sufism,* pp. 203–205. Gulen, *Key Concepts in the Practice of Sufism,* p. 59.

[54] *Muraqaba* is also understood as mediation and the discussion of the how of Muraqaba is not germane to this discussion. For examples of how Muslims meditate, see Scott Kugle (Trans. and Ed.), *Sufi Meditation and Contemplation: Timeless Wisdom from Mughal India* (New York: Suluk press, 2012).

please God or break the law or disengage the servant from his Master. The discipline of the soul that comes about from regular self-evaluation and from training the mind to focus on the divine and to become cognizant of the divine gaze is bound to make an individual a better citizen. This self-improvement or purification through meditation, self-criticism and remembrance of God is also a state of *Ihsan*, one in which one is perfecting or purifying the self. It is perhaps this reality that prompted Prophet Muhammad (pbuh) to say, "One hour of contemplation (*Tafakkur*) is better than one year of worship.[55]"

Both concepts, *Muraqaba* and *Muhasaba*, can be traced to divine attributes and are derived from the 99 names of Allah in the Quran. Muraqaba is an acknowledgment of the divine name *Al-Raqib* (Quran 4:1 and 5:117) that means the watcher or the observer and Muhasaba is a derivative of *Al-Hasib* (Quran 4:6, 4:86, 33:39), which means the reckoner or the accountant.

إِنَّ ٱللَّهَ كَانَ عَلَيْكُمْ رَقِيبًا

Surely Allah is a Watcher over you. (Quran 4:1)

إِنَّ ٱللَّهَ كَانَ عَلَىٰ كُلِّ شَىْءٍ حَسِيبًا

Indeed Allah is over all things an account keeper. (4:86)

The idea that God is watching us and keeping account of our deeds is a central theme in Islamic legal and ethical discourse. This idea of life as a test can also be understood in the context of the Day of Judgment when God will take account of everyone's life, rewarding, punishing and forgiving whom He wills. The reality that God is both *Ash-Shahid*—the witness—(Quran 4:166, 22:17, 41:53, 48:28), and *Mashood*—*the witnessed*—is the dominant view of God and his relationship with his creation, even though it may not be expressed in the terms that I have used. Thus, Muslims as believers witness God (*Shahada*) and God as the Lord of the Day of Judgment (Quran 1:4) bears witness to their actions in this world. While the most beautiful manifestation of the first case is *Ihsan* the most devout awareness of the second reality is *Muraqaba* and *Muhasaba*.

---

[55] Al-Ghazali, *Alchemy of Happiness*, p. 843.

Islamic Society as a Critical Society

Contemporary Western societies, in the wake of European enlightenment and modernization, have been pursuing the idea of creating a critical society.[56] The idea is to create a society that is free from prejudice, social injustice, absence of freedoms and economic exploitation, based on rational knowledge and critical self-examination that allows for continuous self-development. Whether it is Jurgen Habermas' idea of communicative rationality or Herbert Marcuse's Critical theory[57] or the idea of deliberative democracy or even the theories about the importance of critical thinking (particularly in the academic field of education), they are all about creating a *critical public* that will seek to emancipate the self and the public through self-criticism in society. To a great extent, one can argue that the postmodern turn in humanities and to a lesser extent in social sciences along with critical theory also aspires to create an ethos of self-criticism with the goals of emancipation and realization of social justice. Modern social movements that seek various social justice goals from equality for women, freedom from ostracism for people of alternate lifestyles, fair trade practices for underdeveloped societies and oppose international capitalism and imperialism are all part of this global impetus to create a critical juggernaut that will transform the world.

The idea is laudable and many contemporary and modernist Muslim intellectuals, Sir Syed Ahmad Khan, Muhammad Abduh and Asghar Ali Engineer to name but a few of them, have admired this post-enlightenment development and hoped to emulate it in Muslim societies. The critical turn in late modernity is admirable but perhaps not easily imitable. The history of European nationalism, Christianity and its unique experience of modernity and its particular philosophical ideas are essential ingredients of this historical development. While societies are able to import successfully many democratic institutions and processes and even values such as freedom of expression and social trends such as atheism, the fundamental historical struggles that acted as crucibles and went into shaping Western

---

[56] Anthony J. La Vopa, "The Politics of Enlightenment: Friedrich Gedike and German Professional Ideology," *The Journal of Modern History* 62.1 (March 1990): 34–56.

[57] Stephen Eric Bronner and Douglas MacKay Kellner, eds., *Critical Theory and Society: A Reader* (New York: Routledge, 1989). Matthew David, and Iain Wilkinson, "Critical Theory of Society or Self-Critical Society?" *Critical Horizons: A Journal of Philosophy & Social Theory* 3-1 (2002): 131–158. John S. Dryzek, *Deliberative Democracy and Beyond, Liberals, Critics, Contestations* (Oxford University Press, 2000).

present are absent in other societies. Therefore, to a great extent, importation of Western institutions will remain at best synthetic and superficial. The failure of the Arab Spring from 2011 to 2014 is an indication of how the struggles that will shape Muslim futures are different.

In this section, I wish to submit the idea that Muslim societies can and should aspire to create a critical society that will restore social justice, emancipate the public and create a momentum for perpetual development.[58] But while the West is seeking to achieve this on the basis of reason and rationality, Muslim societies can achieve the same thing through their spiritual and mystical ethos. As of late, prominent Western intellectuals too are acknowledging the flaws and limits of the secular aspiration and the power of religion in the public sphere.[59] The practices and vision of *Muraqaba* and *Muhasaba* that have evolved from the concept of *Ihsan* can extend this ethic of self-criticism and self-improvement to the social level and produce a critical society that indulges in public self-criticism in pursuit of perpetual self-purification and development. Thus, *Muraqaba* and *Muhasaba* can bring the culture of public criticism and accountability to both state and society without having to import values or institutions that maybe founded on alien struggles. It will also serve as corrective. Not everything is perfect in Western nations, why then import an alien system that does not work so well even in its native habitat? Why not invest in authentic sources and historically embedded values and institutions that can help reform and rebuild with lesser opposition. Many of these practices are still in vogue, marginalized and proscribed but it will take less effort to revive and revitalize them than to completely destroy what exists and replace it with what is foreign.

MUHABBA|LOVE

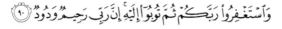

And ask forgiveness of your Lord and then repent to Him.
Indeed, my Lord is Merciful and Loving. (Quran 11:90)

---

[58] See M. A. Muqtedar Khan, "What is Enlightenment? An Islamic Perspective," *Journal of Religion and Society* 16 (2014): 1–8.

[59] Eduardo Mendieta and Jonathan Vanantwerpen, eds., *The Power of Religion in the Public Sphere: Judith Butler, Jurgen Habermas, Charles Taylor, Cornel West* (New York: Columbia University Press, 2011).

One day, when I was very young, I was performing my *wudu* (ablutions) before prayer in my neighborhood's mosque, the Imam who was doing the same by my side asked me, "so how are you *zalim* (tyrant or tormentor)?" I was startled. Not only was I his star pupil, but also very supportive of him and here he was calling me a tyrant. He noticed my confusion and said, "You are not into Urdu poetry are you?" I said on the contrary I enjoy Urdu poetry. The Imam then explained to me that calling me *zalim* was a poetic way of calling me beloved. Since the absence of the beloved is torment, the beloved is also a tormentor. He then asked me why was I tormenting our Lord. By now I was on his wavelength and understood that he was referring to my recent absence from the morning prayers. I promised to be more vigilant with my prayers. But the conversation remained with me and I repeated it to many of my friends who used it as an opportunity to mock me for my distance from our tradition. Too modern, too ignorant and heartless was the verdict. After a few weeks of research (these were pre-Google, pre-Internet days and I was a ninth grader with meager resources), I had an epiphany. I discovered that most of the classical Urdu and Persian poetry was about "True love" (*Ish-e-haqiqi*) as distinct from the metaphorical love (*Ishq-e-majazi*). Urdu poetry it seems has a reverse *double entendre* of its own, the talk was of love and wine and the beloved but actually it was about love for God and a thirst for divine union (*Wisal*). That was a special moment, an awakening, and since then I have always enjoyed the mystical messages behind love poetry in Urdu, which often overlaps with Persian poetry.

Love in the context of Islam is an enigmatic subject. There is clearly a rich tradition of prose and poetry about love in the Islamic culture and yet so little of love is attributed to Islam in the public sphere. There are literally centuries-long traditions of prose and poetry about divine love, but unfortunately the current Muslim obsession with *Shariah* has obscured the importance of love.[60] Islam is about love, not law. Law is there to facilitate not marginalize the expression of love. For the seekers of *Ihsan*, love has always been the central goal of life and purpose of faith. The love that early Sufi Rabia al-Adawiyyah wrote poetry about is well known, as is her distinction between selfish love and selfless love.[61] But none captures the

---

[60] See, for example, Annemarie Schimmel, *As Through a Veil: Mystical Poetry in Islam* (Oxford: Oneworld Publications, 2001). Jalal al-Din Rumi, *The Sufi Path of Love: The Spiritual Teachings of Rumi*, William C. Chittick, ed. (Albany, NY: SUNY Press, 1983)

[61] See Süleyman Derin, *Love in Sufism: From Rabia to Ibn al-Farid* (Istanbul: Insan Publications, 2008), pp. 73–102.

essence of love in Islam better than Ibn Al-Arabi, who described Islam as love in a very beautiful poem included in his collection titled *Tarjuman al-Ashwaq—The Interpreter of Desires*[62]:

> *I profess the religion of love;*
> *Wherever its caravan turns along the way,*
> *That is the belief,*
> *The Faith I keep.*

In this section, I cannot and do not wish to do justice to the place of love in Islam. Fortunately for me, a few recent books, particularly William Chittick's *Divine Love*, Omid Safi's *Radical Love*, have done a far deeper exploration of love in Islam than I can attempt here.[63] My goal is to briefly explore its significance and then try to articulate what role divine love can play to shape the social and public sphere. Those interested in a more in-depth study of divine love in Islam should read the works of William Chittick and Süleyman Derin cited here. For a classical rendering, they can refer to Al-Ghazali's *Ihya*, which includes a chapter called *Kitab al-Mahabbah wa al-Shawq wa al-Uns wa al-Rida—The book of love, desire, intimacy and satisfaction*.[64] Additionally, both Chittick in *Divine Love* and Al-Qushayri in his chapter on love in his *Epistle on Sufism* provide direct access to classical mystical writings on divine love.[65] I will first discuss the divine sources about love and then explore what I see are the four dimensions of love—God's love for humanity and human love for God, for the Prophet and for the rest of humanity.

God's Love for Humanity

Indeed Allah loves those who do Ihsan. (Quran 2:195, 5:13, 3:314, 3:148, 5:93)

As soon as one starts searching the Quran for what Allah says about love, one realizes that indeed God loves those who do *Ihsan*. The Sufis,

---

[62] See the poem "A Garden Among Flames" translated by Michael A. Sells. http://www.ibnarabisociety.org/poetry/ibn-arabi-poetry-index.html.

[63] William C. Chittick, *Divine Love: Islamic Literature and the Path to God* (New Haven, CT: Yale University Press, 2013). Süleyman Derin, *Love in Sufism: From Rabia to Ibn al-Farid* (Istanbul: Insan Publications, 2008). Ghazi bin Muhammad bin Talal, *Love in the Holy Quran* (Chicago, IL: Kazi Publications, 2010). Also see Omid Safi, *Radical Love: Teachings from the Islamic Mystical Tradition* (Yale University Press, 2018).

[64] See Süleyman Derin, *Love in Sufism*, p. 137.

[65] Al-Qushayri, *Epistle on Sufism*, p. 325.

those who have pursued *Ihsan* more diligently than most, however, have built their concept of divine love around the following verse:

يُحِبُّهُمْ وَيُحِبُّونَهُ

He loves them and they love Him. (Quran 5:54)

There are three elements of this verse that appealed to the Sufis. First, it so succinctly expresses the reality of mutual love—God's love for humanity and human love for God. Second, it establishes God as a lover and most importantly it reveals that it was Allah who loved first. One of the beautiful names with which the Quran refers to God is *Al-Wadud*, which means one who loves, one who is affectionate (Quran 19:96, 11:90 and 85:14). In another verse, which is important to the mystics because it establishes the necessity and centrality of Prophet Muhammad (pbuh), and to the orthodoxy because it vindicates the role of *Sunnah* in Islamic *Shariah*, God says if one loves Him, one will follow Prophet Muhammad (pbuh) and through this earn God's love.

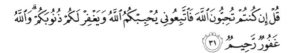

Say, (O Muhammad), "If you should love Allah, then follow me, Allah will love you and forgive your sins. And Allah is most forgiving and most Merciful." (Quran 3:31)

Besides these foundational verses, which reveal God's love for humanity, there are many more verses in the Quran that also articulate God's preferences. We are told whom He loves and whom He does not love. Allah loves those who do *Ihsan*. Allah also loves those who are constantly repentant and pure (in *Muraqaba* and *Muhasaba*, Quran 2:222), who are God conscious (Quran 3:76), who are steadfast and patient (Quran 3:146). Allah loves those who rely on him (Quran 3:159) and those who act justly (Quran 5:42).

Allah does not love those who exceed limits (Quran 2:190), who instigate turmoil (Quran 2:205), who are ungrateful sinners (Quran 2:276), those who deny the truth (Quran 3:32), those who are unjust and oppress others (Quran 3:57), those who are conceited and boastful (Quran 4:36), those who indulge in public utterance of hurtful speech (Quran 4:148), those who are treacherous (Quran 8:58), those who over-express joy (Quran 28:76), those who are corrupt (Quran 28:77) and those who are arrogant boasters (Quran 57:23). These examples of God's expression of love that I have cited are those that explicitly use the verb "he loves." There are many more ways in which God has expressed his love for humanity, specifically using concepts of mercy and forgiveness that will be discussed separately. For a comprehensive and detailed survey of God's love and divine love as expressed and articulated in Islamic sources, see Ghazi bin Talal's *Love in the Holy Quran*.[66]

There are many traditions from the Prophet about God's love for humanity, but the two that have had the most influence on the mystical conception of God's love are these: The Messenger of Allah (saw) said, "Verily Allah ta'ala has said: Whosoever shows enmity to a *wali* (friend) of Mine then I have declared war against him. And My servant does not draw near to Me with anything more loved to Me than the religious duties I have obligated upon him. And My servant continues to draw near to me with supererogatory deeds (nawafil) until I Love him. When I Love him, I am his hearing with which he hears and his sight with which he sees, and his hand with which he strikes, and his foot with which he walks. Were he to ask [something] of Me, I would surely give it to him; and were he to seek refuge with Me, I would surely grant him refuge.[67]" The second tradition that is important to understand God's love for humanity is narrated by Abu Huraira, who reported that Allah's Messenger (pbuh) said: "When Allah loves a servant, He calls Gabriel and says: Verily, I love so and so; you should also love him, and then Gabriel begins to love him. Then he makes an announcement in the heaven saying: Allah loves so and so and you also love him, and then the inhabitants of the Heaven (the Angels) also begin to love him and then there is conferred honor upon him on the earth.[68]" Both these traditions not only describe the love that God has for his servants, who are referred to as *Wali* (friend) but also how this love resonates in the cosmos, making his friend a beloved of the creation.

---

[66] Ghazi bin Muhammad bin Talal, *Love in the Holy Quran* (Chicago, IL: Kazi Publications, 2010).

[67] Both the mystical followers of Islam and the orthodoxy revere this important hadith. It is found in the most authentic collection of traditions, the *Sahih Bukhari*, and is also popularized as the #38th hadith in Imam al-Nawawi's *Arbaeen*. See also Al-Qushayri, *Al-Qushayri's Epistle on Sufism*, pp. 325–326.

[68] This hadith is also a very strong and authentic tradition reported by the canonical *Sahih Muslim*. See Al-Qushayri, *Al-Qushayri's Epistle on Sufism*, p. 326.

Love for God and His Messenger

Love for God and His Messenger is the dominant focus of the faith. All Muslims, mystical and otherwise, are involved in *mujahada* (struggle) to gain *qurbu* (closeness) with God. The path to closeness with God has one door and that is Muhammad (pbuh). Both the sources of Islam, the Quran and the traditions, make the point that one cannot be a true believer unless one loves God and his messenger more than anything else. Love of God and love of his Prophet are both the end and the means of Islam. The most important Quranic source for this is the verse: "Say if you should love Allah then follow me and Allah will love you" (Quran 3:31), which was discussed earlier. And from the many traditions, the one that most strongly advocates love of God and His Messenger is "There are three qualities in which are found the sweetness of faith: that one's love for Allah and His Messenger is more than anything else, that one loves a person only for the sake of Allah, and that one hates to return to unbelief just as he hates to be thrown in the Hellfire."[69]

Finally, when it comes to love for the Prophet, any Muslim who has attended a few sermons at a mosque would surely have heard this tradition: "By Him in whose hands my life is, none of you will have faith till he loves me more than his father, his children and all of humanity.[70]" Many orthodox Muslims privilege the virtue of being God-fearing (*muttaqeen*, understood as one who is *Shariah* compliant) over God-loving. Some are even cynical and suspicious toward the idea of love of God because they see this as a way by which not-so-sincere Muslims escape the obligations specified by the law of God. They also see it as a sign of Sufism, which they reject. However, one can conclude decisively from the sources discussed that love of God and His Messenger is critical to the completion of a Muslim's faith. To reach the state of *Iman*, one must love.

A Believer's Love for Humanity

All men and women are to each other
The limbs of a single body, each of us drawn
from life's shimmering essence, God's perfect pearl;
and when this life we share wounds one of us,

---

[69] See *Sahih Bukhari* Book 2, Hadith #15.
[70] See *Sahih Bukhari* Book 2, Hadith #14.

all share the hurt as if it were our own.
You, who will not feel another's pain,
you forfeit the right to be called human.[71]

Just as witnessing God can be operationalized by witnessing Him in His creation, similarly serving and loving Him can also be operationalized by serving humanity and loving humanity. My goal in this chapter is to develop a political and social philosophy from the cosmology of *Ihsan*, by trying to spiritualize the secular. In order for this claim to be valid, it must be shown to be consistent not only with textual sources, but also with Islamic traditions, at least Sufi traditions of equating love and servant-hood of God with love and service of humanity.[72]

I began this section with a quote from the famous Persian mystic Sheikh Saa'di of Shiraz, who captures the essence of the Quranic verse above in his poetry (Quran 4:36). Incidentally, the quote above is also displayed prominently at the entrance of the Hall of Nations of the United Nations' building in New York. This beautiful verse is commanding us to love and serve humanity—to do beautiful things for them (*Ihsan*). The great poet himself articulates this idea in another succinct and extremely beautiful couplet:

Ibadat ba-juz khidmat-I khalq nist
Ba tasbih-o sajjada-o dalq nist
Worship of God is nothing but service of humanity
It is not about rosary, or the prayer mat or the patched frock.[73]

In a very popular and oft-quoted *Hadith Qudsi*, the Prophet reports that God said: "My love is a right upon those who love each other for my sake. My love is a right upon those who visit each other for my sake. My love is a right upon those who sit together for my sake. My love is a right upon those who maintain relations for My sake." In this tradition, love for God and love for humanity and service to humanity are inextricably linked and when it is read in conjunction with the Quranic verse cited above (4:36), loving God and loving and serving humanity because you love God is *Ihsan*. Imam Al-Nawawi reports in his *Arbaeen*, a tradition (#13) in which

---

[71] Richard J. Newman's select translation from Gulistan. See: http://richardjnewman. com/my-books/selections-from-saadis-gulistan/.

[72] See Chittick, *Divine Love*, p. 242.

[73] See Riazul Islam, *Sufism in South Asia: Impact on 14th Century Muslim Society* (London: Oxford University Press, 2002), p. 325

the Prophet is reported to say: "None of you will believe until you love for your brother what you love for yourself."[74] While some Muslims define "your brother" rather narrowly to say only those who share our beliefs, Sufis and mystics have always understood it in universal terms. I understand it to mean that Muslims will not attain full *Iman* until they treat the rest of humanity with *Ihsan*.

The Sufi approach to life can be described in this way: *Submission to God and service to humanity*. In the sacred realm, a *Muhsin* (one in the state of *Ihsan*) has committed herself completely to the will of her lord and, in the profane sphere, she has devoted herself entirely to doing beautiful things—service to humanity—for the sake of her lord, for she knows that her lord loves those who do beautiful things. Sufis, especially in the Indian subcontinent, advocated a philosophy *of Khidmat-e-Khalq* (the same concept mentioned in the couplet by Sheikh Saa'di).[75] Nizamuddin Awliya (1238–1325 AD), a very prominent Sufi saint of the Chishti order, defined service to humanity as the *raison d'etre* of religion. He thought of fulfillment of rituals as obligatory and service to humanity as supererogatory (*nawafil* that bring one closer to God).[76] This spirit of service to all, regardless of caste, creed, religion or gender, was the motto that defined early Sufism in India and played such a major role in the spread of Islam. In a sound tradition, Prophet Muhammad (pbuh) says, "you will not enter paradise until you love one another, spread peace and beware of hatred.[77]" The following verse captures the essence of the idea of service to humanity as service to God while linking them both to *Ihsan*:

وَٱعۡبُدُواْ ٱللَّهَ وَلَا تُشۡرِكُواْ بِهِۦ شَيۡـًٔا ۖ وَبِٱلۡوَٰلِدَيۡنِ إِحۡسَـٰنًا

وَبِذِى ٱلۡقُرۡبَىٰ وَٱلۡيَتَـٰمَىٰ وَٱلۡمَسَـٰكِينِ وَٱلۡجَارِ ذِى ٱلۡقُرۡبَىٰ

وَٱلۡجَارِ ٱلۡجُنُبِ وَٱلصَّاحِبِ بِٱلۡجَنۢبِ وَٱبۡنِ ٱلسَّبِيلِ وَمَا

مَلَكَتۡ أَيۡمَـٰنُكُمۡ ۗ إِنَّ ٱللَّهَ لَا يُحِبُّ مَن كَانَ مُخۡتَالًا فَخُورًا

---

[74] See Imam Nawawi's *Arbaeen*, #13.

[75] Md. Sirajul Islam, "Civil Society, Solidarity and Social Reformation in the Sufi Perspective," Antonio F. Perez, Semou Pathe Gueye and Fenggang Yang, eds., *Civil Society as Democratic Practice* (Washington, DC: The Council for Research in Values and Philosophy, 2005), p. 236.

[76] See Amir Hasan Sijzi, *Nizamuddin Awliya: Morals of the Heart*, trans. Bruce B. Lawrence (New York: Paulist Press, 1992), pp. 10–11.

[77] See *Al-Adab Al-Mufrad* #260.

> *Serve Allah, and join not any partners with Him; and do* Ihsan *to parents, kinsfolk, orphans, those in need, neighbors who are near, neighbors who are strangers, the companion by your side, the wayfarer (ye meet), and what your right hands possess: For Allah does not love the arrogant, and the boastful.* (Quran 4:36)

Making Love a Societal Virtue

Clearly love of humanity is essential to achieving the state of *Ihsan*. But how does one translate this into a public philosophy? The task is arduous. For centuries now, Muslim orthodoxy has privileged a life of rituals and ritual devotions have become the core of Muslim religious life. It will take a global movement to transform the idea of religiosity as service to humanity. Nothing less than a revival and reform of Sufism can accomplish this challenging task. But in smaller, more educated Muslim communities in the West, where there is also no immediate hope of Muslims coming to power and establishing Islamic states and *Shariah* law, Muslims could be persuaded to carve a niche for themselves as the minority that cares, serves and loves everyone.

Muslim states and societies, especially those that have more developed civil societies and long Sufi heritage like Turkey, Morocco, Egypt, Iran, India, Oman and Pakistan, can advocate a culture of volunteerism. Like military service, perhaps even make a couple of years of social service or *Khidmat-e-Khalq* a mandatory service for all youth or at least give those who volunteer privileges to make it attractive. In the United States, there are many such opportunities for people to serve—Peace Corps, Teach for America, the National Guard, all provide citizens a way to serve their fellow citizens and also benefit from it.[78] There are volunteer movements in the Muslim world whose explicit goal is to gain closeness to God by service to humanity. The Gulen movement, for example, before it got embroiled in politics, was based on this philosophy of service as worship but with a nationalist twist. Indeed, it is also known as the *Hizmet* movement, which is Turkish for service (*Khidmat*).[79] There are social service movements in India that explicitly seek to realize the philosophy of *Khidmat-e-Khalq*. What we need to do is to globalize them, make service as valued and

---

[78] Charles S. Clark, *The New Volunteerism: Is America poised for a surge in good works?* (Washington, DC: Congressional Quarterly, Incorporated, 1996).

[79] M. Hakan Yavuz, *Toward an Islamic Enlightenment: The Gülen Movement* (New York: Oxford University Press, 2013).

desirable as is worship and make Muslims take pride in service as they do in their ritual devotions especially in the month of Ramadan. It will require a sea change in attitudes but the pursuit of *Ihsan* demands nothing less.[80]

HUSN|BEAUTY

إن الله جميل يحب الجمال

Allah is beautiful and he loves beauty.[81]

Both the Quran and the prophetic traditions remind us that God loves those who do beautiful things (Quran 2:195). The theme of beauty, about the beauty of God, of his creation, and his expectations that his vicegerent on earth, the human being, will perform beautiful deeds proliferates everywhere in the Quran, in the traditions and in Muslim history. Many Muslims have taken to heart the prophetic saying that "God is beautiful and he loves beautiful things" and have gone about doing extraordinarily beautiful things in the world. There are four areas of Islamic aesthetics that I want to highlight in this section, whose sole purpose is to make the simple point that any society that seeks virtue must not ignore beauty. Not only is beauty a virtue by itself, it also makes other virtues more beautiful.

The four areas of aesthetics that I find remarkable about the Islamic world are architecture, calligraphy, mystical poetry and *Aqlaq* (manners). Islamic calligraphy is very sophisticated and breathtaking. It, along with Persian and Indian miniatures, is the most famous art form of the Islamic world. Because of theological strictures, Muslim artists have focused more on inanimate art and because of their spiritual leaning combined spirituality with art to produce the beautiful calligraphy that we now behold. Architecture too has been inspired and shaped by Islamic ethos and so we see that the best forms of architecture are mosques and Sufi lodges and

---

[80] I was happy to note that the Jamaat-e-Islami of India has published several books and pamphlets on the concept of *Khidmat-e-Khalq*. There are many charities operating in the Indian subcontinent with that name.

[81] Reported in the collection *Sahih Muslim* #91. Also see M. A. Muqtedar Khan, "God is Beautiful and He Loves Beauty," in *The Huffington Post*, July 25, 2012. http://www.huffingtonpost.com/muqtedar-khan/god-is-beautiful-and-he-loves-beauty_b_1692400.html.

tombs of royalty and saints. I have neither the aptitude nor the desire here to describe Islamic art in detail, but for those who are unfamiliar with it, I invite you to Google images with search words such as Islamic calligraphy and Islamic architecture or beautiful mosques. The results are spectacular. The astonishing Taj Mahal, the grand mosques of Istanbul, the fine tile work of Morocco, the amazing works of Isfahan—together they reveal that Islamic aesthetics does have a touch of the divine.

I am an avid consumer of and occasional contributor to Islamic mystical poetry. In nearly every Muslim language and especially in Persian, Arabic, Urdu and Turkish, mystical poetry has thrived and reached sublime heights. Whether you are reading Rumi or Ghalib, Hafez or Amir Khusroe, Sheikh Saa'di or Sheikh Ibn Arabi, it is impossible to not have your heart melt at the manner in which these great poets have invoked the greatness of God and expressed their love and submission to him. Muslim poetry about Prophet Muhammad (pbuh) too is a spiritual genre capable of taking the audience to heights of ecstasy that simulates divine union. Whether we look at the artwork in the domes of the grand mosques or listen to the delicacy of thought and depth of love in poetry, immerse in the haunting and deeply moving recitations of the Quran and calls for prayers (*Azan*), or simply behold a calligraphic rendering of the Quran—the manifestations of *Ihsan* are inescapable.

Prophet Muhammad (pbuh) has on numerous occasions spoken about the importance of humility, gentleness, kindness, compassion and tolerance in interpersonal communications and dealings. In a famous tradition, he says, "*I have been sent to perfect good character.*[82]" The hadith collections have a vast number of similar traditions that encourage politeness, patience, generosity and good conduct. This element in the Muslim culture has fostered what is known as *Husn-e-Akhlaq*, beautiful character or manners, and shows itself in the manner in which children respect their parents, people deal with their neighbors, foster family values and show generosity and boundless hospitality toward strangers and guests. The advent of modernity has dented this aspect of Islamic aesthetics, but it still remains strong and can be strengthened further to develop civil society, civility and a mutual-help culture based on social bonds.

In a tradition, Prophet Muhammad (pbuh) informs us that God is kind and he loves kindness in all things. In yet another tradition, he tells us "Where there is softness it beautifies that thing and from which it is taken

---

[82] Found in Imam Malik's Hadith collection *Al-Muwatta* #1614.

away it snatches its glamor." In this tradition, the relationship between beauty and softness is emphasized. In a more telling tradition, the Prophet makes it clear that "One who is devoid of kindness is devoid of the good of every kind." All the traditions that I have discussed here are well known and well accepted. They are from *Riyadh al-Saleheen*,[83] which has a whole chapter on beautiful conduct. The Quran too exhorts the believer to be gentle, kind and to adopt manners that are soft, beautiful and fair even when one is engaged in debate.

The most powerful statement on the inherent *Ihsan* that God expects in human interaction is articulated in:

وَلَا تَسْتَوِى ٱلْحَسَنَةُ وَلَا ٱلسَّيِّئَةُ ۚ ٱدْفَعْ بِٱلَّتِى هِىَ

أَحْسَنُ فَإِذَا ٱلَّذِى بَيْنَكَ وَبَيْنَهُۥ عَدَٰوَةٌ كَأَنَّهُۥ وَلِىٌّ حَمِيمٌ

And not equal are the good deed and the bad. Repel [evil] by that [deed] which is better; and thereupon the one who, between you and him is enmity [will become] as though he was a devoted friend. (Quran 41:34)

This verse is often used by Muslim preachers to emphasize the importance of good deeds as instruments of reconciliation. It is the first principle of peacemaking in Islam. The best way to win the heart of those who might despise you or hate you is not only not to respond to evil with evil, but to respond to evil with good. This is *Ihsan*, to do good to even those who might do harm to you. If this virtue becomes a founding pillar of social interaction, then not only will it facilitate harmonious relations but also become the basis for resolving social conflicts and longstanding perceptions of victimization or injustice. As with many such virtues, it too is often the adornment in sermons but not found in institutionalized practices of society.

The late Sufi folk singer Nusrat Fateh Ali Khan (1948–1997) became famous for singing Sufi mystical songs (*Qawwali*)[84], and one of the themes of one of his most famous *Qawwali* in the Urdu language is wishing good for those who wish you evil. I end this section on beauty with a few verses

[83] Imam Al-Nawawi, *Riyadh –al-Saleheen*, trans. S. M. Madani Abbas (Riyadh, Saudi Arabia: International Islamic Publishing House, 2002), pp. 354–357.

[84] Regula Qureshi, *Sufi music of India and Pakistan. sound, context, and meaning in Qawwali* (London: Cambridge University Press, 1986).

from this Sufi *Qawwali* that captures two aspects of the aesthetics of *Ihsan*—poetry and good will.

> *Tera Naam lu zubaan se tere aage sar jhuka doon*
> *Mera ishq kehraha hai, mai tujhe Quda bana loo*
>
> *Teri dillagi ke sadqe tere sangdili pe qurban*
> *Mere gham pe hasne wale tujhe kaunsi dua doon*
>
> I chant your name and I bow before you
> My love commands me that I take you as God
>
> For your love I sacrifice my self to your stone heartedness
> You who laughs at my sorrow, what should I pray for you

This very popular *Qawwali* truly captures the spirit of *Ihsan*.[85] The poet is singing with joy, Oh you who laughs at my misery I pray for you.

MERCY|RAHMAH

My mercy encompasses all things. (Quran 7:156)

If there was one concept that summarizes the essence of Islam it is *Rahmah*—mercy. In the Quran, God repeatedly (114 times) describes himself as the Most Merciful and Most Compassionate, *Al-Rahman* and *Al-Raheem*. While the Quran itself recognizes 99 attributes and names of God, these are the names dearest to God himself. The dominant divine self-perception is that of The Compassionate and The Merciful. The first verse in the Quran (Quran 1:1) is *In the name of Allah, the Most Merciful the Most Compassionate*. This is how Allah wishes to be known. The significance is not lost when it is repeated in the third verse. The first chapter of the Quran, *Al-Fatiha*, is the spiritual heart and the essence of the divine message and without it every prayer is incomplete and it is described as the most often-repeated verse in creation. And in these seven verses that constitute the core of the Quran, God uses two of them to emphasize his

---

[85] This *Qawwali* can be heard on the YouTube here: https://www.youtube.com/watch?v=vN4v4PYgRd4.

mercy and his compassion. God's will to be recognized and acknowledged as Merciful and Compassionate runs across the divine message, invoking many times his unlimited forgiveness and boundless compassion. His benevolence—which enables creation, life and existence—his self-disclosure itself is indicative of his mercy.

According to a very widely known and oft-mentioned tradition, reported by both *Sahih Bukhari* and *Sahih Muslim*, Allah makes a profound promise to Himself before He creates creation—*inna rahmati ghalabath ghadbi*—"My mercy shall prevail over my wrath." This authentic tradition, much treasured by Sufis and constitutive of Islamic mystical thought, is harbinger of good tidings to all, that in the final analysis, Allah is above all Most Merciful and this nature of His will prevail over all His other attributes, including his retribution. This compassion of God moreover is unlimited. None shall despair for his mercy indeed encompasses all things (Quran 7:156). Elsewhere in the Quran, Allah addresses those who disobeyed his laws and sinned as follows:

قُلْ يَٰعِبَادِىَ ٱلَّذِينَ أَسْرَفُوا۟ عَلَىٰٓ أَنفُسِهِمْ لَا تَقْنَطُوا۟ مِن رَّحْمَةِ ۞ ٱللَّهِ ۚ إِنَّ ٱللَّهَ يَغْفِرُ ٱلذُّنُوبَ جَمِيعًا ۚ إِنَّهُۥ هُوَ ٱلْغَفُورُ ٱلرَّحِيمُ

Say, "O My servants who have transgressed against themselves [by sinning] do not despair of the mercy of Allah. Indeed, Allah forgives all sins. Indeed, it is He who is the forgiving and the Merciful." (Quran 39:53)

In the Quran, both the Messenger of God and the message of God are described as mercy. In verse 17:82, the Quran is described as "*Shifa*," healing, and "*Rahmah*," mercy for the believers. And in 21:107, Prophet Muhammad (pbuh) himself is described as mercy to all the worlds. Traditional commentators have understood this verse to mean that Prophet Muhammad (pbuh) has been sent as mercy to all beings including the animal and plant kingdoms.

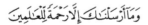

And we have not sent you [O Muhammad], except as mercy to all the worlds.

He is mercy to all because he has come as a messenger from the Most Merciful with the promise of mercy. He was the medium for the divine message and divine revelation and on the Day of Judgment, he will with God's permission intercede on behalf of humanity for God's mercy (Quran 2:255, 20:109). It is through him that we connect with the divine. Unfortunately Islamic orthodoxy often emphasizes a legalistic view of right and wrong and heaven and hell, leading to a legalistic orientation that often ends up portraying God as a wrathful deity that will punish rather than a merciful creator whose defining attribute is compassion.

Allah is also *Al-Ghafur* (Forgiver) and *Al-Afuww* (Pardoner) and often both these attributes appear in conjunction with each other. Indeed Allah is pardoning and forgiving (Quran 4: 99, 22:60, 58:2). Islamic sources, both the Quran and hadith, in many ways emphasize how forgiving God is. Indeed in 73 verses, both these attributes are combined to describe Allah as *Ghafurur Raheem*, Forgiving and Merciful (e.g. see 5:3, 4:152, 4:106). Witnessing God's forgiveness and mercy is *Ihsan*. There are innumerable traditions on forgiveness as they are on mercy but this *Hadith Qudsi* captures divine forgiveness in all its *husn* (beauty).

> *Allah the Exalted said: O son of Adam, if you call upon me and place your hope in me, I will forgive you without any reservation. O son of Adam, if you have sins piling up to the clouds and then ask for my forgiveness, I will forgive you without any reservation. O son of Adam, if you come to me with enough sins to fill the earth and you meet me without associating a partner with me, I will come to you with enough forgiveness to fill the earth.*[86]

Forgiveness is undoubtedly an important element of mercy. While divine mercy is about God's benevolence, compassion and forgiveness, human mercy, which does not include God's benevolence but can to some extent replicate forgiveness, has an alternate element and that is *Sadaqah* or charity. *Sadaqah* must be understood separate from *Zakat*, one of the five pillars of Islam. *Zakat* is a religious obligation and the refusal to pay it might jeopardize a believer's legal status as a believer, but *Sadaqah* is charity or charitable acts performed over and beyond the obligatory.

In an authentic tradition, both forgiveness and charity are connected. *Sahih Muslim* (#2588) reports that "Charity does not decrease wealth, no one forgives another except that Allah increases his honor, and no one humbles himself for the sake of Allah except that Allah raises his status." This tradition treats both forgiveness and charity as similar.

---

[86] Sunan Al-Tirmidhi, 3540.

Like that tradition, a verse in the Quran ties forgiveness, charity and mercy together, in a way completely defining the concept of mercy.

> *Do they not know that Allah accepts repentance from His servants and receives the charities, and that Allah is the Oft-forgiving, the most Merciful?* (Quran 9:104)

Additionally, the Quran insists that those who give charity do not use it to remind or chide or insult the beneficiary (2:254, 2:264); it is displeasing to God and in God's eyes nullifies the virtue of charity. *Ihsan* is not only to give charity but also to maintain the ethics of charity. It is supposed to help and assist without depriving the beneficiaries of their inherent dignity. Most of what I have written here about God's mercy in essence can be distilled from the teachings of Sufi saints and other mystical scholars. The key question however remains, how do we translate this into public policy? What would a public philosophy that is based on mercy be like?

Conservative politicians like President George W. Bush in the United States and Prime Minister David Cameron in the United Kingdom have used the idea of "compassionate conservatism" to suggest that compassion plays a role in shaping their public policy.[87] While intuitively it might suggest that finally conservatives have recognized the lack of compassion in their pro-market politics, what they meant was that they believed conservatism was indeed good for the poor and the left behind. The idea exists but was not very compelling. Nevertheless, I think it is important for social harmony that compassion plays a role in public policy.

There are many areas in which a *culture of giving and forgiving* can be inculcated. Forgiveness of loans, of protracted punishments, compassion for first-time offenders are all good public policies. A tax system that not only encourages but rewards charity and a social system that rewards and holds sacrifice, service and charitable acts in great esteem can be easily nurtured. We live in a consumer age in which self-worth is measured through accumulation of wealth and goods. What we need is reversal or deconstruction of this culture of materialized self-worth and a move toward a public narrative that valorizes those who give and forgive and not those who accumulate and

---

[87] Jesse Norman, and Jana Ganesh, "Compassionate Conservatism," *London: Policy Exchange* (2006).

hoard. We need to appreciate not just self-worth but also the worth of others as equal to self. As Prophet Muhammad (pbuh) said, "you are incomplete until you desire for others what you desire for yourself." Ultimately it is the Quran that inspires mercy by promising that indeed the mercy of God is with those who do *Ihsan* (7:56).

$$ إِنَّ رَحْمَتَ ٱللَّهِ قَرِيبٌ مِّنَ ٱلْمُحْسِنِينَ $$

Indeed the Mercy of Allah is near those who do beautiful things (Ihsan).

IHSAN AS EPISTEMOLOGY|MAA'RIFAH

Knowledge of God is essential to achieving *Ihsan*. Indeed to be in a state of *Ihsan* is to be in a state of such acute awareness of the divine presence that it is as if one is actually seeing God. After all, the purpose of God's self-disclosure or creation of the creation and in it a sentient being capable of knowing is so that He is known. Remember the famous tradition we have already discussed—*I was a hidden treasure, I wanted to be known, therefore I created creation.* One may know him directly or one may know him through the knowledge of the self. According to a hadith, the Prophet said, "*man arafa nafsahu faqad 'arafa Rabbahu,* Whosoever knows himself knows his Lord." While mystical practices have made the awareness of God a phenomenological issue especially in the popular form of Sufism through remembrance rituals (*Zikr*), *Ihsan* is also a state of knowledge and not just a state of being. I submit that *Ihsan* contains, if not constitutes, an epistemology in itself. It is both a *state of being* and a *state of knowing*. It is a theory of knowledge and a theory of existence at the same time. Both epistemology and ontology in one idea.

Chittick writes in *The Sufi Path of Knowledge*, "God's self-disclosure appears in two modes—ontological and cognitive, or as existence and knowledge..." He is explaining the way Ibn Arabi, the Andalusian Sufi master, often sees *being* and *finding* existence and knowledge as the same.[88] Mystical pursuit of knowledge is driven by three core principles—one that there is a God, two that the purpose of existence is to know God and three that the knowledge of God can be had only as a blessing of God, who reveals Himself to his servant through His light or self-disclosure.

---

[88] See William Chittick, *The Sufi Path of Knowledge*, p. 212.

While most mystical practitioners do not have an explicit theory of knowledge or a developed discourse on epistemology, the works of mystical scholars like Ibn Arabi and Al-Ghazali, to just name two, have left enough source material to recognize and articulate the highly sophisticated understanding of epistemology that underpins Islamic mysticism. One would not be entirely off the mark if one asserted that *Ilm Al-Tasawwuf*, the science of mysticism, is basically a theory of knowledge of the divine (gnosis) with its own methods and means of verification and authentication of findings. I will resist the strong temptation to immerse in a lengthy discussion of this knowledge form known as gnosis (*ma'rifah*)—the epistemology of *Ihsan*—primarily because that is not the goal of this book and others have already done a better job than I can do here. Mehdi H. Yazdi in *The Principles of Epistemology in Islamic Philosophy: Knowledge by Presence*, Syed Hussain Nasr in *Knowledge and the Sacred*, William Chittick in *The Sufi Path of Knowledge*, Ibrahim Kalin in *Knowledge in Later Islamic Philosophy*, Omid Safi in *The Politics of Knowledge in Premodern Islam* are some contemporary scholars who have all explored the concept of knowledge in Islamic mystical thought. There are many ways of knowing the Divine and *Ihsan* is a state of knowing the divine and being with the divine and that is the main point I want to make here.

There are various levels of knowing. The most common characterization is the three levels of certainty that nearly all mystical orders subscribe to—*Ilm Al-Yaqeen* (certainty based on knowledge), *Ayn Al-Yaqeen* (certainty based on seeing) and *Haqq Al-Yaqeen* (certainty based on experience or reality or unity with the divine). According to the epistemology of *Ihsan*, different methodologies lead to different levels of certainty and *Ihsan* is the highest form of certainty. The two most important principles of mystical epistemology are as follows: first, reason and scientific methods are not sufficient to reach *Haq Al-Yaqeen*, and second, true knowledge of The Real (*Al-Haq*) is bestowed as a divine disclosure, revelation or opening to the seeker by divine grace and mercy. And when one is blessed with such mercy only then one reaches the station where one knows the Creator and His creation. According to a *Hadith Qudsi* much cherished by Islamic mystics, when God loves someone, He becomes his ears, his eyes, his tongue and his hands: "When I love him, then I shall be his ears with which he listens, his eyes with which he sees, his tongue with which he speaks, and his hands with which he holds; if he calls Me, I shall answer him, and if he asks Me, I shall give him." When one is in a state of *Ihsan*, one knows God and His names, and this creation is just a manifestation of

His essence. Thus, *Ihsan* is also an epistemology, a way of knowing the ultimate truth and the many truths that it encompasses. A Sufi master in Chicago while encouraging me to write this book said, "when God loves you my son, he shares his secrets with you, so as you set out to write this book, first earn his love."

The essence of *Ihsan* as epistemology is often derived by Sufis from the verse about allegories (*Mutashabihaat*) in the Quran.

> *He it is Who has sent down to thee the Book:*
> *In it are verses basic and clear; they are the foundation of the Book: others are allegorical. But those in whose hearts is perversity follow the part thereof that is allegorical, seeking discord, and searching for its hidden meanings, but no one knows its hidden meanings except Allah. And those who are firmly grounded in knowledge say: "We believe in the Book; the whole of it is from our Lord:" and none will grasp the Message except men of understanding.*
> (Quran 3:7)

This verse has profound implication for understanding the Quran in general and to the mystics in particular. Both Al-Qushayri and Al-Tustari understand that the Quran possesses both exoteric and esoteric meanings and while the former are clear and are the foundational principles of the faith, the latter are hidden in allegories. The spiritual and allegorical truth can only be comprehended and received by those who have achieved *Ihsan* and have purified their hearts. This knowledge is obtained directly from God through inspiration (*Ilham*) or spiritual awareness (*Irfan*) or through mystical awakening and opening (*Ilm Al-Ladunni*). In essence, it means that esoteric knowledge is not a function of learning or product of rational research methodology but a byproduct of spiritual condition (*haal*). At different spiritual levels, you comprehend different levels of truth and, in the state of *Ihsan*, one is blessed with *Haqq Al-Yaqeen*.

The Quran clearly recognizes the possibility of multiple meanings and multiple understanding and also acknowledges that some interpretations are better than others. It goes further and commands Muslims to extract the best understanding from the sacred texts (*ahsanuhu*). In chapter Al-Zumar, we find a very fascinating verse that says:

> *Those who listen to the Word, and follow the best (meaning) in it:*
> *those are the ones whom Allah has guided, and those are the ones endowed with understanding.* (Quran 39:18)

This one verse is an interpretive philosophy in itself. Even when you encounter sacred sources, interpret them in a state of *Ihsan*—take the most beautiful meaning from them. This idea is also repeated in verse 7:145, which states that the Torah was revealed to Moses and commands his people to take the (*ahsanuha*) best from it and act upon it. Maulana Mufti Muhammad Shafi, in his exegetical discussion of 39:18, not only confirms the meaning that I am giving to this verse but also states that this was the understanding of many including Ibn Kathir and Ashraf Ali Thanvi.[89]

Epistemology and Public Policy

Does how we construct knowledge inform how we make public policy? The answer to this difficult question is yes. If ideology can inform both political structure and public policy, then so can epistemology. Politics in a democracy with competing political parties and perspectives is premised on the belief that ideas can shape reality. Epistemology is a paradigm or essentially a complex idea and we know that ideas do impact reality, human behavior and choices, and constitute society. For thousands of years, humans have labored to articulate ethical philosophies and normative paradigms, not to mention nurture religious traditions. The goal was always to produce a common public good by cultivating choices and actions informed by normative values.

Ihsan too can and should inform public policy. The ontological understanding of existence as unfolding of divine mercy and the epistemology of understanding this mercy makes the pursuit of power, wealth and prestige seem trivial. The nothingness of human individuality in contrast with the majesty and infinity of the divine redefines the purpose of society as an enabler of the discovery of The Real (*Al-Haqq*). Discovering the divine truth and witnessing good in the constitution of society involve *erring on the side of compassion* while making laws and policies. While this is not a venue to discuss specific policies in detail, one can apprehend my point by comparing it to the American criminal justice system, which errs on the side of the offender in order to not risk punishing the innocent, also

---

[89] See Maulana Mufti Muhammad Shafi, *Ma'riful Qur'an*, Vol. 7 (Karachi: Maktaba-e-Darul-Uloom, 2003), pp. 554–555.

known as *Blackstone's Formulation*.[90] While there may be many flaws and biases in how it is executed, the principle in essence is informed by *Ihsan*. Thus, policies that seek to address illegal immigration can also err on the side of amnesty, just as those that deal with loan defaults by the poor can err on the side of forgiveness. Once the population is educated in the meaning and virtues of *Ihsan*, it will not be difficult to develop a society that aspires to institutionalize compassion.

COMPLETE SUBMISSION|*FANAA*

Mutu, qabla anta mutu.
Die before you die.

Ihsan is that state in which one serves the creation and worships the Creator as if one is seeing God. But while this understanding of *Ihsan* describes what *Ihsan* is, it does not fully convey what the consequence of *Ihsan* is and what happens when one is in a state as if one is seeing God. That state is understood by Sufis as the state of *Fanaa*—complete submission of the self to the divine. When one beholds the divine in His entire glory, what else is there to see, remember or know. The entire creation is His creation. He alone is the true reality; everything else exists by His virtue. Nothing precedes Him or matters and, in the light of His being, everything else pales into nonexistence. How can the beholder retain his or her sense of the self or of being when in the presence of the Creator? There is nothing else from infinity to infinity except Allah and even though the seeker beholds Him, he is in such a state of submission that it is like adding a drop to the ocean and the drop completely disappears—*Fanaa fi Allah*—is annihilated in Allah.

Thus, the consequence of achieving *Ihsan* is a moment of such submission, such union with True Being (*Al-Hayy*), True Reality (*Al-Haqq*) that the seeker ceases to exist and is annihilated in his or her self and now remains only in union with God—*Baqa fi Allah*. In a rather curious way, both Muslim contentions that one can see God and that one cannot see God are true in the state of *Fanaa*. One witnesses the One but before one can do that, one submits and completely surrenders the self to the point of nonexistence and, in this state, one sees with eyes of the divine (recall the tradition When God loves someone he sees with God's eyes, listens with

---

[90] Vidar Halvorsen, "Is it better that ten guilty persons go free than that one innocent person be convicted?," *Criminal Justice Ethics* 23.2 (2004): 3–13.

God's ears and so forth), and thus in a way, only God sees Himself since the seeker who is *Fanaa fi Allah* does not exist but in Allah. This is the ultimate moment of simultaneous selflessness and fulfillment, in a way that only mystics can articulate. The idea of annihilation in God is articulated as to "die before one dies." This paradoxical statement actually calls for one to pass away into God before one passes away from this world.

Both Schimmel and Chittick have explained the meaning of *Fanaa* with references to the classical masters of *Tasawwuf* and I owe them a great debt as I began my efforts to understand Fana through their works. Here I want to share the two definitions of *Fanaa* advanced by the classical scholar Al-Qushayri in his *Epistle on Sufism*. He describes *Fanaa* as die in God and *Baqa'a* as subsisting in God after being annihilated in God. In fact, he describes *Fanaa* as triple death and cites a Sufi poet to make his point. In the first instance, the seeker loses his self or his attributes and subsists with divine attributes. In the second death, the seeker loses even the divine attributes and survives only through love of God and then finally he dies and is subsumed in God and subsists in Him. He quotes an unknown Sufi poet who says[91]:

> *Some people wander across the land by the desert*
> *While others wander in the arena of his love*
> *Annihilate yourself thrice*
> *And subsist close to the Lord.*

Fanaa, understood as mystical death, may be difficult to discuss in political and practical terms. However, Al-Qushayri also provides a simpler and indeed more operational definition of *Fanaa*. He defines *Fanaa* as the disappearance of blameworthy qualities and the appearance or ascendance of praiseworthy qualities. Essentially, the good in the soul prevails over the evil, and the seeker becomes a *Muhsin*, a doer of beautiful deeds. So how do we combine both the manifestation of good character and the annihilation of the self so that it can become the basis for public policy?

Society Where Others Matter

وَيُؤْثِرُونَ عَلَىٰٓ أَنفُسِهِمْ

And prefer others to themselves. (Quran 59:9)

---

[91] Al-Qushayri, *Epistle on Sufism*, p. 91.

I submit that the best way to achieve *Fanaa* is in a community setting and not in the state of ascetic retreat that mystics sometimes achieve. By privileging other-regarding behavior and politics over self-regarding politics, we can achieve *Fanaa* in this world. Politics and often public policy are driven by the self-interest of dominant political actors and forces. Enlightened societies try to advance the idea of a "common good," a shared interest that advances the interest of all in the society. But often what really transpires is that the very idea of common good is essentially partisan interests of the dominant forces in the society articulated in the form of common interests. Surely in deliberative democracy and in free societies, the idea of the common good can be debated and the underlying vested and partisan interests can be exposed. But exposing vested interests is one thing and eliminating the impact of these forces is quite another.

But if in a society there are many who pursue *Ihsan*, those who have reached some degree of *Fanaa*, then we have a possibility of politics in which the activist engages the public sphere not in the pursuit of self-interest but in the interests of others, standing up for the marginalized and the powerless, struggling for social justice and for advancing not just some version of common good but the interests of the most vulnerable and the oppressed. Critics might suggest that there are already social movements and groups that are indeed engaging in such politics, and they will be right. They are indeed those who are in the state of *Ihsan*. While one can find many examples of selfless dedication to service today in every society, traditional Muslim societies were often anchored by the selfless services provided by mystical orders and mystics.

For centuries, before the colonial experience and the subsequent modern revivalist Islamic movements undermined the role of Sufi Islam in much of the Muslim world, Sufi orders and Sufi Sheikhs played a very important role in Muslim societies. There was the Sultan and his authority. He maintained order and the people obeyed him in matters concerning this world. And then there was the Sufi master, the Sheikh, who had his own charismatic appeal and spiritual authority and he was the guide and master as the believer walked the path behind the master to the other world. The two authorities together constituted a premodern version of the modern state and society.

This premodern society was infused with Sufi values and led by Sufi virtues. While the sultans advanced the interests of the dynasties they belonged to and built their legacies with grand architectural projects or conquests, the Sufi masters lived lives that exemplified self-sacrifice. They shared wealth and accumulated nothing. They built bridges of love and service, opened their doors for all—the poor or the rich, the powerful or the weak—none were turned away. Sometimes they guided temporal authority and at other times they stood up to its excesses. While the sultans built empires of power, the Sufi masters build empires of piety filled with love and spirituality. They were repositories of knowledge and centers of the social, cultural and spiritual lives of their society. These Sufi Sheikhs, through their negation of self-interests, advanced the spiritual and sometimes even material interests of the subaltern. Through their example, they taught how a society can be nurtured where the elite pursue the interests of others.

The verse of the Quran with which we began this section (59:9) refers to the citizens of Madinah who embraced Prophet Muhammad (pbuh) and his fellow migrants from Mecca with open arms and open hearts. The Quran praises them for loving the others and sharing with them even at the risk of self-deprivation. The verse ends with—*wa man yuqa shuhha nafsihi faulaaika humu almuflihoon*—Those who transcend self-interest and saves their souls from it, will be among those who are successful. Allah says in the Quran that ultimately everything will perish (*Fanaa*), and what will remain (*Baqaa*) is the glorious and majestic face of your Lord (Quran 55:26–27).

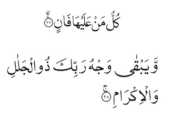

CHAPTER 6

Islamic Political Philosophy:
A Critical Genealogy

Say, "O Allah, Owner of Sovereignty, You give sovereignty to whom You will and You take sovereignty away from whom You will." (Quran 3:26)

In this chapter, I propose to provide a critical reading of the history of Islamic political thought. I am not seeking to provide a comprehensive account of every important political thinker or trend in the 1400 plus years of Islamic history; such a project would necessarily be encyclopedic and some very competent scholars have already attempted that with reasonable success.[1] My goal here is to identify the *different iconic perspectives and approaches* that Islamic thinkers have adopted in their efforts to conceptualize and study politics and governance, power and authority, and provide a summary and a critique of their work in order to show the diversity of thought and plurality of approaches within the umbrella that can be properly called as Islamic political philosophy.

Islamic political philosophy and thought, as I have argued elsewhere, remains an underdeveloped and understudied subject,[2] especially among practicing Muslims. It is only lately that we have seen a spike in the

---

[1] See Antony Black, *History of Islamic Political Thought: From the Prophet to the Present: From the Prophet to the Present* (Edinburgh University Press, 2011).

[2] See M. A. Muqtedar Khan, "The political philosophy of Islamic resurgence," *Cultural Dynamics* 13.2 (2001): 211–229.

© The Author(s) 2019
M. A. M. Khan, *Islam and Good Governance*,
https://doi.org/10.1057/978-1-137-54832-0_6

academic interest in Islamic political thought as scholars have sought to understand the conceptual origins and historical context of the role of Islam in politics and the language of political Islam with the rise of many Islamic agencies—states such as Iran, movements such as the Muslim Brotherhood, militant groups such as Al-Qaeda, quasi-governing bodies like Hamas in Gaza and radical state entities like *Daesh* (Islamic State) operating on the stage of world politics. It is my contention that the rapid development of Islamic law and its canonization as divine law had marginalized and subordinated all other branches of Islamic knowledge. Islam and *Shariah* are often equated as one and the same and therefore knowledge of Islam has become synonymous with knowledge of Islamic *Shariah*. Islamic disciplines and epistemes that do not deal with legal issues specifically are often treated as marginal, trivial or even unnecessary distractions. I have pointed this out in the earlier chapters of this book and argued that this is one of the reasons why applied knowledge of *Ihsan* was so sparse. The same is unfortunately true of Islamic political philosophy which too remains underdeveloped, dwarfed by the significance attached to law and the study of law by Muslims.[3]

Most practicing Muslims are more concerned with Islamic legal rulings that deal with daily mundane issues than with political philosophy. This may be the case because for many Muslims political philosophical issues are "settled" and they are merely concerned with immediate challenges. Many Muslims live either in societies transitioning to democracy and hence are more concerned with elements of democratic theory or in non-Islamic authoritarian regimes and have little opportunity to participate in discussions that are about fundamental principles or political philosophy. Those who live in so-called Islamic states do not have the freedom to advance a critical perspective. Islamic scholars and intellectuals until the advent of modernity did not feel the need to revisit what they considered settled issues in Islamic political philosophy. The Muslim community was the *Ummah*, it was governed by a *Caliph*, who ruled them by the revealed *Shariah* law as articulated by the Ulema (legal scholars) using the process of *Shura* (consultative governance). The changes that needed to be addressed were addressed through *Ijtihad* within the legal schools. That was it, a consensual, settled and rarely contested political paradigm.

---

[3] M. A. Muqtedar Khan, "The Political Philosophy of Islamic Resurgence," *Cultural Dynamics* 13.2 (2001): 211–229. Abdullahi A. An-Na'im, *Islam and the secular state: Negotiating the future of Sharia* (Harvard University Press, 2009).

Until the advent of modernity, Islamic political thought developed episodically and often minimally, usually driven by a political crisis that also involved religious elements. New ideas emerged only in response to crisis of legitimacy and not as an ongoing response to the needs for good governance. The crystallization of the theory of Caliphate by Al-Mawardi (it will be discussed in greater detail in the section about Al-Mawardi) was in response to the decline of the power of the Abbasid Caliphs in relation to other emerging tribal warlords.[4] But with the challenge of modernity one witnessed an explosion in Islamic political thinking and we witnessed the emergence of a new chapter in Islamic political thought as Muslim thinkers began to shift their level of analysis from empire to state, from Caliphate to Islamic state.[5] My critical review of Islamic political thought will therefore be in two parts. The first part will explore *key thinkers* representing major trends in the premodern period when Islam was more or less dominant and the second part will explore *key theories* representing important trends in Islamic political thought as it struggles to respond to the dual challenges posed by modernity and the rise of the politically and intellectually powerful modern West. In the past, I have employed this rupture in the development of Islamic thought to identify the different theories of authority and state that have been developed under the rubric of Islam.[6]

The critical perspective of Islamic political thought that I seek to offer here is from the point of view of *Ihsan*. This perspective is not as complex as other poststructural or postmodern genealogies that seek to expose complex dynamics of knowledge and power. In my genealogy of Islamic political thought, I seek to demonstrate the following:

1. There have been, in the past, several different normative and epistemological approaches to understanding and theorizing Islamic politics. There was no single Islamic political philosophy; on the contrary, there were many perspectives and traditions.
2. Modernity has caused a significant rupture in the evolution of Islamic political thinking. Many claims to authenticity by Islamist theorists notwithstanding, contemporary Islamic political thought is as modern as the modernity it rejects and despises.

[4] W. Montgomery Watt, "Islamic political thought" (1968).
[5] M. A. Muqtedar Khan, "The Political Philosophy of Islamic Resurgence," *Cultural Dynamics* 13.2 (2001): 211–229.
[6] M. A. Muqtedar Khan, "Political Authority in Islam," in Kabir Hassan and Mervyn K. Lewis, eds., *Handbook on Islam and Economy* (London: Edward Elgar Publishing Ltd., 2014).

3. There always was a mystical approach to politics in the Islamic past. I will argue that Islamic mysticism or Sufi political thought was veiled behind a form of Islamic secularity when it came to politics and also concealed in forms of poetry rather than systematic theory or philosophy. While overt Islamism has always privileged Islamic symbolism, used Islamic lexicon, trumpeted Islamic *Shariah*, mystical Islam was always more concerned with substance than form, service rather than symbolism and *Tariqah* rather than *Shariah*—the way rather than the law. The term *Shariah* actually means the way.

4. The idea of an Islamic state or Islamic governance that Muslims sought, primarily because of their desire to live in a divinely ordained order and enjoy true justice, has failed to materialize. Wherever Islamists have come to power, they have failed in their efforts to bring order, peace and justice; on the contrary, they have ushered in authoritarianism and divisions within Muslim communities and between Muslims and non-Muslims.[7]

Prologue to Political Philosophy

But before I offer my critical perspective, I will, as a prologue, touch upon two cardinal issues that serve as uncontested foundational maxims of Islamic political thought coming from traditional sources and traditional scholars. The first is the assumption that there is no separation of religion and politics in Islam and the second is the canonization of the precedence of the Rashidun Caliphs.

Islam and Secularism

I would like to explore the issue of Islam's compatibility or conformity with secularism to clarify some basic issues. The debate on Islam and secularism continues to unfold with finer and finer nuances being added to the already complex and deeply contested juxta-positioning of Islam and secularism.[8] The latest twist to the discourse is Islamic arguments for secular-

---

[7] Olivier Roy, and Carol Volk, *The failure of political Islam* (Harvard University Press, 1996). M. A. Muqtedar Khan, "Islam, Democracy and Islamism After the Counterrevolution in Egypt," *Middle East Policy* 21.1 (2014): 75–86.

[8] Abdullahi A. An-Na'im, "Islam and secularism," *Comparative secularisms in a global age* (2010): 217–28. Azzam Tamimi, and John L. Esposito, *Islam and secularism in the Middle East* (NYU Press, 2000). M. A. Muqtedar Khan, "The Myth of Secularism," in Dionne, E. J., Jean Bethke Elshtain, and Kayla Meltzer Drogosz, eds., *One Electorate Under God? A Dialogue on Religion and American Politics* (Brookings Institution Press, 2004).

ism and a rather important claim that Islam or at least Muslims do have a long history of secular political thought, which was hitherto ignored by those who saw Muslim history only through Islamist lenses.[9] But the issue of Islam's compatibility or lack thereof with secularism is a modern concern brought about by the postcolonial revival of Islamic political thought which is overshadowed and to a great extent shaped by modern Western political thought. In the premodern era, this was not a concern for Muslims. Muslims took the role of religion in both shaping the law of the land and in matters of governance as given; they were mostly concerned with the fidelity with which Islamic values were implemented or corrupted by good or bad rulers.

The Islamic-leaning historians of Islamic politics and Islamists maintain that Islamic states and societies must implement Islamic laws and values and therefore Islamic polities cannot be really secular. In the premodern era, nearly all Islamic empires, the Rashidun, the Umayyads, the Abbasids and the Ottomans, relied on using implementation of Islamic law as a legitimizing device.[10] In modern times, Iran, Saudi Arabia, Malaysia, Sudan, Afghanistan under Taliban, Pakistan under Zia al-Haq are examples of states that claimed to be Islamic and who eschew or eschewed secularism as an anathema. In recent years after Egypt gained some respite from dictatorship, the Islamist led reforms rejected the idea of a secular state opting to make Islam the official religion of the state and the constitution enshrined Islamic law as the source of the state's political values.[11] There are enough scriptural sources to defend this claim scholastically and the history of the last ten years of the life of Prophet Muhammad (pbuh) and the era of the first four Caliphs also cement the idea that secularism is not an Islamic virtue. As a result of this, both political authority and political legitimacy in Muslim kingdoms, empires and countries have primarily come from within Islamic sources.

The key to understanding the intertwining of religion and politics to the concept of political authority in Islam are the multiple roles of Prophet Muhammad (pbuh) as a religious founder, political leader, head of state and spiritual guide and his unparalleled success in establishing his religion

[9] Abdullahi A. An-Na'im, *Islam and the secular state: Negotiating the future of Sharia* (Harvard University Press, 2009), Mehrzad Boroujerdi, ed., *Mirror for the Muslim Prince: Islam and the Theory of Statecraft* (Syracuse University Press, 2013).

[10] Ira M. Lapidus, *A history of Islamic societies* (Cambridge University Press, 2014). Wael B. Hallaq, *The origins and evolution of Islamic law*, Vol. 1 (Cambridge University Press, 2005).

[11] M. A. Muqtedar Khan, "Islam, Democracy and Islamism After the Counterrevolution in Egypt," *Middle East Policy* 21.1 (2014): 75–86.

as the foundation of a state and society in a little over a decade. In 622 AD, about 12 years after he declared his prophethood, Prophet Muhammad (pbuh) migrated from Mecca to Medina and established an Islamic society and state at the invitation of the various tribes that lived in Medina (then known as *Yathrib*). His embryonic state was based on a treaty or social contract referred to as the *Dastur-Al-Madinah* (Constitution of Medina).[12] The Constitution of Medina establishes the importance of consent and cooperation for governance. According to this compact, Muslims and non-Muslims were equal citizens of Medina, with identical rights and duties. Communities with different religious orientations enjoyed religious autonomy, which amounted to essentially choice of legal system based on their religion.

This prophetic precedence has made the inseparability of religion and politics an enduring aspect of Islamic political thought and practice. The status of Muhammad (pbuh) as the Prophet of God as well as the ruler of Medina has established the significance of religion in statecraft and the role of religion in shaping the character and identity of the political community. The objective of forming a political community is also seen in terms of religious needs and religious obligations. Thus, when contemporary political theorists talk of an Islamic state they imagine it as an ideological instrument designed for the explicit purpose of advancing an Islamic religious agenda, even though the very objectives of the Islamic law (*Maqasid al-Shariah*) are widely understood as those guiding principles which enable the individual and the community to live a virtuous life in a society determined to establish social justice and public welfare, both understood according to the Islamic paradigm.[13]

Even this book assumes a fundamental relationship between religious values and principles and politics. It does not assert or conclude that secularism is necessarily superior to polities that are influenced by religious values. But it also does not advocate a regime that is theocratic in structure or run by the clergy or even designed to enforce religious values. Indeed, I believe that nothing is more tyrannical than forcing religion on people. It is like

[12] See Muhammad Husayn Haykal, *The Life of Muhammad*, trans. Ismael R. al Faruqi (New Delhi: Crescent Publishing Company, 1976), pp. 181–183. See also Nazih Ayubi, *Political Islam*, p. 6. See the chapter "The Compact of Medina and its Democratic Foundations," in M. A. Muqtedar Khan, American Muslims: Bridging Faith and Freedom (Beltsville, MD: Amana Publishers, 2002), pp. 98–101.

[13] For a lucid discussion of the objectives of the *Shariah*, see M. Umer Chapra, *Islam and the Economic Challenge* (Herndon, VA: International Institutive of Islamic Thought and The Islamic Foundation, 1992), p. 7. Also see Fathi Osman, *Sharia in Contemporary Society* (Los Angeles, CA: Multimedia Vera International, 1994).

making God a partner in oppression. Indeed, it is clear that compulsion in religion is persecution. But what then is the purpose of this book? It is to make the case that religious values that are based on the principles of *Ihsan* can bring out the best in the human being, making her a force for good in society—educating, transforming, reforming and serving selflessly. *Ihsan* and its manifestations will appeal to the noble and the good that is fundamental to humanity and will attract human agents to act according to these values in pursuit of perfection and self-elevation. Using state machinery to force people to act in a noble fashion would undermine the very purpose of these values. Truth is self-evident, the Quran says, and hence there is no need for compulsion in religion (*la ikraha fi al-deen*; Quran 2:256).

Religion in my humble opinion serves humanity best when it is a moral motivator that seeks the good of others. Secularism, designed to protect the state from religion as in the case of the French laicism or protect religion from the state as in the case of American secularism, does not necessarily guarantee good governance or the creation of ethical society. Secularism is not by itself a virtue; it is just a means to create an open space for them who may not subscribe to the state's preferred religion. But can states remain without a moral purpose or can society survive without a fundamental ethical foundation? Where will these values come from, the will of the majority? Will it then be forced upon everyone? Non-religious values—ideologies—can be as oppressive and tyrannical as religious values when states become their instruments of oppression. History has already witnessed the extremism that such ideological states are capable of under Nazi fascism and Soviet communism.

THE RASHIDUN CALIPHATE (632–662 AD)

The example of the first four Caliphs of Islam, celebrated as the *Rashidun Caliphate*, the rightly guided Caliphs (*Al-Khulafa Al-Rashidun* in Arabic), has remained a major precedent and source for Islamic political thought for centuries. Their rule, their methods and principles and their character have been canonized as the best in Islamic, if not human, history by Muslim historians and have since served as the benchmark for Islamic governance for most Sunni political thinkers.[14] Shia theologians primarily privilege the

---

[14] This privileging of historical events as sacred principles of government practice can be best seen in Al-Mawardi's development of the principles of Caliphate. See Abu'l Hasan Al-Mawardi, *Al-Ahkam as-Sultaniyyah*, trans. Asadullah Yate (London: Ta-Ha Publishers, 1996), pp. 23–26.

rule of the fourth Caliph, Ali Ibn Abi Talib, as the only one that enjoyed sacred legitimacy and the era of the first three Caliphs to them is not a source of political values. It is this historical construction of the Rashidun Caliphate as the best era of the best generation of Muslims and above all the best example of the implementation of Islamic values in political and social arena that inspires political Islam in their quest for reviving the Islamic Caliphate or adjusting their demands according to the modern realities and seeking to establish an Islamic state instead of a unified Caliphate. All groups, whether they are moderate, radical or enlightened, who seek to establish an Islamic polity derive not just inspiration but principles and even political structures and processes from this period. Some groups actually seek to replicate and not emulate this period, which has led many serious scholars to reject their efforts as futile and impossible.[15]

The canonization of the era of the Rashidun Caliphs presents both opportunities and pitfalls for contemporary Sunni political philosophers and theorists. When it serves the purpose of contemporary thinkers, the early precedents are used as sacred principles to advance a particular idea or political principle. For example, many Islamic liberal thinkers who maintain that Islam is democratic or that Islam and democracy are compatible (yours truly included) buttress their argument by using the example of the Rashidun Caliphs as democratically elected rulers. Since this was the best example of the implementation of Islam, Islam is democratic because the Rashidun Caliphs were elected and not hereditary monarchs.[16] But the sacred status of this era prevents contemporary Sunni thinkers from advancing a critical historical analysis of the early formation and fragmentation of the Islamic polity without losing the attention of Muslim readers. Any attempts to explain or analyze the collapse or end of the Rashidun Caliphate as a consequence of bad decisions or bad governing practices can spell the end of a scholar or at least the utility and potential impact of his or her analysis to the believing masses. As a result of this theo-political constraint,

---

[15] See Abdelilah Belkeziz, *The State in Contemporary Islamic Thought* (London: I. B. Taurus, 2009). Noah Feldman, *The fall and rise of the Islamic state* (Princeton, NJ: Princeton University Press, 2012). See Hugh Kennedy, *The Prophet and the Age of the Caliphates* (London: Longman, 1986).

[16] John L. Esposito, and John O. Voll, *Islam and Democracy* (London: Oxford University Press, 2001). Also see M. A. Muqtedar Khan, ed., *Islamic Democratic Discourse: theory, debates, and philosophical perspectives* (Lanham, MD: Lexington Books, 2006). M. A. Muqtedar Khan, "Islamic Governance and Democracy," in Shiping Hua, ed., *Islam and Democratization in Asia* (NY: Cambria Press, 2009): 13–27.

Muslims today are unable to benefit from the lessons that can be drawn, both positive and negative, from the formative period of Islamic polity.[17] The only serious contemporary critique of the theory of Caliphate from within Islamic sources was advanced by an Egyptian scholar and intellectual Ali Abdel-Raziq (1888–1966) in the early twentieth century who rejected the idea that Islamic sources prescribe a system of governance. But his impact was limited to academic debates and it did not stem the demand for the revival of the Caliphate/Islamic state.[18]

The idea that there is a "real and true Islam" and that it was best implemented by the Rashidun Caliphs is deeply engraved in the consciousness of a vast majority of Muslims. The more devout and more engaged they are with their tradition and with the religious establishment, the stronger is this conviction. I have already acknowledged that this tendency is partially useful to political thinkers and that it has been exploited by Islamist thinkers who have shaped demands for the creation of Islamic state and the revival of the Caliphate based on this sacred history. Secular and liberal thinkers too have used it and when political thinkers across the spectrum employ this as a "*daleel*" or proof of arguments to make their cases they further reify the era and strengthen its claims to sacredness.

But, for the sake of argument, if we abandon this assumption and rather than insisting that it was the best implementation of Islam, we assume that the era of the Rashidun Caliphate was the *best and the most sincere attempt* to implement Islam as taught by the Prophet Muhammad (pbuh), we open up opportunities to learn from that era that can be quite beneficial. Take, for example, the issue of nomination of successors. Prophet Muhammad (pbuh) had not appointed a specific political or religious successor to his mission. But Abu Bakr As-Siddiq the first Caliph did appoint Umar Ibn Khattab the second Caliph as his successor. In turn, the second Caliph appointed not a successor but an electoral college of six most prominent companions of Prophet Muhammad (pbuh) (later this became the basis for a special concept: *ahl al-hal wal-aqd*) and charged them with the task of electing one of themselves as his successor. Al-Mawardi and subsequent scholars then made this precedent an important principle of Islamic governance, an elite who could select and remove the Caliph, something like the Guardian Council in

---

[17] See Marshall G. S. Hodges, *The Venture of Islam: The Classical Age of Islam* (Chicago: University of Chicago Press, 1974), pp. 195–217, for a not so sacred rendering of this period.

[18] Souad T. Ali, *A Religion, not a State. Ali' Abd ul-Raziq's Islamic Justification of Political Secularism* (Salt Lake, Utah: University of Utah Press, 2009).

today's Iran. The third Caliph Uthman Ibn Affan, even though he ruled for the longest period, was assassinated before he could unveil a succession process. If we unpack these series of decisions alone, we can see that no specific Sunnah of the Prophet or of the previous Caliph was being followed by anyone in the matter of succession. But rather each Caliph was *innovating* with sincere intentions to make the best decision for the *Ummah* in the light of Islamic teachings and the unique political circumstances that they faced.

If we accept this conclusion, then it opens the door for several interesting ideas and principles. First, it implies that there is a progressive dimension to implementation of Islam. We can abandon the previous example for a more democratic or a more pragmatic or even a more inclusive solution. That is the precedent (*Sunnah*) of the Rashidun; their willingness to abandon the previous Sunnah in favor of contextual wisdom and pragmatism (*Hikmah*) or necessity. This also opens the door for social science and places it on par with history. Thus, Islamic political philosophy now need not depend on just recanting, reproducing or reinterpreting sacred past as the sole guiding framework of contemporary politics. It can also employ empirical social sciences and rational political theories to infer or deduce the best possible governing structures and processes for a political time and place and implement it rather than attempting to mangle the present to reproduce a distant past. Political thinkers in our era can now come to terms with modernity, adapt to the irreversible historical and structural developments of modernity and think in the present and plan for the future.

One remarkable feature of the era of the Rashidun Caliphate is its territorial and cultural expansion. As the Islamic polity, which started as an *Islamopolis*—a city-state in Medina—rapidly transformed itself into an expansive empire that included people from different cultures and languages, Islamic governance faced newer and newer challenges of diversity and complexity. For example, the second Caliph had to contend with Persians and the third Caliph had to deal with Egyptians who were both new to the polity and the religion. That is why the era of the most successful of them, that is, of Umar Ibn Khattab, is full of *innovation* and *adaptation*. Muslims consider Umar Ibn Khattab as the best leader Muslims have ever had after the Prophet himself. His rule was remarkable for its stability and for territorial expansion. But above all his reign is exemplary for the numerous innovative methods of governance introduced by him that were completely alien to the Arab political practices. For example, he adopted the Persian *Diwan* system, created a standing army, built garrison towns to host his military and provided pensions from the state treasury. These are just a few innovations that were not practiced by the Prophet or the first Caliph but instituted by Umar Ibn Khattab. Indeed, if every Muslim leader was an Umar, then Islamic history would be one of continuous development; innovation and adaptation would be routine and both politics and culture would be progressive and forward-looking not conservative and backward-looking.[19]

But thanks to the success of Islamism, Islamic politics today is either about replication and copying the early Caliphs or just implementing the so-called *Shariah* laws—laws that were articulated and developed to serve the needs of the society by scholars centuries ago. The foundational thinkers of modern Islamism, such as Maulana Maududi and Syed Qutb, basically relied on the works of Al-Mawardi, Ibn Taymiyyah and a selective reading of the era of the Rashidun Caliphate to develop a modern concept of an Islamic state that is procedurally democratic but substantively authoritative, whose constitutive dimension was implementing an already articulated Islamic law. Thus, a modern Islamic state, which is yet to come into existence, is envisioned as a state that applies Islamic laws that already exist. But a critical reading of the era of the Rashidun Caliphate would reveal that the early rulers did not apply an already given law but actually articulated and developed Islamic laws as and when the need arose for them. When they faced a new situation, they tried their best to come up with a wise solution that was consistent, in their view, with Islamic values. And this led to the development of practices, principles and procedures which contemporary Islamists privilege as divine law whose implementation is a litmus test that any state claiming to be Islamic must meet. Thus, ironically even when advocates of Islamic states recommend producing a state like that of the Rashidun Caliphate, they are not willing to let the new state develop a new understanding of the divine principles and articulate laws more apropos of contemporary realities. If they are willing to do that and accept the democratic nature of the Rashidun Caliphate, then the modern Islamic state will look no different from a liberal and democratic welfare state.

---

[19] M. I. Moosa, "The Diwan of Umar Ibn Al-Khattab," *Studies in Islam* 11.2 (1965). Tarik Unal, *Umar Ibn Al-Khattab: Exemplar of Truth and Justice* (Istanbul: Tughra Books, 2014). Also see Al-Qudsy, S. H. S. I., and A. A. Rahman, "Effective Governance in the Era of Caliph 'Umar Ibn Al Khattab (634-644)," *European Journal of Social Sciences* 18.4 (2011). 612–624.

PART I: ISLAMIC THEORIES OF POLITY AND GOVERNANCE

While Islamic thought is multilayered and very rich, the tradition of political theory and philosophy remains thin and underdeveloped.[20] Perhaps this could be explained by the hegemonic nature of Islamic legal thought that has always sought to colonize Islamic thinking at the expense of metaphysics, mysticism, philosophy and literature.[21] Even contemporary Islamic legal scholars often tend to equate Islam itself with Islamic legal thinking as if there is nothing outside the law (and the study of *Shariah*). Nevertheless, the premodern era did witness several political thinkers of whom Al-Farabi, Al-Mawardi, Ibn Taymiyyah, Ibn Khaldun, Abu Hamid Al-Ghazali, Ibn Rushd, Nasiruddin Al-Tusi, Ibn Sina, remain very prominent. While a comprehensive review of their political thought can be found elsewhere,[22] here I choose to critically review only five classical Muslim thinkers who contributed to Islamic political thought and Islamic political values but from entirely distinct and different perspectives. Al-Farabi was a philosopher and his approach was normative. Al-Mawardi was a jurist in the service of the Abbasid Caliphate and he approached Islamic political thought from clearly a legalistic perceptive.

Ibn Taymiyyah was a theologian and a polemicist and he approached politics from the perspective of theology. Ibn Khaldun was many things but what was most outstanding about his thought was his emphasis on empiricism. I classify his approach as sociological realism and therefore his perspective as sociology of polity. And finally, Sheikh Saa'di Shirazi, a Persian Sufi poet, who in my view came very close to articulating a mystical view of political theory.

AL-FARABI: PHILOSOPHY, GOVERNANCE AND DEMOCRACY

Abu Nasr Al-Farabi (872–950 AD) is widely recognized as one of the most important philosophers of not just Islamic but all of political philosophy. His debt is acknowledged by both Western and Islamic philosophical

---

[20] For discussion of the diversity and nature of Islamic discourses, see M. A. Muqtedar Khan, "Islam as an Ethical Tradition of International Relations," *Islam and Christian-Muslim Relations* 8.2 (Summer 1997): 173–188.

[21] See M. A. Muqtedar Khan, "Political Philosophy of Islamic Resurgence," *Cultural Dynamic* 13.2 (Summer 2001): 213–231.

[22] Erwin Isak Jakob Rosenthal, *Political thought in medieval Islam: an introductory outline.* CUP Archive, 1958. Antony Black, *The History of Islamic political thought: from the Prophet to the present* (Edinburgh University Press, 2011).

and political traditions. Al-Farabi is, in my view, the best representative of the tradition of Islamic philosophy (*Falsafa*) which boasts of stars like Ibn Rushd, Ibn Sina, among classical thinkers and Seyyed Hossein Nasr, Abdullahi A. An-Na'im and Abdolkarim Soroush among contemporary ones. In his *Mabadi ara al-Madinat al-Fadilah* (Opinions of the Citizens of the Excellent City), Al-Farabi develops his ideas linking metaphysics and cosmology with social ethics and political community. He develops a typology of polities and discusses how a sense of collective purpose, informed by a consciousness of the divine, can enable human beings to develop virtuous cities and polities which will not only be governed in a just and noble fashion but will also enable their citizens to work toward the perfection of the self.[23]

While reading Al-Farabi one is immediately struck by the contemporary relevance of his theories. Al-Farabi conceived of the possibility of establishing ideal polities at three levels—global, national and city. He actually thought that political unity and ethical governance were possible not only at the level of a city-state but also on a global scale.[24] Three elements can be identified as crucial to Al-Farabi's vision of an ideal state—a knowledgeable population, the presence of choice/freedom and the role of a philosopher or philosophers. Al-Farabi clearly believed that whatever a city became, virtuous or ignorant or even wicked, it must do so through free choice of its people. Thus, in a sense freedom of conscience more than anything else or rather the freedom to choose or eschew an ethical path was important for Al-Farabi and it is a lesson that contemporary Islamists must not ignore. A state where citizens are coerced into pursuing an ethical path would be meaningless since the virtue of virtue is in its independent realization as a result of knowledge and communion with the divine (in Al-Farabi's terms with the active intellect).[25]

---

[23] See Abu Nasr Al Farabi, *Mabadi ara ahl al-Madinat al-Fadilah* (*On the Perfect State*), trans. Richard Walzer (Chicago: Great Books of the Islamic World, 1998). See Muhammad Saghir Hassan al-Ma'sumi, "Al-Farabi," in M. M. Sharif, ed., *A History of Muslim Philosophy I* (Karachi: Royal Book Company, 1963), pp. 704–716. Also see Deborah L. Black, "Al-Farabi," in Seyyed Hossein Nasr and Oliver Leaman, eds., *History of Islamic Philosophy I* (London: Routledge, 1996), pp. 178–197.

[24] While it remains beyond the scope of the discussion in this conversation, it must be noted that in an era of globalization it is really exciting to find a classical philosopher who conceived of not only of the possibility of global governance but also of establishing a global ethical polity.

[25] See Al-Farabi, *On the Perfect State*, p. 231.

Al-Farabi imagined the state as a cooperative effort of free and willing citizens seeking a common purpose—ultimate happiness through contact with the active intellect. In essence the state for Al-Farabi, whatever the collective goal—prosperity or perfection, was an instrument to solve collective action problems. In his discussion of the nature of a state, he previews two important contemporary theories, namely, the systems theory and the Weberian conception of the modern state as a product of rationalization, division of labor and specialization. Al-Farabi compares the state to a human body and argues that just as each organ through perfecting its own function and integrating with the whole creates a functional body, so should various elements of society perfect their roles and integrate to create the state. It is in the rationalization of the state and in treating it as a system that Al-Farabi introduces his Platonic Republicanism by talking of hierarchical roles from the noble to the ignoble in his idyllic society. He places the philosophers on top of the hierarchy. He argued that their knowledge, wisdom and nobility were necessary for any city to achieve a virtuous status.[26]

Unlike contemporary political theory where the emphasis is on perfecting structure and process, Al-Farabi concentrates on the nature and character of the governors in arguing the possibility of realizing virtue in society. It is when virtuous individuals govern that we have a virtuous society. Social virtue for Al-Farabi is a personality effect and not a systemic effect.[27] Needless to say, contemporary theorists who live in far more complex societies would disagree with this premise. But we must remember that Al-Farabi's work was only the beginning of Islamic political theorizing.

Al-Farabi was the first Muslim thinker to explore the virtues of democracy. Al-Farabi places democracy in the category of ignorant cities. Ignorant cities are those cities that collectively are not aware of God (the First Cause). They also do not have a single purpose. He recognizes that since democracies are free societies there will be multiple objectives that the citizens of a democracy will seek. He also suggests that if people who seek security dominate the polity a democracy can become a national security state (Al-Farabi talks in terms of cities of war and peace). But he also makes a very interesting observation which is perhaps the most important lesson contemporary

---

[26] See Al-Farabi, *On the Perfect State*, p. 231.

[27] For a discussion on the two paths to good governance, through good systems and/or good leaders, see the chapter on "Good Governance," in M. A. Muqtedar Khan, *American Muslims*, pp. 111–114.

Muslim thinkers can take from him. Al-Farabi suggests that because democracies are free societies and are also non-homogenous, there will be people who will excel in good as well as people who will excel in evil. But the fact that one can find the pursuit of perfection present within a democracy, a democracy has the best chance of all ignorant cities of becoming a virtuous city. This is a cautionary but powerful endorsement of democracy when the options available to societies largely fall in the ignorant category (monarchies, dictatorships, etc.).[28]

Al-Farabi was not a secular thinker in the modern sense of the term. He believed that the virtuous cities were best governed and did lead to their citizens gaining ultimate happiness because philosopher-kings or Prophet-legislators ruled them. He imagined these philosopher kings as those capable of combining governance with wisdom and true knowledge of the divine and of what makes humans happy. But this knowledge is acquired not just through reason but also revelations and hence the first ruler who establishes the virtuous city must be a prophet-legislator who can connect the political with the divine, governance with epistemology and truth with reality. There is no doubt that Al-Farabi was thinking of Prophet Muhammad (pbuh) as the founding ruler of the virtuous city and then subsequently he imagined that philosophers could succeed him.[29]

Revelation was necessary for the founding of the virtuous city but thereafter reason would suffice, as it would process the revelation and facilitate good governance by drawing on the wisdom of the divine (revelations). In his *Madinat al-Fadilah*, Al-Farabi explicitly uses the term Imam to describe the first ruler and I reproduce the entire statement here since it so succinctly summarizes his vision:

> *He is the sovereign over who no other human being has any sovereignty whatsoever; he is the Imam; the first sovereign* (wa hua Imam, al rais al awwal) *of the excellent city, he is the sovereign of the excellent nation and the sovereign of the universal state.*[30]

[28] For an excellent discussion of Al Farabi's understanding of democracy, see Muhsin Mahdi, "Al Farabi," in Leo Straus and Joseph Cropsey, ed., *History of Political Philosophy* (Chicago, IL: University of Chicago Press, 1987), pp. 224–226. See Al-Farabi, *On the Perfect State*, p. 315. Also see Muhsin S. Mahdi, *Alfarabi and the Foundation of Islamic Political Philosophy* (Chicago, IL: University of Chicago Press, 2001), pp. 144–146.

[29] Muhsin S. Mahdi, *Alfarabi and the Foundation of Islamic Political Philosophy* (Chicago, IL: University of Chicago Press, 2001), pp. 130–132.

[30] Abu Nasi Al-Farabi, *On the Perfect State*, Great Books of Islamic World, 1998, trans. Richard Walzer (New York: Oxford University Press, 1998), p. 247.

The ruler needed to understand both divine law and human law, recognize the superiority of the divine law which included both laws about actions and laws about morality, and comprehend what was good in the philosophical sense. Thus, Al-Farabi's philosopher king personified the wisdom that made divine law accessible and embedded in the opinions of the citizens that enabled them to pursue perfection and establish a virtuous city.

As I read and reread Al-Farabi, it is impossible to escape the mystical undertones to Al-Farabi's ideas and philosophy. The pursuit of perfection and virtue that he sought to see both in individual thought and especially in sociopolitical reality can also be understood as similar to the Sufi pursuit of perfection of the human soul that can mirror the divine—*realization of Ihsan*. At the risk of undermining the unique nature of my book, I submit that Al-Farabi's political ideas can be viewed as an early philosophical attempt to articulate a politics based on *Ihsan*.

AL-MAWARDI: ISLAMIC JURISPRUDENCE AND THE THEORY OF CALIPHATE

Abu al-Hasan Al-Mawardi (972 to 1058 AD), a prominent Islamic jurist, who worked for the Abbasid Caliphs Al-Qaim and Al-Qadir sought to preserve and restore the institution of the Caliphate. He wrote his famous canonical treatise *The Ordinances of the Government* (*Al Ahkam as-Sultaniyyah*)[31] between 1045 and 1058, during a crucial time when there appeared the possibility that through an alliance with the rising Seljuks the Abbasids Caliphate could regain its past glory and power. Much of Al-Mawardi's work is mundane and deals mostly with practical aspects of governance and public administration. But a small part of his work deals with the theory of the Caliphate. It is a mixture of legalistic manipulation and political theology with the clear objective of assigning exclusive religious legitimacy to the Caliph and working to restore his sociopolitical status and legal authority.[32] In trying to legitimize the Caliphate on religious grounds, Al-Mawardi tied political authority to religious sources in such a tight knot that Muslims have failed to untie it since.

---

[31] See W. Montgomery Watt, *Islamic Political Thought* (Edinburgh: Edinburgh University Press, 1968), pp. 99–104.

[32] See Muhammad Qamaruddin, "Al-Mawardi," in M. M. Sharif, ed., *A History of Muslim Philosophy I* (Karachi: Royal Book Company, 1963), pp. 717–731.

Al-Mawardi was by training a jurist. Islamic jurists in general look at governance from a purely legal perspective in that they privilege laws and try to develop ideas about political structures and practices based on laws which are already given. Their primary goal is to articulate Islamic laws from Islamic sources (such as the Quran and Sunnah) and demand that both governance structures and practices conform to these laws. Abu Abdullah Al-Shafii (767–820 AD) was a prominent jurist who first systematized Islamic jurisprudential thinking. It is his development of jurisprudence, which made governance in Islam primarily a legalistic exercise. Al-Shafii sought and most Islamic jurists seek to minimize the use of reason and *ijtihad* (independent thinking) in the articulation and application of the law.[33] He sought to privilege the text of sacred sources above reason. To a great extent, Al-Mawardi remained true to his tradition and used sacred text with great felicity to privilege the authority of the Caliph above all others.

His *Al-Ahkam As-Sultaniyyah* is not a theory of the state in any sense of the term. It does not offer any conception of what the ultimate purpose of political community is or why states exist and what are just and good states. His focus is to advance a theoretical argument to legitimize the claim of the Abbasid Caliphate to legitimate power over the entire Muslim community and especially to the exclusion of all other rulers, regimes and claims.[34] In one sense, his theory of the Caliphate is a repudiation of Shiite claims. This political objective becomes clearer in one particular principle that he advances with regard to who can be the Caliph. Al-Mawardi argues that if there is more than one person qualified to become the Caliph, then it is *not* necessary that the best one should become the Caliph. It is acceptable for anyone of the qualified people to be chosen as the Caliph and the Electoral College, which can consist of even one individual, does not need to offer an explanation as to why they chose the inferior candidate over the superior candidate. This is clearly a *Sunni* defense against the *Shiite* claims that no one was more superior to the descendants of the Prophet when it came to religious legitimacy. This gift from Al-Mawardi and other Sunni jurists to this day remains an excuse for the tons of incompetent rulers that have plagued the Muslim world.[35]

---

[33] M. A. Muqtedar Khan, "Reason and Personal Reasoning," *American Journal of Islamic Social Sciences* 16.3 (1999).

[34] Abu'l Hasan Al-Mawardi, *Al-Ahkam as-Sultaniyyah*, trans. Asadullah Yate (London: Ta-Ha Publishers, 1996), pp. 23–26.

[35] For an excellent critique of the Al Mawardi work, see, M. Qamaruddin Khan, "Al Mawardi" in M. M. Sharif, ed., *A History of Muslim Philosophy I* (Karachi: Royal Book Company, 1963), pp. 717–732.

Al-Mawardi's methodology was rather simplistic. He basically studied the history of the early Caliphate and based his theories on this early Islamic period. The first four Caliphs are considered as the rightly guided Caliphs by Muslims generally and even though this claim is not based on the Quran it is so widely accepted by Islamic scholars that it has become a religious cannon. Since the early Caliphs were considered as righteous, many of their practices and actions are also taken as righteous principles. Thus, Al-Mawardi's theory of Caliphate is an articulation of selective historical episodes as theoretical principles of Islamic government.[36]

Al-Mawardi also insisted on some rather dubious criteria in his theory of the Caliphate. For example, he insisted that only a member of the tribe of Quraysh could become a Caliph. This stipulation was to exclude the *Buwayhids,* the *Fatimids* and the *Seljuks* from usurping the title of the Caliph. It did not matter to him that it was completely in contradiction to the universalism characteristic of the message of Islam. It also did not matter to him that he was reducing Islamic political theology to crass tribalism and parochialism.[37] It is apparent from his other works in the field of jurisprudence and even in sociology that Al-Mawardi was an excellent thinker and scholar. But his inability to rescue his political theology from his partisan politics demands that his contribution, regardless of its popularity with contemporary Islamists, must be viewed with caution.[38]

IBN TAYMIYYAH AND *SIYYASAH SHARAIYYAH*: *SHARIAH*-BASED GOVERNANCE

Ibn Taymiyyah lived at a time when the Muslim world experienced a high degree of insecurity. The Mongols and the Crusaders were threatening the integrity of Muslim lands and many new religious practices inspired by

---

[36] See Abu Al-Hasan Al-Mawardi, *The Ordinances of Government,* trans. Wafaa H. Wahba (NY: Ithaca Press, 2000). Also see L. Carl Brown, *Religion and State: The Muslim Approach to Politics* (New York: Columbia University Press, 2000). Also

[37] In his last sermon, which is considered as a will and testament that Muslims must uphold, the Prophet specifically instructed his followers not to distinguish between an Arab and a non-Arab. Making tribal distinctions for purposes of legitimacy was clearly self-serving (for the Quraysh and the Abbasids who belonged to the Quraysh tribe) and antithetical to the Message of Muhammad. See Abdul Hameed Siddiqui, *Life of Muhammad* (Des Plaines, IL: Library of Islam, 1991), pp. 288–289.

[38] For a useful summary of Al Mawardi's Theory of the Caliphate, see Antony Black, *The History of Islamic Political Thought,* pp. 81–91.

eclectic mysticism and Neoplatonist philosophers were in Ibn Taymiyyah's view, threatening the integrity of Islam as a faith. Just as Al-Mawardi's theory of the Caliphate was inspired by the threats to the Caliphate, Ibn Taymiyyah's ideas of the state were also inspired by a deeply felt insecurity of the future of Islam as a faith and Islam as an empire. It is important to remember that while Al-Farabi and later Ibn Khaldun's attempt to theorize the state were inspired more by intellectual curiosity than temporal politics; the theories of Al-Mawardi and Ibn Taymiyyah were firmly embedded in the politics of their time and were clearly designed to advance certain partisan positions. While Al-Mawardi sought to restore the glory of the Caliphate, Ibn Taymiyyah sought to restore the global dominance of the Islamic civilization and domestic domination of Islamic *Shariah*.[39]

Their theories may have been reasonable for their times but are certainly not portable across time and in my view should not be treated as transcendent moral principles. But unfortunately, their theories of Caliphate and governance continue to resonate today. Sunnis accept Al-Mawardi's conception of the Caliphate widely, and Ibn Taymiyyah's ideas of Islamic governance based on Islamic law dominate the thinking of political Islamists and *Jihadist* of our times. The ideologies of the Kingdom of Saudi Arabia, the extremist entity called Islamic State of Iraq and Syria (ISIS) and to some extent even Al-Qaeda have been shaped by Ibn Taymiyyah's conception of Caliphate and *Jihad*.[40] I have also shown in the second chapter while discussing blasphemy how intolerance and violent responses to alleged cases of blasphemy in Pakistan are a direct consequence of the work of Ibn Taymiyyah. It is Ibn Taymiyyah more than anyone else from whom modern-day Islamists get the idea that an Islamic state is an Islamic state only because it implements Islamic law. This idea in modern times has been advanced most vigorously by Maulana Maududi and Syed Qutb and through their Islamic movements *Jamaat-e-Islami* in South Asia and the Muslim Brotherhood in the Arab world.

---

[39] See the chapter "*Ibn Taymiyya: Sharia Governance,*" in Antony Black, *The History of Islamic Political Thought*, pp. 154–159. Qamaruddin Khan, *The Political Thought of Ibn Taymiyah* (New Delhi: Adam Publishers, 1982). Also see Ibn Taymiyya, *Public Duties in Islam: The Institution of the Hisbah*, trans. Mukhtar Holland (Leicester, UK: The Islamic Foundation, 1985).

[40] Mona Hassan, "Modern interpretations and misinterpretations of a medieval scholar: Apprehending the political thought of Ibn Taymiyya," in Yossef Rapaport and Shahab Ahmed, eds., *Ibn Taymiyya and His Times* (2010), pp. 338–366.

Ibn Taymiyyah's approach was a significant departure from traditional scholarship. His methodology was a mixture of selective use of tradition and past scholarship and a direct use of the Quran unlike say Al-Mawardi who relies primarily on the traditions and historical narratives about the early period of Islam. One of the reasons why Ibn Taymiyyah's rather ideological and stark conceptualization of the purpose of the state has so much appeal for so many is the raw nature of his discourse. He relies on direct and literalist use of the Quran and his selection of Quranic verses gives a quality to his discourse, which his followers find compelling (I am aware that some critics may argue that I too employ this methodology in this book). After all, if he is using so many words of God, then it stands to reason that his discourse must be more authentic than others whose discussions are corrupted by their reason and interpretation. Ibn Taymiyyah also describes the ideological objectives of the state in minimal and simple terms, and this clarity of discourse adds to his appeal and influence even today. While Al-Mawardi's limitations are readily apparent, Al-Farabi's and Ibn Khaldun's analyses have an erudite quality, which easily alienates simplistic readers. The two make intellectual demands of their reader, especially Al-Farabi whose writings are complex and philosophical. But Ibn Taymiyyah is clear, dogmatic and simple.

Ibn Taymiyyah was convinced that Islamic duties such as encouraging good and forbidding evil could not be fulfilled without state power. He also felt that several Islamic obligations such as *Jihad* (struggle) against sin and disobedience to God, enforcement of Islamic law and even fulfillment of collective obligations such as establishing justice needed the power and machinery of the state. Arguing that religion needed the state to realize itself, Ibn Taymiyyah provided for the first time the argument for a religious necessity of the state. Thus, unlike previous Muslim thinkers like, Al-Farabi who believed that religious knowledge was necessary for political excellence, Ibn Taymiyyah argued that political power was necessary for religious excellence.[41]

Ibn Taymiyyah's enduring and to some extent problematic characterization of the Islamic state as one that enforces the *Shariah* is his most distinct contribution to Islamic political thought. Today this character has become the defining characteristic of the Islamic state for most Islamic thinkers and nearly all Islamic movements. Today Muslim states and politicians use the symbolic application of the *Shariah* (which is often operationalized as the

---

[41] Qamaruddin Khan, *The Political Thought of Ibn Taymiyah*, pp. 23–51.

application of stringent Islamic laws known as *hudud laws* against crimes such as adultery, theft and apostasy) along with banning of interest as a litmus test to determine the Islamic nature of states.[42]

Ibn Taymiyyah emphasized the coercive dimension of statecraft. It is in this arena that he departs considerably from the Quranic injunction that "there is no compulsion in religion" (Quran 2:256); and essentially sees the state as a coercive means to expand and spread Islam beyond its borders and maintain the doctrinal purity of how Islam is practiced within its borders. His idea of the state is a Hobbesian Leviathan that rules with an iron fist. Ibn Taymiyyah errs on the side of severity and shows little affinity to compassion or forgiveness. For example, he narrates a tradition according to which Prophet Muhammad (pbuh) the amputation of the hand of a man who stole another man's mantle. When the owner of the mantle who had brought the thief to the Prophet heard the judgment, he intervened and said that he gives the mantle to the thief so that he could escape the punishment. But Prophet Muhammad (pbuh) insisted that the punishment should be executed and forgiveness was possible only before the theft was reported.[43] Ibn Taymiyyah's then uses this episode to argue that the *Shariah* must be implemented no matter what. It was the will of God. When I read this, I was first surprised by the lack of forgiveness that Ibn Taymiyyah sees in Islamic law.

Then I thought of the Quranic verse (21:107), which says: *And We have not sent you, [O Muhammad], except as a mercy to the worlds.* Clearly this episode was not very consistent with that injunction or the many other reminders of God's compassion and mercy that I discussed in the chapter on *Ihsan*. I also recalled another more prominent tradition in which a woman from Ghamid came and confessed to Prophet Muhammad (pbuh) that she had committed adultery.[44] The tradition is remarkable in the great reluctance (that stretched over more than two years) the Prophet exhibited in execution of the punishment for adultery insisting that she seek Allah's forgiveness instead. If Ibn Taymiyyah had included such traditions in his deliberations, he would have been less severe and would have shown more compassion in his understanding of Islamic law. In another instance, he advocates death to those who do not pray regularly, taking a position

---

[42] Qamaruddin Khan, *The Political Thought of Ibn Taymiyah*, pp. 23–51.

[43] See Imam Ibn Taymiyyah, *The Political Shariah on Reforming the Ruler and the Ruled* (London: Dar al-Fiqh 2012), pp. 97–100.

[44] See hadith in *Sahih Muslim*, Book 17, #4206

contrary to the Quranic message that there is no compulsion in religion (Quran 2:256).[45] He brought a severity to the business of establishing Islam, and this approach to religion without compassion has become the trademark of neoconservative movements such as the *Salafi* movement and the *Wahhabi* movement who see Ibn Taymiyyah as a great reviver and resuscitator of purity in Islam. Clearly, Ibn Taymiyyah's Islam is one, which is deeply motivated by insecurity and fear that the faith and its polity are under siege and about to be destroyed. This insecurity more than anything else is the cause for his imagination of the state as an Islamic leviathan that exercises absolute power within and ferociously attacks threats from without.

Finally, Ibn Taymiyyah placed great emphasis on the principle of *Jihad*. Indeed, in his contemptuous criticism of Sufis he suggests that the biggest difference between Sufis and those who follow the true way of Islam (a modern term for this group would be Salafis) was *Jihad*.[46] He argues that the real aim of people who hold positions of power in an Islamic polity is to ensure that religion is only for Allah—a justification for discrimination against people of other faiths since the goal is to eliminate other religions—so that the word of Allah remains uppermost. He invokes the verse 57:25 in the Quran that refers to God's revelation of the book and creation of iron for military power and argues that the preservation of religion can only be done with the help of the book and the sword.[47] He also cites several traditions from the hadith literature to glorify *Jihad* understood very clearly as fighting. If anyone reads him and accepts his interpretation of Islam, one would conclude that there is nothing greater and more pleasing to God than fighting for his religion.[48]

In several *Fatwas*, variously knows as the Mardin fatwa and the anti-Mongol fatwas, Ibn Taymiyyah provides the legalistic justification for using violence even against Muslims in Muslim lands, an argument that has been used, or misappropriated according to some, by Al-Qaeda, ISIS and other groups; most famously by the one that assassinated Egyptian President Anwar Sadat in 1981.[49] Some contemporary scholars like Yahya

---

[45] See Imam Ibn Taymiyyah, *The Political Shariah on Reforming the Ruler and the Ruled* (London: Dar al-Fiqh 2012), p. 197.

[46] Yahya Michot, *Ibn Taymiyyah against Extremisms* (Beirut: Dar Albouraq, 2012), p. 187.

[47] See Imam Ibn Taymiyyah, *The Political Shariah on Reforming the Ruler and the Ruled* (London: Dar al-Fiqh 2012), p. 35.

[48] See Imam Ibn Taymiyyah, *The Political Shariah on Reforming the Ruler and the Ruled* (London: Dar al-Fiqh 2012), p. 111.

[49] Mona Hassan, "Modern interpretations and misinterpretations of a medieval scholar: Apprehending the political thought of Ibn Taymiyya," in Yossef Rapoport and Shahab Ahmed, eds., *Ibn Taymiyya and His Times* (2010), pp. 338–366.

Michot have argued that terrorists have misappropriated Ibn Taymiyyah; and others like Abdullah Bin Bayah, have tried to salvage his image but negate his message.[50] Regardless of how those fatwas are interpreted, the fact remains that defining an Islamic polity, as one that merely implements a medieval understanding of Islamic law, is problematic to say the least. This theory of the state offers little by way of good governance for contemporary societies except to offer harsh punishments that govern sexual relations and a few crimes and encourage bellicose postures toward others.

IBN KHALDUN AND THE REALITY OF POLITICAL AUTHORITY AND GOOD GOVERNANCE

Ibn Khaldun's approach was unique and far more empirical than any of the three theorists that we have considered so far. While Al-Farabi, Al-Mawardi and Ibn Taymiyyah were all normative and prescriptive, Ibn Khaldun was empirical, historical and descriptive in his analysis of the origin and decline of states and societies. He is the only early Muslim scholar who to some extent provides alternative and secular justifications for political authority by focusing on its social necessity and its cultural advantages. He was less interested in describing desirable qualities in states and was rather occupied in understanding the natural laws that shaped the origin, growth and decline of cultures and civilizations.[51] Unlike others, Ibn Khaldun was unique in his assumptions that history played a role in shaping political reality. And therefore in order to understand political reality one had to understad the rules that shaped historical development. Thus, in an effort to understand and even develop a political science, Ibn Khaldun ended up creating sociology and philosophy of history.

---

[50] Yahya Michot, "Ibn Taymiyya's "New Mardin Fatwa". Is genetically modified Islam (GMI) carcinogenic?," *The Muslim World* 101.2 (2011): 130–181.

[51] See Ibn Khaldun, *Muqaddimah*, trans. Franz Rosenthal (Princeton, NJ: Princeton University Press, 1969). Also see Muhsin S. Mahdi, *Ibn Khaldun's Philosophy of History* (Chicago, IL: Chicago University Press, 1957). See Abderrahmane Lakhsassi, "Ibn Khaldun," in Seyyed Hossein Nasr and Oliver Leaman, eds., *History of Islamic Philosophy I* (London: Routledge, 1996), pp. 350–366. Also see Muhsin S. Mahdi, "Ibn Khaldun," in M. M. Sharif, ed., *A History of Muslim Philosophy II* (Karachi: Royal Book Company, 1963), and pp. 888–903. See also the chapter "Ibn Khaldun (1332–1406): The Science of Civilization and Governance of Islam," in Antony Black, *The History of Islamic Political Philosophy*, pp. 165–182.

Ibn Khaldun argued that there were three types of states or polities.[52] They are states that are *natural,* those that are *rational* and the third type was the Caliphate. Natural states were those where political power and authority were assumed by kings and tribal leaders, in pursuit of natural desires untamed by reason or religion. Rational states were states where political authority was moderated by reason and sought to advance the material and this worldly benefits and interests of its people. In the natural state, only the worldly interests of the rulers were advanced but in the rational state, that ruled based on the wisdom derived from rational political laws, the worldly interests of the entire population were accrued. The goal of the Caliphate was to realize both this worldly and the otherworldly interests of its people. Thus, the Caliph armed by the knowledge of the divine law (received through revelation) would ensure that the community was enjoying a successful life here and would also be successful in the hereafter. Thus, while reason could safeguard worldly interests only religion could guard both temporal and eternal interests.

Ibn Khaldun's take on the concept of the Caliphate is also more nuanced and more modern than those of his classical cohort. He imagined the Caliphate as composed of two types of sovereignties—the royal political authority, the kind that is possessed by natural and rational state rulers and the *Imamate,* a religious form of authority that came from religion, and knowledge of religious laws. Thus, for Ibn Khaldun political authority of the Caliph was invested with both divine and temporal, sacred and secular, authority or sovereignty. To him this idea of the merging of political and sacred authority, which he acknowledges was also envisaged by philosophers (Al-Farabi in particular), was best manifest in Prophet Muhammad (pbuh). I find this interesting because with further development Islamic political theory could have recognized the virtues of secular governance when religious authority becomes corrupt.[53]

Ibn Khaldun in a very interesting section advances an idea of good governance that can be seen as criticism of religion-based governance. He describes good governance or "good rulership" as mildness, moderation, kindness and beneficence toward the subjects. He argues that if the ruler "counts the sins" of his subjects and treats and punishes them harshly, it will lead to discontent

---

[52] See Abdelilah Belkeziz, "The State in Contemporary Islamic Thought" (London: I. B. Taurus, 2009), pp. 95–96. Also see Ibn Khaldun, *The Muqaddimah,* trans. Franz Rosenthal (Princeton, NJ: Princeton University Press, 1969), pp. 154–155.

[53] Ibn Khaldun, *Muqaddimah,* trans. Franz Rosenthal (Princeton, NJ: Princeton University Press, 1969), pp. 154–165.

and even rebellion. It is quite interesting that Ibn Khaldun, who was born four years after the death of Ibn Taymiyyah in 1328 AD, lived in essentially the same sociopolitical context as Ibn Taymiyyah advances a diametrically opposite view. Ibn Taymiyyah advocated severity in applying religion and Ibn Khaldun considered it antithetical to good governance.[54]

Ibn Khaldun's key concept was the idea of *asabiyyah* or solidarity. He like Al-Farabi also saw the state as an expression of a group's collective desire to achieve a singular goal and the necessary convergence of interests that leads to the recognition of a common goal comes from the emergence of group solidarity or tribal kinship—*asabiyyah*. Ibn Khaldun's theory of the state is essentially a discussion of how tribes, which live in rural and nomadic conditions band together under the relations and rules of kinship, and when this *asabiyyah* is territorialized through conquest, they establish a state. The emergence of cities and urban lifestyle is the beginning of the establishment of culture and civilization, which lead to the stages of contentment and corruption and the collapse of solidarity and the state. Ibn Khaldun argued that the development of the state had five stages: (1) emergence of solidarity in tribal and nomadic people leading to territorial conquest, (2) the capture of territory and the establishment of the state with the tribal head as the leader, (3) consolidation of power and sovereignty and the establishment of cities, (4) emergence of culture, civilization and the state of contentment as citizens of the city enjoy the fruits of civilization and conquest and (5) decline of solidarity and the decline of the state and the emergence of threats on the outskirts of the city as alternate tribes, freshly rejuvenated by the emergence of their own solidarity seek to establish their own state. Ibn Khaldun suggested that while tribal identity and kinship may work as *asabiyyah* in formative and rural stages, religion was the only cement that could keep a civilization alive and thriving. The solidarity that is so necessary to maintain the territorial integrity and the cultural momentum of the civilization could come only from religion and he too like Al-Farabi posits religion as a necessity for the state.

More than his specific and substantive contribution, it is Ibn Khaldun's approach and epistemological contribution that is worth noting. Even today most of Islamic political thought coming from traditional scholars is entirely normative and bereft of any empirical content. Even when they review history, it is hagiographic and preachy. The absence of critical perspectives

---

[54] Ibn Khaldun, *Muqaddimah*, trans. Franz Rosenthal (Princeton, NJ: Princeton University Press, 1969), p. 153.

makes the normative contributions just utopian and honestly inapplicable in today's time and place. It is important to note that all the four prominent classical Muslim political thinkers saw religion playing an important role in the formation, maintenance, governance and sustenance of the state. For Al-Farabi, religion brought a foundational and epistemological quality to the polity, for Al-Mawardi it was a legitimizing principle, for Ibn Taymiyyah state was necessary for religion itself and for Ibn Khaldun religion was the cement that kept the state and society intact.[55] Needless to say none of these theorists have advanced a decisive treatise on the state. They are all remarkably similar in one way and that is they are all formative approaches to studying the state from different perspectives: political, sociocultural, legal and theological. It is one of the limitations of Islamic political thought that very little work has been done subsequently to pursue the philosophical and sociological approaches to the state that were initiated by Al-Farabi and Ibn Khaldun. It is also an indication of the insecurity overshadowing contemporary Muslim thought that Al-Mawardi and Ibn Taymiyyah play such a prominent role in the theories of the Islamic state that are being advanced in the postcolonial era.

SHEIKH SAA'DI OF SHIRAZ: SUFISM AND ISLAMIC GOVERNANCE

The political revivalist discourse has been the dominant Muslim response to modernity; the modern state and the Western-dominated global order. This revivalist discourse, developed by thinkers such as Jamaluddin Al-Afghani, Maulana Maududi, Rashid Rida, Syed Qutb and Taqiuddin Al-Nabbhani, has been fundamentally shaped by ideologues influenced primarily by Shariah-based politics thinkers—Al-Mawardi and Ibn Taymiyyah. With "*Shariah* implementation" becoming both the goal and the litmus test of Islamic states, the historical role of Sufis and Sufi thought in Islamic governance and empires has been ignored, marginalized and even forgotten. The rise of two competing tendencies in Islamic societies, the reformist tendency represented by

---

[55] For a sense of how Ibn Khaldun's ideas are still relevant, see Akbar Ahmad, "Ibn Khaldun's Understanding of Civilizations and the Dilemmas of Islam and the West Today," *Middle East Journal* 56.1 (Winter 2002): 20–45. Also see Robert Cox, "Towards a post-hegemonic conceptualization of world order: reflections on the relevancy of Ibn Khaldun," in James Rosenau and Ernst-Otto Czempiel, eds., *Governance without Government: Order and Change in World Politics* (Cambridge: Cambridge University Press, 1992).

Islamist movements such as The Muslim Brotherhood and *Jamaat-e-Islami* and puritanical movements represented by the Salafi Wahhabi movements have both targeted and attacked Sufism, Sufi practices and Sufi ethos. The reformist saw Sufism as too fatalistic and therefore an impediment to their efforts to revive and reform Muslim societies. The puritanical movements see Sufism as something even more dangerous—they loathe its tolerance, its acceptance of others, specially its religious pluralism and its preference to not adhere to the letter of the law in its quest for realizing the spirit and the higher purposes of revelation.[56]

Additionally, the widely held and popular understanding of Sufism, which is in many ways emphasized by the lifestyle of many contemporary Sufi masters, is that it eschews engagement with worldly issues, specially politics. Because Sufism is often mistaken for asceticism, insights and theories on politics are not expected from Sufi quarters. In the past few years some governments (most prominently the British government) have taken to promoting Sufism as an antidote to *Jihadism* or the so-called Islamic radicalism.[57] Also in recent years a few scholars have paid serious attention to the political ideas that Sufis bring to Islamic political thought. But neither these studies have been systematic nor have the Sufis left theoretical discourses that are amenable to study political thought in the usual way we examine perspectives and schools of thought.[58] Most of the Sufi writings are in aphorisms or poetry or in flashes/reflections that appear as if they are streams of consciousness. Some like Ibn Arabi have written serious and philosophically dense text but not systematically about politics or in a way that political philosophers and theorists would recognize as speaking to them. Sayid Rizvi in his magnum opus *A History of Sufism in India*, Mehrzad Boroujerdi in his fine collection titled *Mirror for the Muslim Prince* and Omid Safi in his *The Politics of Knowledge in Premodern Islam* have paid attention to this genre. In the past few decades, we have seen a great deal of work on Sufism and translations of Sufi classics, but not on Sufi political theory.[59]

[56] Elizabeth Sirriyeh, *Sufis and Anti-Sufis: The Defence, Rethinking and Rejection of Sufism in the Modern World* (New York: Routledge, 2014).

[57] See, for example, Jane Lampman, "Sufism may be powerful antidote to Islamic Extremism," *The Christian Science Monitor*, Dec. 5, 2007. On the World Wide Web at: http://www.csmonitor.com/2007/1205/p13s02-lire.html.

[58] See Muzaffar Alam, *Languages of Political Islam in India 1200–1800* (London: Orient Blackswan, 2004). And also see Saiyid Athar Abbas Rizvi, "A History of Sufism in India, 2 Vols," (New Delhi: Munshiram Manoharlal, 1978).

[59] Mehrzad Boroujerdi, ed., *Mirror for the Muslim Prince: Islam and the Theory of Statecraft* (NY: Syracuse University Press, 2013). Omid Safi, *The politics of knowledge in premodern Islam: negotiating ideology and religious inquiry* (Durham, NC: University of North Carolina Press, 2006).

It was difficult selecting a single Sufi master as representative of Sufi political thought who had expressed his ideas in a modality that is conducive to such studies. Some colleagues I consulted recommended Nizam al-Mulk (1018–1092 AD),[60] his star disciple Abu Hamid Al-Ghazali (1058–1111 AD) and Nasiruddin al-Tusi (1201–1274 AD). I am not persuaded that we can use al-Mulk and al-Tusi as representative of Sufism. They may have dabbled with Sufism and even supported it, but while the former was more of a theologian-jurist, the later was a polymath who also dabbled in giving advice to Sultans. Al-Ghazali was the favorite but the more I read his work, the more I was convinced that it is difficult to separate the early Al-Ghazali who was a realist policy wonk from the later mystical Al-Ghazali. In the end, I selected Sheikh Saa'di of Shiraz persuaded by Shomali and Boroujerdi's excellent analysis of his work and my own personal connection to Sheikh Saa'di.[61] When I was growing up, Saa'di was a household name in Muslim families of India. Whenever she got into an argument with my grandfather, my maternal grandmother, to our great delight, would demand that he speak to her with respect since she had studied Saa'di's *Bustan* and *Gulistan* in Persian. One of Sheikh Saa'di's paeans about Prophet Muhammad (pbuh) has been my favorite since childhood and I often recite it in my lectures during Mewlid celebrations even to this day. The paean was about Prophet Muhammad's (pbuh) mystical night journey and it goes this way:

Balaghal-'ula be-kamaal-e-hi,
Kashafad-duja be-jamaal-e-hi,
Hasunat jamee'u khisaal-e-hi,
Sallu 'alae-hi wa aal-e-hi ...

He reached great heights by his own virtue
He dispatched darkness by his goodness
Every attribute of his is beautiful
May Allah shower his blessings on him and his family.

---

[60] Nizam Al-Mulk, Hubert Darke, trans., *The Book of Government or Rules for Kings* (London: Curzon, Books, 1960).

[61] See Alireza Shomali and Mehrzad Boroujerdi, "Sa'di's Treatise on Advice to the Kings," in Mehrzad Boroujerdi, ed., *Mirror for the Muslim Prince: Islam and the Theory of Statecraft* (NY: Syracuse University Press, 2013), pp. 45–81.

Additionally, it was delightful to note that in the very first tale, in Book One, in fact in the second paragraph of his book *Gulistan* Saa'di begins his advice to Kings by quoting a verse from the Quran that is about *Ihsan*: ... *Who restrain anger and who pardon the people—and Allah loves those who do* Ihsan *(Muhsineen)* (Quran, 3:134). How can a book about *Ihsan* not be partial to a scholar who starts his own book by invoking a verse from the Quran about *Ihsan?*

Shomali and Boroujerdi in their excellent analysis correctly locate Saa'di's work on politics within the genre of advice to Sultan or Mirrors to Princes, which was a prominent form of political advice literature in the Persian-Islamic societies during the heydays of Muslim Sultans and emperors from *Andalus* (Spain) to Hindustan (India).[62] But they chose to emphasize the secular nature of Saa'di's work and this is the only issue on which I wish to quibble with them.[63] Clearly Saa'di's work is markedly different from Al-Mawardi's *Ahkam* or Ibn Taymiyyah's *Shariah* politics. I do not however think that it is secular. The political ethos and values that underpin and radiate from Saa'di's work are in my view Islamic but from the Sufi tradition and because the Sufi perspective is based on an esoteric understanding of the *Shariah*, it is not as legalistic as the advice that comes from traditional orthodox Ulema. Traditional *Shariah* scholars had only one way of thinking—apply the law and do not waver too far from the sacred texts. Sufis and philosophers on the other hand also recognized the role of *Hikmah* (wisdom), *aql* (reason) and *ma'rifah* (gnosis) in divining the deeper meanings of the legal text and applied it to serve the material and spiritual interests of both the rulers and the ruled.

Sacred Is Secular

The beauty of Sufi thought is that it persuades rulers to follow Islamic values and to seek outcomes consistent with Islamic notions of justice unlike the *Shariah*-based politics approach which advocates rulers to apply the law forcefully on the populace and rather than the social outcomes themselves they are more interested in the realization of the letter of the

---

[62] More than half a century ago Reuben Levy translated and located Saa'di's work within the Mirrors for the Princess genre. Reuben Levy, *Stories from Sa'di's Bustan and Gulistan* (New York: Frederick A. Stokes Company Publishers, 1928). See also See Reuben Levy, A Mirror for Princes: *The Qabus Nama by Ksi Kaus Ibn Iskandar,* (New York: E. P. Dutton, 1951).

[63] See Alireza Shomali and Mehrzad Boroujerdi, "Sadi's Treatise on Advice to the Kings," pp. 45–81.

law. It is precisely because of this wisdom that Sufi political values appear to be secular and not religious. There are no secular ends in Islamic view; both secular and spiritual ends are either realized explicitly through legal means (*Shariah* politics) or through subtle means, which persuade rather than coerce rulers and the ruled to realize the good that is good in this and the other world.

The Sufi ideal that subverts or deconstructs the distinction between secular and religious by actually equating sacred to secular and mundane reality is best captured in this statement by Saa'di:

> *Religion consists alone in the service of the people; it finds no place in rosary, or prayer rug, or tattered garment. Be a King in Sovereignty and a devotee in purity of morals. Action, not words, is demanded by religion, for words without action are void of substance.*

The idea is also expressed by the prominent Sufi from India, Nizamuddin Awliya, when he states that the sole purpose of religion is to be of service to humanity regardless of religion, creed, race or nationality.[64] By reducing religion to service of humanity (*Khidmat-e-Khalq*), Sufis privilege the ruled over and above the ruler, since they are more demanding of the rulers and want the rulers to follow certain norms and ethics in order to do good for the ruled. Indeed, the spiritual and the otherworldly good of the rulers are subordinated to this worldly good of the ruled.

> *The administration of the state is a tremendous responsibility. It requires vigilance and prudence and also, continuous prayer to God so that what happens by the King's will, tongue, hands, and pen, will be productive to the dominion and to religion and (thus) accord with God's consent.*[65]

Sufi Advice Is More Comprehensive Than a Mirror for a Prince

The genre of mirror to the Princes or advice to sultans should not be understood as works of political philosophy rather they should be seen as policy recommendations for good governance. While the text *Nasihah al-Mulk* is indeed advice to Kings and recommends realism and even explores the idea of a social contract between the King and his subjects as Shomali

---

[64] See Nizamuddin Awliya, *Morals of the Heart*, trans. Bruce Lawrence (New York: Paulist Press, 1992), pp. 10–11.

[65] Shomali and Boroujerdi, p. 64.

and Boroujerdi recommend, it does not represent Saa'di's entire political philosophy. In *Gulistan* (Rose Garden), perhaps it is a metaphor for a happy and well (divinely) governed state and *Bustan* (Orchard), Saa'di advises not just the rulers, the ruled and the *Dervishes* the intellectual and spiritual elite of the society too are showered with his advice.[66] It is interesting that he does not speak much of or to traditional Islamic orthodox Ulema recognizing that they were not his audience. In these two books, Saa'di is clearly concerned with establishing a peaceful, stable, content and ethically sound and spiritually rich society. In many ways, Saa'di is a humanitarian *par excellence* and along with his love of God his single most important concern was for the material and spiritual well-being of all people. This philosophy is best captured in this famous stanza from *Gulistan*:

> *All men and women are to each other*
> *the limbs of a single body, each of us drawn*
> *from life's shimmering essence, God's perfect pearl;*
> *and when this life we share wounds one of us,*
> *all share the hurt as if it were our own.*
> *You, who will not feel another's pain,*
> *you forfeit the right to be called human.*

This poem of Saa'di has received much attention. It adorns the entrance to the United Nations' building in New York. It not only emphasizes the universalist and humanist tradition that underpins Islamic mysticism but it also is based directly on Islamic sources. The poem basically paraphrases a famous tradition of Prophet Muhammad (pbuh), quoted below, which itself is based on the Quran (9:71 and 59:9).

> *The example of the believers in their affection, mercy, and compassion for each other is that of a body. When any limb aches, the whole body reacts with sleeplessness and fever.*[67]

But Saa'di's entire philosophy of life and governance can be summarized in one short Surah or chapter of the Quran—*Al-Asr* (103) that reads as follows;

---

[66] See Omar Ali-Shah Saadi, trans., *The Rose Garden (Gulistan)* (Reno, Nevada: Tractus Books, 1997). Hart Edwards, *The Bustan of Sadi* (Los Angeles, CA: Indo-European Publishing, 2012).

[67] *Sahih Bukhari* 5665, *Sahih Muslim* 2586

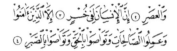

By time, indeed all of humanity is lost. Except those who believe, who do righteous deeds and advise each other to truth and advise each other to patience.

A Society Without War or Rebellion

Saa'di's philosophy will not appeal to those who are deeply frustrated and discontented with status quo and seek radical and rapid change. It is not revolutionary in fact it can be labeled as anti-revolution. He uses the threat of possible discontent and rebellion to insist that kings be considerate and caring; just and fair, and eschew oppression and tyranny (for their own good). But he also advises the ruled to be content; satisfied with what they have and be grateful to their Lord for they could be worse off than they are. There is no room for revolution or *Jihad* of any kind in Saa'di's politics. He does not advise the king to expand his realm, and he has no suggestions on how the king can rally his troops behind the flag to expand his reach and territory. Saa'di imagined a utopia in which the rulers were benign and just, the ruled content and forbearing and the *dervishes* (Sufis) selfless and ready to serve both the ruler and the ruled.

What is clear from Saa'di's contribution is that while Sufis may not have much to say about the structure and the organization of a state, they do have much advice to give for good governance and good living and good here is understood as good in this life as well as in the hereafter. It is also clear that they see the worldly well-being of the population as a higher priority for the ruler than the implementation of *Shariah* or any specific set of laws. Thus, the approval and contentment of the population are the litmus test for Sufi conceptions of an Islamic polity—and this alternate conception of an Islamic state is something that appeals to me more than an arbitrary implementation of laws potentially in a coercive setting. A Sufi state is one in which good governance is the ultimate good. It is a state of goodness—*Ihsan*.

PART II: THEORIES OF ISLAMIC POLITY AND ISLAMIC GOVERNANCE

Classic Islamic thinkers that we have studied so far were interested either in understanding how to establish a good government or how to establish the legitimacy of governments through implementation of Islamic laws.

Contemporary Islamic political thinkers are more interested in a comprehensive, meaning political, cultural and religious, revival of Muslim societies and they see an Islamic polity as either a part of that revival or a vehicle that will precipitate an Islamic revival. Their intellectual quest has more complications than that of their predecessors. They not only are trying to find a form of Islamic polity and governance suited for their time and place but they're also trying to simultaneously deal with the decline of Islamic power, rise of the Western, and with the political ideas, culture and structural changes that modernity brought to modern times.[68] Many Muslims, intellectuals and lay people, believe that it was the departure from the "Islamic way" which was the cause for the decline of the Islamic civilization and a return would once again herald the reawakening of Islamic civilizational glory. The Islamic state was envisioned as the vehicle of change that would realize these aspirations.[69]

Four Responses to Postcolonial Reality

There have been four distinct theoretical directions that Muslim thinkers have sought to shape the Muslim world's postcolonial political reality. The first and the most dominant response remains by secular Muslims who basically sought only political freedom from the West while culturally and intellectually embracing the West. Many of these Westernized secular elite replaced foreign colonization with internal colonization and in effect continued with the same regimes as the past. Indeed, in some cases, such as Turkey and Tunisia, they sought to introduce and establish Western cultures in Muslim societies with much gusto. In much of the Muslim Middle East, independence and modernization went hand in hand with Westernization.[70] These secular elites over the years have proven to be corrupt, more inclined to sell out national interests in pursuit of power and wealth and in spite of their Western intellectual allegiance extremely authoritarian and undemocratic. This Western secular authoritarian elite today rule much of the Muslim world. The limits of their

[68] Ali Rahnema, ed., *Pioneers of Islamic revival* (London: Zed Books, 2006). John L. Esposito, *Voices of resurgent Islam* (London: Oxford University Press, 1983).

[69] See Nazih Ayubi, *Political Islam*, pp. 1–24. Muhammad Asad, *The Principles of State and Government in Islam* (Gibraltar: Dar Al-Andalus, 1981). Also see Hamid Enayat, *Modern Islamic Political Thought* (Austin, Texas: University of Texas Press, 1991). Also see Mumtaz Ahmad, ed., *State Politics and Islam* (Indianapolis, IN: American Trust Publications, 1986).

[70] Mardin Serif, "Turkey: Islam and westernization," *Religions and societies: Asia and the Middle East* (1982): 171–198. M. Hakan Yavuz, "Cleansing Islam from the public sphere," *Journal of International Affairs* 54.1 (2000): 21.

vision and the poverty of their commitment is perhaps one of the major causes of the present crisis in the Muslim world. A century and half of Islamic revivalism and the momentous "Arab Spring" from 2010 to 2013 have resulted in a few quasi-Islamic states, Iran, Saudi Arabia and Sudan and a few Islamic democracies such as Pakistan, Turkey, Malaysia and Indonesia, but the goal of revival and global ascendance of Islam remains unrealized.[71]

The power and influence that the secularists wield along with their perennial failure to provide clean and good governance can be seen in the post–Arab Spring condition of Iraq, Syria, Egypt, Tunisia and Libya. But to date the best example of success of Muslim secularism remains Turkey. Turkey is easily the best governed and one of the most democratic of Muslim countries. It has been governed by an Islamist-leaning party (AK Party) since 2002, but continues to retain its secular and constitutional democratic character. Many commentators argue that the continued presence of democracy in Turkey is a credit to Turkish Islamists, who have truly realized the Islamic democracy that Islamic modernists dream about. Others argue that it is a credit to the legacy of nearly 80 years of aggressive secularism that has had such an enduring impact on Turkey that even Turkish Islamists advocate secularism. Regardless of what is true, Turkey's experience is not replicable. As the successor of the Ottoman Empire and the seat of the empire for centuries, it had experienced a degree of modernization, development and Europeanization that other Muslim countries had not experienced. So, while the Turkish model may be desirable to both secularists who are willing to live with Islamists and Islamists who are willing to share power with secularists, it may not be easy to reproduce in other Muslim countries. Finally, one reason why Turkey's experience and Turkish Islamism are different from that of Arab and South Asian Islamism is because Turkish Islamists by and large come from Sufi backgrounds whereas other Islamists tend to be more Salafi and are often anti-Sufi. I am aware that the founder of the Muslim Brotherhood, Hasan Al-Banna, belonged to a Sufi order, but when he founded the Muslim Brotherhood, he did not see it as a spiritual order, on the contrary saw it as one that was to engage the world order.

---

[71] Jean-François Létourneau, "Explaining the Muslim Brotherhood's Rise and Fall in Egypt," *Mediterranean Politics* (2016): 1–8. Frédéric Volpi and Ewan Stein, "Islamism and the state after the Arab uprisings: Between people power and state power," *Democratization* 22.2 (2015): 276–293. M. A. Muqtedar Khan, "The Arab Fall: War of All Against All," *Turkey Agenda* (2015). M. A. Muqtedar Khan, "Islam, Democracy and Islamism After the Counterrevolution in Egypt," *Middle East Policy* 21.1 (2014): 75–86.

The second and the third direction that Muslims are pursuing are both Islamic and non-secular in nature. They are the efforts to either establish an Islamic state or revive the old institution of the Caliphate. The Islamic state and the Caliphate though similar are actually mutually exclusive ideas. It was the recognition by leading Muslim thinkers such as Maulana Maududi and Rashid Rida that the possibility of reinstituting the Caliphate was impossible which led them to settle for a limited Caliphate accepting the postcolonial order of nation states and advancing the idea of the Islamic state. The theory of the Islamic state in principle accepts the world of nation states and is also a deferment of the utopian goal of global political integration of the Muslim world. It is possible that they hoped to first establish an Islamic state and then use it as a vehicle to unite Muslims, through persuasion or conquest and reconstruct the Islamic Caliphate.

The Movement for the Caliphate

The most prominent theorist with some contemporary influence in advocating the revival of the Caliphate was Taqiuddin Al-Nabbhani the founder of the political Islamist movement, *Hizb ut-Tahrir*. Al-Nabbhani has provided the Caliphate (*Khilafah*) movement the intellectual framework for their ideology. He produced a grand narrative about the virtues of the Caliphate that are far removed from historical reality. He believed that until the British and the Turks destroyed the institution of the *Khilafah* the entire Muslim world was under one rule. Details such as the presence of three simultaneous Caliphs, the *Abbasids* in Baghdad, the *Fatimids* in Egypt and the *Umayyads* in Spain during the tenth and the eleventh centuries, or the long wars between Muslim empires and the presence of numerous dynasties such as the Mughals in India or the Safavids in Iran, are irrelevant to his claim that a unified Caliph ruled uninterrupted from the first successor to Prophet Muhammad (pbuh) until 1924.[72] He seems to be laboring under a simplistic belief that all Muslims have to do is declare the *Khilafah* and Islam and Islamic civilization will regain its lost glory. He obviously does not bother to explain how, if *Khilafah* alone is the panacea of all problems, this glory was lost in the first place even while the *Khilafah* existed.[73]

---

[72] See Taqiuddin Al-Nabbhani, *The Islamic State* (Walnut, CA: The Islamic Cultural Workshop, 1996), pp. 128–133.

[73] See Taqiuddin Al-Nabbhani, *The Islamic State* (Walnut, CA: The Islamic Cultural Workshop, 1996).

Al-Nabbhani's book *The Islamic State* is full of historical inaccuracies, confusion between description and prescription and is more an expression of anger and frustration at the Muslim condition than a systematic theory of an Islamic polity. His usage of the term Islamic state interchangeably with the global Caliphate further heightens this confusion. He however does advance a sample constitution; this itself is a departure from the practice of the original Caliphate that was never a constitutional polity. The constitution he proposes is a muddled mixture of liberal democratic ideas and Islamist rhetoric. This idea is now advanced by mostly disenfranchised and disgruntled Muslim youth who use it to express their frustration with modernity and the powerlessness of the *Ummah* in the face of Western domination.

Al-Nabbhani advocated military *Jihad* as a means to establishing the Caliphate and as one of the key functions that the Caliphate will perform. He clearly argues that it is the duty of the Caliphate to conquer more lands in order to spread Islam and save the citizens of those countries from their own miserable lives. If one needs a footnote from a Muslim scholar to support the claim that "Islam was spread by the sword," then one need not look further than Al-Nabbhani.[74] If one were to read Al-Mawardi, Ibn Taymiyyah and Al-Nabbhani together then one can easily understand the political philosophy of the so-called Islamic State (*Daesh*) that has ravaged Iraq and Syria and wreaked havoc all over the world. It is possible that Al-Nabbhani would have been critical of some of the more egregious atrocities committed by the Islamic State but in principle he would admire both its emergence and its goals. It is clearly a natural consequence of his ideas and the movement that he launched.

The Islamic State (*Daesh*) is reviled by vast majority of Muslims according to a Pew study.[75] But it also has a tremendous appeal for many Muslims both in the West where they have enjoyed the fruits of modernity, democracy, pluralism and capitalism, and in Muslim societies especially in the Arab states. The brutality of the regime and its use of terrorism as its main strategy to conquer territory, take female slaves, attack civilians with suicide bombers and coordinated shooting rampages both in Europe and Muslim countries has shocked the world and triggered a wave of global

---

[74] See Taqiuddin Al-Nabbhani, *The Islamic State* (Walnut, CA: The Islamic Cultural Workshop, 1996), pp. 147–168.

[75] Jacob Poushter, "In Nations with significant Muslim Populations, much Disdain for ISIS," *Pew Research Center*, November 17, 2015. http://www.pewresearch.org/fact-tank/2015/11/17/in-nations-with-significant-muslim-populations-much-disdain-for-isis/.

Islamophobia, millions of refugees and devastated cities. In fact, the Islamic State (*Daesh*) has brought only infamy to Islam and devastation to Muslims. If their application of their understanding of Islamic law pleases God, it is not clear as to why then are the areas that they governed the worst places to live in the world today. Indeed, millions of Muslims have voted with their feet, through mass migration, that they would rather live in non-Muslim countries governed by secular democratic laws than the Islamic law implemented by the new Caliphate.[76]

The Quest for the Islamic State

The sister idea of the Islamic Caliphate is the revival of the Islamic state. Readers must remember that while I am treating them as two distinct ideas it is possible that in the minds of many of its advocates the two concepts may very well be the same. Jamaluddin Afghani, whose most important goal in life was to decolonize Muslim lands and Muslim culture, raised the first modern call for a political revival of the Muslim community. He wanted Muslims to become independent of the West politically as well as culturally and he envisaged an Islamic polity that would act as this beacon of freedom from Western occupation. Even though Afghani did not actually theorize about an Islamic state, his ideas of political independence from the West remain key foundations for the subsequent call for an Islamic state made by Maududi and Iqbal in South Asia and echoed in Egypt by Rashid Rida, Hassan al-Banna and Syed Qutb.[77]

Afghani and his disciples such as Muhammad Abduh were basically Islamic modernists. They accepted several aspects of modernity such as the importance of rational thought and science. Afghani and Abduh succeeded to some extent in reviving the rationalist tradition of the early *Mutazzalites*. But Afghani's most important impact was his ability to incite Muslim nationalism and awaken the desire for political freedom. But even at this time, late nineteenth century and early twentieth century, Muslim intellectuals were still talking of the *Ummah*, of the Muslim community as one global political entity and they hoped to unite them all under one banner.

[76] Michael Weiss, and Hassan Hassan, *ISIS: Inside the Army of Terror* (New York: Simon and Schuster, 2015). Daniel Byman, *Al Qaeda, the Islamic State, and the Global Jihadist Movement: What Everyone Needs to Know* (New York: Oxford University Press, 2015).

[77] See Ali Rahnema, ed., *Pioneers of Islamic Revival* (London: Zed Books, 1994) and also John O. Voll and John L. Esposito, *Makers of Contemporary Islam* (New York: Oxford University Press, 2001).

This call for a global political unity became temporarily more urgent and popular in the late 1920s after dissolution of the institution of the Caliphate. Until now the Caliphate had served as a symbol of Muslim political unity and with its dissolution ended the dream of a unified free *Ummah*.[78]

The earliest articulation of the Islamic state was made in South Asia by Maulana Maududi, the founder of *Jamaat-e-Islami*, a movement seeking to revive Islamic civilization through the establishment of an Islamic state, and Muhammad Iqbal who is considered as the intellectual architect of Pakistan. The independence movement in India had generated a sense of insecurity among Muslims who feared that they would be marginalized and dominated by the Hindu majority in the region after independence. This insecurity and the mishandling of Muslim fears by India's Hindu leaders led to the call for a separate state for Muslims in South Asia. Pakistan was thus conceived as a safe haven for Muslims—a Muslim home- land. Both Iqbal and Maududi, however, hoped not just to create a Muslim homeland but also an Islamic state.[79]

For Iqbal, an Islamic state was the expression of the Muslim spiritual self that sought to excel morally in all spheres including the political arena. He envisaged the Islamic state as a culmination of Muslim pursuit of per- fection and also submission to the will of God. He saw it as a vessel of Muslim identity and manifestation of Islamic civilization. Maududi, how- ever, imagined the Islamic state as an ideological instrument that sought to establish the "sovereignty of God" (*Al-Hakimiyyah*) on earth. This was the first and also the most sophisticated theorization of an Islamic state. For Maududi the objective of the Islamic state was to enforce the will of Allah and this was to be operationalized by applying the *Shariah* as the law of the land. Both Iqbal and Maududi accepted the territoriality of the Islamic state as opposed to the globality of the *Ummah* and they also were in favor of democracy at least at a procedural level. Iqbal sought to limit the franchise to those who were intellectually developed and knowledge- able and Maududi sought to make democracy ultimately subordinate to the *Shariah*. In essence they were willing to embrace the democratic process but not the democratic spirit.[80]

---

[78] For an understanding of Afghani's work and its impact, see Nikki R. Keddie, *An Islamic Response to Imperialism: Political and Religious Writing of Sayyid Jamal ad-Din "al-Afghani"* (Los Angeles, CA: University of California Press, 1983).

[79] For an understanding of Muhammad Iqbal's ideas on the Islamic state, see John L. Esposito, "Muhammad Iqbal and the Islamic State," in John L. Esposito, ed., *Voices of Resurgent Islam* (New York: Oxford University Press, 1983).

[80] To review Maulana Maududi's ideas on the Islamic state, see Syed Abul A'la Maududi, *Islamic Law and Constitution* (Lahore: Islamic Publications, 1992). See Masudul Hasan,

There are five important characteristics that are common to all these theorists. First, they saw the Islamic state as an ideological actor seeking to rescue the Muslim *Ummah* from Western domination. For most of these theorists the concept of a malevolent, imperial, Judeo-Christian and anti-Islamic West was the threat against which the Islamic state was expected to emerge and resist. Second, for the first time Islamic political theorists felt the need to assert that religion and politics are not separate. Thus, the Islamic state became a vehicle to reject secularism and secular humanism. Third, Islamic state was represented as a political arrangement wherein God and God alone was sovereign and legislator. Once again this was conceived in opposition to Western democracies where it was assumed that human will was sovereign and thus denying the possibility of pro-scribing politics within moral absolutes. Fourth, the ideological purpose of the Islamic state was seen as applying the *Shariah* within its borders and a commitment to *Jihad* (struggle) to spread Islam abroad. Finally, nearly all theorists of the Islamic state including Maududi, Qutb, Iqbal, Rida and Khomeini, their criticism of democracy notwithstanding, advocated the embrace of democratic procedures in selecting rulers and legislators and even in collective decision making.

The key to the idea of Islamic state and its legitimacy remains in the notion of applying the divine *Shariah*. The modern trajectory of this idea can be traced to Maududi, who borrowed it from Ibn Taymiyyah, to the Indian scholar Ali Mian Nadwi, who transmitted it to Syed Qutb.[81] From Maududi and Qutb the two Islamic movements, *Jamaat-e-Islami* and the Muslim Brotherhood have since globalized this concept of *Shariah* politics in the past 80 odd years. Maududi's admiration and endorsement of Ibn Taymiyyah as perhaps the most important reviver of Islam can be found in his widely translated and read work on Islamic revivalism. It is remarkable how Maududi singles out Ibn Taymiyyah for incredible praise:

Only Ibn Taymiyyah had the distinction of explaining the Islamic beliefs and injunctions in their right perspective and their true import.[82]

Sayyid Abul A'ala Maududi and His Thought (Lahore: Islamic Publications, 1984). Also see S. Vali Nasr, *Maududi and the making of Islamic Revivalism* (New York: Oxford University Press, 1997).

[81] See Asyraf hj. A. B. Rahman and Nooraihan Ali, "The Influence of Al-Mawdudi and the Jamaa'at Al Islami Movement on Sayyid Qutb Writings," *World Journal of Islamic History and Civilization* 2.4 (2012): 232–236.

[82] Syed Abul A'la Maududi, *A Short History of The Revivalist Movement in Islam* (Kuala Lumpur: The Other Press, 2002), p. 57.

It is obvious that except for Al-Nabbhani who is a modernized replica of Al-Mawardi, most other theorists of the Islamic state are modern versions of Ibn Taymiyyah in their conception of the application of the *Shariah* as the definitive characteristic of an Islamic state. Even the Islamic State (*Daesh*) and its leadership are heavily influenced by Ibn Taymiyyah. While the *Jamaat*'s and the Muslim Brotherhood's appropriation of the medieval scholar is mediated by Maududi and Qutb, *Daesh* accesses him directly and much of their communications quote him and his students to establish the Islamic credentials of their actions. Perhaps all of them see themselves like Ibn Taymiyyah, living in times when Muslims felt insecure about their borders from Western imperialism and the dilution of their Islamic identity from the globalization of Western culture. The added dimension that in an Islamic state God alone is sovereign is merely another way of registering their resistance to Western domination, which still continues even after decolonization. When Islamist theories say God is sovereign, what they basically mean is that *Shariah* is applied and Western influences must be expelled.[83]

Contemporary Impact of the Demand for Islamic State

Islamic revivalism and the campaign for an Islamic polity have not been very beneficial to the Muslim world. *Jihadi* groups such as Al-Qaeda, Boko Haram and Islamic State (*Daesh*) have unleashed violence and terrorism in Muslim countries killing and destabilizing states wherever they are. They also invite the Western powers to attack these countries by committing acts of terrorism in the West. Their actions have become so egregious and gratuitous that vast majorities of Muslims have literally disowned them and now scholars are rushing to issue fatwas declaring these movements as un-Islamic and anti-Islamic. They have not established any justice or moral order anywhere except produce chaos, mayhem and destruction. In addition, they have incited a discourse of Islamophobia that makes the lives of ordinary Muslims in a globalized world very difficult. *Jihadism* has no doubt both failed catastrophically but has also proven counterproductive. It has set back all societies, rather than revive and renew, that came within its orbit.

The peaceful revivalist movements have not had any success so far either. The Jamaat-e-Islami of Pakistan has been campaigning for decades in Pakistan, advocating the Islamization of its polity and economy. Decades

---

[83] Daniel Byman, *Al Qaeda, the Islamic State, and the Global Jihadist Movement: What Everyone Needs to Know* (New York: Oxford University Press, 2015).

of Islamization rhetoric have merely resulted in a nation proliferated by *Jihadi* groups, the Taliban and a culture of religious intolerance and sectarian strife. The loss of life, property and potential for development as a result of terrorism at home and abroad has been incredible. But one positive aspect of that country is the fact that despite the debilitating impact of Islamist groups, democracy, relative freedom of speech and diversity in practice of Islam still remain in Pakistan. The best aspects of Pakistan are those, which have not yet been affected by Islamic groups like the Taliban and the Lashkars and the *Jamaat* itself.[84]

In the Arab world, the Muslim Brotherhood has been struggling for ninety years to establish an Islamic state. They got their opportunity after secular dictatorships collapsed under the weight of their tyranny in Tunisia, Egypt and Libya. The Muslim Brothers won elections in Tunisia and Egypt and got their chance to both govern and design the new nations. In Tunisia, *Al-Nahda*, an Islamist party, was the biggest electoral victor and formed the government and had a chance to impact the writing of the new constitution. In Egypt, the Muslim Brothers had bigger electoral success and had complete control on the writing of the new constitution. Unfortunately, both in Egypt and Tunisia complex political circumstances and the limits of the Islamist vision and their failure to provide good governance all combined to close the window that had opened for the Islamic state. It is not the goal of this chapter to examine how and why it happened, but what happened is that not only has the Islamic state not been realized in these societies but also they are now neither more democratic nor more Islamic. The supporters of the Muslim Brothers will dispute this conclusion vehemently, but the fact remains that majorities in Egypt and in Tunisia have rejected the Shariah-based politics model and in Egypt have preferred to return to dictatorship rather than live under the rule of Muslim Brothers.[85]

[84] Husain Haqqani, *Pakistan: Between mosque and military* (Washington, DC: Carnegie Endowment, 2010). Husain Haqqani, "The role of Islam in Pakistan's future," *Washington Quarterly* 28.1 (2004): 83–96. Nadia Mushtaq Abbasi, "Impact of terrorism on Pakistan," *Strategic Studies* 23 (2013): 33–68.

[85] M. A. Muqtedar Khan, "Islam, Democracy and Islamism After the Counterrevolution in Egypt," *Middle East Policy* 21.1 (2014): 75–86. Jason Brownlee, Tarek Masoud and Andrew Reynolds, *The Arab Spring: Pathways of Repression and Reform* (Oxford University Press, 2015). John L. Esposito, Tamara Sonn, and John O. Voll, *Islam and Democracy after the Arab Spring* (Oxford University Press, 2015).

The Modernist Vision of Islamic Democracy

The fourth Muslim response to the postcolonial realities is that perspective which maintains that democracy is indispensable for Islamic governance and striving for democracy and Islamic governance is one and the same thing. The democracy deficit in the Muslim world has been mitigated by efforts at democratization in Indonesia, Malaysia, Pakistan, Iran, Tunisia, Morocco, Bangladesh and Turkey. Nevertheless, democracy is glaringly absent from most of the Arab world.[86] There are commentators in the West and in the Muslim world who share common interests in asserting that Islam and democracy are incompatible. Some Western scholars argue that Islam is incompatible with modernity, and in particular democracy, and insist that Muslims must either abandon Islam or reform Islam in order to join the "modern world."[87] Some Muslim scholars and militants reject democracy, arguing that it is contrary to the way of God (the Islamic *Shariah*), and in their eagerness to reject Western cultural and political domination they also reject democracy, falsely believing that democracy is something uniquely Western.[88] Fortunately, these arguments have been soundly rebutted. Many scholars have systematically demonstrated that Islam can coexist with the democratic process, and by highlighting the presence of democracy in several Muslim countries and the presence of Muslims in the West and in other places like India where democracy is well established, they have drawn attention to the fact that Islam and Muslims can thrive in democratic societies.[89]

Before my mystical turn I too was firmly grounded in this genre making the case for the compatibility of democracy and Islam, for faith and freedom. I approached democracy from within Islamic thought and described

---

[86] See Noah Feldman, *After Jihad: America and the Struggle for Islamic Democracy* (New York: Farrar, Straus & Giroux, 2003).

[87] See, for example, Bernard Lewis, "Islam and Liberal Democracy," *Atlantic Monthly* 27.2 (1993): 89.

[88] See Abdelwahab El-Affendi, "Democracy and its Muslim Critics: An Islamic alternative to Democracy?," in M. A. Muqtedar Khan, ed., *Islamic Democratic Discourse: Theory, Debates and Philosophical Perspectives* (Lanham, MD: Lexington Books, 2006), pp. 227–56.

[89] For this line of reasoning, see Mumtaz Ahmad, "Islam and Democracy: The Emerging Consensus," Islamonline.net (May 6, 2002). On the World Wide Web: http://www.islamonline.net/english/Contemporary/2002/05/Article15.shtml. Also see the collection of essays in Khaled Abou El Fadl, Joshua Cohen, and Deborah Chasman, eds., *Islam and the Challenge of Democracy* (Princeton, NJ: Princeton University Press, 2004), and in M. A. Muqtedar Khan, ed., *Islamic Democratic Discourse: Theory, Debates and Philosophical Perspectives* (Lanham, MD: Lexington Books, 2006).

the broad principles of Islamic governance. The key features of Islamic governance that I have found in Islamic sources, the Quran and the prophetic precedence (*Sunnah*) and contemporary Muslim discussions on the Islamic state are constitution, consent and consultation. Muslims who seek to implement the *Shariah* are obliged to emulate the Prophet's precedence and given the rather narrow definitions of *Shariah* and Sunnah that most Islamist operate with, there is no escape for them from the three key principles identified here. While these principles need to be explored and articulated in the specific sociocultural context of different Muslim societies, it is important to understand that they are essential.

Constitution

After Prophet Muhammad (pbuh) migrated from Mecca to Medina in 622 CE, he established the first Islamic state. For ten years, Prophet Muhammad (pbuh) was not only the leader of the emerging Muslim community in Arabia but also the political head of the state of Medina. As the leader of Medina, Prophet Muhammad (pbuh) exercised jurisdiction over Muslims as well as non-Muslims. The legitimacy of his sovereignty over Medina was based on his status as the Prophet of Islam as well as on the basis of the compact of Medina. As Prophet of God he had sovereignty over all Muslims by divine decree. But Prophet Muhammad (pbuh) did not rule over the non-Muslims of Medina because he was the messenger of Allah. He ruled over them by virtue of the compact that was signed by the *Muhajirun* (Muslim immigrants from Mecca), the *Ansar* (indigenous Muslims of Medina) and the *Yahud* (several Jewish tribes that lived in and around Medina). It is interesting to note that Jews were constitutional partners in the making of the first Islamic state.[90]

The compact of Medina can be read as both a social contract and a constitution. A social contract, an idea developed by English philosophers Thomas Hobbes and John Locke, is an imaginary agreement between people in the state of nature that leads to the establishment of a community or a state. In the state of nature people are free and are not obliged to follow any rules or laws. They are essentially sovereign individuals. But through the social contract, they surrender their individual sovereignty to a collective and create a community or a state.

[90] For the entire text of the Compact of Medina, see M. H. Haykal, *The Life of Muhammad*, trans. Ismael R. Al Faruqi (Indianapolis: NAIT, 1988), pp. 180–83.

The second idea that the compact of Medina manifests is that of a constitution. In many ways the constitution is the document that enshrines the conditions of the social contract upon which any society is founded. The compact of Medina clearly served a constitutional function since it was the constitutive document for the first Islamic state. Thus, we can argue that the compact of Medina serves the dual function of a social contract and a constitution. Clearly, the compact of Medina by itself cannot serve as a modern constitution. It would be quite inadequate since it is a historically specific document and quite limited in its scope. However, it can serve as a guiding principle to be emulated rather than a manual to be duplicated. Today Muslims worldwide can emulate Prophet Muhammad (pbuh) and draw up their own constitutions, historically and temporally specific to their conditions.

Consent

An important principle of the Constitution of Medina was that Prophet Muhammad (pbuh) governed the city-state of Medina by virtue of the consent of its citizens. He was invited to govern and his authority to govern was enshrined in the social contract.[91] The constitution of Medina established the importance of consent and cooperation for governance. The process of *bayah*, or the pledging of allegiance, was an important institution that sought to formalize the consent of the governed. In those days, when a ruler failed to gain the consent of the ruled through a formal and direct process of pledging of allegiance, the ruler's authority was not fully legitimized.[92] This was an Arab custom that predates Islam but like many Arab customs was incorporated within Islamic traditions. Just as Prophet Muhammad (pbuh) had done, the early Caliphs of Islam too practiced the process of *bayah* after rudimentary forms of electoral colleges had nominated the Caliph, in order to legitimize the authority of the Caliph. One does not need to stretch one's imagination too far to recognize that in polities that have millions rather than hundreds of citizens; the process of nomination followed by elections can serve as a necessary modernization of the process of *bayah*. Replacing *bayah* with ballots makes the process of pledging allegiance simple and universal. Elections therefore are neither a departure from Islamic principles and traditions nor inherently un-Islamic in any form.

[91] See A. H. Siddiqui, *The Life of Muhammad* (Des Plaines, IL: Library of Islam, 1991), pp. 117–32.

[92] See Khaled Abou El Fadl et al., *Islam and the Challenge of Democracy*, p. 11.

The Quran too recognizes the authority of those who have been chosen as leaders and in a sense extends divine legitimacy to those who have legitimate authority.

O you who believe! Obey Allah and obey the Messenger and those in authority from among you. (Quran 4:59)

Consultation

The third key principle of Islamic governance is consultation or *Shura* in Arabic. This is a very widely known concept and many Islamic scholars have advanced the Islamic concept of *Shura* as evidence for Islam's democratic credentials. Indeed, many scholars actually equate democracy with *Shura*.[93]

...and consult them in affairs (of moment). Then, when thou hast taken a decision put thy trust in Allah. (Quran 3:159)

[righteous are those] ... who conduct their affairs through [shura baynahum] mutual Consultation. (Quran 42:38)

Muslim scholars dispute whether the Quranic injunction for consultation is advisory or mandatory, but it nevertheless remains a divine sanction. Pro-democracy Muslims see it as necessary and those who fear democratic freedoms and prefer authoritarianism interpret these injunctions as divine suggestions and not divine fiats. The Prophet himself left behind a very important tradition that emphasized the importance of collective and democratic decision-making. He said, "the community of Muhammed will never agree upon error."[94] Consultative governance therefore is the preferred form of governance in Islam and any Muslim who chooses to stay true to her sacred sources cannot but prefer a democratic structure to all others to realize the justice and well-being promised in Islamic sources.

Contemporary Academic Contributions

In recent years, a few academics in the West have advanced interesting perspectives on Islamic political thought and even advanced their own models

---

[93] See, for example, John L. Esposito and John O. Voll, *Islam and Democracy* (New York: Oxford University Press, 1996).

[94] See the hadith collection Imam Al-Tirmidhi (4:2167).

on how Muslims could build a polity that accommodates both Islam and to some extent democracy and secularism. They include Abdullahi A. An-Na'im, Khaled Abou El-Fadl, Abdolkarim Soroush, Nader Hashmi, Abdelwahab El-Affendi and Wael Hallaq. All of them offer very interesting and sophisticated perspectives. El-Fadl and Soroush in my view are the poles and the rest fall in between. El-Fadl advances a strong juristic case for the compatibility of Islam and democracy and Soroush offers a philosophical perspective. Soroush is closer to Al-Farabi in his style and perspective and even though El-Fadl is more like Al-Mawardi in his approach, his conclusions are very different; moderated by a clear normative preference for tolerance and democracy and influenced by Western discourse on human rights. Despite their varying perspectives, both El-Fadl and Soroush make the case for the compatibility of Islam and democracy. I have discussed and engaged these scholars extensively in the past and my own thinking has been enriched by their thoughtful contributions.[95]

Hashmi's *Islam, Secularism and Liberal Democracy* is more about the compatibility of religion and liberal democracy in spite of the fundamental relationship between secularism and liberal democracy.[96] It is a very good example of how Western political thought can impact and permeate Muslim political theory. Hashmi's book sometimes reads more like a book about Western liberal political thought than one that seeks to define a system of government or governance for Muslims. He has interesting insights on the more complex ways of thinking about secularism and he highlights how Muslims must come to terms with this idea before they can articulate a conception of democracy. Wael Hallaq's *The Impossible State* is a very sophisticated legal and philosophical conversation about modernity and the modern state.[97] He highlights some of the fundamental incompatibilities in the premodern conceptions of law and polity in Muslim thinking and modern structural conditions. In a sense, he is arguing that the Islamic state, state understood in modern terms, did not ever exist and

---

[95] Abdolkarim Soroush, *Reason, freedom, and democracy in Islam: Essential writings of Abdolkarim Soroush* (New York: Oxford University Press, 2000). Khaled Abou El Fadl, *Islam and the Challenge of Democracy: A "Boston Review" Book* (Princeton, NJ: Princeton University Press, 2004). Also see M. A. Muqtedar Khan, "Islamic Democratic Theory: Between Political Philosophy and Jurisprudence," *Global Dialogue* 6.1/2 (2004): 44–52.

[96] Nader Hashemi, *Islam, Secularism, and Liberal Democracy: Toward a Democratic theory for Muslim Societies* (New York: Oxford University Press, 2009).

[97] Wael B. Hallaq, *The impossible state: Islam, politics, and modernity's moral predicament* (New York: Columbia University Press, 2014).

may not be possible to realize. He recommends that Muslims first adjust to the modern state and its metaphysical and ethical preferences and then work slowly to build a moral community that may gradually realize Islamic laws and values.

An-Na'im in *Islam and the Secular State* and El-Affendi in his *Who Needs an Islamic State?* advance a very similar thesis even though they look at things very differently.[98] Both of them are making the same argument that Muslims can produce an Islamic polity without having to either impose the *Shariah* or have an ideological state. They seem to argue that a secular state that allows the existence of a religious society and community can serve Muslim aspirations. Muslims do not have to impose Islamic law in order to construct a virtuous state and society. A free society that allows its citizens to build a moral and ethical culture and community is in my view a more virtuous state than one that coerces its population into following a moral code. Both of them provide a very nuanced critique of contemporary Islamist thinking and the demand for a *Shariah* state. I find them the most compelling of contemporary academic scholars. I wish academics impacted Muslim masses, the same way as Islamist ideologues do.

CONCLUSION

In this chapter, I sought to provide a brief genealogy of Islamic political thought and philosophy. I divided the history of Islamic political thought into two eras, premodern and postcolonial. In the premodern era, I sought to show the diversity in approaches to political thought within the Islamic intellectual tradition. While the work of jurist-theologians like Al-Mawardi and Ibn Taymiyyah has dominated contemporary Islamic political revival, I want to remind us that there are other legitimate and important Muslim contributions to understanding politics and achieving the Islamic goals to establish justice, dignity and protect freedom of religion—essentially good governance. When Muslims talk of Islamic governance, they automatically talk of the juristic-theologian perspective as if it is the only approach. We should not forget that both Al-Farabi and Ibn Khaldun also provided alternate approaches to Islamic governance which

---

[98] Abdullahi A. An-Na'im, *Islam and the Secular State: Negotiating the future of Shari'a* (Boston: Harvard University Press, 2008). Abdelwahab El-Affendi, *Who needs an Islamic state?* (London: Malaysiathinktank, 2008).

may actually be more compatible with modern times than the Al-Mawardi and Ibn Taymiyyah approaches. I have also shown that even though the Sufis have not articulated political theory in a systematic fashion; through poetry, mystical aphorisms, parables and even advice literature they have provided another distinct perspective on Islamic governance.

In the second part, I examined the approaches to politics adopted by Muslim political thinkers in the postcolonial era. Unfortunately, the plot I write is a tragedy. Except for the Islamic democracy approach, which has seen very limited success in Pakistan, Turkey, Iran, Malaysia and Indonesia, the Islamist approaches of Islamic Caliphate and Islamic state have so far shown very little promise of success. Indeed, much of the Arab world today is mired in a struggle between authoritarian regimes and extremist movements seeking to establish totalitarian regimes.[99] This struggle is spilling over into Muslim states where democracy has a hope (Turkey and Pakistan) and is threatening to undermine its prospects there. I find classical Islamic thinkers more promising. They were original and true not only to their sources but also to their time and place and one can easily see how they were all responding to their challenges. Contemporary thinkers are however constrained by not only the pressure to remain consistent with the Islamic heritage but also to articulate a vision at a time when there is so much intellectual pressure from Western political thought and success of Western political models. While the classical thinkers were in tune with their moment in history, many of the contemporary Islamic thinkers struggle to come to terms with modernity. The biggest challenge that remains for them is to separate Western culture and ideology from the irreversible structural conditions of modernity. The former can be critiqued and deconstructed but the latter must be accommodated and adjusted to.

---

[99] The sole exception is Tunisia where the inability of Islamists to dominate the politics as they did in post–Arab Spring Egypt has allowed secular democratic forces to balance them and this has resulted in a tenuous but still enduring democratic Tunisia. But Tunisian democracy is more secular and not what I would describe as an Islamic democracy.

CHAPTER 7

Ihsan and Good Governance

Indeed, Allah has commanded Justice with Ihsan. (Quran 16:90)

In this chapter, I shall propose a broad model of good governance that seeks
to realize the highest virtues in Islamic ethos—*Ihsan*. At the outset, I want
to touch upon a simple 'level of analysis' issue. The concept of *Ihsan*, the
highest state and virtue that a believer can aspire for, is one that has traditionally been conceived of and understood at an individual level. Here I am
proposing that we realize *Ihsan* not just at an individual level but also at a
collective level. Thus, we seek to establish social and structural conditions
that can facilitate the emergence of a society of *Muhsins*—those who have
attained the personal state of *Ihsan* and wish to establish a community or
State of *Ihsan*. It is possible to imagine a society composed of and led by
virtuous individuals and all religious and normative political theories did so.
Al-Farabi's vision of a virtuous republic too imagined a society of individuals
with laudable virtues. But here I am arguing that we also need to envision a
state that is virtuous and to do so we need virtuous governance and we need
to identify the structural characteristics of this virtuous state. Therefore, in
this chapter, I will discuss what constitutes a *State of Ihsan* and advance an
alternate vision of Islamic governance that goes beyond the elementary idea
that Islamic governance is just the implementation of Islamic laws, but
rather that Islamic governance is the realization of virtuous outcomes such
as social justice, tolerance, acceptance, compassion and peace.

© The Author(s) 2019   209
M. A. M. Khan, *Islam and Good Governance*,
https://doi.org/10.1057/978-1-137-54832-0_7

Muslims who seek to engage in politics and shape the political system itself must balance their endeavors according to the following two Quranic commands: *Let there be no compulsion in religion, truth stands out clear from error* (2:256) and *You are the best nation produced for humanity. You encourage what is good and forbid what is evil* (3:110). Those Muslim thinkers who privilege 2:256 argue that no compulsion in religion clearly advocates a secular state, which does not enforce religious values over its population. What is the point of belief if this belief is coerced by the state? Thus, while criminal activity can be prosecuted, the state must stay out of matters of belief and *Ibadah* (worship). On the other hand, some scholars have interpreted the command to encourage or order good and forbid evil as implementation of *Shariah*, since it is the *Shariah* that informs Muslims about what is right and what is wrong. Thus, a *Shariah*-based state cannot be secular since it has the moral preference for *Shariah*, which must be implemented.[1]

A believing Muslim must abide by Islamic *Shariah*. She and specially the knowledgeable ones in the community have the freedom to interpret and reinterpret the *Shariah*, but they must have faith in the *Shariah*, which is part of becoming a Muslim—submitting to Allah. So, in essence, the believers must balance the two commands: let there be no compulsion in religion and yet there must be a community that advocates good and forbids evil. Indeed, the partial approaches of either interpretation that privileges one command while ignoring the other are in violation of the spirit of the Quran. The Quran clearly forbids selective application of the scriptures (Quran 2:85). The only way in which one can imagine the simultaneous realization of both those principles is to adopt the solution recommended by Abdullahi A. An-Na'im,[2] establish a secular state—a state that does not compel its people to follow a religion—and yet encourage the establishment of a religious society enriched and infused by Islamic values through endeavors anchored in civil society. Similarly, a State of *Ihsan* can be imagined as a secular state that does not seek to enforce or implement religion and religious values but creates an intimidation-free environment that allows various ethical and virtuous communities and even movements to advocate the pursuit of individual and societal perfection. A society in

---

[1] See, for example, Mustafa Köylü, "Religion and Citizenship education: The Case of Turkey," in Ednan Aslan and Marcia Hermansen, eds., *Islam and Citizenship Education* (New York: Springer 2015), pp. 201–201. See also M. A. Muqtedar Khan, "Islamic governance and democracy," *Islam and Democratization in Asia* (2009): 13–27.

[2] See An-Na'im, *Islam and the Secular State*.

which individuals seek to perfect their souls and their moral conduct and pursue a life that will witness the divine goodness by manifesting it in their actions can potentially become the virtuous society that philosophers from Plato to Al-Farabi and mystics like Saa'di dreamed of.

Imagine a modern polity to be composed of two important halves, the state and the society; premodern thinkers often conceptualized this segmentation as that between rulers and the ruled. I propose five normative and *Ihsan*-based principles that in my view should shape the structure and nature of the state and five similarly ethical and mystical *Ihsan*-based principles that should inform the constitution of the society. The purpose of these principles is to enable us to start thinking about Islamic governance in ways that will incorporate the essence of *Ihsan* into the processes of governance. In the review of Islamic political philosophy, we found that Muslim thinkers devoted much ink and thought to the nature and structure of the rulers/state/Caliphate and very little to that of the ruled/citizens. The emphasis on the citizens to obey was asserted from the Quran—*Obey Allah, his messenger and those in authority amongst you* (4:59)—and the assumption that the state or the rulers will determine the nature of the political community was taken for granted.[3] They assumed that the nature of the state was constitutive of the political community. The structure of the polity was seen as top down. The political community composed of rulers and the ruled was understood as a product of obedient and believing but passive subjects and the nature of the rulers and the structure of the government as alone deterministic of the ultimate nature of the state. I am now recognizing that both the state and the society have power to shape their collective reality and therefore the political community is co-constituted by both the state and the society. They shape each other and they coproduce their political reality. The reality that political community is a historically evolving product of the continuous interaction of the state and the society also emphasizes the futility of articulating blueprints for perfect states. So rather than designing a blueprint for a virtuous state as my predecessors have done, I shall limit myself to articulating a few guiding principles. The principles that I propose are based on my unveiling of *Ihsan*—from a cosmic view to a worldview—and the political philosophical thoughts, poetry and musings of *Ahl Al-Tasawwuf* (the Sufis) such as Saa'di of Shiraz. These principles I submit, if realized by the state and the society, could produce a virtuous political reality—a State of *Ihsan*.

---

[3] Asma Afsaruddin, "Obedience to Political Authority: An Evolutionary Concept," *Islamic Democratic Discourse: Theory, Debates, and Philosophical Perspectives* (2006): 37.

THE STATE OF *IHSAN*

This book does not seek to advance a utopian project that will instantaneously transform the world or the Muslim society that adopts it magically. Suddenly justice and peace are not going to appear as soon as this model is invoked. Honestly no model has delivered in such a way. Historically, we can only find that some models are better and more successful than others while challenges to peace, harmony and justice remain in every society and in every era. History in a sense is driven by the perpetually arising challenges to justice, and human development is a consequence of this continuous struggle to face them. Nor am I suggesting that we press some mythical "reset button" that will erase the past and allow a desirable present and future to appear. We have to start from where we are. The following are the five principles of good governance, at the level of the state and government structure, that I submit that can help establish a *State of Ihsan*. I discuss these principles as illustrating a transition from the extant principles to what I am proposing. Therefore, they are all cast in the form of "from something" to "something else."

From Tawheed *to Sovereignty*

إِنَّنِي أَنَا ٱللَّهُ لَآ إِلَٰهَ إِلَّآ أَنَا۟ فَٱعْبُدْنِي وَأَقِمِ ٱلصَّلَوٰةَ لِذِكْرِيٓ

Indeed, I am Allah. There is no deity except Me, so worship me and establish prayer for My remembrance. (Quran 20:14)

The principle of *Tawheed*, which is belief in the oneness of God or monotheism, is the most important belief in Islam. Everything else is secondary to testifying the oneness of God. God is One; He alone is worthy of worship—*There is No God but Allah* (Quran 112:1). He is eternal, unchanging and permanent, and He alone created the entire creation (Quran 112:2 and 32:4). He created sentient beings for the sole purpose of worshipping Him and Him alone without any partners (Quran 51:56). The fundamental goal of creation is to witness Him and glorify Him. In essence, the singular purpose of all things that exist is to testify to His oneness (Quran 22:18). Fascinatingly, God is unity but His creation is the realm of multiplicity. He created multiple beings—humans, jinn and angels. He created multiple life forms—humans, animals and plants. He created multiplicity in humanity: as different races, tribes and nations, and even faiths. If He wanted, He could create them all the same and make them believe in Him, but even in matters of belief in Him, He created diversity—those who believe, those who doubt, those who deny and those who take partners (Quran 49:13, 10:99 and 5:48). Thus, the defining characteristic of the creator is unity and the defining characteristic of creation is multiplicity. This is the central creedal belief of Islam across all of its many sects. Initially, Muslims understood *Tawheed* as oneness of God, but after encountering the Christian doctrine of Trinity, the concept took another dimension, unity of God, implying the indivisibility of the divine and thus God is One, absolute and indivisible. The principle of *Tawheed* not only has spiritual implications but also sociopolitical implications for Muslim societies. All Muslim political theorists of Islamic polities will agree that ultimately the most important normative goal of Muslims is the preservation, realization and institutionalization of *Tawheed*. It is the core of Islamic schools of thought and Islamic ideologies.

But the people of *Ihsan* provide an interesting interpretation to this principle. One of Allah's 99 names is *Al-Haq*, mentioned in several verses in the Quran (6:62, 22:6, 24:25). *Al-Haq* means both "The Truth" and "The Real." Many Sufis believe that God is the only absolute reality and everything else that exist other than Him has no reality except a conditional existence contingent on the mercy and benevolence of *The Real*.[4] He is and He is like nothing else (Quran 112:4 and 42:11). There is a fundamental opposition in the ontology of the Creator and the creation; the former is eternal and permanent, while the latter is temporal and contingent. God is One but His creation is multiple. Yet, unity is invisible and multiplicity is manifest. While philosophically it is difficult to fully understand as to how things can exist and be unreal at the same time, some of the aspects of multiplicity that are more germane to political systems, such as differences in race, gender, ethnicity, nationality and religion, can be understood as unreal in the sense that they are socially constructed and not given. Thus, unity is invisible but given and multiplicity is visible but socially and historically constructed. In a well-known tradition, Prophet Muhammad (pbuh) says as much when he says that all are born as believers but it is their parents who bring people up as Jews or Christians, hinting at a universal identity and socially constructed difference.[5]

---

[4] See Murata and Chittick, *Vision of Islam*, pp. 60–62.
[5] See the collection in *Sahih Bukhari*, Book 33, and #6426.

This metaphysical and mystical prelude is necessary for a discussion of sovereignty, which is so central to modern Islamic thought as it is used to distinguish Islamic polities, wherein God alone is sovereign, from modern nation states, where people are sovereign. But a reading of the development of the modern concept of sovereignty based on the work of philosophers Jean Bodin, Thomas Hobbes, Jean Jacques Rousseau, John Locke and Immanuel Kant, and several contemporary theorists such as Nicholas Onuf, I have shown that the modern concept of sovereignty essentially argues that sovereignty is "absolute, indivisible and inalienable."[6] It reads like the Islamic concept of *Tawheed* and thus the power to make laws that many Muslim theorists argued was God's prerogative alone was now vested in the modern state. But what these theorists, specially Maulana Maududi of Pakistan and Syed Qutb of Egypt, who made *Al-Hakimiyyah*, God's sovereignty, a distinguishing feature of Islamic state, did not comprehend was that God bestowed sovereignty to humanity to act as His vicegerents on earth (Quran 2:30) and thus they possessed *Wilayah* or authority to act on his behalf. The modern state is just a device that enables the sovereign human to act on earth as witness to her Lord (when she is a believer) and as witness against herself when she is a disbeliever. In both cases, within the Islamic cosmology, she is acting only because God has empowered her to act.

The conclusion of this discussion is that the modern state is neither acting for God nor acting against God, just as the Islamic Caliphates neither acted for God nor acted against God. Both the modern state and the premodern empires, sultanates and Caliphates, no matter what their ideological or political claims, acted as devices of those in power and were designed to serve their interests whatever they may be—sacred or mundane. Our collective beliefs can be shaped by the more powerful modern states and even our identities can be constituted by them to a great extent, but our ability to reason, to deconstruct and to commit to normative goals can empower us to reconstitute even the modern states. The wave of democratization in Eastern Europe after the collapse of the Soviet Union in 1991 is one excellent example of how it has been done successfully in recent times. The Arab Spring, which has failed (barring Tunisia to some extent), was an excellent opportunity to reconstitute the nature of polities in the Middle East. That failure, however, does not mean that Arabs will never be able to reconstitute their polities. Human agency (vicegerency) is a powerful force that drives our history.[7]

[6] See M. A. Muqtedar Khan, "Sovereignty in Modernity and Islam," *East-West Review* 1.2 (Summer 1995): 43–57.

[7] M. A. Muqtedar Khan, "Sovereignty in Islam as Human Agency," *Ijtihad*. Available from: http://www.ijtihad.org/sovt.htm (Dec 30, 1999).

My first principle is to submit that we can think of the modern concept of sovereignty in the same vein as one thought of *Tawheed* in the political sense. And sovereignty is essentially the institutionalization of the collective will of people within a polity. Thus, in order to uphold the idea of unity of God in the political realm, we need not assume that God's sovereignty is somehow at odds with the will of the people rather to recognize that the will of the people is essentially God's granting of agency or *Khilafah* to human actors. It is only because human beings possess agency that they can be expected to create a virtuous society on earth and can be judged for the kind of political systems they produce. Without agency, there is no sovereignty and, without sovereignty, there is no polity. It is time Muslims recognized that God has granted them agency to act and must act to bear witness to Him in the political sense.

From Righteous Caliphs to Prophet

As discussed in the previous chapter, the theory of Caliphate based on the historical precedence of the rightly guided Caliphs (*Al-Khulafa Al-Rashidun*) has become the basis for much of *Shariah*-based Islamic models of government. The entire philosophical project treats the first 30 years of Islamic history after the death of Prophet Muhammad (pbuh) as the perfect model of governance that must be replicated or modeled in order for any Islamic form of government to be legitimate. It is because of this logic that Islamic governments implement Islamic laws and it is the belief of those who advocate *Shariah*-based governments that this was done best by the rightly guided Caliphs. I submit that the problem with this model is that it treats the first four Caliphs as models for emulation. But the Quran on the other hand says that it is the Prophet (pbuh) who has been sent as a model for Muslims to emulate.

لَّقَدْ كَانَ لَكُمْ فِى رَسُولِ ٱللَّهِ أُسْوَةٌ حَسَنَةٌ

Certainly the Messenger of Allah is the best example (model) for you. (Quran 33:21)

The word used for the term model is a conjugate of *Ihsan* and can also be understood as the most beautiful example. While one can maintain that the period of the rightly guided Caliphs was the best implementation of Islam after the Prophet's death, the best application of Islam in history would have to be under the sovereignty of Prophet Muhammad (pbuh) who governed with the dual benefit of divine revelation and the active participation of Angel Gabriel, who was always there to advise him and facilitate communications with God. Therefore, I submit that Muslims, in order to articulate Islamic governance, return to the prophetic example (Sunnah) and not privilege the example of the rightly guided Caliphs over that of the prophetic model. This is not to deny that within the particularities of time and space, the actions and choices of the rightly guided Caliphs were the best realizations of the prophetic model.

So, what does this paradigmatic shift mean? What it means is that one starts looking explicitly and exclusively at the prophetic example for principles of good governance and political community rather than any other era. We work with the original blueprint. We understand that structural conditions have changed significantly in the last 1400 years but nevertheless the methodology or approach of Prophet Muhammad (pbuh) to governance, not necessarily specific rulings or decisions, can serve as the best normative model for Muslims with which they can inform their contemporary political theory. The biggest benefit to Muslims from this paradigmatic shift is the tradition of constitutionalism. Prophet Muhammad (pbuh) governed the nascent state of Medina based on a clearly articulated constitution known as *Al-Dastur Al-Madinah*[8] and we are in possession of its text. It is not a draft that can be practically implemented today; it has its limitations but the principles of governance and political community that it enshrines can be beacons of guidance for us today. For example, it does not specify the architecture of government or the mechanics and locations of power and authority and its execution. That is why the first four Caliphs had a different process in each of their pathways to power and authority.

But the nascent state of Medina does privilege and provide sacred sanction to the idea of a social contract and constitution, to governance by consent and to mutual consultation. It also provides the prophetic precedence of treating people of different communities as citizens with equal rights. The constitution of Medina explicitly calls Jews and Muslims as constituting one *Ummah* (one nation) in article #25 and also stipulates same rights and responsibilities for all communities that are party to the constitution.[9] Additionally, the prophetic model prescribes less than the caliphal

---

[8] M. A. Muqtedar Khan, "The Compact of Medina: A Constitutional Theory of the Islamic State," *The International Mirror* (2001). M. A. Muqtedar Khan, "Islamic governance and democracy," *Islam and Democratization in Asia* (2009): 13–27.

[9] The full text of the English translation of the constitution of Medina can be read here: http://www.constitution.org/cons/medina/con_medina.htm.

model, thus enabling Muslims in different eras and different circumstances to be at liberty to develop and adopt systems of governance that are best suited to them as long as they respect the prophetic example of constitutionalism, consent and inclusiveness, and treat the example of other Muslims as advisory and informative rather than sacred and mandatory. Therefore, my second governance principle is to privilege the example of the Prophet above all others and use the constitution that Prophet Muhammad (pbuh) used as a guide to good governance.

From Structure to Process: Government to Governance

Two things stand out from our brief review of the history of Islamic political thought. For many Muslim thinkers the structure of the state and the application of divine law by the state were paramount, except for philosophers and those who were part of the advice to Sultans genre and Ibn Khaldun. For modern thinkers, the structure of the government became the most important element as they struggled to balance the demands of governing a complex modern society in a highly competitive and hostile international environment with values and laws articulated and canonized centuries before to serve medieval societies and their leaders. Every modern model advanced by Muslims tried to create a structure of government that would reconstitute either the global Caliphate or a state-level Caliphate with the powers and authority of the Rashidun Caliph and thus the focus on the Caliphate, the Islamic state or the Islamic democracy.[10]

Only two processes received any attention: the process of *Shura*, consultation, and the process of *Ijtihad*, the rethinking of Islamic edicts to suit new circumstances. For some, the process of consultation and rethinking was limited and, for the modernists, it was certainly expansive and they did talk of *Shura* as nothing short of democracy and *Ijtihad* as a surrogate term for modernization of Islamic laws.[11] Even when thinking of Islamic democracies in theory, contemporary jurists limited both consultation and rethinking as the preserve of jurists alone and subordinated democracy to

---

[10] Hamid Enayat, *Modern Islamic political thought* (London: I. B. Tauris, 2005). Antony Black, *The history of Islamic political thought: From the Prophet to the present* (London: Edinburgh University Press, 2011). Patricia Crone, *God's rule: Government and Islam* (New York: Columbia University Press, 2004).

[11] See Ahmad Al-Raysuni, *Al-Shura: The Quranic Principle of Consultation* (Herndon, VA: IIIT, 2011). Taha Jabir al-Alwani, *Ijtihad* (London: International Institute of Islamic Thought, 1993).

limits of the *Shariah* already defined by the tradition in the past. I think that this is a profound limitation in extant Islamic political thought—the inability to play outside the sandbox whose boundaries have been delineated by Al-Mawardi and Ibn Taymiyyah.

I would like to submit that Muslim thinkers stop attaching too much significance to the structure and architecture of government. What is the point of getting the structure right if it does not deliver? This raises another question: what is the deliverable? In my view, good governance is the deliverable and *Muslims should focus on Islamic (good) governance rather than Islamic government.* It does not matter what the form of the government is if it does not deliver good governance. Additionally, governmental structures evolve over time and fundamental changes in them require revolutions that can be bloody and not necessarily successful. If the Arab Spring has taught one thing, then it is the fact that revolutions do not necessarily guarantee positive outcomes. They can lead to and have led to collapse of the political order, chaos and devastation. Structures can be changed gradually if there is a need and the need can be determined by privileging good governance rather than religious symbolism as the product of governments and states.

So for now, I recommend that Muslim societies proceed with the working hypothesis that the collective wisdom of humanity, which considers democratic governance as a desirable form of government, cannot be entirely wrong and pursue gradual democratization with emphasis on Islamic or good governance. Muslims will fail if they ignore the overwhelming accumulation of empirical evidence. Democracies have proven to be enduring (the American system has existed for over 240 years across three centuries with only 27 amendments), adaptable to different cultures and values, and desirable to people of all faiths and even those who do not believe in God. Hindus in India, Jews in Israel, Christians and Atheists in America and Europe, and even large segments of Muslims find democratic forms of government desirable.[12] The so-called system of Caliphate has no appeal to those who are not Muslims. How can one convince Hindus, Buddhists and Jews that the best and virtuous heads of states can only come from the Arab tribe of the Quraysh? Will this system appeal to them as democracy does? Muslims too abandoned this system

---

[12] See Pew Studies Survey, which found that large percentages of Muslims prefer democracy. *Most Muslims Want Democracy, Personal Freedoms, and Islam in Political Life* (Washington, DC: Pew Research Center, July 10, 2012). http://www.pewglobal. org/2012/07/10/chapter-2-views-of-democracy/.

after trying it for 30 years only. Even the Quran encourages Muslims to learn from history and the experience of other nations and civilizations— *so travel through the Earth and observe the demise of nations that denied the truth before you* (Quran 6:11 and 3:137).

It is a fact that democratic governance has greater appeal for Muslims than dictatorships or monarchies. Some Muslims yearn for benevolent dictatorships, but that is in my view an oxymoron. We live in an era where it is assumed that democracy is the best form of government. Having lived all my life in democracies—the first 25 years in the largest democracy (India) and the next in the oldest democracy (the United States)—I have witnessed enough bad governance to conclude that democratic structures are not a guarantee of good governance. Democracy may be the best form of conflict resolution in domestic politics when the democratic system is truly inclusive and open. And democracies come with protection of human rights and many freedoms including freedom of religion and therefore and without a doubt they are the least oppressive of all forms of government as long as you qualify as a citizen and have access to the rights and freedoms guaranteed by the state's constitution. But the democratic structure of a state is not a guarantee of good governance; ask African Americans in the United States, Muslims in India and France or the Palestinians in Israel. Social science and political theory scholars have examined both the virtues and the limits of democratic governance and they have much to say about both aspects. All these conversations are essentially driven by the empirical evidence that we now have about the advantages and deficiencies of democracy. Muslim societies can only benefit from this accumulated fountain of knowledge if they too institute democratic governance, but until then we are limited to discussing the promise of *Shura* and praising the model of *Siyyasah Sharaiyyah*, which probably never existed in history.

If Muslim activists and theorists start focusing more on processes rather than structures, on good governance rather than symbolic policies that buttress the identity of Islamic states as Islamic, then both governance and government, society and state will improve. The focus on process will allow Muslims to institute, develop and modernize the processes of *Shura, Ijtihad, Muraqaba, Muhasaba* and even *Ijma*. I can easily imagine that over time a society regardless of its initial governing structure, democratic or monarchic, will definitely become more deliberative, inclusive, responsive, accountable, consensual and sensitive to aspects of social justice if it allows processes of *Shura* (consultation and deliberation), *Ijtihad* (rethinking laws and policies based on empirical reality), *Muraqaba* (self-criticism), *Muhasaba* (accountability) and *Ijma* (consensus building) to flower. All these normative processes that I have enumerated based on Islamic sources are similar to the benchmarks of good governance developed by empirical social sciences.[13] Nations like Jordan and Morocco, which are constitutional democracies, will probably benefit more from incremental and gradual commitment to good governance than sudden revolutionary changes to their structure that could lead to violence and perhaps even civil wars as in Iraq and Syria. Even states in various stages of transition to democracy such as Pakistan, Bangladesh, Malaysia, Indonesia, Iran and Turkey can benefit significantly from an increased emphasis on good governance and processes of government. In this age of *fitna*—crisis, chaos and civil war—a focus on governance, which can gradually improve the product of government, is better than sudden revolutionary upheavals.

National Interest to National Virtue

The arena of global politics has always been dominated by great power rivalry and the struggle to control territory, water and resources, all often subsumed under the term *realpolitik* or high politics. National and international security has always been an important issue and will remain so in the future, especially with the rise in terrorism and civil wars. But students of global politics are also aware of the intellectual struggle, particularly since World War II, to find an alternate means of thinking about global politics that contests the ontology of power struggle and emphasizes interdependence, emerging global governance and the enormous degree of cooperation that now exists between states to argue that not only does realist thinking not fully capture the nature of global politics but it may well be a part of the problem that exacerbates global politics. Additionally, along with liberal analysis, which focuses on cooperation rather than conflict, we have also seen the emergence of perspectives that emphasize the role of identities and cultures in shaping global politics. Thus, along with protecting *national interest*, narrowly

---

[13] Alina Mungiu-Pippidi, *The Quest for Good Governance: How Societies Develop Control of Corruption* (London: Cambridge University Press, 2015). See also M. A. Muqtedar Khan, "Islamic Governance and Democracy," *Islam and Democratization in Asia* (2009): 13–27. Abdul Rashid Moten, "Striving for Islamic Governance: Varying Contexts, Different Strategies," *American Journal of Islamic Social Sciences* (Spring 2015): 68–99.

construed to mean national and international security, states are now also seen as protecting national culture, national identity and national interests understood broadly to include the environment, economic interests and global order.[14]

Muslim nations too have been motivated by either national security understood in the realist sense or by the desire to protect national culture and national identity, especially those states that claim to be Islamic states. Many of Iran's foreign policy decisions since 1979 after its Islamic revolution and Saudi Arabia's support for Islam globally can be understood as a consequence of national interest understood in terms of defending Islamic identity. Many Muslim countries that claim to be Islamic invest in symbolic projects and policies designed specifically to project their Islamic identity.[15] In recent years, we have seen how Turkey, under the governance of an Islamist-leaning party (AKP), has used its foreign policy to defend its claim as a Muslim state interested in leading the global Muslim *Ummah*.[16]

In my vision, the *State of Ihsan* will be more concerned with *national virtue* than national identity. The difference is *in becoming* rather than *appearing to be so*. Machiavelli famously advised the prince that it was not important to be just; what was important was to be seen to be just. In the State of *Ihsan*, it would be the opposite. Virtue is valued for its inherent value and not for its ability to help acquire and keep power. Thus, the state would be geared toward encouraging its citizens to be virtuous for the sake of virtue. Just as modern states encourage their citizens to give charity to participate in volunteerism, the State of *Ihsan* will also seek to pursue national virtue as if it was of vital national interest. One meaning of the term *Ihsan* is to make more beautiful or to become better. For the people of *Ihsan*, life is about perfecting virtue, perfecting the soul in order that it becomes worthy of mirroring the divine and acting as a perfect mirror in which the divine can contemplate itself. Thus, the purpose of the State of *Ihsan* is to provide the security and the freedoms that can enable its citizens to perfect virtue.

---

[14] Martha Finnemore, *National Interests in International Society* (London: Cambridge University Press, 1996). Peter J. Katzenstein, ed., *The Culture of National Security: Norms and identity in world politics* (New York: Columbia University Press, 1996).

[15] For a discussion of Iranian and Saudi Arabian foreign policies, see M. A. Muqtedar Khan, *Jihad for Jerusalem: identity and strategy in international relations* (New York: Praeger, 2004).

[16] M. Hakan Yavuz, "Turkish identity and foreign policy in flux: The rise of Neo-Ottomanism," *Critique: Journal for Critical Studies of the Middle East* 7.12 (1998): 19–41.

Justice: From Virtue to Social Condition

اَعْدِلُوْاهُوَأَقْرَبُ لِلتَّقْوَىٰٓ

Be Just it is close to piety. (Quran 5:8)

The Quran commands the believers to be just, to pursue justice in all their affairs and to judge between people with fairness over 60 times. In a verse that has much political-philosophical relevance, in that it both extends *de jure* sovereignty to humanity on earth to act on behalf of God, the Quran once again emphasizes the expectations that human agents will act on behalf as God with justice and not in pursuit of self-interest. This verse addresses Prophet David and says:

> *O' David, indeed we have made you a vicegerent (Khalifah) upon the Earth, so judge between people with truth and justice and do not follow your own desires.* (Quran 38:26)

Verse 4:58, which is one of the most used verses by Islamic political thinkers, from Ibn Taymiyyah to al-Maududi, also commands justice and as does the widely quoted verse 4:135, which commands Muslims to stand up for justice even if it is against one's own parents and peoples. Verse 5:42 commands Prophet Muhammad (pbuh) to judge with justice if he chooses to act as a judge for the people who come to him for judgment. This verse also adds that *Allah loves those who act justly.* Once a person asked Prophet Muhammad (pbuh) to summarize the essence of Islamic teachings and in answer to his query, the Prophet recited the verse with which we began this chapter—*Indeed Allah has commanded justice with Ihsan* (Quran 16:90)—thus placing both *Ihsan* and justice (*Adl*) front and center of Islamic values. Prophet Muhammad (pbuh) emphasized the importance of justice by also mentioning that on the Day of Judgment, the one dearest to God and nearest to himself in station will be a ruler who ruled justly (*Al-Tirmidhi* #1334).

Clearly, the importance of justice in Islamic primary sources cannot be emphasized more. But it is a bit surprising as to how in the later development of Islam, at least Sunni Islam, the concept of justice has been underplayed. For example, the Sunni conception of "pillars of Islam" does not include justice, whereas the Shia conception of the pillars of Islam does include the concept of justice. In fact, the Islamic juristic understanding of justice is more or less based on a definition widely attributed to Imam Ali:

"Justice puts things in their places.[17]" This definition of justice is no different from that of Plato, who defined justice as giving each person his due.[18] None of the six authentic books of prophetic traditions (*Kutub al-Sittah*) and the earliest collection *Al-Muwatta* include a section on justice. None of the collectors who collated traditions according to various topics, including *Jihad* and menstruation, felt the need to collate hadith under the subtitle of justice. There are 93 books in the *Sahih Bukhari* collection and 43 in *Sahih Muslim*, and none of them is on justice.

This is not just a mere oversight in tabulation. Islamic jurists have, to a great extent, sidelined the concept of justice. For example, *Maqasid al-Shariah* approach to Islamic law, an approach that seeks to first identify the higher or more fundamental and transcendent purposes of Islamic law and then derives specific rulings in ways that safeguard the said higher purposes, also ignores justice. Surprisingly it is the consensus of the Islamic jurists that justice is not one of the higher purposes of Islamic law. The five higher purposes that all agree upon are the preservation of *Deen* (religion), *nafs* (life), *nasl* (lineage), *aql* (intellect) and *maal* (property). This listing of higher purposes of Islamic law includes "lineage" but not justice. I find this profoundly shocking, especially given the emphasis on justice in the Quran. It is not difficult to understand how jurists, who placed lineage over justice, excluded mercy and compassion from their rulings as I discussed earlier in this book. Jasser Auda, a renowned expert in the *Maqasid al-Shariah* approach, concedes that the traditional approach "did not include the most universal and basic values, such as justice and freedom."[19] The very prominent Azhari scholar Muhammad Al-Ghazali made a similar observation when he argued that the five original intents are of secondary nature and both justice and freedom are of primary value and must be added to the *Maqasid*, especially since they were intended as such in prophetic messages.[20]

Islamic political thinkers who are seen as part of the orthodoxy, such as al-Mawardi, Ibn Taymiyyah and most modern Islamists, also do not discuss or explore justice in any depth. They refer to it in two contexts: as an

[17] See M. Ali Lakhani, ed., *The Sacred Foundations of Justice in Islam: The Teaching so Ali Ibn Abi Talib* (Vancouver, Canada: World Wisdom, 2006), p. 27.

[18] Plato, *The Republic of Plato*, Vol. 30 (New York: Oxford University Press, 1945).

[19] See Jasser Auda, *Maqasid Al-Shariah: A Beginner's Guide* (London: International Institute of Islamic Thought, 2008), p. 7.

[20] See Gamal Eldin Attia, *Towards Realization of the Higher Intents of Islamic Law: Maqasid Al-Shariah: A Functional Approach* (London: International Institute of Islamic Thought, 2008), p. 83.

attribute of a desired ruler and as something that should be safeguarded while making judgments. For such legalistic scholars, justice is more of a quality of judgment than a sociopolitical condition. They do not see justice as a desired state of society. El Fadl, a jurist himself, makes a very interesting observation about this dilemma and begs the questions: "does the divine law define justice or does justice define divine law?" Clearly in his assessment, justice is defined by what is now understood as *Shariah* law and if we were to reverse that assumption and grasp the idea of justice in the Quran and then define divine law as that which is shaped by the divine concept of justice, in El Fadl's view, it would take a profound paradigm shift. In this book, I am indeed calling for such a paradigm shift because I find that the current legal corpus, understood as Islamic law or *Shariah* law, has strayed away from the mercy, the compassion and the justice that is so overwhelmingly dominant in the Quranic discourse.

The discourse on Islamic state and the Caliphate essentially operates with an unstated assumption that *Shariah* law is the most just of all other systems of laws devised by human beings and therefore the Islamic state, a state where Islamic laws are fully implemented, must necessarily be more just than any other form of government. They do not feel the need to either substantiate or explore this claim. It is stated as a truism. But the problem with this position is that the set of laws that are being presented as divine are essentially a product of human *Ijtihad* or intellectual product based on divine sources for sure but viewed in very specific historical and political contexts. It is essential that Muslims revisit these assumptions that they have until now held as sacred. Take Syed Qutb for example. He actually wrote a book with the title *Islam and Social Justice*. He argues that Islam offers a comprehensive and superior concept of social justice and it is based on the following three foundations:

1. absolute freedom of conscience,
2. the complete equality of all men and
3. the firm mutual responsibility of society

He just states these three elements with little critical explanation. This is what he concludes about freedom of conscience:

> *Thus, Islam approaches the question of freedom from every angle and from all points of view; it undertakes a complete emancipation of the conscience.*[21]

[21] Syed Qutb, Social Justice in Islam, p. 67.

If this is true, then how does he square the punishment for apostasy that jurists claim is part of the *Shariah*? The first Caliph even waged wars against those who were deemed as apostates (*Riddah* wars); how is that consistent with this claim of absolute freedom of conscience? Why privilege the tribe of Quraysh, if equality is fundamental to Islam, as the only people with the right to be Caliphs? Qutb, of course, does not explore these issues at all. Similarly, consider the claim that in Islam "all men" are equal (we shall assume that sexism is unintended and interpret "all men" as all human beings). He claims that Islam guarantees women "complete equality" to men and then proceeds to enumerate and justify several instances where the *Shariah* does not do so. He explores the unequal inheritance and the treatment of women as unequal witnesses, and explains them away as based on the unequal physical attributes and responsibilities of men and women. He does not discuss polygamy. It would have been interesting to see how he would have maintained the complete equality of men and women based on physical attributes justifying polygamy for men and not for women. Ideological rhetoric like Qutb's is an easy target and I do not want to belabor it here. I just want to point out how uncritical it is of its own claims. Qutb repeatedly claims that in matters of religion, men and women are equal. Well, if a woman's *Shahada* (witnessing) of God is equal to a man's *Shahada* of God, then how can he justify the rule that a women's witness in court is not equal to a man's witness in court?

It is my assessment that we have this anomaly because justice is being seen as an aspect of individual personality and not social condition. Therefore, whether describing the court-appointed judge (*Qadi*), or an Imam or even the Caliph, it was always stipulated that one of the attributes of the candidate must be that he is just. Jurists understood this as "obedience to God," which meant obedience to the law and thus once again justice became subservient to law.[22] Individuals are not just; the decisions they make, within the limits of the information available to them, are either just or not just. But what jurists have not explored is the systemic aspect of justice; legal, ethical and institutional frameworks can be unfair and unjust in the manner in which they distribute roles and resources and create conditions that are discriminatory. I submit that in the State of *Ihsan*, justice must be rescued from the limiting influence of law and it should be the Quranic conception of justice that defines both state and

---

[22] See Majid Khadduri, *The Islamic Conception of Justice* (Baltimore: Johns Hopkins University Press, 1984), p. 145.

state laws rather than law defining the state and the concept of justice. I conclude this section with a beautiful poem from the Sufi poet Jami on the role of justice and religion in politics. He argues that justice without religion is better than religion when it is accompanied by tyranny.

> *Adl wa insaf dan na kufr wa na din*
> *Anche dar hifz-i-mulk dar kar ast*
> *Adl be din nizam 'alam ra*
> *Bihtar az zulm-i-Shah dindar ast." Jami. Biharistan.*

Be aware that justice and equity, not unbelief nor religion
Are needed for the maintenance of the kingdom
Justice without religion, for the next world Is better than the tyranny of a religious
Shah!—Poet Jami

THE SOCIETY OF *MUHSINS*

As discussed earlier in this chapter, I am seeking to realize *Ihsan* both at the level of the state and at the level of the society. I have already identified the five principles that I feel should shape the nature of a state, and in this section, I will spell out five principles that I feel that society must cultivate to ultimately realize a virtuous state that can deliver good governance. In a sense, this is my theory of good citizenship necessary for good governance. The principles I articulate are basically derived from the unveiling of *Ihsan* in Chap. 5. While they may, at first reading, appear esoteric because I am deriving them from esoteric mysticism, they are practical and not only have they been discussed by many ethical theorists but also practiced in various forms in many societies in the past and in the present. These principles cannot exist in a society without the presence of political virtues that I attributed to the State of *Ihsan*. I also submit that the five principles of the State of *Ihsan* that I described earlier cannot be realized in a society without *Muhsins*. So, in a way, these two aspects—virtues of the state and virtues of the society—co-constitute each other. There cannot be one without the other, and they must both emerge simultaneously in elementary forms, perhaps at the behest of an activist agency consciously seeking good governance, and then gradually blossom as they support, strengthen and nurture each other. To Islamic social theorists, this mutual co-constitution of state and society, structure and agency, in pursuit of transformative change is an exegesis of the Quran's verse on change (Quran 13:11):

Indeed, Allah will not change the condition of a people until they change what is in themselves

In this verse, structural change is tied to change in agency. The Quran states clearly that existing condition of a society will not change until there is a change within the citizens themselves. Hence I identify the changes that must be instituted in the society in order to reshape the state. The five principles that in my vision characterize a society of *Muhsins* are (1) citizenship as witnessing the divine, (2) citizens as character builders, (3) citizens as lawmakers, (4) citizenship as self-regulation and (5) citizens as rulers: from God governance to good governance.

Citizens as Witnesses

In Chap. 5, I explored *Mushahada*, or witnessing, as the mystical understanding that *Ihsan* is indeed worshipping or serving God as if you are seeing Him. In a way, being in the mystical state of *Ihsan* is to bear witness to God (take *shahada*). As citizens of the State of *Ihsan*, we also bear witness to God about the state of governance. Thus, citizens who are aware, socially and politically engaged, who participate in dialogue with the state, who are willing to hold the state accountable to its laws and values are bearing witness to God about the state. In a very well-known tradition (the seventh hadith in Imam Nawawi's collection), Prophet Muhammad (pbuh) describes religion in a very succinct way, *"Al-Deen Al-Naseehah,"* meaning religion is advice or sincerity. I prefer the way Aishah Bewley translated this hadith— *The way (Al-Deen) is good counsel.*[23] When the Prophet was asked to whom, he responded by saying "to God, his book, his messenger, rulers of Muslims and their common folk." I understand this hadith in the light of *Ihsan* to mean that our faith commands us to be sincere to God, His book and His messenger and to sincerely counsel our rulers (the state) and fellow citizens.

The concept of *Al-Naseehah* is a complex idea. When viewed through the lens of *Ihsan*, *Al-Naseehah* includes the twin concepts of self-witnessing, *Muraqaba and Muhasaba*. *Muraqaba* involves vigilance, watchfulness, to be self-aware, awake and critical of the self. *Muhasaba* is about holding the self to account.[24] So, when one is striving to achieve *Ihsan* in one's personal

---

[23] Ibn Al-Arabi, *On the Mysteries of Bearing Witness to the Oneness of God and Messengership of Muhammad*, trans. Aisha Bewley (Chicago: Kazi Publications, 2010).

[24] Annemarie Schimmel, *Mystical Dimensions of Islam* (Durham, NC: University of North Carolina Press, 1975), pp. 100–101.

life, one is vigilant and watchful of one's action, thoughts and even desires, and holds oneself accountable to the highest of virtues. One is giving sincere advice to oneself through the spiritual practices of *Muraqaba* and *Muhasaba*. One is bearing witness against oneself to God.[25]

When we translate this principle of sincere advice to the public realm, we are talking about engagement that includes public involvement, voting, attending town hall meetings with one's leaders and consulting with them, critiquing and advising them, testifying in parliaments and partaking in policy debates—being vigilant about how our rulers govern and holding them accountable. But this concerned citizenship can be taken up a notch through the creation of institutions of civil society that conduct *Muraqaba*—public deliberations and vigilance—but also *Muhasaba*—hold the government accountable. Thus, a society of *Muhsins* is a critical society that holds a mirror to its government in pursuit of good and virtuous governance. It is through the emergence of concerned and engaged citizens and network of organizations that do the same (civil society) that citizenship becomes an act of "witnessing" (*Mushahada*).

The link between citizenship and the act of witnessing has been made by some political theorists but the context and their treatment of the idea are much different from what I am suggesting here.[26] Critics might read this and suggest that in the end the society of *Muhsins* looks no different from that of a healthy liberal democracy with a vibrant civil society.[27] After all, advance democratic societies are proliferating with non-government organizations that pursue goodness, charity and welfare, defend civil rights and conduct research in the public interest and hold government officials accountable.[28] Without the private pursuit of good, there may be no public good or good governance in many democracies. Perhaps it is so, and maybe that is why democratic nations with rich civic culture are stable and prosperous. However, when we read some of the moral and social objectives of these citizens—pursuit of virtue and goodness in governance—

---

[25] This discussion is partly informed by Ibn Arabi's discussion of the hadith of good counsel. Ibn Al-Arabi, *On the Mysteries of Bearing Witness to the Oneness of God and Messengership of Muhammad*, trans. Aisha Bewley (Chicago: Kazi Publications, 2010), pp. 97–101.

[26] Schudson Michael, *The Good Citizen: A History of American civic life* (London: Oxford University Press, 2001). David Batstone, *The Good Citizen* (London: Routledge, 2014).

[27] Andrew F. March, *Islam and liberal Citizenship: The Search for an overlapping consensus* (Oxford University Press, 2011).

[28] Claire Mercer, "NGOs, civil society and democratization: a critical review of the literature," *Progress in development studies* 2.1 (2002): 5–22. Marina Ottaway and Thomas Carothers, *Funding virtue: civil society aid and democracy promotion* (Carnegie Endowment, 2000).

then perhaps we may detect a subtle difference. As I envision it, for Muslims who are seeking to realize *Ihsan* in their personal and public lives, this is the path to take. The beauty of this vision of citizenship as witnessing is that unlike the citizenship imagined by traditional Islamic scholars that necessitates an Islamic state implementing the *Shariah* law,[29] one can be a good citizen, a *Muhsin* in a state, regardless of whether it is Islamic or not, whether it is a Muslim majority state or not. But this civic engagement in pursuit of good is not the entire idea; it is one of five characteristics of the society of *Muhsins*. Citizenship thus becomes a moral and divine obligation to self and society as one bears witness against self and society.

Citizens as Character Builders

إِنَّ اللهَ جَمِيلٌ يُحِبُّ الْجَمَالَ

Allah is beautiful, He loves beauty.[30]

The word *Ihsan* is a conjugate of the Arabic world for beauty *husn* and therefore to do *Ihsan* is also to do beautiful things. In the Islamic sources, the idea of beauty is central to understanding God and His creation. God is the paragon of beauty. He is beautiful and all beauty flows from Him. God is beautiful as is His creation. The material world is beautiful as is the world of ideas and ideals. One can be beautiful on the exterior as well as on the interior. Indeed, I understand the Islamic mystical tradition as an exercise in interior decoration—purification and beautification of the soul, the spirit and the world of thoughts. The relationship between *Ihsan* and beauty has been explored comprehensively in Chap. 5; here I merely explore how this could be operationalized in the political arena.

In the past, the Islamic civilization has been inextricably linked to beauty—the most beautiful architecture as exemplified by the Taj Mahal, the beautiful poetry that enriches human souls across cultures and centuries like that of Mevlana Rumi and the uniquely Islamic calligraphy that more explicitly links devotion and beauty. Muslim mystical music, art and the mystical practices that shape the culture of Sufi communities resonate the appreciation for beauty in Islamic ethos. But unfortunately, the past few decades of Islamic history have been infused with an ugliness that is

---

[29] Mohammad Hashim Kamali, *Citizenship and accountability of government: an Islamic perspective* (Islamic Texts Society, 2011).

[30] Authentic Hadith from the collection *Sahih Muslim* #91 and *Al-Mu'jam al-Awsaṭ* #6902.

difficult to ignore or comprehend. The scourge of terrorism, the culture of extremism and the proliferation of intolerance are making the current era the ugliest in Islamic history. In the name of religion Muslims are committing crimes against humanity, against their fellow believers and against the legacy of beauty that embellishes the Islamic civilization. Abou El Fadl captures this ugliness in all its facets in a powerful essay titled "The ugly modern and the modern ugly: Reclaiming the beautiful in Islam," and I refer everyone who wishes to understand this negative aesthetic turn to read it.[31]

To do *Ihsan* is to bear witness to the beauty that is God and the beauty that He has created for us. His signature is *husn* and those who truly wish to live a life of *Ihsan* not only bear witness to the beauty that is creation itself but also seek to manifest beauty in everything they do. Some countries in the Muslim world today are rich and they are investing in building beautiful mosques, museums and other physical things of aesthetic value. But true beauty comes not from brick and mortar but from the protection of humanity and its dignity and from building societies that are peaceful and tolerant, advance social justice and pursue a high quality of life. Thanks to the United Nations Development Programme (UNDP), we have a measure of quality of life that goes beyond measuring wealth and income per capita; it is known as the Human Development Index (HDI).[32] The State of *Ihsan* would in my view employ a similar index but besides income, education, health and equality, it will include indicators for spiritual health. The very existence of the measure HDI suggests that human beings have an intuitive idea of the good life and are aspiring to measure it and articulate policies to realize it. It is also clear that this notion of a good life is understood both in material and non-material terms. The inclusion of indicators of gender equality and income distribution is also a sign that we are becoming more holistic and idealistic in our aspirations. The State of *Ihsan* will try its best to improve on its HDI, supplemented with opening of social spaces for pursuit of spirituality.

The idea is not to build or possess beautiful things; it is not a problem if you do, but the key goal is to live a beautiful life. The modern age is obsessed with success measured often in accumulation of wealth and fame.

---

[31] See Khaled Abou El Fadl, "The ugly modern and the modern ugly: Reclaiming the beautiful in Islam," *Progressive Muslims: On justice, gender, and pluralism* (Oxford: Oneworld, 2003), p. 45. Also see Khaled Abou El Fadl, *The search for beauty in Islam: A conference of the books* (Lanham, MD: Rowman & Littlefield, 2001).

[32] See the webpage of UNDP: http://hdr.undp.org/en.

It ignores the more spiritual and humanistic needs that are as necessary to a good life as are security and amenities. Prophet Muhammad (pbuh) said that he was sent to perfect good character. Elsewhere he is reported to have said that he was sent only to perfect moral character and do beautiful deeds. There are many such reports which all indicate that the purpose of Islamic teachings and prophetic examples is to internalize beauty and manifest it in our manners, our culture, our society and our nations.[33] Just as the State of *Ihsan* pursues national virtue as an important component of national security, so will its citizens the *Muhsins* emphasize the perfection of national and individual character. The society of *Muhsins* would pursue this not through legislation or coercive tools of the state but through civil society initiatives that will educate and proliferate the desire to be good and to do good. It is how Prophet Muhammad (pbuh) understood his mission and none exemplified *Ihsan* better than him.

Shariah *by* Shura: *Citizens as Lawmakers and Policymakers*

In previous discussions, particularly those in Chaps. 2 and 6, I have tried to show how the idea of Islamic *Shariah* and the need for its implementation have become the central conceptual vehicle for the realization of the Islamic state by modern Islamists. Political philosophy and theory, which seek to understand what are virtuous and good regimes and what are the public goods that a regime must offer, have been sidelined to privilege Islamic law. The articulation of Islamic law has become the most common way to operationalize justice, leading to a paradigm that is tautological[34]; justice is what Islamic law seeks to realize and justice is what Islamic law says justice is. Therefore, there is very little critical examination of what passes for Islamic law using an independent conception of justice as a yardstick. Indeed, to an extent, faith itself has been reduced to the adherence to law, making Islam itself and its practices subordinate to the dictates of legal maxims. *Given the centrality of* Shariah, *as a proxy for both faith and government, it is critical that we revisit how we accept what Islamic law is.* The State of *Ihsan* will have laws, and they will be based on Islamic mystical

---

[33] See Abu Amina Elias, "Good Character is the path to salvation in Islam," on the World Wide Web at: https://abuaminaelias.com/good-character-is-the-path-to-salvation/.

[34] Mohammad Hashim Kamali, *Principles of Islamic jurisprudence* (Cambridge, UK: Islamic Texts Society, 2003). Also see Mohammad Hashim Kamali, *Shari'ah law: An Introduction* (London, UK: Oneworld Publications).

principles and ethics for certain, but the key question is how will they be different in substance and in process of legislation from those of the Islamic state envisioned by political Islamists?

This discussion is not going to be a foray into another reinvention of *Usul Al-Din* (sources of Islam) and/or *Usul al-Fiqh* (sources of Islamic jurisprudence); I shall leave that discussion for another day. It is sufficient for my purpose to acknowledge that there exist many schools of Islamic jurisprudence, both classical ones like the Hanafi, the Maliki, the Shafii, the Hanbali and various non-Sunni schools, and contemporary ones like the *Maqasid al-Shariah* school, the Liberal Islam school and the Progressive Muslims initiative, all of which advance different conceptions of Islamic laws and ethos. Additionally, there are many contemporary attempts at rearticulating the methodology of *Ijtihad* and the sources of Islamic law itself, thereby attempting to reach different, even more modern understanding of Islam and Islamic law without meddling with the fundamental sources—the Quran and the authentic Sunnah. The proliferation of old and new schools of law provides a Muslim seeking an Islamic ruling on any issue with a bewildering array of methodologies, perspectives and rulings.[35] This, by itself, is not a bad thing as a well-known and oft-cited tradition attests that difference of opinion is a mercy from God.

So how does one, in a market place of competing interpretations, go about determining what exactly is the best or the most appropriate or valid interpretation of the *Shariah* ruling? Which interpretation should become law and guide the policies and the politics of the state? Laws are important for governance and so if we are interested in discovering what is good governance based on Islamic principles then how do we select which interpretation of the *Shariah* is most consistent with the beauty, compassion and goodness enjoined by *Ihsan*? In the presence of multiplicity of interpretations, which interpretation should prevail? In a society which is free from intimidation, independent thinking is encouraged and freedom of thought and conscience is safeguarded, there will be multiplicity of interpretations (Islamic history and extant schools testify to this possibility) on

---

[35] See for classical schools, Wael B. Hallaq, *A History of Islamic Legal Theories: An Introduction to Sunni usul al-fiqh* (London: Cambridge University Press, 1999). For liberal Islam, see Charles Kurzman, ed., *Liberal Islam: a source book* (New York: Oxford University Press, 1998). And for Progressive Islam, see Omid Safi, ed., *Progressive Muslims: On Justice, Gender and Pluralism* (Oxford: Oneworld Oxford, 2003). For the Maqasid school, see Jasser Auda, *Maqasid al-Shariah as philosophy of Islamic law: a systems approach* (Herndon, VA: International Institute of Islamic Thought, 2008).

what is the best policy to pursue in any given situation. To resolve this challenge, I submit that in the *State of Ihsan*, the government and the citizens arrive at *Shariah by Shura*.

I can imagine many readers reacting in amazement to this idea, *Shariah* is from God not humans, they might say. But on reflection one will realize that Muslims have always judged between competing interpretations and often the criteria for preference has been methodological. Some preferred interpretations are based on literal texts of the Quran, while others have balanced the Quranic text with what they considered authentic traditions and some have preferred the interpretive opinions of the first three generations of Muslims over rational and philosophical arguments to determine the best interpretation of what *Shariah* is. In Chap. 5 of this book, I discuss *Ihsan* as epistemology and argue based on the Quranic verse 30:18 that those seeking to realize *Ihsan* will seek to advance the most beautiful interpretation of the *Shariah* and beauty here will be determined by the abundance of virtues such as love, tolerance, social justice, charity, compassion and mercy in the interpretation of the divine message.

Thus, a society of *Muhsins* will employ *Shura* at two levels to arrive at *Shariah* rulings. First, scholars, lawyers, opinion makers, policymakers and religious teachers will seek to maximize *Ihsan* when they interpret religious sources to arrive at *Shariah* rulings, and then people will apply the same criteria of *Ihsan* (discussed in detail in the section *Ihsan* as Epistemology) to select through consultation the most beautiful understanding of the divine message from the multiplicity of interpretations advanced by civil society. This is not some fanciful or idealistic and utopian imagination; this is a divine command—*listen to the Quran and derive the most beautiful meaning from it* (Quran 39:18). People will measure competing interpretations against the yardstick of *Ihsan* and choose. Islamists' interpretations that privilege law (often over love and compassion) insist that they are seeking to establish justice. But the critical thing that they ignore (even though most practicing Muslims are reminded of it every Friday)[36] is that God/s command to implement justice comes with the added injunction that justice must be moderated by *Ihsan*—*Inna Allah ya'muru bi al-adli wa al-Ihsan*—Indeed Allah commands justice with *Ihsan* (Quran 16:90).

At the level of the State, the same process shall be employed. In order to articulate policies and adopt laws, the state will consult with its citizens—the first *Shura*—which fulfills the Islamic mandate to conduct their affairs

---

[36] Most Friday sermons end with the recitation of the Quranic injunction to balance justice with *Ihsan* (Quranic verse 16:90).

through mutual consultation (*Wa amrhum shura baynahum*, Quran 42:38) and then consult among those who have the authority to make laws and govern (*Ulul Al-Amr*, Quran 4:59)—the second *Shura*—to decide the best course of action. Once again this is not new; we have witnessed the use of town hall meetings to consult with the people and hearings organized by parliamentary committees to consult with experts. Thus, I submit that this two-step model of consultation will not only cultivate a culture of consultative governance often described by modern theorists as deliberative democracy,[37] but it will also foster a deep investment of the civil society in governance through consultation both at the stage of conception and at the stage of implementation of laws as well as policies. The State of *Ihsan* will in a way implement the *Shariah* but the beauty (*Ihsan*) is in the way it will arrive at what *Shariah* is, *through Shura*.

There are several precedents in Islamic history that indicate that Muslims have indeed arrived at what is assumed to be a *Shariah* ruling through the process of consultation. An example that readily comes to mind is the advent of the *Azaan*, the call for prayer, which is such an integral part of Islamic worship. It was arrived upon through a process of *Shura* between Prophet Muhammad (pbuh) and his companions. They came up with many ideas and settled for the most beautiful of many suggestions and Muslims have abided by it ever since. It was through consultation that Umar Ibn Khattab put an end to the practice of giving *Zakat* to non-Muslims to soften their hearts toward Islam (*Muallafah Al-Qulub*).[38] This is a Quranic rule that has been overturned by *Shura*. The process of establishing a political successor to Prophet Muhammad (pbuh) after his death, which led to the election of Abu Bakr as the first Al-Rashidun Caliph at the convention in the *Saqifah* of *Banu Saidah*, is another example of how what Muslims later deemed as *Shariah* emerged from *Shura*.[39]

In my view, this two-step *Shura* process guided by a commitment to articulating and adopting the most beautiful understanding of the divine command is the key operating procedure of the State of *Ihsan*. It incorporates inclusivity, privileges democracy and egalitarianism, and advocates

---

[37] James Bohman, ed., *Deliberative democracy: Essays on reason and politics* (Cambridge, MA: MIT Press, 1997).

[38] Quran 9:60: Zakah expenditures are only for the poor and for the needy and for those employed to collect [Zakah] *and for bringing hearts together* [for Islam] and for freeing captives [or slaves] and for those in debt and for the cause of Allah and for the [stranded] traveler—an obligation [imposed] by Allah. And Allah is Knowing and Wise.

[39] See Ahmad Al-Raysuni, *Al-Shura: The Qur'anic Principle of Consultation* (Herndon, VA: International Institute of Islamic Thought, 2011).

for *Ihsan* in politics. It safeguards both democracy and Islam and indeed recognizes that democratic governance is necessary for Islamic political outcomes. Muslim scholars have in the past privileged the idea of *Maslaha* (public interest or the common good) as the normative criteria for making interpretive preferences.[40] Those interpretations that advanced the most *Maslaha* were considered the best interpretations. In my *Shariah by Shura* model, I am advocating the same except I define the common good as *Ihsan*. The public benefit that must be maximized in my model is the good (understood as *Ihsan*) of all people.

Ultimately, we must remember that legitimate and authoritative interpretations of Islam have emerged not because of argumentation or debate but because of the development of Ijma or consensus around certain interpretations.[41] Many Islamic scholars have argued that Ijma of Muslims is *Shariah* and at times it can be used to extend preference for one opinion (*hukm*) over other. A process of *Istihsan* conducted through *Shura* to arrive at an Ijma can be very powerful legislation. Therefore, in the final analysis of these competing interpretations, regardless of what criteria are used to measure their quality—*Maslaha* or *Ihsan*—an Ijma or consensus will have to emerge around a specific interpretation before it becomes the dominant paradigm. It is quite possible that one may see the emergence of competing political camps, those who lean more toward realism and argue for *Maslaha* and those who are determined that the most beautiful of ideals prevail, arguing for *Ihsan*. Hence, the two-step *Shura* process is to my mind the best way to govern. It transfers law and policy making from state to society; it brings in inclusion and democracy through consultation and authority, and legitimacy through consensus.

---

[40] See Tariq Ramadan, "*Ijtihad* and Maslaha: The Foundations of Governance," in M. A. Muqtedar Khan, ed., *Islamic Democratic Discourse: Theory, Debates, and Philosophical Perspectives* (Lanham, MD: Lexington Books, 2006), pp. 3–20. Also see Felicitas Opwis, "Maslaha in contemporary Islamic legal theory," *Islamic law and society* 12.2 (2005): 182–223. See also Asma Afsaruddin, "Maslahah as a Political Concept," in Mehrzad Boroujerdi, ed., *Mirror for the Muslim Prince: Islam and the Theory of Statecraft* (Syracuse, NY: Syracuse University Press, 2013), pp. 16–44.

[41] For a summary of the argument that the real source of authority in Islamic law comes from consensus or Ijma, see Wael Hallaq, "On the authoritativeness of Sunni consensus," *International Journal of Middle East Studies* 18.4 (1986): 427–454. See also George F. Hourani, "The basis of authority of consensus in Sunnite Islam," *Studia Islamica* 21 (1964): 13–60.

From Law Enforcement to Self-Regulation:
Citizenship as Freedom

I began this chapter by explaining the need to balance the two commandments in the Quran: one that says there is no compulsion in religion (Quran 2:256) and the other that encourages Muslims to become change agents and to advocate for good and forbid evil (Quran 3:110). For centuries, Muslim jurists like Ibn Taymiyyah have used this commandment to justify the creation of an Islamic state whose purpose is to enforce Islamic law.[42] Since Islamic law is both just and good, and since it is articulated by God Himself, the rulers in an Islamic state would not be tyrannical even if they were to enforce this law. Such notions of divine law do not consider the reality that much of what passes for Islamic law is essentially human interpretations of divine sources. The modern-day political Islamists too have relied on this understanding or fallacy to argue that an Islamic state must enforce the *Shariah*. Islamic modernists who believe in democracy and freedom, however, have relied on the no compulsion verse to advocate for a system that allows for freedom of conscience and religion.[43] In this section, I hope to resolve this tension between the two commandments by conceiving of citizenship as self-regulating freedom.

The value and concept of freedom remains one of the most under-addressed themes in premodern Islamic political thought.[44] It is this deficit that has contributed to the slow embrace of modern concepts of democracy and human rights in much of the contemporary Muslim world. Freedom, understood as freedom from the authority of the state, has remained somewhat alien to Islamic political thought since Islamic jurists have for centuries glorified Islamic law and the states that enforce it. The philosophy of freedom posits state authority as more or less a necessary evil and the state as a potential villain that can become tyrannical and must be restrained by constitutional and other means (such as cutting taxes and resources available to it). The philosophy of divine law sees the state as a hero that alone can bring justice by implementing divine law and therefore

---

[42] M. A. Muqtedar Khan, "The Islamic States," *Routledge Encyclopedia of Political Science* (2004).

[43] See, for example, Fathi Osman, "Islam in a Modern State: Democracy and the concept of Shura," *MF Osman, Islam in a Modern State: Democracy and the Concept of Shura (Occasional papers series)* (2001): 3–23.

[44] Mohammad Hashim Kamali, *Freedom, equality and justice in Islam* (Cambridge: Islamic Texts Society, 2002), pp. 2–3.

is both necessary and desirable. Freedom, on the other hand, has always been viewed with suspicion by orthodox theologians and jurists who fear that freedom will enable people to pursue their own whims rather than obey the will of God.

Muslim scholars in the premodern era have examined the idea of freedom (*hurriyah*) in the context of theology (*Kalam*) while debating free will and predestination. They have understood *hurriyah* in opposition to slavery. Freedom as the opposite of slavery has received the most attention from Islamic jurists. The Sufis have paid the greatest attention to the idea of freedom, but more in the context of freedom from wants and desires than freedom from an oppressive state. The most eloquent of them was the Andalusi mystic Ibn Al-Arabi, who argued that a true believer enjoys absolute freedom since she is slave only to God and therefore slave to none. But his conception of freedom too was within the context of slavery and servitude. Philosophers like Al-Farabi have explored freedom in the political sense. He explored the concept of freedom in the context of democratic cities but not as something that is either characteristic or necessary for his virtuous republic. I have discussed Al-Farabi's thoughts in much more detail in Chap. 6. Freedom, as it is understood today in advanced democratic societies, was explored and even valorized by political Islamists like Maulana Maududi of Pakistan and Syed Qutb of Egypt. Living in the era of authoritarian and postcolonial states, Islamists seeking political space to advance their conception of Islam, politics and statehood naturally found the idea of political freedom, which would give them an opportunity to propagate their ideas, quite appealing.[45] They subscribed to the idea in a very limited way without adding any depth to the idea. I have already discussed Qutb's ideas on freedom earlier in this chapter.

In recent times, many Muslim political theorists have discussed the importance of freedom, democracy and human rights but within the broad rubric of liberal democracy, including yours truly until now, thus making freedom one of the end goals of their political quest. Some like Hashim Kamali, Abdulaziz Sachedina, Abdullahi A. An-Na'im, M. A. Muqtedar Khan and Khaled Abou El Fadl rely on Islamic sources to make their case, while others like Nader Hashmi and Abdolkarim Soroush rely more on

---

[45] See Franz Rosenthal, *The Muslim concept of freedom prior to the nineteenth century* (London, Brill, 1960). Also see Michael Cook, "Freedom," in Richard Bulliet et al., eds., *The Princeton Encyclopedia of Islamic Political Thought* (Princeton, NJ: Princeton University Press, 2012), pp. 174–175.

Western or rational political thought.[46] In this book, I am seeking freedom to create a state and society where politics will be in pursuit of *Ihsan*. Here freedom is not a goal but a necessary condition to enable the politics of *Ihsan*. I have advocated for democracy and argued the compatibility of democracy and Islam for two decades. But the political realities of the twenty-first century have now given me a pause. I am appalled at the rise of populist authoritarianism in the United States and India, the world's oldest and the world's biggest democracies. And after listening to liberals in the West insist that Israel is a democracy despite its systematic oppression of Palestinians, I am convinced that democratic institutions and processes are in themselves not sufficient to bring justice and goodness to society. Democracies clearly can allow oppression, racism, religious discrimination and intolerance. They can very quickly turn into majoritarian autocracies. Al-Farabi was right; democratic polities can lead to good as well as bad and I now believe that to ensure a good polity, we need democratic structures and something more—a public philosophy of virtue and morality. Hence, my quest for the political philosophy of *Ihsan* as the software in a system whose hardware is democratic.

Quran and Freedom

I am persuaded that based on several verses in the Quran, a case for the Islamic ideal of freedom can be made. In verse 2:256, the Quran flatly states that there can be no compulsion in religion since truth is now manifestly clear from falsehood. The point that this verse is making is not only to insist that the state not meddle in matters of religion but it also suggests that freedom can be based on dialogue since it also stipulates that truth can be separated from falsehood. In verse 10:99, the Quran once again affirms the principle of non-compulsion and adds that the diversity of faiths and belief are by divine design. In verses 21–22 of chapter 88, the

---

[46] Mohammad Hashim Kamali, *Freedom, equality and justice in Islam* (Cambridge: Islamic Texts Society, 2002). Abdullahi A. An-Na'im, *Islam and the Secular State* (Cambridge: Harvard University Press, 2008). Abdulaziz Sachedina, *The Islamic roots of democratic pluralism* (New York: Oxford University Press, 2001). Khaled Abou El Fadl, ed., *Islam and the Challenge of Democracy* (Princeton, New Jersey: Princeton University Press, 2015). Abdolkarim Soroush, *Reason, freedom, and democracy in Islam: Essential writings of Abdolkarim Soroush* (New York: Oxford University Press, 2002). M. A. Muqtedar Khan, ed., *Islamic democratic discourse: theory, debates, and philosophical perspectives* (Lanham, MD: Lexington Books, 2006). Nader Hashmi, *Islam, secularism, and liberal democracy: Toward a democratic theory for Muslim Societies* (New York: Oxford University Press, 2009).

Quran makes it very clear that our role is merely to remind people of their divine and moral duties but not to exercise control over them. These verses in my view provide a straightforward resolution to the tension between the two commandments: no compulsion in religion, and to adjoin good and forbid evil. I read these verses as commanding that we must encourage good and forbid evil but only through reminders and suggestions and not through coercion.[47]

I think of freedom as absence of internal and external infringements and constraints to pursue *Ihsan*. This is a similar idea to Isaiah Berlin's concept of negative liberty.[48] By external constrains, I am referring to the limits that states can impose on religious and political activism and the intolerance of dominant political or religious ideologies that suffocate alternate visions. Internal constrains are those identified by the Sufis and described in the Quran as false gods (*taghut*). They are the self-regarding motivators such as pursuit of power, wealth and fame that can impede the individual's and group's pursuit of *Ihsan*. My goal is to aspire for an intimidation-free society where people fear not the law but fear their own demons. They pursue *Ihsan* not because the state insists on it but because they are responding to the call to witness their Lord. They obey the divine commandments not from fear of a punitive state but because they themselves aspire to submit to the divine will. There is nothing new or unique about this virtue. Muslims in the West already are self-regulating when they abstain from alcohol consumption, eat halal food, women wearing hijabs, praying and fasting, and even paying *Zakat*. None of this is mandated by the state but Muslims as self-regulating moral agents observe these Islamic principles. Even people of other faiths (such as Hindu vegetarians) and atheists (who are vegans for example) and all the billions of people who live by their own ethical codes, to give charity, to volunteer, to help their neighbors, all of these actions not demanded by law demonstrate the capacity for self-regulation. Self-regulation is a sign of enlightenment. The State of

---

[47] Quran 2:256: There shall be no compulsion in [acceptance of] the religion. The right course has become clear from the wrong. So, whoever disbelieves in *taghut* (false deities) and believes in Allah has grasped the most trustworthy handhold with no break in it. And Allah is Hearing and Knowing. Quran 10:99: And had your Lord willed, those on earth would have believed—all of them entirely. Then, [O Muhammad], would you compel the people in order that they become believers? Quran 88:21–22: So, remind, [O Muhammad]; you are only a reminder. You are not over them a controller.

[48] Isaiah Berlin, *Two concepts of liberty: an inaugural lecture delivered before the University of Oxford on 31 October 1958* (Oxford: Clarendon Press, 1959).

Ihsan is one where the state does not impose virtue. It is a state where citizens are self-regulating, *a free state where self-regulating citizens seek to maximize national virtue willingly and without compulsion.* The State of *Ihsan* therefore is not so much an enabler of *Ihsan* but one that does not disable anyone from pursuing it.

Four Freedoms in the State of Ihsan
I believe that for the State of *Ihsan* to become a reality, these four freedoms must be available to its citizens so that they can become self-regulating *Muhsins.* The four freedoms are (1) freedom to do *Ijtihad,* (2) freedom to challenge existing Ijma, (3) freedom to be or not to be a Muslim and (4) freedom to be a partner in governance. Freedom for *Ijtihad* is absolutely necessary to allow political theorists to advance visions of good governance and virtuous republics, which will entail systematic critique of the existing political order and political elite. Without this freedom, even jurists will not be able to perform their functions. Indeed, without the *freedom to do Ijtihad,* no form of Islamic state will be able to operate. Freedom to think, research and argue for better governance and a better society and critique status quo is the first step to good governance. Without freedom, there can be no faith or faith-based governance. There are many ways of conceptualizing *Ijtihad* itself. Some think of *Ijtihad* in very narrow terms, such as limited analogical thinking (*Qiyas* by *muqallids*), while others think of it in vastly expansive ways that encompass civilizational revival itself.[49] I am insisting on freedom for *Ijtihad* and the freedom to define *Ijtihad.* Those definitions with merit will survive and the frivolous ones will fall—after all, God has guaranteed that believers will never agree upon error. Prophet Muhammad (pbuh) said that those who do *Ijtihad* and get it wrong are blessed and those who do *Ijtihad* and get it right are blessed twice. This is in my mind an unrestrained license to think and do *Ijtihad.*[50] The State of *Ihsan* at best will encourage and enable *Ijtihad* and at worst not present any barriers to *Ijtihad.*

---

[49] M. A. Muqtedar Khan, "Two Theories of *Ijtihad,*" *Common Ground News Service* (2006). Taha Jabir Al-Alwani, *Ijtihad* (Herndon, VA: International Institute of Islamic Thought, 1993). Tariq Ramadan, "*Ijtihad* and Maslaha: The Foundations of Governance," in M. A. Muqtedar Khan, ed., *Islamic Democratic Discourse: Theory, Debates, and Philosophical Perspectives* (Lanham, MD: 2006): 3–20.

[50] Mohammad Hashim Kamali, *Freedom of expression in Islam* (Cambridge: Islamic Texts Society, 1997).

The concept of freedom of thought and/or expression and speech in liberal democracies includes freedom for *Ijtihad*, but by describing it specifically as freedom for *Ijtihad*, I want to make it clear that this freedom does not just include freedom to think on religious issues but is designed explicitly to protect the freedom of critical religious thought. *Freedom for challenging Ijma* also, it can be argued, is covered under the general idea of freedom of religion or under the freedom for *Ijtihad*. I fear that in the past few hundred years, Islamic thought has become backward-looking and the past is glorified and made sacred with ever-increasing fervor. Even if societies allow freedom of *Ijtihad*, I fear they will treat real or imagined past consensus as out of bounds for critical reexamination today. Therefore, I insist on recognizing the freedom to challenge the past consensus as necessary and fundamental to a society where citizens can be self-regulating pursuing self-purifying rather than fearful of the state and wallowing in blind obedience. Challenging past Ijma is not necessarily a rejection of the past; it may result in better understanding of past logic and reasoning and may even reinforce past consensus but this time with fresh and contemporaneous reasons and arguments, and breathe more life into faith and its traditions. Renewal and continuous renewal are not possible without continuous self-examination (*Muraqaba*). A self-critical society is a society of *Muhsins* who are self-regulating citizens of the State of *Ihsan*.

Freedom to be or not to be is my way of arguing that unlike the Islamic state, as imagined by contemporary Islamists, the State of *Ihsan* will not force its citizens to practice Islam or any other faith. Islamic states today go to great lengths to discipline the lives of their citizens, often of women and often in superficial ways to signal their religious identity—imposing the hijab and the chador for women, restricting the preaching of other faiths, making conversion out of Islam illegal and so on and so forth. It appears that these states are worried that without the ever-present stick of the state their citizens would abandon Islam. The State of *Ihsan* does not seek citizens who practice out of fear of state reprisals. It will be composed of citizens who choose to follow Islamic values because they are in love with their Lord and want to please their Lord and gain proximity to Him. They do not need a state to incentivize their faith; they need it to get out of their way as they march along the various way stations to *Ihsan*. It is a desire to be one with the One and not a desire to stay out of prison that motivates the self-regulating *Muhsins* in the State of *Ihsan*.

The demand for *freedom to be a partner in governance* should not come as a surprise to any Muslim who ponders the role of Islam in governance. This is just another way of stating that Muslims as believers have the right to consultative governance and thus have a right to have a say in how they are governed. In a State of *Ihsan*, where citizens are self-regulating, *there will be a transfer of governance from state to society* and individuals, thus making states weak and civil society strong. The more seriously policymaking, law-making and governance are taken by citizens, the more participatory governance will become. I expect that in a truly developed State of *Ihsan*, the civil society will be so developed and so engaged that governance will become ubiquitous and invisible as virtuous citizens with a very strong culture of self-regulation will make the state so thin that it will become invisible, as will governance itself. Citizens of the State of *Ihsan* will fulfill the Quranic commandment to advocate for good and campaign against evil in their pursuit of *Ihsan* and there will be no need for compulsion whatsoever.

God Governance to Good(ness) Governance: Citizens as Consumers of Public Goods

وَتَعَاوَنُواْ عَلَى ٱلْبِرِّ

And cooperate with one another in goodness. (Quran 5:2)

While some Muslims today are clamoring for the establishment of Islamic states, others are looking for secular democracies, and some even for Islamic democracies. Unfortunately, this focus on the structure of government is precluding them from calling for what they actual need, which is good governance. I believe that Muslim aspirations are misdirected, because they believe that the security, prosperity and well-being that they are seeking, will be delivered by one of these models. For decades, they have experienced authoritarian dictatorships and monarchies and they are more than ready for change and are looking for a magic formula that will transform their reality. I understand and appreciate the desire of Muslim masses to shed the shackles of authoritarian government and to let faith, culture and commerce thrive unencumbered by ideology or dictators. But I fear that Muslims pursuing and privileging any specific structure of government are in for a disappointment.

The Egyptian experiment after the Arab Spring, moving from a military dictatorship to an ideology-driven majoritarian democracy, and its failure attests to this reality. Egyptians from 2010 to 2013 rejected dictatorship, democracy and Islamism.[51] They also rejected the idea of the Islamic state

---

[51] Hisham A. Hellyer, *A Revolution Undone: Egypt's Road Beyond Revolt* (Oxford University Press, 2017). Also see Bahgat Korany, and Rabab El-Mahdi, eds., *Arab Spring in Egypt: revolution and beyond* (American University in Cairo Press, 2012).

as even the most ardent advocates of the Islamic state—the Muslim Brotherhood—did not press for it and instead chose a democratic structure of government. Thus in 2011 with the collapse of the military regime of Hosni Mubarak, Egyptians rejected military dictatorship and by not even considering the creation of an Islamic state as an alternative, they signaled a preference for some form of popular democratic governance. Unfortunately, that political experiment failed and the Egyptian reality in 2018 does not look very different from that of 2010. Egyptians are still looking for a government that can deliver the public goods they desire.

But democracy as a structure of government alone is not a guarantor that all segments of society will benefit from the state. There are democratic states where governance is far from good. Minorities are suffering from neglect and sometimes from state-sponsored discrimination. Income gaps are increasing and education standards are declining. Health care is far from what is needed and even children in schools are not safe from violence and massacres. One can find all these trends in the United States, which for centuries has been the poster child for democracy. There are authoritarian states like Singapore that are providing better governance for their citizens. Security, growth and environment are all better in this non-democracy than in the United States. The point that I am trying to make is that structures of government are not enough by themselves. Establishing democracy without pursuing good governance will lead to dissatisfaction and political instability. Citizens must demand more from their governments and governing elite. While some authoritarian states might deliver some public goods better than democratic states, the absence of freedoms takes away from the material benefits of good governance.

What Muslims need to be seeking is a system of government that can deliver the public goods that they seek without loss of freedom of any kind. A vast majority of Muslims, whether in Egypt or Malaysia, Michigan or England, understand this intuitively. But then there are those who want God to be sovereign and those who do believe that Islamic values can help bring about a better state and society. This section is specifically for them. The conversations in Muslim politics must be about *what the public needs from its governments and not what God needs from his people*. God does not need anything. He is *Al-Ghani* (self-sufficient, free from need). What the public needs from its rulers is good governance. Ultimately, one must recognize that the role of government is not to govern but to facilitate self-governance, both in the spiritual and the mundane spheres. We do not want the government to tell us what to believe and what to do. We want the government to deliver what we need and not become a barrier to its citizens' spiritual, ideational and material aspirations as long as these aspirations do not infringe on the basic rights of others and do not obstruct the aspirations of others.

The key is to understand the difference between God-centric and God governance. The latter is a legal fiction, a juristic charade maintained by jurists who claim that God rules if God's laws, which in reality are essentially interpretations of jurists and their view of what constitutes God's *Shariah*, are enforced and the emphasis is on enforced. God-centric is what this book is about—make the desire to bear witness willingly through voluntary submission to God (*Mushahada*) a state and social aspiration. The difference may appear to be semantic but in reality it is profound. It is a shift from the authoritarian model of governance to a more democratic model. In the former, the elite (jurists) define what is *Shariah* and enforce it with or without the consent of the population, Muslim or non-Muslim. The little lip service given to democracy in this *Islamic state* is basically procedural. In the latter, the *State of Ihsan*, the citizens are God-centered and so is the society, but the state itself is more focused on good governance—the good here is understood more in the sense of goodness or *Ihsan* and all the values that have been described in the previous chapter and in this one.

IHSAN AND GOOD(NESS) GOVERNANCE

In the last three decades, a regime of public policy research and domestic and international benchmarks have emerged to identify the best practices of governance to create a prolific discourse on good governance.[52] These benchmarks are used by international organizations, lending and development agencies, to provide loans, grants and other forms of support to developing nations. They are also used by politicians to tout their own success and by governments to reward subunits, local government units and even departments for good performance. Governance is essentially the delivery of public goods and services; they can be as profound and complex such as providing universal health care, Internet access and free education nationwide, to as simple as taking care of potholes and broken street lamps

---

[52] John Graham, Timothy Wynne Plumptre and Bruce Amos, *Principles for good governance in the 21st century* (Ottawa: Institute on Governance, 2003). David Levi-Faur, ed., *The Oxford handbook of governance* (London: Oxford University Press, 2012).

in your neighborhood. Governance is not about identity politics, altering history, promoting religious conversion, taking revenge against its own citizens for historical acts of real or perceived injustices or even policing thought and conscience of citizens. Governance is about delivery of public goods and services to all citizens equally. Even the few Muslim theorists who have studied good governance in recent years have all been informed by a *Shariah*-centric approach—meaning they view quality of governance based on *God governance and not goodness in governance*.[53]

Some of the broadly agreed upon public goods are public safety, criminal justice, education, defense, public safety, economic development, social justice, health care, political equality and social welfare. When these public goods and services are delivered efficiently, effectively, inclusively, with transparency, without corruption and in accordance with the law, then we can acknowledge that good governance is in place. Good governance is essentially about the processes by which public institutions deliver public goods and manage public resources.

Muslim scholars of governance, the few that existed, have also viewed public responsibilities as a trust from God (*Amanah*) and this model of governance as trusteeship has guided them in emphasizing honesty and transparency in governance. Even a cursory examination of the benchmarks of good governance and historical Muslim practices of governance will reveal that some of its values such as accountability, rule of law, consultation and consensus building have always been valued even when they have not been fully realized. Efficiency, effectiveness, transparency and responsiveness have not received much attention and neither has participatory governance. The primary reason in my mind for this neglect is the use of *Shariah* law and its implementation as a way of gaining legitimacy, thus replacing the delivery of public goods and public services, or inclusivity and social justice as the yardstick for evaluating governance and legitimacy.

Even in recent times, illegitimate leaders and regimes have used implementation of a few symbolic *Shariah* rulings as a justification rather than efficient and effective delivery of public goods. This ploy has worked and continues to work with Muslim masses because large segments assume that the purpose for which governments exist is to implement God's rules,

[53] See Maszlee Malik, *Foundations of Islamic Governance: A Southeast Asian Perspective* (London: Taylor & Francis, 2016). Joseph J. Kaminski, *The Contemporary Islamic Governed State* (London: Palgrave Macmillan, 2017). See also Abdul Rashid Moten, "Solving for Islamic governance: Varying Contexts, Different Strategies." *American Journal of Islamic Social Sciences* 32.2 (2015): 68.

even defend God's religion and His Prophet (pbuh) from their enemies. Far from realizing a State of *Ihsan*, Muslims will not enjoy any degree of good governance until they change their philosophy of governance and think of ruling institutions not as *God Government but Good Governance.* Use of religious symbolism by governments and leaders should be viewed with suspicion rather than acceptance. In my experience, governments usually use religious symbolism if they come to power in suspicious ways (i.e. without the full consent of the governed) or if their policies to deliver public goods and services have begun to go south.

But the purpose of the State of *Ihsan* is not limited to good governance, as understood by contemporary political theory. It includes the delivery of public goods and services but it also includes the creation of an environment in which citizens can be self-governing and pursue goodness or *Ihsan*. I do not see the role of the state as implementing or enforcing *Ihsan* but enabling all the structural and societal features described here to allow beauty or goodness or *Ihsan* to become a reality. Thus, the good in good governance in the worldview of *Ihsan* becomes goodness.

Muslims, like all people, deserve to be governed well. I wish to see them governed beautifully (*Ihsan*). This will not happen until Muslims disentangle governance from imposition of religious symbols and identity politics and start seeking substantive improvements in the quality of material and spiritual life. The key is that society must habitually expect delivery of services and demand it and states must develop the habit of delivering public goods and services demanded by *all* their citizens. Muslims need to first move from expecting the realization of religious symbolism to demanding good governance and then to aspiring for the State of *Ihsan* and good(ness) governance.

CHAPTER 8

Closing Thoughts

لَّلْعَٰلَمِينَ رَحْمَةً إِلَّا أَرْسَلْنَٰكَ وَمَآ

We have sent you as nothing but mercy to all the worlds. (Quran 21:107)

I end this journey toward *Ihsan* with a few closing thoughts that encapsulate and summarize my argument in this book. In this book, I have tried to advance a vision of Islamic political philosophy anchored by the concept of *Ihsan*, which I argue is the most beautiful way of understanding Islam and its worldview. I present *Ihsan* as a spiritual state in which the *Muhsin* seeks to perform beautiful deeds in order to earn a vision of the divine. I also argued that *Ihsan* is a complex concept—a cosmology by itself—that has many components including an epistemology, and a set of normative preferences such as love over law, and mercy and forgiveness over retribution. The Quran teaches us that God sent both his messenger and his message as mercy to humanity.[1] In this age when Islamophobia is rampant, it is important for Muslims to actualize this divine promise so that rather than fearing Islam and Muslims, the world is reassured that Islam and Muslims are here to bring love, compassion and comfort to others. Muslims in the State of *Ihsan* can be nothing but mercy to all of humanity.

I have clearly relied on the key concept of *Ihsan* and leaned heavily on the Sufi understanding and teachings of its deeper meanings, to develop an Islamic political philosophy of good governance. While I am advocating that

[1] See verses 21.107 and 17.82 in the Holy Quran.

© The Author(s) 2019
M. A. M. Khan, *Islam and Good Governance*,
https://doi.org/10.1057/978-1-137-54832-0_8

all Muslims, at both individual and institutional/national level, inculcate the virtues of *Ihsan*, I am not calling for all Muslims to become Sufis. While Sufi thought, music and poetry, not to mention the philosophical and mystical works of Jalaluddin Rumi, Ibn Arabi, Al-Ghazali and Khawaja Nizamuddin, inspire and enrich me, I remain skeptical of the Sufi orders and their contemporary practices. Sufi orders these days are engrossed in rituals and hagiography of their teachers. They are too busy listening to stories about the service and struggles for social justice of their past teachers and have little time to go out and engage in that same service and struggles themselves. To me *Ihsan* is about doing beautiful things in difficult circumstances. It is engaging with the world in pursuit of social justice and not remaining silent in retreats in the face of oppression. So, in a way I am recommending that we embrace the Sufi understanding of *Ihsan* and not apply for membership in Sufi orders. I want *Ihsan* to be realized in the public sphere and do not want it to be quarantined in the Sufi lodges.

Muslims all over the world are feeling victimized by the existing global order. They want change and they want it now. Islamic states like Iran have tried to bring about change through foreign policies that are counter-hegemonic and radical groups like Al-Qaeda and Daesh have resorted to terrorism in pursuit of change. Islamist movements have tried to bring about change from within and they too have adopted both violent and counter-hegemonic tactics at the domestic level, in Pakistan, Afghanistan, Indonesia, Philippines, Palestine and Egypt. The demand for justice, for a new order, is strident. In *Islam and Good Governance*, I have tried to articulate a new form of politics that emphasizes compassion and love, and without denying the need for change, I have merely advocated a change in the means for change.

I have taken the Quranic injunction to pursue justice through *Ihsan* (Quran 16:90) and underscored the point that justice is not enough. Islam teaches that God expects us to pursue justice in the most beautiful way. Thus, while the goal is a just order, the means must be based on the principles of *Ihsan*. I think Muslim political agencies, whether they are states, militants or social movements, are so convinced of the holiness of their goals—to establish a divine order, the kingdom of God, the *Shariah*-based Islamic state—that they are willing to overlook the manner in which these goals are pursued. Some of the tactics used by Islamists, the Taliban in Afghanistan and Pakistan and Jihadis in Iraq and Syria, for example, would make anyone who cares about humanity recoil in horror. How can one bear witness to God and act as if he is seeing us and we are seeing him when one wears a suicide vest and walks into a school or a mosque or shoots a young girl in the face? By emphasizing the importance of *Ihsan* in the pursuit of justice, as taught by the Quran, I want Muslims to realize that Islamic ethics are deontological. Ethical actions are what Islam is about, not some imaginary just outcome regardless of how one arrives at it. Every element of good governance that I have outlined in the chapter "*Ihsan* and Good Governance" seeks to infuse the virtue of *Ihsan* in the legislation of *Shariah*, in the conception of citizenship, in the delineation of the purpose of the state and in guiding the activism of civil society.

Islamic movements and Islamic states have failed in achieving the goals they had set for themselves—a revival of the Islamic civilization and escape from the cultural and political hegemony of the West. But they have succeeded to a great extent in reducing Islam to an identity and have created a global demand for symbols of Islamic identity. Many Muslims seem to be living in two worlds, the real one where they have to deal with the world of nation states and existing laws and then the imaginary one wherein they talk about Islamic identity, Muslim world and Islamic things that exist as ideals or existed in an idealized memory of the past. They live in an identity shroud that they wrap around themselves. This reduction of Islam to an identity is superficial and external. I wish to move away from the "Islam of symbols" and toward an "Islam of substance" an Islam where the practice of values matters rather than symbolism. Islam should be a reservoir of values that shapes Muslims' actions, not an identity that feeds their discourses and rhetoric. In trying to imagine the *Muhsin* as a self-critical citizen, I want to move Islam from the outside to the inside and make it the epicenter of our ethics and not the flag that we fly everywhere.

I do believe that Islamic teachings have much to offer to society and one way to do so is to channel the concept of *Ihsan* and advocate for good governance in Muslim societies. All societies and nations desire similar goals, self-determination, preservation of culture, wealth and nationhood and the freedom to celebrate one's history, and identity. While other societies are welcome to pursue these goals through a combination of their particular history and the discoveries of science and social science, I believe that Muslims too can and should be allowed to advocate for these goals within the particular context that they find most meaningful. I am convinced that Muslims can find dignity for themselves collectively and for all individuals who live in their societies, but not through a process of enforcing values and marginalizing difference but through opening spaces for everyone to bear witness in their own unique ways. I hope this book sparks conversations that inspire us all to do beautiful things in our lives, including in the public arena. I hope the book invites people to live as if they are in a thrall of the divine vision, and for those who are not as blessed, let them know that there is a divine witness to their deeds.

BIBLIOGRAPHY

Abbas, Shemeem Burney. *Pakistan's Blasphemy Laws: From Islamic Empires to the Taliban.* Austin, TX: University of Texas Press, 2013.

Abbasi, Nadia Mushtaq. "Impact of Terrorism on Pakistan." *Strategic Studies* 33, no. 2 (2013).

Abduh, Muhammad, and Kamran Talattof. "The Necessity of Religious Reform." In *Contemporary Debates in Islam: An Anthology of Fundamentalist Thought*, edited by Mansoor Moaddel and Kamran Talattof, 45–52. New York: St. Martin's Press, 2000.

Abou El Fadl, Khaled. *Conference of the Books: The Search for Beauty in Islam.* Lanham, MD: Rowman and Littlefield, 2005.

———. *The Great Theft: Wrestling Islam from the Extremists.* New York: Harper Collins, 2007.

———. *Speaking in God's Name: Islamic Law, Authority and Women.* Oxford: Oneworld, 2014.

Abu-Rabi', Ibrahim M. *Intellectual Origins of Islamic Resurgence in the Modern Arab World.* Albany: SUNY Press, 1996.

Afsaruddin, Asma. "Obedience to Political Authority: An Evolutionary Concept." *Islamic Democratic Discourse: Theory, Debates, and Philosophical Perspectives* (2006): 37–60.

Ahmad, Mumtaz, ed. *State Politics and Islam.* Indianapolis, IN: American Trust Publications, 1986.

———. "Islamic Fundamentalism in South Asia: The Jamaat-i-Islami and the Tablighi Jamaat of South Asia." In *Fundamentalisms Observed*, edited by Martin Marty and Scott R. Appleby, vol. 1, 457–530. Chicago: University of Chicago Press, 1991.

© The Author(s) 2019
M. A. M. Khan, *Islam and Good Governance*,
https://doi.org/10.1057/978-1-137-54832-0

Ahmed, Leila. *Women and Gender in Islam: Historical Roots of a Modern Debate.* New Haven, CT: Yale University Press, 1992.

Ahmed, Akbar. "Ibn Khaldun's Understanding of Civilizations and the Dilemmas of Islam and the West Today." *The Middle East Journal* 56, no. 1 (Winter, 2002): 20–45.

Ahmed, M. Basheer, Syed A. Ahsani, and Dilnawaz Ahmed Siddiqui. *Muslim Contributions to World Civilization.* Herndon, VA: International Institute of Islamic Thought (IIIT), 2005.

Akbarzadeh, Shahram, ed. *Routledge Handbook of Political Islam.* London: Taylor & Francis, 2012.

Al-Alwani, Taha Jabir. *Ijtihad.* Herndon, VA: International Institute of Islamic Thought (IIIT), 1993.

Alam, Muzaffar. *Languages of Political Islam in India 1200–1800.* London: Orient Blackswan, 2004.

Al-Arabi, Ibn. *On the Mysteries of Bearing Witness to the Oneness of God and Messengership of Muhammad.* Translated by Aisha Bewley. Chicago: Kazi Publications, 2010.

Al-Farabi, Abu Nasr. *On the Perfect State.* Translated by Richard Walzer. New York: Oxford University Press, 1998.

Al-Ghazali, Abu Hamid. *The Inner Dimensions of Islamic Prayer.* Translated by M. Holland. Leicester, UK: Islamic Foundation, 1983.

———. *Ihya Uloom al-Deen.* Translated by Allama Faiz Ahmed Owaisi. New Delhi: Maktabah Radhwiyyah, 1999.

———. *Al-Ghazali's Path to Sufism: His Deliverance from Error [Al-Munqidh Min Al-Dalal] and Five Key Texts.* Translated by R.J. McCarthy. Louisville, KY: Fons Vitae, 2000.

Al-Ghazali, Abu Hamid, and Claud Field. *The Alchemy of Happiness.* Armonk, NY: M.E. Sharpe, 1991.

Ali, Jan. "Islamic Revivalism: The Case of the Tablighi Jamaat." *Journal of Muslim Minority Affairs* 23, no. 1 (2003): 173–181.

Ali, Souad T. *A Religion, Not a State: Ali'Abd Al-Raziq's Islamic Justification of Political Secularism.* Salt Lake: University of Utah, 2009.

Al-Jilani, Abd al-Qadir. *The Secret of Secrets.* Translated by Tosun Bayrak al-Jerrahi Al-Halveti. Cambridge: Islamic Texts Society, 1992.

Allawi, Ali A. *The Crisis of Islamic Civilization.* New Haven: Yale University Press, 2009.

al-Ma'sumi, Muhammad Saghir Hassan. "Al-Farabi." In *A History of Muslim Philosophy I*, edited by M.M. Sharif, 704–716. Karachi: Royal Book Company, 1963.

Al-Mawardi, Abu'l Hasan. *Al-Ahkam as-Sultaniyyah: The Laws of Islamic Governance.* Translated by Asadullah Yate. London: Ta-Ha Publishers, 1996.

Al-Mawardi, Abu al-Ḥasan. *The Ordinances of Government.* Translated by Wafaa H. Wahba. New York: Ithaca Press, 2000.

al-Mulk, Nizam. *The Book of Government or Rules for Kings*. Translated by Hubert Darke. London: Curzon Books, 1960.

An-Na'im, Abdullahi A. *Islam and the Secular State*. Cambridge: Harvard University Press, 2008.

Al-Nawawi, Imam. *Riyadh–al-Saleheen*. Translated by S.M. Abbas. Madani. Riyadh, Saudi Arabia: International Islamic Publishing House, 2002.

Al-Qaradawi, Yusuf. *Approaching the Sunnah: Comprehension & Controversy*. Herndon, VA: International Institute of Islamic Thought (IIIT), 2006.

Al-Qudsy, S.H.S.I., and A.A. Rahman. "Effective Governance in the Era of Caliphate Umar Ibn Al-Khattab (634–644)." *European Journal of Social Sciences* 18, no. 4 (2011): 612–624.

al-Qushayri, Abu 'l-Qasim. *Al-Qushayri's Epistle on Sufism: Al-Risala Al-Qushayriyya Fi 'Ilm Al-Tasawwuf*. Translated by Alexander D. Knysh. Reading: Garnet Publishing, 2007.

Al-Raysuni, Ahmad. *Al-Shura: The Qur'anic Principle of Consultation*. Herndon, VA: International Institute of Islamic Thought (IIIT), 2011.

Al-Razi, Fakruddin. *Tafsir Al-Fakr Al-Razi*. Vol. 5. Beirut, Lebanon: Dar Al-Fikr, 2003.

Al-Tustai, Sahl B. Abd Allah. *Tafsir Al-Tustari: Great Commentaries on the Holy Quran*. Translated by Annabel Keeler and Ali Keeler. Louisville, KY: Fons Vitae, 2011.

Al-Zamakhshari, Mahmud bin Umar. *Al-Kashaf*. Beirut, Lebanon: Dar Al-Kitab, 2008.

Amin, Qasim. "The Liberation of Women." In *Contemporary Debates in Islam: An Anthology of Fundamentalist Thought*, edited by Mansoor Moaddel and Kamran Talattof, 163–182. New York: St. Martin's Press, 2000.

Al-Nabbhani, Taqiuddin. *The Islamic State*. Walnut, CA: The Islamic Cultural Workshop, 1996.

An-Na'im, Abdullahi A. *Toward an Islamic Reformation: Civil Liberties, Human Rights, and International Law*. Syracuse, NY: Syracuse University Press, 1990.

———. "Islam and Secularism." In *Comparative Secularisms in a Global Age*, edited by Linell E. Cady and Elizabeth Shakman Hurd. Basingstoke: Palgrave Macmillan, 2010.

An-Nawawi, Sheikh M. *Al-Arbaeen Al-Nawawi*. Chicago: Kazi Publications, 1982.

An-Nawawi, Imam. *An-Nawawi's Forty Hadith*. Translated by Ezzedine Ibrahim and Denys Johnson-Davies. Riyadh, KSA: International Publishers House, 1992.

Arabi, Muhyi-Al-Din Ibn. *Tafsir Ibn Arabi*. Beirut, Lebanon: Dar Sader Publishers, 2002.

Arnold, Thomas Walker. *The Preaching of Islam: A History of the Propagation of the Muslim Faith*. Delhi; L. P. Publications, 1990.

Asad, Muhammad. *The Principles of State and Government in Islam.* Gibraltar: Dar Al-Andalus, 1981.

As-Sa'di, Sheikh Abd-Ar-Rahman b Nasir. *Tafsir as-Sadi.* Translated by S. Abd Al-Hamid. Floral Park, NY: Islamic Literary Foundation, 2012.

Attia, Gamal Eldin. *Towards Realization of the Higher Intents of Islamic Law; Maqasid Al-Shari'ah: A Functional Approach.* Herndon, VA: International Institute of Islamic Thought, 2007.

Auda, Jasser. *Maqasid Al-Shariah as Philosophy of Islamic Law: A Systems Approach.* Herndon, VA: International Institute of Islamic Thought (IIIT), 2008a.

———. *Maqasid Al-Shariah: A Beginner's Guide.* Vol. 14. International Institute of Islamic Thought (IIIT), 2008b.

Austin, Ralph William Julius. *The Bezels of Wisdom.* Mahwah, NJ: Paulist Press, 1980.

Awliya, Nizamuddin. *Morals for the Heart.* Translated by Bruce B. Lawrence. New York: Paulist Press, 1992.

Ayoob, Mohammed. *The Many Faces of Political Islam: Religion and Politics in the Muslim World.* Ann Arbor: University of Michigan Press, 2007.

Ayubi, Nazih. *Political Islam: Religion and Politics in the Arab World.* London: Taylor & Francis, 2004.

Badran, Margot, ed. *Feminism in Islam: Secular and Religious Convergences.* Oxford: Oneworld Publications, 2009.

Bakhtiar, Laleh, and Kevin Reinhart. *Encyclopedia of Islamic Law: A Compendium of the Major Schools.* Chicago: Kazi Publications, 1996.

Balqazīz, 'Abd al-Ilāh. *The State in Contemporary Islamic Thought: A Historical Survey of the Major Muslim Political Thinkers of the Modern Era.* London: I. B. Tauris, 2009.

Barlas, Asma. *"Believing Women" in Islam: Unreading Patriarchal Interpretations of the Qur'an.* Austin, TX: University of Texas Press, 2002.

Batstone, David B., and Eduardo Mendieta. *The Good Citizen.* New York: Routledge, 1999.

Baumgartner, Frederic J. *Longing for the End: A History of Millennialism in Western Civilization.* Boulder, CO: St. Martin's Press, 1999.

Belkeziz, Abdelilah. "The State in Contemporary Islamic Thought." *A Historical Survey of the Major Muslim Political Thinkers of the Modern Era* 49 (2009): 70.

Bennabi, Malek. *The Question of Culture.* Translated by Abdul Wahid Lu'lu'a. Kuala Lumpur: The International Institute of Islamic Thought, 2003.

Berlin, Isaiah. *Two Concepts of Liberty: An Inaugural Lecture Delivered Before the University of Oxford on 31 October 1958.* Oxford: Clarendon, 1959.

Bhatnagar, Shyam Krishna, and Aligarh Muslim University. *History of the M.A.O. College, Aligarh.* [Bombay]: [Published for] Sir Syed Hall, Aligarh Muslim University [by] Asia Pub. House, 1969.

Bhutto, Benazir. *Reconciliation: Islam, Democracy, and the West.* New York: Harper, 2008.

Black, Deborah L. "Al-Farabi." In *History of Islamic Philosophy I*, edited by Seyyed Hossein Nasr and Oliver Leaman, 178–197. London: Routledge, 1996.

Black, Antony. "Ibn Khaldun (1332–1406): The Science of Civilisation and the Governance of Islam." In *A. Black, The History of Islamic Political Thought: From the Prophet to the Present*, 165–182. London: Routledge, 2001.

———. *The History of Islamic Political Thought: From the Prophet to the Present*. Edinburgh: Edinburgh University Press, 2011.

Bohman, James, ed. *Deliberative Democracy: Essays on Reason and Politics*. Cambridge, MA: MIT Press, 1997.

Braudel, Fernand. *On History*. Translated by Sarah Matthews. Chicago: University of Chicago Press, 1982.

Bronner, Stephen Eric, and Douglas Kellner, eds. *Critical Theory and Society: A Reader*. New York: Routledge, 1989.

Browers, Michaelle. *Political Ideology in the Arab World: Accommodation and Transformation*. Cambridge, UK: Cambridge University Press, 2009.

Brown, L. Carl. *Religion and State: The Muslim Approach to Politics*. New York: Columbia University Press, 2001.

Brown, Jonathan A.C. *Hadith: Muhammad's Legacy in the Medieval and Modern World*. Oxford: Oneworld Publications, 2009.

Brownlee, Jason, Tarek E. Masoud, and Andrew Reynolds. *The Arab Spring: Pathways of Repression and Reform*. USA: Oxford University Press, 2015.

Buchanan, Patrick J. *The Death of the West: How Dying Populations and Immigrant Invasions Imperil Our Country and Civilization*. Boulder, CO: St. Martin's Griffin, 2002.

Burgat, Francois. *Face to Face with Political Islam*. London: I. B. Tauris, 2003.

Butler, Judith, Jurgen Habermas, Charles Taylor, Cornel West, Eduardo Mendieta, Jonathan VanAntwerpen, and Craig Calhoun. *The Power of Religion in the Public Sphere*. New York: Columbia University Press, 2011.

Byman, Daniel. *Al Qaeda, the Islamic State, and the Global Jihadist Movement: What Everyone Needs to Know*. New York: Oxford University Press, 2015.

Chapra, M. Umer. *Islam and the Economic Challenge*. Herndon, VA: International Institute of Islamic Thought and The Islamic Foundation, 1992.

———. *Muslim Civilization: The Causes of Decline and the Need for Reform*. Leicester, UK: Islamic Foundation, 2010.

Cheema, Umar. "Only Five Out of Fifty Four Muslim States Have Tough Blasphemy Laws." https://www.geo.tv/latest/16721-only-five-out-of-54-muslim-states-have-tough-blasphemy-laws.

Chittick, William C. "Divine Love: Islamic Literature and the Path to God." http://public.eblib.com/choice/publicfullrecord.aspx?p=4585770.

———. *The Sufi Path of Knowledge: Ibn Al-'Arabi's Metaphysics of Imagination*. Albany, NY: State University of New York Press, 1989.

———. *Faith and Practice of Islam: Three Thirteenth-Century Sufi Texts*. Albany, NY: SUNY Press, 1992.

————. *Sufism: A Beginner's Guide.* Oxford: Oneworld Publications, 2005.

Claire, Mercer. "NGOs, Civil Society and Democratization: A Critical Review of the Literature." *Progress in Development Studies* 2, no. 1 (2002): 5–22.

Clark, Charles S. *The New Voluntarism: Is America Poised for a Surge in Good Works?* Washington, DC: Congressional Quarterly, Incorporated, 1996.

Cohen, Joshua, and Deborah Chasman, eds. *Islam and the Challenge of Democracy.* Princeton: Princeton University Press, 2004.

Colby, Frederick Stephen "The Subtleties of the Ascension: Al-Sulamī on the Miraj of the Prophet Muhammad." *Studia Islamica* (2002): 167–183.

————. *Narrating Muḥammad's Night Journey: Tracing the Development of the Ibn ʿAbbās Ascension Discourse.* Albany: SUNY Press, 2008.

Cook, Michael. "Freedom." In *The Princeton Encyclopedia of Islamic Political Thought*, edited by Richard Bulliet, David Cook, Roxanne L. Euben, Khaled Fahmy, Frank Griffel, Bernard Haykel, Robert W. Hefner, Timur Kuran, Jane McAuliffe, and Ebrahim Moosa, 174–175. New Jersey: Princeton University Press, 2012.

Cornford, Francis MacDonald. *The Republic of Plato.* Vol. 30. Oxford: Oxford University Press, 1945.

Cox, Robert W. "Towards a Post-Hegemonic Conceptualization of World Order: Reflections on the Relevancy of Ibn Khaldun." In *Governance Without Government: Order and Change in World Politics*, edited by James Rosenau and Ernst-Otto Czempiel, 132–159. Cambridge: Cambridge University Press, 1992.

Crone, Patricia. *God's Rule: Government and Islam.* New York: Columbia University Press, 2004.

Dabashi, Hamid. *The Green Movement in Iran.* New York: Transaction Publishers, 2011.

Daniel, Norman. *Islam and the West: The Making of an Image.* Oxford: Oneworld, 2009.

Daryabadi, Abdul Majid. *The Glorious Quran: Text, Translation and Commentary.* Leicester, UK: Islamic Foundation, 2000.

David, Matthew, and Iain Wilkinson. "Critical Theory of Society or Self-Critical Society?" *Critical Horizons: A Journal of Philosophy & Social Theory* 3, no. 1 (2015): 131–158.

Davison, Andrew, and Joel Weinsheimer. *Secularism and Revivalism in Turkey: A Hermeneutic Reconsideration.* New Haven, CT: Yale University Press, 1998.

Dawud, Abu. *Sunan Abu Dawud: English-Arabic Text, Vol V.* Translated by Muhammed Mahdi, Al-Shariaf. Beirut, Lebanon: Dar Al-Kotob Al-Ilmiyyah, 2008.

Delong-Bas, Natana J. *Wahhabi Islam: From Revival and Reform to Global Jihad.* London: I. B. Taurus, 2007.

Derin, Süleyman. *Love in Sufism: From Rabia to Ibn Al-Farid.* Istanbul: Insan, 2008.

Diner, Dan. *Lost in the Sacred: Why the Muslim World Stood Still*. Translated by Steven Rendall. Princeton, NJ: Princeton University Press, 2009.

Dryzek, John S. *Deliberative Democracy and Beyond: Liberals, Critics, Contestations*. Oxford; New York: Oxford University Press, 2000.

Edwards, A. Hart. *The Bustan of Sadi*. Los Angeles, CA: Indo-European Publishing, 2012.

El Fadl, Khaled Abou. "The Ugly Modern and the Modern Ugly: Reclaiming the Beautiful in Islam." In *Progressive Muslims: On Justice, Gender and Pluralism*, edited by Omid Safi. Oxford: Oneworld Publications, 2003.

———. *Islam and the Challenge of Democracy: A Boston Review Book*. Princeton: Princeton University Press, 2004.

———, ed. *Islam and the Challenge of Democracy: A Boston Review Book*. New Jersey: Princeton University Press, 2015.

El-Affendi, Abdelwahab. "Democracy and Its (Muslim) Critics: An Islamic Alternative to Democracy?" In *Islamic Democratic Discourse: Theory, Debates, and Philosophical Perspectives*, edited by M.A. Muqtedar Khan, 227–257. Oxford: Lexington Books, 2006.

———. *Who Needs an Islamic State?* London: Malaysia Think Tank, 2008.

Enayat, Hamid. *Modern Islamic Political Thought*. Austin, Texas: University of Texas Press, 1991.

Esposito, John L. "Muhammad Iqbal and the Islamic State." In *Voices of Resurgent Islam*, edited by John L. Esposito, vol. 183, 40–51. New York: Oxford University Press, 1983a.

———., ed. *Voices of Resurgent Islam*. New York: Oxford University Press, 1983b.

———., ed. *Political Islam: Revolution, Radicalism, or Reform?* Boulder, CO: Lynne Rienner Publishers London, 1997.

———. *Islam: The Straight Path*. New York: Oxford University Press, 1998.

Esposito, John L., and John Obert Voll. *Islam and Democracy*. New York: Oxford University Press, 1996.

———. *Makers of Contemporary Islam*. New York: Oxford University Press, 2001.

Esposito, John L., Tamara Sonn, and John O. Voll. *Islam and Democracy After the Arab Spring*. Oxford University Press, 2015.

Feldman, Noah. *After Jihad: America and the Struggle for Islamic Democracy*. New York: Farrar, Straus and Giroux, 2003.

———. *The Fall and Rise of the Islamic State*. Princeton, NJ: Princeton University Press, 2009.

———. *The Fall and Rise of the Islamic State*. Princeton, NJ: Princeton University Press, 2012.

Finnemore, Martha. *National Interests in International Society*. Ithaca, NY: Cornell University Press, 1996.

Ghamidi, Javed A. "The Punishment for Blasphemy Against the Prophet (Sws)." http://www.ghamidi.net/article/Punishment%20for%20Blasphemy.pdf.

Giddens, Anthony. *The Consequences of Modernity.* Stanford, CA: Stanford University Press, 1990.

———. *Modernity and Self-Identity: Self and Society in the Late Modern Age.* Stanford, CA: Stanford University Press, 1991.

Gottschalk, Peter, and Gabriel Greenberg. "From Muhammad to Obama: Caricatures, Cartoons and Stereotypes of Muslims." In *Islamophobia: The Challenge of Pluralism in the 21st Century,* edited by John L. Esposito and Ibrahim Kalin, 191–210. New York: Oxford University Press, 2010.

Graham, John, Timothy Wynne Plumptre, and Bruce Amos. *Principles for Good Governance in the 21st Century.* Ottawa: Institute on Governance, 2003.

Guillaume, A. *The Life of Muhammad.* Karachi: Oxford University Press, 1967.

Gulen, Fethullah. *Key Concepts in the Practice of Sufism.* Clifton: Tughra Books, 2007.

Habermas, Jürgen, and Frederick G. Lawrence. *The Philosophical Discourse of Modernity.* Boston: The MIT Press, 1990.

Haddad, Yvonne Yazbeck. *Contemporary Islam and the Challenge of History.* Albany, NY: State University of New York Press, 1982.

Haddad, Yvonne Yazbeck, John Obert Voll, and John L. Esposito. *The Contemporary Islamic Revival: A Critical Survey and Bibliography.* Westport, CT: Greenwood Publishing Group, 1991.

Hallaq, Wael B. "On the Authoritativeness of Sunni Consensus." *International Journal of Middle East Studies* 18, no. 4 (1986): 427–454.

———. *A History of Islamic Legal Theories: An Introduction to Sunni Usul Al-Fiqh.* London: Cambridge University Press, 1999.

———. *The Origins and Evolution of Islamic Law.* Cambridge, UK; New York: Cambridge University Press, 2005.

———. *The Impossible State: Islam, Politics, and Modernity's Moral Predicament.* New York, NY: Columbia University Press, 2013.

Halvorsen, Vidar. "Is It Better That Ten Guilty Persons Go Free than That One Innocent Person Be Convicted?" *Criminal Justice Ethics Criminal Justice Ethics* 23, no. 2 (2004): 3–13.

Haq, Mufti A. *The Tablighi Jamaat Movement.* Lahore, Pakistan: Aziz Printing House, 1987.

Haqqani, Husain. "The Role of Islam in Pakistan's Future." *The Washington Quarterly* 28, no. 1 (2004): 83–96.

———. *Pakistan: Between Mosque and Military.* Washington, DC: Carnegie Endowment, 2010.

Hasan, Masudul. *Sayyid Abul A'ala Maududi and His Thought.* Lahore: Islamic Publications, 1984.

Hashemi, Nader. *Islam, Secularism, and Liberal Democracy: Toward a Democratic Theory for Muslim Societies.* Oxford; New York: Oxford University Press, 2009.

Hassaballa, Hesham A. "Why We Muslims Are Angry." http://www.beliefnet.com/Faiths/Islam/2006/02/Why-We-Muslims-Are-Angry.aspx.

Hassan, Mona. "Modern Interpretations and Misinterpretations of a Medieval Scholar: Apprehending the Political Thought of Ibn Taymiyya." In *Ibn Taymiyya and His Times*, edited by Yossef Rapaport and Shahab Ahmed, 338–366. Oxford [etc.]: Oxford University Press, 2010.

Haykal, Muḥammad Ḥusayn. *The Life of Muḥammad*. Translated by Ismaʿil Ragi Al-Faruqi. New Delhi: Crescent Publishing Co, 1976.

Hefner, Robert W., ed. *Shari'a Politics: Islamic Law and Society in the Modern World*. Bloomington, IN: Indiana University Press, 2011.

Hellyer, Hisham A. *A Revolution Undone: Egypt's Road Beyond Revolt*. Oxford: Oxford University Press, 2017.

Hodgson, Marshall G.S. *The Venture of Islam: The Classical Age of Islam*. Chicago: University of Chicago Press, 1974.

Hourani, George F. "The Basis of Authority of Consensus in Sunnite Islam." *Studia Islamica*, no. 21 (1964): 13–60.

Hourani, Albert. *Arabic Thought in the Liberal Age 1798–1939*. New York: Cambridge University Press, 1984.

Hua, Shiping. *Islam and Democratization in Asia*. Amherst, MA: Cambria Press, 2009.

Huntington, Samuel P. "The Clash of Civilizations?" *Foreign Affairs* 72, no. 3 (Summer, 1993): 22–49.

Hussain, Ahmad Iftheqar. "First Contemporary Muslim Philosopher's Conference." *American Journal of Islamic Social Sciences* 15, no. 3 (Fall, 1998): 167–172.

Ibn al-'Arabi, Aisha Abdurrahman Bewley, and Laleh Bakhtiar. *Ibn Al-'Arabī on the Mysteries of Bearing Witness to the Oneness of God and Messengership of Muhammad: From the Futūhāt Al-Makkiyya (Meccan Revelations)*. [S.l.]; Chicago, IL: Great Books of the Islamic World, Inc.: Distributed by KAZI Publications, Inc., 2010.

Ibn Ashur, Muhammad al-Tahir. *Treatise on Maqasid Al-Shari'ah*. Herndon, VA: International Institute of Islamic Thought, 2006.

Ibn Ṭalal, Ghazi ibn Muḥammad. *Love in the Holy Qur'an*. Chicago, IL: Kazi Publications, 2010.

Ibn Taymiyyah, Naseer Al-Din Albani. *Kitab Al-Iman*. Beirut, Lebanon: Al-Maktab Al-Islami, 1992.

Ibn-Arabi, Muhammad. *Divine Sayings: Mishkat Al-Anwar Oxford*. Translated by Stephen Hirtenstein and Martin Notcutt. Oxford: Anqa Publishing, 2008.

Ibrahim, Saad Eddin. "The Causes of Muslim Countries?: Poor Record of Human Rights." In *Islam and Human Rights: Advancing a US-Muslim Dialogue*, edited by Shireen Hunter, Kirk W. Larsen T. Hunter, and Huma Malik, 100–109. Washington, DC: CSIS, 2005.

'Ināyat, Ḥamīd. *Modern Islamic Political Thought*. London: I. B. Tauris, 2005.

Iṣlāḥī, Muḥammad Yūsuf. *Everyday Fiqh*. Vol. II. Lahore: Islamic Publications, 1991.

Islam, Riazul. *Sufism in South Asia: Impact on Fourteenth Century Muslim Society*. Karachi: Oxford University Press, 2002.

Islam, Md Sirajul. "Civil Society, Solidarity and Social Reformation in the Sufi Perspective." In *Civil Society as Democratic Practice*, edited by Antonio F. Perez, Semou Pathe Gueye, and Fenggang Yang. Washington, DC: The Council for Research in Values and Philosophy, 2005.

Ismail, Farrag. "A Salafi Tremor in Egypt—Founding a Party, Recognizing a Civil State and Granting Copts the Right to Refer to Their Religion." *Al Arabiya News*, June 02, 2011. http://www.alarabiya.net/articles/2011/06/02/151576.html.

Jamal, Mahmood. *Islamic Mystical Poetry: Sufi Verse from the Early Mystics to Rumi.* UK: Penguin, 2009.

Jan, Abid Ullah. *The End of Democracy.* Pragmatic Publishing, 2003.

Kabbani, Sheikh Hisham. *Self-Purification and the State of Excellence.* Mountain View, CA: As-Sunnah Foundation of America, 1998.

Kalabadhi, Abu Bakr. *The Doctrine of the Sufis.* Translated by Arthur John Arberry. Lahore, Pakistan: Suhail Academy, 2011.

Kamali, Mohammad Hashim. *Principles of Islamic Jurisprudence.* Cambridge: Islamic Texts Society, 1991.

———. *Freedom of Expression in Islam.* Vol. 4. Cambridge: Islamic Texts Society, 1997.

———. *Freedom, Equality, and Justice.* Vol. 47. Cambridge: The Islamic Texts Society, 2002.

———. *A Textbook of Hadith Studies: Authenticity, Compilation, Classification and Criticism of Hadith.* Leicestershire: The Islamic Foundation, 2005.

———. *Citizenship and Accountability of Government: An Islamic Perspective.* Cambridge: Islamic Texts Society, 2011a.

———. *Shari'Ah Law: An Introduction.* Oxford: Oneworld Publications, 2011b.

Kaminski, Joseph J. *The Contemporary Islamic Governed State: A Reconceptualization.* London: Palgrave Macmillan, 2017.

Karamustafa, Ahmet T. *Knowledge of God in Classical Sufism: Foundations of Islamic Mystical Theology.* Mahwah, NJ: Paulist Press, 2004.

Kathir, Ibn. *Tafsir Ibn Kathir.* Translated by Sheikh S. Al-Mubarakpuri. Vol. 4. Jeddah, KSA: Darussalam Books, 2003.

Kathir, Ibn, and Saifur Rahman Mubarakpuri. *Tafsir Ibn Kathir.* Vol. 9. Jeddah, KSA: Darussalam, 2003.

Katzenstein, Peter J., ed. *The Culture of National Security: Norms and Identity in World Politics.* New York: Columbia University Press, 1996.

Keddie, Nikki R., and Jamāl al-Dīn Afghānī. *An Islamic Response to Imperialism: Political and Religious Writings of Sayyid Jamal Ad-Din "Al-Afghani".* Vol. 21. New York: University of California Press, 1983.

Kennedy, Hugh. *The Prophet and the Age of the Caliphates.* London: Longman, 1986.

Khadduri, Majid. *The Islamic Conception of Justice.* Baltimore: Johns Hopkins University Press, 1984.

Khadduri, Majid, and Herbert J. Liebesny, eds. *Origin and Development of Islamic Law*. New York: The Lawbook Exchange, Ltd., 1955.

Khaldun, Ibn. *The Muqaddimah*. Translated by Franz Rosenthal. Princeton, NJ: Princeton University Press, 1969.

Khaldun, Ibn, and N.J. Dawood, eds. *Muqaddimah: An Introduction to History*. Translated by Franz Rosenthal. Princeton, NJ: Princeton University Press, 1989.

Khan, Israr Ahmad. *Authentication of Hadith: Redefining the Criteria*. Herndon, VA: International Institute of Islamic Thought, 2010.

Khan, M.A. Muqtedar. "Sovereignty in Modernity and Islam." *East-West Review* 1 (Summer, 1995): 43–57.

———. "Islam as an Ethical Tradition of International Relations." *Islam and Christian-Muslim Relations* 8, no. 2 (Summer, 1997): 177–192.

———. "Constructing Identity in Global Politics." *American Journal of Islamic Social Sciences* 15, no. 3 (Fall, 1998a): 81–106.

———. "The Need to Revive Islamic Philosophy." *Intellectual Discourse* 6, no. 1 (Spring, 1998b).

———. "Reason and Personal Reasoning." *American Journal of Islamic Social Sciences* 16, no. 3 (1999a).

———. "Sovereignty in Islam as Human Agency." *Ijtihad*, Dec 30, 1999b. http://www.ijtihad.org/sovt.htm.

———. "Islam in America: Islamic Identity and the Two Faces of the West." *The Washington Report on Middle East Affairs* 19, no. 7 (2000): 71.

———. "The Political Philosophy of Islamic Resurgence." *Cultural Dynamics* 13, no. 2 (Summer, 2001a): 211–229.

———. "The Compact of Medina: A Constitutional Theory of the Islamic State." *Mirror International*, May 30, 2001b.

———. *American Muslims: Bridging Faith and Freedom*. Beltsville, MD: Amana Publications, 2002.

———. "Constructing the American Muslim Community." In *Religion and Immigration: Christian, Jewish, and Muslim Experiences in the United States*, edited by Y. Haddad, Jane I. Smith, and John L. Esposito, 175–198. New York: Rowman Altamira, 2003.

———. "The Myth of Secularism." In *One Electorate Under God?: A Dialogue on Religion and American Politics*, edited by E.J. Dionne, Jean Bethke Elshtain, and Kayla Meltzer Drogosz. Washington, DC: Brookings Institution Press, 2004a.

———. "The Islamic States." In *Routledge Encyclopedia of Political Science*, edited by M. Hawkesworth and M. Kogan, 265–278. New York: Routledge, 2004b.

———. *Jihad for Jerusalem: Identity and Strategy in International Relations*. Westport, CT: Praeger, 2004c.

———, ed. *Islamic Democratic Discourse: Theory, Debates, and Philosophical Perspectives*. Lanham, MD: Lexington Books, 2006.

———, ed. *Debating Moderate Islam: The Geopolitics of Islam and the West*. Salt Lake City: University of Utah Press, 2007a.

———. "Islamic Democratic Theory: Between Political Philosophy and Jurisprudence." In *Beyond Textual Islam*. New Delhi: Serial Publications, 2008.

———. "Islamic Governance and Democracy." In *Islam and Democratization in Asia*, edited by Shiping Hua, 13–27. New York: Cambria Press, 2009.

———. "The Quran Burning: Sing of Things to Come." http://newsweek.washingtonpost.com/onfaith/panelists/muqtedar_khan/2010/09/the_quran_burning_sign_of_things_to_come.html.

———. "The Verbal Assault on Islam." http://newsweek.washingtonpost.com/onfaith/panelists/muqtedar_khan/2010/05/freedom_of_expression_burqa_muhammed_and_cartoons.html.

———. "Islam and the Political Theology of Blasphemy." The Summer Scholars Institute at IIIT, Aug 12, 2011.

———. "God Is Beautiful and He Loves Beauty." *The Huffington Post*, Jul 25, 2012. http://www.huffingtonpost.com/muqtedar-khan/god-is-beautiful-and-he-loves-beauty_b_1692400.html.

———. "Prophet Muhammad Was the Best of Muhsins." *The Huffington Post*, Jan 01, 2013.

———. "Islam, Democracy and Islamism After the Counterrevolution in Egypt." *Middle East Policy* 21, no. 1 (2014a): 75–86.

———. "Political Authority in Islam." In *Handbook on Islam and Economic Life*, edited by Kabir Hassan and Mervyn Lewis. London: Edward Elgar Publishing Ltd., 2014b.

———. "The Arab Fall: War of All Against All." *Turkey Agenda*, 2015.

———. "Common Ground: Two Theories of Ijtihad." https://www.upi.com/Common-Ground-Two-theories-of-ijtihad/47791143060954/.

Khan, Qamaruddin M. "Al Mawardi." In *A History of Muslim Philosophy I*, edited by M.M. Sharif, 717–732. Karachi: Royal Book Company, 1963.

———. *The Political Thought of Ibn Taymiyah*. New Delhi: Adam Publishers, 2007b.

Korany, Bahgat, and Rabab El-Mahdi, eds. *Arab Spring in Egypt: Revolution and Beyond*. Cairo: American University in Cairo Press, 2012.

Köylü, Mustafa. "Religion and Citizenship Education: The Case of Turkey." In *Islam and Citizenship Education*, edited by Ednan Aslan and Marcia Hermansen. New York: Springer, 2015.

Kugle, Scott Alan, ed. *Sufi Meditation and Contemplation: Timeless Wisdom from Mughal India*. Translated by Scott Alan Kugle and Carl W. Ernst. New York: Suluk Press, 2012.

Kurzman, Charles, ed. *Liberal Islam: A Source Book*. New York: Oxford University Press, 1998.

———, ed. *Modernist Islam: A Source Book*. Oxford: Oxford University Press, 2002.

La Vopa, Anthony J. "The Politics of Enlightenment: Friedrich Gedike and German Professional Ideology." *The Journal of Modern History* 62, no. 1 (1990): 34–56.

Lakhani, M. Ali, Reza Shah-Kazemi, and Leonard Lewisohn, eds. *The Sacred Foundations of Justice in Islam: The Teachings of ʿAlī Ibn Abī Ṭālib*. Vancouver, Canada: World Wisdom, Inc., 2006.

Lakhsassi, Abderrahmane. "Ibn Khaldun." In *History of Islamic Philosophy I*, edited by Seyyed Hossein Nasr and Oliver Leaman, 350–366. London: Routledge, 1996.

Lampman, Jane. "Sufism May Be Powerful Antidote to Islamic Extremism." *The Christian Science Monitor*, Dec 5, 2007.

Lapidus, Ira M. *A History of Islamic Societies*. Cambridge, UK: Cambridge University Press, 1988.

Lauzière, Henri. "Post-Islamism and the Religious Discourse of Abd Al-Salam Yasin." *International Journal of Middle East Studies* 37, no. 2 (2005): 241–261.

Létourneau, Jean-François. "Explaining the Muslim Brotherhood's Rise and Fall in Egypt." *Mediterranean Politics* 21, no. 2 (2016): 300–307.

Levi-Faur, David, ed. *The Oxford Handbook of Governance*. Oxford: Oxford University Press, 2012.

Levy, Reuben. *Stories from SaʿDí's Bustán and Gulistán*. New York: Frederick A. Stokes Company Publishers, 1928.

———. *A Mirror for Princes: The Qabus Nama by Ksi Kaus Ibn Iskandar*. New York: E. P. Dutton, 1951.

Lewis, Bernard. "Islam and Liberal Democracy." *Atlantic Monthly* 271, no. 2 (1993): 89–97.

———. *Islam and the West*. Oxford: Oxford University Press, 1994.

Linde-Laursen, Anders. "Is Something Rotten in the State of Denmark? The Muhammad Cartoons and Danish Political Culture." *Contemporary Islam* 1, no. 3 (Fall, 2007): 265–274.

Lings, Martin Muhammad. *His Life Based on the Earliest Sources*. Rochester, Vermont: Inner Traditions International, Ltd, 1983.

Loxley, James. *Performativity*. New York: Routledge, 2006.

Lumbard, Joseph E.B., ed. *Islam, Fundamentalism, and the Betrayal of Tradition: Essays by Western Muslim Scholars*. Bloomington, IN: World Wisdom, Inc., 2004.

Lynch, Marc. "The Big Think Behind the Arab Spring." *Foreign Policy* no. 190 (2011): 46.

Mahdi, Muhsin S. *Ibn Khaldun's Philosophy of History: A Study in the Philosophic Foundation of the Science of Culture*. London: G. Allen and Unwin, 1957.

———. "Ibn Khaldun." In *A History of Muslim Philosophy II*, edited by M.M. Sharif, 888–903. Karachi: Royal Book Company, 1963.

———. "Al Farabi." In *History of Political Philosophy*, edited by Leo Strauss and Joseph Cropsey. Chicago, IL: University of Chicago Press, 1987.

———. *Alfarabi and the Foundation of Islamic Political Philosophy.* Chicago, IL: University of Chicago Press, 2001.

Mahmood, Saba. *Politics of Piety.* Princeton, NJ: Princeton University Press, 2005.

Malik, Maszlee. *Foundations of Islamic Governance: A Southeast Asian Perspective.* London: Taylor & Francis, 2016.

Mango, Andrew. *Ataturk.* London: John Murray, 1999.

March, Andrew F. *Islam and Liberal Citizenship: The Search for an Overlapping Consensus.* New York: Oxford University Press, 2009.

Maududi, Syed Abul A'la. *The Islamic Law and Constitution.* Lahore: Islamic Publications, 1992.

———. *The Meaning of the Quran, Vol. IV–VI.* Translated by Muhammad Ch Akbar. Lahore, Pakistan: Islamic Publications, 1993.

———. "Self-Destructiveness of Western Civilization." In *Modernist and Fundamentalist Debates in Islam,* edited by Mansoor Moaddel and Kamran Talattof, 325–331. New York: Springer, 2000.

———. *A Short History of the Revivalist Movement in Islam.* Kuala Lumpur: The Other Press, 2002.

McDonough, Sheila. *Muslim Ethics and Modernity: A Comparative Study of the Ethical Thought of Sayyid Ahmad Khan and Mawlana Mawdudi.* Waterloo, Canada: Wilfrid Laurier University Press, 1984.

Mernissi, Fatima. *Beyond the Veil: Male-Female Dynamics in Modern Muslim Society.* Vol. 423. Bloomington, IN: Indiana University Press, 1987.

Michot, Yahya. "Ibn Taymiyya's "New Mardin Fatwa". Is Genetically Modified Islam (GMI) Carcinogenic?" *The Muslim World* 101, no. 2 (2011): 130–181.

———. *Ibn Taymiyya Against Extremism.* Beirut: Albouraq Editions, 2012.

Moosa, M.I. "The Diwan of Umar Ibn Al-Khattab." *Studies in Islam* 11, no. 2 (1965).

Moten, Abdul Rashid. "Striving for Islamic Governance: Varying Contexts, Different Strategies." *The American Journal of Islamic Social Sciences* 32, no. 2 (2015): 68–89.

Muhammad, Asad. *The Message of the Quran.* 1980.

Muhammad, Yasien. *Fitrah: Islamic Concept of Human Nature.* London: Ta-Ha Publishers, 1996.

Mungiu-Pippidi, Alina. *The Quest for Good Governance: How Societies Develop Control of Corruption.* London: Cambridge University Press, 2015.

Murata, Sachiko, and William C. Chittick. *The Vision of Islam.* New York: Paragon House, 1994.

Muslim, Imam. *Sahih Muslim.* Translated by Abdul Hamid Siddiqui. Vol. 1. New Delhi, India: Idara Isha'at-e-Diniyat, 2007.

Nadwi, Sayyed Abul Hasan Ali. *Islam and the West.* Lucknow: Academy of Islamic Research and Publications, 1991.

———. *Islam and the World: The Rise and Decline of Muslims and its Effect on Mankind.* London: UK Islamic Academy, 2003.

Na'īm, 'Abd Allāh Aḥmad. *Islam and the Secular State: Negotiating the Future of Shari'a*. Cambridge, MA: Harvard University Press, 2008.

Nasr, Seyyed Hossein. *Ideals and Realities of Islam*. London: George Allen and Unwin, 1966.

———. *Traditional Islam in the Modern World*. London: KPI Publication, 1987.

———. *Knowledge and the Sacred*. Albany: SUNY Press, 1989.

———. *The Need for a Sacred Science*. Albany, NY: SUNY Press, 1993.

Nasr, Seyyed Vali Reza. *The Vanguard of the Islamic Revolution: The Jama'at-i Islami of Pakistan*. Berkley, CA: University of California Press, 1994.

———. *Mawdudi and the Making of Islamic Revivalism*. New York: Oxford University Press, 1997.

———. *Islamic Leviathan: Islam and the Making of State Power*. Oxford; New York: Oxford University Press, 2001.

Nettler, Ronald L., Mohamed Mahmoud, and John Cooper, eds. *Islam and Modernity: Muslim Intellectuals Respond*. London: I. B. Taurus, 1998.

Nicholson, Reynold. *Mathnawi of Jalaluddin Rumi*. London: Gibb Memorial Trust, 1926.

Norman, Jesse, and Jana Ganesh. *Compassionate Conservatism*. London: Policy Exchange, 2006.

Nyazee, Imran Ahsan Khan. *Islamic Jurisprudence (Usul Al-Fiqh)*. Islamabad, Pakistan: International Institute of Islamic Thought, 2000.

Opwis, Felicitas. "Maslaha in Contemporary Islamic Legal Theory." *Islamic Law and Society* 12, no. 2 (2005): 182–223.

Osman, Fathi. "Islam in a Modern State: Democracy and the Concept of Shura." *Occasional Papers Series, Center for Muslim-Christian Understanding, History and International Affairs, Edmund A. Walsh School of Foreign Service, Georgetown University, USA* (2001): 3–23.

Ottaway, Marina, and Thomas Carothers. *Funding Virtue: Civil Society Aid and Democracy Promotion*. Washington, DC: Carnegie Endowment, 2000.

Pasha, Mustapha Kamal. "Ibn Khaldun and World Order." In *Innovation and Transformation in International Studies*, edited by Stephen Gill and James H. Mittelman, 56–70. London: Cambridge University Press, 1997.

Poushter, Jacob. "In Nations with Significant Muslim Populations, Much Disdain for ISIS." *Pew Research Center*, Nov 17, 2015. http://www.pewresearch.org/fact-tank/2015/11/17/in-nations-with-significant-muslim-populations-much-disdain-for-isis/.

Qureshi, Regula. *Sufi Music of India and Pakistan: Sound, Context, and Meaning in Qawwali*. Cambridge; New York: Cambridge University Press, 1986.

Quṭb, Sayyid. *Milestones*. Damascus, Syria: Dar Al-Ilm, 2000a.

———. *Social Justice in Islam*. Oneonta, NY: Islamic Publications International, 2000b.

Rahman, Fazlur. "Islamic Modernism: Its Scope, Method and Alternatives." *Intejmiddeaststu International Journal of Middle East Studies* 1, no. 4 (Winter, 1970): 317–333.

———. *Islam.* Chicago: University of Chicago Press, 1979.

———. *Islam and Modernity: Transformation of an Intellectual Tradition.* Chicago: University of Chicago Press, 1982.

———. *Revival and Reform in Islam.* London: Oneworld Publications, 1999.

———. *Revival and Reform in Islam: A Study of Islamic Fundamentalism.* Oxford: Oneworld, 2000.

Rahman, A., and Nooraihan Ali. "The Influence of Al-Mawdudi and the Jama'At Al Islami Movement on Sayyid Qutb Writings." *World Journal of Islamic History and Civilization* 2, no. 4 (2012): 232–236.

Rahnema, Ali, ed. *Pioneers of Islamic Revival.* London: Zed Books, 1994.

Rais, Rasul Bakhsh. "What Kind of Pakistan Do We Want?" *The Express Tribune,* May 31, 2011. http://tribune.com.pk/story/178863/what-kind-of-pakistan-do-we-want/.

Ramadan, Tariq. *Islam, the West and the Challenges of Modernity.* Leicester: Islamic Foundation, 2001.

———. "Ijtihad and Maslaha: The Foundations of Governance." In *Islamic Democratic Discourse: Theory, Debates, and Philosophical Perspectives,* edited by M.A. Muqtedar Khan, 3. Lanham, MD: Lexington Books, 2006.

———. *In the Footsteps of the Prophet: Lessons from the Life of Muhammad.* London: Oxford University Press, 2007.

———. *Radical Reform: Islamic Ethics and Liberation.* London: Oxford University Press, 2009.

Reetz, Dietrich. "Enlightenment and Islam: Sayyid Ahmad Khan's Plea to Indian Muslims for Reason." *Indian Historical Review* 14, no. 1–2 (1988): 206–218.

Rizvi, Saiyid Athar Abbas. *A History of Sufism in India.* 2 Vols. New Delhi: Munshiram Manoharlal, 1978.

Rosenthal, Franz. *The Muslim Concept of Freedom Prior to the 19th Century.* London: Brill, 1960.

Rosenthal, Erwin Isak Jakob. *Political Thought in Medieval Islam: An Introductory Outline.* Cambridge: Cambridge University Press Archive, 1962.

Roy, Olivier. *The Failure of Political Islam.* Cambridge, MA: Harvard University Press, 1994.

Rubin, Uri. "The Assassination of Ka'b B. Al-Ashraf." *Oriens* 32, (1990): 65–71.

Rumi, Jalal al-Din. *The Masnavi: Book One.* Translated by Jawid Mojaddedi. New York: Oxford University Press, 2004.

Saadi, S. *The Rose Garden (Gulistan).* Translated by Ali-Shah, Omar. Reno, Nevada: Tractus Books, 1997.

Sachedina, Abdulaziz. *The Islamic Roots of Democratic Pluralism.* New York: Oxford University Press, 2001.

————. *Islam and the Challenge of Human Rights*. New York: Oxford University Press, 2009.

Sadaqat, Muhammad. "Girl Accused of Blasphemy for a Spelling Error." *The Express Tribune*, Sep 25, 2011. http://tribune.com.pk/story/259907/girl-accused-of-blasphemy-for-a-spelling-error/.

Saeed, Abdullah. *Islamic Thought: An Introduction*. New York: Routledge, 2006.

Ṣāfī, Lu'ayy. *Tensions and Transitions in the Muslim World*. Lanham, MD: University Press of America, 2003.

Safi, Omid, ed. *Progressive Muslims: On Justice, Gender and Pluralism*. Oxford: Oneworld, 2003.

————. *The Politics of Knowledge in Premodern Islam: Negotiating Ideology and Religious Inquiry*. Durham, NC: University of North Carolina Press, 2006.

Salem, Paul. "The Rise and Fall of Secularism in the Arab World." *Middle East Policy* 4, no. 3 (1996): 147–160.

Sardar, Ziauddin. *Reading the Qur'an: The Contemporary Relevance of the Sacred Text of Islam*. New York: Oxford University Press, 2011.

Sayeed, Khalid Bin. *Western Dominance and Political Islam: Challenge and Response*. Albany, NY: SUNY Press, 2009.

Schimmel, Annemarie. *Mystical Dimensions of Islam*. Durham, NC: University of North Carolina Press, 1975.

————. *As Through a Veil: Mystical Poetry in Islam*. Oxford: Oneworld Publications, 2001.

————. *And Muhammad Is His Messenger: The Veneration of the Prophet in Islamic Piety*. Chapel Hill, NC: UNC Press Books, 2014.

Schudson, Michael. *The Good Citizen: A History of American Civic Life*. Cambridge, MA: Harvard University Press, 1999.

Schuon, Frithjof. *Understanding Islam*. Bloomington, IN: World Wisdom Books, 1994.

Şerif, Mardin. "Turkey: Islam and Westernization." In *Religions and Societies: Asia and the Middle East*, edited by Carlo Caldarola, 171–198. Berlin: Mouton Publishers, 1982.

Shafi, Maulana Mufti Muhammad. *Mariful Quran*. Vol. 7. Karachi: Maktaba-e-Darul-Uloom, 2003.

————. *Ma'riful Qur'an: A Comprehensive Commentary on the Holy Quran*. Translated by Muhammad Hasan Askari and Muhammad Shameem. Karachi, Pakistan: Maktaba-e-Darul-uloom, 2005.

Shomali, Alireza, and Mehrzad Boroujerdi. "On Sadi's Treatise on Advice to the Kings." In *Mirror for the Muslim Prince: Islam and the Theory of Statecraft*, edited by Mehrzad Boroujerdi, 45–81. New York: Syracuse University Press, 2013.

Siddiqui, A.H. *The Life of Muhammad*. Des Plaines, IL: Library of Islam, 1991.

Sirriyeh, Elizabeth. *Sufis and Anti-Sufis: The Defence, Rethinking and Rejection of Sufism in the Modern World*. New York: Routledge, 2014.

Soguk, Nevzat. *Globalization and Islamism: Beyond Fundamentalism.* New York: Rowman & Littlefield Publisher Inc., 2011.

Soroush, Abdolkarim. *Reason, Freedom, and Democracy in Islam: Essential Writings of Abdolkarim Soroush.* New York: Oxford University Press, 2000.

Stephen, Toulmin. *Cosmopolis: The Hidden Agenda of Modernity.* Chicago: The University of Chicago Press, 1990.

Stillman, Norman A. *The Jews of Arab Lands.* Philadelphia: Jewish Publication Society, 1979.

Tahir, Muhammed. *The History of Jamaate Tabligh.* Karachi: Printing Press Karachi, 1987.

Tamimi, Azzam, and John L. Esposito, eds. *Islam and Secularism in the Middle East.* New York: New York University Press, 2000.

Tarik, Unal. *Umar Ibn Al-Khattab: Exemplar of Truth and Justice.* Istanbul: Tughra Books, 2014.

Taymiyyah, Ibn. *Public Duties in Islam: The Institution of the Hisbah.* Translated by Mukhtar Holland. Leicester, UK: The Islamic Foundation, 1985.

———. *Kitab Al-Iman: Book of Faith.* Translated by Salman Hassan Al-Ani and Ahmad Tel. Selangor, Malaysia: Islamic Book Trust, 1999.

———. *The Political Shariah on Reforming the Ruler and the Ruled.* London: Dar al-Fiqh, 2012.

Torab, Azam. *Performing Islam: Gender and Ritual in Iran.* Amsterdam: Brill, 2006.

Uddin, Asma T. "Blasphemy Laws in Muslim-Majority Countries." *The Review of Faith & International Affairs the Review of Faith & International Affairs* 9, no. 2 (2011): 47–55.

Uthman, Fathi. *Sharia in Contemporary Society: The Dynamics of Change in the Islamic Law.* Los Angeles, CA: Multimedia Vera International, 1994.

Van Bruinessen, Martin, and Julia Day Howell, eds. *Sufism and the 'Modern' in Islam.* Vol. 67. New York: I. B. Tauris, 2007.

van Ess, Josef. "Vision and Ascension: Surat Al-Najm and Its Relationship with Muhammad's Miraj." *Journal of Qur'anic Studies* 1, no. 1 (1999): 47–62. http://www.jstor.org/stable/25727943.

Volpi, Frédéric, and Ewan Stein. "Islamism and the State After the Arab Uprisings: Between People Power and State Power." *Democratization* 22, no. 2 (2015): 276–293.

Wadud, Amina. *Qur'an and Woman: Rereading the Sacred Text from a Woman's Perspective.* New York: Oxford University Press, 1999.

Watt, W. Montgomery. *Islamic Political Thought.* Edinburgh: Edinburgh University Press, 1968.

Weiss, Michael, and Hassan Hassan. *ISIS: Inside the Army of the Terror.* New York: Simon and Schuster, 2015.

Yalman, Nur. "Some Observations on Secularism in Islam: The Cultural Revolution in Turkey." *Daedalus* 102, no. 1 (Winter, 1973): 139–168.

Yamaguchi, Hiroichi, and Haruka Yanagisawa, eds. *Tradition and Modernity: India and Japan Towards the Twenty-First Century*. New Delhi: Munshiram Manoharlal Publishers Pvt. Ltd., 1997.

Yared, Nazik Saba. *Secularism and the Arab World: 1850–1939*. London: Saqi Books, 2002.

Yassine, Sheikh Abdessalam. *Al-Ihsan*. Casablanca, Morocco: Matbooaat Al-Afaq, 1998.

Yavuz, M. Hakan. "Turkish Identity and Foreign Policy in Flux: The Rise of Neo-Ottomanism." *Critique: Journal for Critical Studies of the Middle East* 7, no. 12 (1998): 19–41.

———. "Intricacies of Identity – Cleansing Islam from the Public Sphere." *Journal of International Affairs* 54, no. 1 (2000): 21.

———. *Secularism and Muslim Democracy in Turkey*. Vol. 28. Cambridge, UK: Cambridge University Press, 2009.

———. *Toward an Islamic Enlightenment: The Gulen Movement*. Oxford; New York: Oxford University Press, 2013.

Zaheer, Khalid. "The Real Blasphemers." *The Express Tribune,* Jan 2, 2011. http://tribune.com.pk/story/96867/the-real-blasphemers/.

Zaman, Muhammad Qasim. "Pakistan: Shari'a and the State." In *Sharia Politics: Islamic Law and Society in the Modern World*, edited by Robert W. Hefner, 207–243. Bloomington, IN: Indiana University Press, 2011.

Index[1]

A

Abu Bakr, 99, 169, 234
Abu Haneefah, 32
Adam, 23, 111, 112, 128–131, 150
Aesthetic, 2, 87, 96, 125, 145, 146, 148, 230
Afghanistan, viii, 12, 23, 53, 165, 248
Ahadith, 14, 81n5, 90, 114
Ahmad Khan, Sir Syed, 59, 66, 71, 135
Aligarh Muslim University, 60
Allah, 9, 11, 19, 21–23, 23n25, 25, 32, 33, 35–37, 43, 46, 68, 73, 80, 80n4, 91, 93, 95, 99, 105, 109–114, 117, 120–122, 125–128, 130, 132–134, 138–141, 144, 145, 148–152, 154, 156, 157, 159, 181, 182, 188, 189, 198, 203, 205, 209, 210, 212, 213, 215, 222, 227, 229, 233, 234n38, 239n47
Andalusia, 5

Arab Spring, ix, 5–7, 51, 54–56, 58, 101, 136, 194, 214, 218, 242
Asghar Ali Engineer, 135
Authoritarianism, 1, 53, 55, 56, 164, 205, 238
Ayn Al-Yaqeen, 131, 153
Al-Azhar, 108n8

B

Baqa, 88, 120, 121, 159
Bayrak, Tosun, 94
Beautiful, 1–4, 12, 21–23, 25, 39, 41, 77–79, 85, 88, 89, 94, 97, 99, 110, 112, 113, 115–117, 119n21, 122, 125, 134, 138, 139, 142, 143, 145–147, 152, 155, 157, 188, 215, 221, 226, 229–231, 233–235, 247, 248, 250
Beauty, 2, 5, 15, 21, 25, 77–79, 84, 89, 97, 99, 113, 118, 122, 127, 145–148, 150, 189, 229–234, 246

---

[1] Note: Page numbers followed by 'n' refer to notes.

CPSIA information can be obtained
at www.ICGtesting.com
Printed in the USA
BVHW042214270519
549333BV00027B/97/P